be recalled before the date stamped below.
eturn it when it is recalled or you will be fined.

Aspects of Educational and Training Technology XXVIII

Aspects of Education and Training Technology XXVIII

Computer Assisted and Open Access Education

Edited for the Association for Educational and Training Technology by

Fred Percival, Ray Land and Denis Edgar-Nevill

Kogan Page Ltd, London

First published in 1995

Reprinted 1996

Kogan Page Limited
120 Pentonville Road
London N1 9JN

British Library Cataloguing in Publication Data

A CIP record for this book is available from the British Library

ISBN 0 7494 1414 6
ISSN 1350-1933

Printed and bound in Great Britain by
Biddles Ltd, Guildford and King's Lynn

Contents

Editorial

This volume represents the Proceedings of the Association for Educational and Training Technology's (AETT) 1994 International Conference. The Conference was hosted by Napier University, Edinburgh and was attended by over 180 delegates from 15 countries. The papers, workshops and other Conference contributions explored the theme 'Computer Assisted and Open Access Education.'

The last few years have seen unprecedented expansion in the range and use of computer technologies in education. The last year alone has witnessed a dramatic fall in the costs of hardware, bringing new learning tools within the reach of educational institutions for the first time. Growing interest is reflected in the number of major projects that are currently being funded in this field. Examples include the *Teaching and Learning Technology Programme (TLTP)*, the *Computers in Teaching Initiative (CTI)*, the *Information Technology Training Initiative (ITTI)*, the *Flexibility in Teaching and Learning Scheme (FITLS)*, and the *Effective Teaching and Assessment Programme (ETAP)*. The Conference theme was therefore both timely and topical.

As professional educators come to terms with the implications of multimedia, hypertext and virtual reality it is becoming clear that these new technologies are offering solutions that will profoundly transform our educational institutions and ways of working by the end of the century. But what will be the nature of these new technologies? How will they transform the learning experience? What will be their effect upon the role of the teacher? What are the implications for the culture and management of our organisations?

These changes come at a time when institutions are also seeking to develop wider access for students through more flexible provision. The temporal and spatial barriers that currently constrain access may well be overcome by innovations in educational technology. The pace of development is accelerating but change may prove problematic if it is not responsibly managed and if quality is not maintained.

The organisation of these Proceedings reflects that of the Conference. The editors struggled with alternative section titles, but in the end settled for these rather arbitrary divisions. We are aware that many of the contributions straddle more than one area, and we apologise to those authors who feel that their work has been misplaced!

Around 85 sessions ran at the Conference. Such was the response that the editors have been unable to include all of them in these Proceedings. However, we have attempted to give a rounded flavour of the Conference by inclusion, in Section 5, of abstracts of papers not reproduced in full. Full versions of these papers are available from the contributors or the editors of this volume.

We would like to thank all those who contributed to the success of AETT 94, including the organisers, the support staff and the Conference delegates. Special thanks are due to Guiti Saberi, the Conference Administrator, for months of sterling work, and also to Kate Campbell for her help with the final preparation of this volume.

Fred Percival, Ray Land and Denis Edgar-Nevill
Napier University, Edinburgh

Index of contributors

Section 1 :   Perspectives on Teaching and Learning

1.   Education in the Year 2000: Will We Recognise it?

Jonathan Darby, *Computers in Teaching Initiative, University of Oxford*

Summary
I want to take the opportunity to explore the future with you: not precisely what the technology will look like and be capable of, but rather the complex web of forces that will determine how the technology is used.

Looking back over past experiences we see many false dawns but also numerous developments that took us by surprise. Who, for example, predicted a decade ago that by today the fax machine would be almost as ubiquitous as the telephone? In higher education we are still teaching pretty much as we did 50 years ago, yet there have been confident predictions since the seventies that Computer-Based Learning would soon enter the educational mainstream. The proliferation of names and three letter acronyms (CAI, CAL, CBT, CBL, CML, etc) to denote computers in teaching are an indication that something has gone badly wrong. It is like some shady company which changes its name at frequent intervals to escape its debts and reputation but whose sharp practices remain the same.

The speed of change in higher education is now increasing but little of this change is due to the influence of technology. Instead it is old fashioned financial sticks and carrots that are driving the change, both directly and by the pressure of rising student numbers stimulated by the funding regime. The picture is very different in industry where in some companies there is wholesale reliance on learning technology but there the cost/benefit equation works out very differently.

When predicting the future the message of history is confused. The only thing we can say with any certainty is that the future will surprise us. We do however have a rich vein of experience to tap in the UK and it is fruitful to examine it when contemplating the way forward. The first phase of the Computers in teaching Initiative (CTI) demonstrated that the computer could be a powerful tool in teaching all subjects but it failed to produce academically portable materials. CTI Phase 2, by creating a UK-wide discipline-based information and support infrastructure, has dramatically lowered the entry cost to academics of becoming competent learning technologists but is unable to be effective where suitable materials to do already exist. The jury is still out on the Teaching and Learning Technology Programme but the Programme cannot succeed in its declared aim of bringing learning technology into the mainstream of higher education without the active support of many other players in the higher education system.

Given the experiences of the past it is a brave person who predicts sweeping changes but I shall stick my neck out nevertheless. I believe that the next five years will see sweeping changes. The technology is already capable of teaching students more cheaply than conventional means but it is not in the interests of lecturers in higher education to see this happen. The key to the changes will not be technology but Modularisation, credit Accumulation and Transfer (MoCAT). This will enable a new breed of small entrepreneurial education providers to exploit information and communication technology to deliver higher education modules at a lower cost than conventional universities and colleges. Students will not only find the new providers more affordable but they will also be attracted by the ability to study at a time and place of their choosing.

A STUDENT'S LIFE

"The first thing Carlos does after breakfast is to check his mail. There are the usual multimedia advertisements that he glances at briefly before disposing of, a voice message from his tutor reminding him of the evening seminar and an annotated copy from Jane of the first draft of their joint project. Carlos reduces the mail system to an icon, which will flash if any more mail arrived, and turns his attention to Module PM207 which is on *Company Ethics*.

His workstation, which he uses for most of his studying, connects to the academic network using the facilities of his cable TV company and accesses the next unit. Carlos likes to see and hear the presenter so he opens a video window in addition to the presentation notes window. Carlos stops the presentation every so often to make his own notes next to those of the presenter. At one point he has difficulty with the presentation and repeats a section of it. It is still not clear so he highlights the notes that he is not following and selects "Explain" from the "Guidance" menu. Carlos is asked a few questions and is then offered a choice of three items of background material. 5 minutes with the first of them is enough to explain the concept he had not previously encountered and he is able to proceed with the unit.

At 10 he breaks off from his study to go to work. Much of his work is done from home, but today he has a number of meetings to attend. Carlos is completing his higher education in a way that has become the norm. He receives a full-time salary but his work hours are two thirds of normal. The remainder of his time is spent studying. His employer receives a grant from the education department to cover the cost of his study.

Higher education is now totally modularised. Carlos's degree is made up of a variety of different types and lengths of modules. Some are offered by his employer, others by local companies and colleges. However most of Carlos's studies are with the Open Network University (ONU).

The ONU is international with students in almost every country of the world. All materials are delivered to students' homes or workplaces via the international academic network and local telecommunication facilities. Student workstations can reproduce sound and video, and are equipped with a small video camera above the screen. Students can use the module materials in a variety of ways. Some like to print them as booklets to skim or to read right through. Others prefer the linear tutorial mode with the option of a presenter's voice and video presence to accompany it. However most use is made of the interactive multimedia mode in which students work through the material following their own sequence with the help of concept maps and extensive cross references. All modules contain frequent self assessment tests to enable students to check their understanding of the topic.

That evening Carlos has a seminar with 5 other students and his tutor. As it happens each of them is in another country and the seminar is conducted using teleconferencing. Carlos has six windows on his screen each displaying the video image of the other seminar participants. The video camera on top of his monitor transmits his image to the others. A lively discussion ensues on the ethics of insider dealing and very quickly the distance that divides the participants is forgotten. In addition to the 6 video windows there is a "table top" window which is used from time to time to show items of interest to the others. The seminar ends when Carlos's tutor Annette points out that they have over-run their time by 20 minutes.

Annette works in an old-style university but teaches part-time for the ONU. Students consistently rate her highly for the quality of her teaching and it was because of this that she was asked to join the ONU. As an author she started by transferring some of her existing courses to the new media but soon realised that she could now include material she had previously considered too difficult by taking advantage of the added interaction now available to her and the ability to cross reference to other materials.

Higher education has become highly competitive. Students can assemble their degree courses by taking modules from a variety of providers. An informal course assessment network has sprung up and potential students can check the comments and ratings of past students before selecting a module. Annette regularly checks the ratings for her modules and those of her competitors. She knows that if she does not regularly update her courses student enrolment will drop.

Keeping her courses up to date is not as difficult a task as it used to be. In 1995 a consortium of 27 universities from 14 different countries started to buy the rights to utilise resource materials in computer based and text based teaching materials. This proved so advantageous that the consortium expanded rapidly. Today over 5000 universities and other higher education providers belong to the consortium, representing a third of the global higher education sector. Course developers and tutors in member institutions access this information via intelligent agents that hunt out material of specific interest to them. Students too are able to access this resource base when researching for assignments.

Annette finds her work with the ONU more satisfying than her main job. Despite not meeting her ONU students face to face she finds she gets to know them better than her other students, and her interactions with them tend to be at a higher level because they come to their tutorials better prepared. She prefers putting her energies into developing multimedia course materials to repeating old lecture courses.

Carlos is enthusiastic about his mode of studying. He finds it hard to conceive how his parents sat through several hours of lectures a day when they were students. He has the freedom to study what he wants, when he wants, where he wants. He also enjoys excellent interaction with his tutors and fellow students even though he knows most of them through electronic mail and teleconferencing links. Even his parents concede that he is able to find out more in ten minutes than they were able to in an afternoon in the university library" (Darby & Kjöllerström, 1994)

LESSONS OF THE PAST

Looking back over past experiences we see many false dawns but also numerous developments that took us by surprise. Who, for example, predicted a decade ago that by today the fax machine would be almost as ubiquitous as the telephone? In higher education we are still teaching pretty much as we did 50 years ago, yet there have been confident predictions since the seventies that Computer Based Learning would soon enter the educational mainstream. The proliferation of names and three letter acronyms (CAI, CAL, CBT, CBL, CML, etc) to denote computers in teaching are an indication that something has gone badly wrong. It is like some shady company which changes its name at frequent intervals to escape its debts and reputation but whose sharp practices remain the same.

The speed of change in higher education is now increasing but little of this change is due to the influence of technology. Instead it is old fashioned financial sticks and carrots that are driving the change, both directly and by the pressure of rising student numbers stimulated by the funding regime. The picture is very different in industry where in some companies there is wholesale reliance on learning technology but there the cost/benefit equation works out very differently.

When predicting the future the message of history is confused. The only thing we can say with any certainty is that the future will surprise us. We do however have a rich vein of experience to tap in the UK and it is fruitful to examine it when contemplating the way forward. The first phase of the Computers in Teaching Initiative (CTI) demonstrated that the computer could be a powerful tool in teaching *all* subjects but it failed to produce academically portable materials. CTI Phase 2, by creating a UK-wide discipline based information and support infrastructure, has dramatically lowered the *entry cost* to academics of becoming competent learning technologists but is unable to be effective where suitable materials do not already exist. The jury is still out on the Teaching and Learning Technology Programme but the Programme cannot succeed in its declared aim of bringing learning technology into the mainstream of higher education without the active support of many other players in the higher education system.

THE FUTURE OF PUBLISHING

Academics publish in order to establish and enhance their reputations. In the past this has necessitated striking a deal with publishers in which the academic assigns to the publisher copyright, and with it exploitation rights, and the publisher bears the cost of printing, distributing and marketing the academic's works. Now that an all pervasive global academic network is effectively in place academics have an alternative to consigning their work to a publisher. At no direct cost to themselves, or anyone else, they can publish over the Internet. This has two further immediate advantages. It reaches a larger audience and it avoids the usual delays of paper publishing. With tools like World Wide Web text can be formatted and illustrations can be included. The MIME standard for document transmission even allows for the inclusion of sound and video in documents. Online collections of working papers are proliferating. This summer will see the launch of the UK's first fully refereed electronic journal. It seems inevitable that the advantages to academics in publishing electronically will lead to a rapid marginalisation of academic publishing companies unless they can find new roles for themselves.

Such a shift in publishing patterns would have immediate implications for teaching and learning. It would lead to the creation of large amounts of material where the copyright resided with academics themselves or their host institutions. Students would be able to access much of it directly and course designers would be able to rapidly assemble readers for their students. One vision of how this could be done (by a librarian) is contained in the report of the Joint Funding Councils' Libraries Review Group (Follett, 1993).

The librarian has a meeting first thing with the group responsible for a new course on "Redesigning the Inner City", for which he has assembled a package of materials written within the department, along with a wide range of other resources. These include review articles, some commercially published for which copyright clearance has been paid, and some from "MasterClass" and "Improf", the collaborative inter-university resource banks. They also comprise links to the main library catalogues and the relevant abstracting services to which the university subscribes, sample sets of demographic data, previous examination papers, and a range of example dissertations from previous years. With another colleague in Information Systems, a software specialist, all this has been loaded into the departmental server, and wrapped into a brief hypertext overview of the course.

HIGHER EDUCATION UNDER PRESSURE

Given the experiences of the past it is a brave person who predicts sweeping changes but I shall stick my neck out never-the-less. I believe that the next five years *will* see sweeping changes. The technology is already capable of teaching students more cheaply than conventional means but it is not in the interests of lecturers in higher education to see this happen. The key to the changes will not be technology but Modularisation, Credit Accumulation and Transfer (MoCAT). This will enable a new breed of small entrepreneurial education provider to exploit information and communication technology to deliver higher education modules at a lower cost than conventional universities and colleges. Students will not only find the new providers more affordable but they will also be attracted by the ability to study at a time and place of their choosing. Few universities and colleges will be immune to the pressure this will place them under.

References

Darby, J. & Kjöllerström, B. (1994). A student's life 1998 in *"Higher Education 1998 Transformed by Learning Technology"*. Oxford: CTISS Publications. (Reproduced with permission)

Follett, B. (1993). *Joint Funding Councils' Libraries Review Group: Report*. Bristol: HEFCE.

2. Innovative Teaching at a Scottish University

Henry Ellington and Bill McIntosh, *The Robert Gordon University, Aberdeen*

Summary
In 1993, a comprehensive survey of innovations in teaching and learning within the Faculty of Management was carried out at Aberdeen's Robert Gordon University. This paper presents the results of the survey, showing how over 140 recently-introduced or planned innovations of a wide range of types were reported, and describing representative examples of these. It also shows how the survey provided evidence of the success within the Faculty of the University's 5-year 'Enterprise' programme in helping students to develop transferable process and IT skills, of an increasingly student-centred approach to instruction, and of increasing development of external links. The paper concludes by identifying some of the benefits that can accrue from wide-ranging surveys of this type within a Higher Education Institution.

INTRODUCTION

In April 1993, all Course Leaders within the Faculty of Management at Aberdeen's Robert Gordon University were asked to complete a questionnaire. This solicited information regarding all changes to teaching/learning introduced during the previous three years,the reasons for making these changes, and a brief evaluation of their success; it also asked them to list any further changes planned during the following twelve months. This paper presents the results of the survey and discusses their implications.

THE OVERALL RESULTS OF THE SURVEY

The Faculty of Management at The Robert Gordon University comprises three Schools (Business, Librarianship and Information Studies, and Public Administration and Law) plus the academic sections of the University's Educational Development Unit. At the time of the survey, its portfolio of courses included seven undergraduate degrees (six with honours programmes), one postgraduate certificate, four postgraduate diplomas (three with linked masters programmes) and a Master of Business Administration run jointly with the University of Aberdeen. In all, 145 different innovations were reported in respect of these 13 courses, of which 118 had actually been implemented and 27 were planned.

In order to give the report on the survey a logical structure and thus facilitate reference, the various innovations were classified under six broad headings,each with its own sub-headings. Note that some innovations were included in more than one category, so that the total number of entries (173) was greater than the total number of innovations reported. These various sections and subsections are listed below, together with the number of innovations described in each.

Section 1: Innovations involving individualised learning (17)
  1.1 Changes to existing self-study courses/course units (2)
  1.2 Courses/course units changed to self-study form (4)
  1.3 Self-study programmes built into traditional courses (4)
  1.4 Use of exercises/packages involving individual study (7)

Section 2: Innovations involving group learning (43)
  2.1 Innovations in seminars/tutorials/class discussions (15)

2.3 Use of mediated feedback with classes (2)
2.4 Use of group projects/exercises/case studies (16)

Section 3: Innovations designed to develop 'enterprise' skills (58)
3.1 Development of written communication skills (8)
3.2 Development of oral communication/presentation skills (20)
3.3 Development of group/interpersonal/leadership skills (8)
3.4 Development of problem-solving and related skills (12)
3.5 Development of general management/business skills (10)

Section 4: Innovations involving use of information technology (24)
4.1 Use of the computer as a vehicle for instruction (8)
4.2 Use of the computer as an aid to calculations (6)
4.3 Use o the computer as a database (9)
4.4 Use of telecommunications in course delivery (1)

Section 5: Innovations involving external links (17)
5.1 Innovations involving European links, visits, etc. (4)
5.2 Formation of external links within the UK (4)
5.3 Use of residential courses within the UK (3)
5.4 External visits, projects etc. within the UK (6)

Section 6: Other innovations (14)
6.1 Changes in form of lectures (4)
6.2 Establishment of links between/within courses (6)
6.3 Other innovations (4)

Note that the above classification was by no means a rigorous one, since some innovations that were allocated to a particular section or sub-section could equally well have been allocated to another - or, in some cases, to more than one.

EXAMPLES OF THE INNOVATIONS REPORTED

Since the main body of the report on the survey ran to more than 40 pages, it is clearly not possible to give anything more than a flavour of its contents in a paper of this type. This will be done by describing one typical innovation from each of the first five sections listed above.

Example 1 : An innovation involving individualised learning (from Section 1.2)

The introductory 'Economics' courses in two of the Business School's degrees have been reorganised as a series of open-learning modules and units based on textual materials. Lectures have been reduced to one per week, and tutorials to one per fortnight. Students are able to monitor their progress via self-assessment questions at the end of each unit. Initial teething problems now appear to have been overcome, and the programmes are proving both effective and popular with students.

Example 2 : An innovation involving group learning (from Section 2.1)

In order to encourage students to take a broader view of the material presented on the course, encourage reading, and develop analytical skills, the delivery and assessment programme of the second-year 'Political Analysis' course in one of the School of Public Administration and Law's degrees has been radically restructured. Delivery now centres on seminar discussion and analysis of selected texts with assessment being largely based on student performance in such exercises. Students have reported that they prefer the new system to the old.

Example 3 : An 'enterprise'-related innovation (from Section 3.5)

Students joining the first year of the 'Business Studies' degree now undergo a Business Skills Induction Week during which they are helped to develop basic research, IT, time-management, team, leadership and presentation skills. Working in teams, they are required to produce a market intelligence report and present their findings. This involves devising their own programme, sorting out their priorities and allocating responsibilities. The innovation appears to be working well.

Example 4 : An innovation involving IT (from Section 4.1)

Postgraduate students studying 'Information Retrieval' in the School of Librarianship and Information Studies now have access to hypermedia packages for self-instruction and remedial support. Feedback from students indicates that the packages have proved helpful and popular. Their availability (on an open-access basis) also releases staff time previously needed for repetitive revision with individual students.

Example 5 : An innovation involving external links (from Section 5.1)

A 3-day marketing exercise involving speakers from industry and students communicating (in French and German) with French and German companies has been introduced into the first year of the 'European Business Administration with Languages' degree. The object is to allow students to practise their language skills in real-life situations and introduce them to the wide world of business. The innovation is proving effective, and is highly popular with students.

SOME OF THE CONCLUSIONS DRAWN FROM THE SURVEY

The results of the survey show that staff of The Robert Gordon University's Faculty of Management have been both highly ingenious and highly diverse in introducing innovations into the various courses for which they are responsible. Not surprisingly, considering the vast amount of time, money and other resources that were devoted to the promotion of an 'enterprise culture' in the University between 1988 and 1993 through the Government's Enterprise in Higher Education Programme', a large number of these are directly or indirectly related to the development of the various skills that this programme was designed to promote (transferable process skills, communication skills, IT skills and general 'life' skills of all types). Ample evidence for the success of the University's 'Enterprise' programme within the Faculty can be found in the report.

The report also indicates that Course Teams have been moving towards a much more student-centred approach to instruction than has been the case in the past, as evidenced by the extensive use that has been made of innovative group-learning techniques, and, to a lesser extent, individualised-learning methods and methods based on the use of information technology. Both of the latter are likely to be major growth areas during the remainder of the 1990's, particularly if the recommendations of the MacFarlane Report (CSUP, 1993) are put into practice. The innovative work already carried out in these two areas should provide an excellent foundation for further developments.

Finally, the report shows that some Course Teams have made considerable progress in developing new types of external links, both within the UK and within the wider context of the European Community. Formation of such links is likely to become increasingly important, and the innovative work already carried out should provide useful examples for others to emulate. Indeed, this is true of all the examples of innovative teaching developments described in the report.

SOME OF THE BENEFITS OF SUCH A SURVEY

The authors believe that two main benefits can accrue from carrying out wide-ranging surveys of the type described within a Higher Education Institution.

First, such a survey identifies good practice and raises general awareness of same. This has certainly been the case within the Faculty of Management at The Robert Gordon University, where all Course Teams have now had the opportunity to see the sort of interesting things that their colleagues on other Course Teams are doing. It is confidently expected that this will lead to a spread of these new ideas throughout the Faculty, with obvious benefit to students. Nor are such benefits limited to the particular section of an Institution within which the survey is carried out. In The Robert Gordon University, for example, the report on teaching innovations in the Faculty of Management has been widely disseminated among other staff. Also, plans are currently being made to carry out similar surveys in the University's other three Faculties with a view to producing a University-wide data base on innovative teaching.

Second, surveys of this type provide documentary evidence of good teaching and innovative thinking that can be cited in both internal and external quality assessment events. Since 1993, all of Britain's Higher Education Institutions have been subject to two new types of external quality assessment, namely, subject-based assessments of the quality of their course delivery carried out by their National Funding Body, and global audits of their quality-assurance and quality-control processes carried out by the (UK-wide) Higher Education Quality Council. The results of the survey described in this paper - and of the further surveys currently being planned - will undoubtedly prove extremely useful in both of these contexts.

Reference

CSUP (1993) *Teaching and Learning in an Expanding Higher Education System.* The Committee of Scottish University Principals, Polton House Press, Midlothian, Scotland.

Note

Anyone wishing to see a copy of the report on the survey of teaching innovations described in the paper should contact the Faculty Administrative Officer, Faculty of Management, The Robert Gordon University, Hilton Campus, Aberdeen.

3. Gender and Age Effects in Secondary School Pupils' Use of and Attitudes Towards Computers

P Glissov, G Siann and A Durndell, *Glasgow Caledonian University*

Summary

This paper describes the findings of a questionnaire survey of pupils' use of and attitudes to computers, carried out in five Scottish secondary schools.

A questionnaire measuring school and home use of computers, as well as attitudes towards computers, was completed by 429 pupils in their first, third, or fifth year. Significant differences were found between the sexes in a number of areas.

In general girls reported a narrower experience of using computers at school in a variety of areas, though there were no difference between the genders in the number of pupils who reported using computers for playing games. Boys were significantly more likely to own computers and also reported using computers more frequently outside school, with the exception of word processing.

Further analyses carried out on a subset of 196 pupils indicated significant gender differences on an attitudinal scale, with boys relatively more likely to hold positive views about computer use. Significant age related differences were also found on this subset, with a general decline in positive views of computers with age for both girls and boys.

It was argued that the findings have implications for school policy with regard to the participation of girls in the area of computer based subjects.

INTRODUCTION

The 'gender gap' associated with the under representation of women and girls in careers and courses in science and technology continues to cause concern. However, there is some indication that this gap is narrowing and that female students are beginning to achieve comparable standards to male students in mathematical and scientific subject areas, though the gender gap in the area of computing studies at school and in higher education has tended to widen (Dain 1991). A 1993 government White Paper, *Realising Our Potential: A Strategy for Science, Engineering and Technology* indicated a notable lack of women in promoted levels in technological fields.

Whilst these facts are rarely disputed the reasons under–lying the facts are a matter for debate. There is now research evidence linking the gender gap in computing to experiential, contextual and attitudinal factors.

EXPERIENTIAL FACTORS

Girls have consistently been shown to be less likely to own a computer, less likely to have access to one at home and less likely to use one at school (e.g. Miura 1987; Levin & Gordon 1989).

SOCIAL CONTEXT FACTORS

Previous research also suggests that the gender gap may result from an interaction between the level of experience and the social context in which computers are used. Particularly, the gender composition of the dyad or group working at the computer has received attention in the literature (e.g. Fisher 1984; Siann et al. 1990). The findings of these studies are supported by Beynon's (1988) study of girls and boys working in groups of 2 girls and 2 boys at a computer in a primary school classroom. He found that the advantage exerted by the boys showed itself in their dominance of the physical space in front of the computer and through psychological means like ridiculing girls when they made mistakes.

The continuing association in many schools of computers with mathematical and scientific disciplines also contributes to the gender gap in reinforcing the stereotype of computers as a male domain (Collis & Ollila 1990). This is important in so far as a preference for science and mathematics subjects has repeatedly been found to be positively correlated with liking of computers (Bear et al. 1987; Loyd et al. 1987).

ATTITUDE FACTORS

Research consistently shows that girls and boys both like computers (Glissov, 1992). The question therefore is why this is not transferred into personal agency as regards computer usage? This question was expressed by Collis (1985) as the "I can't, but we can" paradox, based on the generally held belief amongst girls that as a group girls and woman can be equally good at using computers in comparison with males, but for a variety of reasons females believe that computers are of little consequence to them. This view resonates with the findings that females are more likely to view computers as useful tools rather than as objects of intrinsic interest (Siann et al. 1990), and that such attitudes have implications for women's and girls' perception of computing as a discipline (Durndell 1990). It has been suggested that this aspect of women's attitudes to computers is more aptly termed the "I can, but I don't want to" syndrome (Lightbody & Durndell 1993).

The present paper focuses particularly on gender related differences with respect to pupils' experience of computers, their attitudes towards computers and their school year.

The research reported in this paper was part of a broader study of social and motivational aspects of the gender gap in computer use. The effect of sociocultural background and single sex education is not covered here as they have been reported elsewhere (Glissov, 1991 and 1992) and some of the findings of this paper have also been reported in Durndell et al. (in press).

METHOD

Schools

The 5 schools selected were all situated in the same city and reflected variables relevant to factors not under consideration here. Three of the schools were from the fee paying private sector, owned and administered by the same Merchant Company Trust, one a girls only, one a boys only, and one a co-educational school. The other two schools were from the state sector, both co-educational comprehensives, one of which serves an area of considerable social deprivation and the other of which draws its pupils from a socially diverse catchment area. Table 3.1 shows the sample sizes by year and gender.

Table 3.1:   Sample by Gender and School Year

	First	Third	Sixth	Total
Girls	66	74	66	206
Boys	85	87	51	223
Total	151	161	117	429

Questionnaire

A questionnaire was developed from one used previously by Macleod et al. (1988) and other similar instruments, and piloted at one of the participating co-educational schools on a small sample of pupils that did not take part in the questionnaire survey (see Glissov 1992 for details).

The questionnaire consisted of four sections:

1. Experience of computer usage, with items relating the kind of use respondents had made of computers (a) within school, and (b) outside school, e.g. at home and at friends.

    Two   variables   were   computed   from   the   responses   to   this   section.

    (a)   **schoolUSE** aggregated the items referring to the extent to which computers were used at school; and
    (b)   **homeUSE** aggregated items referring to computer use outside school. On both usage scales the maximum possible score was 10 and the minimum 0 with higher scores indicating more use. Analyses of variance were performed on both scales with gender and school year as independent variables.

2. Attitudes towards computers and their use were the target of the second section containing 55 statements which required responses on a five point Likert scale ranging from 'strongly agree' to 'strongly disagree'. The items covered interest in computers, personal feelings when respondents worked with computers and the kind of personal characteristics that respondents believed would be necessary to be successful in working with computers, for example: 'Computers are great toys', 'I would like to know more about computers' and 'I don't think I'll ever get used to working with computers'.

    A scale measuring the range of positive and negative attitudes (**compATT**) was computed as follows. The scores on 7 items that expressed a positive attitude to computers were aggregated and from this sum the scores of 7 items that expressed a negative attitude to computers were subtracted. The maximum and minimum scores obtainable on this computer attitude scale were 14 and -14 respectively, with the more positive attitude represented by the higher scores.

3. & 4. The last two sections sought respondents' views on statements relating to gender appropriate behaviour and their views on school life and the questionnaire administration.

    The results of these two sections will be reported elsewhere, see Durndell et al. (in press).

Chi-square analyses were carried out on the data relating to all 429 pupils' experience of computers (questionnaire section 1) and analyses of variance were performed on a subset of 196 pupils on the attitudinal variable (questionnaire section 2) with gender and school year as independent variables. The two state schools were excluded from the analyses of variance mainly because the very low number of sixth year pupil's in these schools would defeat the assumption of normal distribution.

RESULTS

(A)   Experience of computers

School use

Generally boys were significantly more likely than girls to have used various computer hard and soft ware as is evident in Table 2. It was also found that significantly more boys indicated that they had made use of the school's computers outside lessons.

Table 3.2:   **Gender Differences and Computer Use at School: Percentage of girls and boys ticking 'Yes' options.**

	Girls	Boys	Total	$X^2 p$
Play game for fun	84.0	79.4	81.6	ns
Play game to learn	73.8	75.7	74.8	ns
Used disk drive	61.0	78.0	69.9	.001
Used Mouse	19.4	27.5	23.6	.06
Used printer	57.8	72.2	65.3	.002
Used spreadsheet	05.5	12.3	09.0	.02
Written	a			computer
program:	33.5	57.0	45.7	.001
Used	a			computer
outside lessons:	56.4	69.5	63.2	006
N=	206	223	429	

NB: Yates correction applied in each case.

Contrary to expectations there were no gender related differences in games playing at school.
  In addition to the above items, respondents were also asked how many pieces of text, e.g. letters, notes, assignments, they had produced at school using a wordprocessor. Nearly half of all pupils said that they had produced nothing on a wordprocessor (Table 3.3). Of those that had produced a piece of work on the wordprocessor, fewer girls than boys reported to have produced more than 10.

Table 3.3.   **Gender Differences and Wordprocessor Usage: Percentage of respondents ticking the various levels.**

	None	1-5	6-10	>10	*N*
Girls	54.3	34.0	5.1	06.6	*197*
Boys	45.4	27.6	8.7	18.3	*218*
Total	49.6	30.6	7.0	12.8	*415*

Chi-square=16.22; df=3; p_.001.

Turning to the results on the aggregated scores of computer use, the analysis of variance indicated that in all three years at school for the selected subset boys made significantly more use of computers, and computers were used least by the youngest pupils (Table N4).

Table 3.4:   **Means of Scores on Aggregated Scale of Computer Use at School (schoolUSE) by Gender and School Year**

	First	Third	Sixth
Girls	1.58	1.98	2.40
Boys	2.74	3.37	3.30

N=197. Analysis of variance for Gender was significant, $p<.001$. Year: difference significant , $p<.012$. Interaction between Gender and Year was not significant.

Home computer use

The expected significant differences in computer ownership were found, with 68% of boys and 38% of girls reporting that they 'have a computer of their own'. It is hardly surprising therefore that boys also reported using computers on a significantly more regular basis than girls. For example 42% of girls reported that they never use a computer outside the school, compared with 15% of boys, and 4% of girls indicated that they use computers daily, compared with 23% of boys (Table 3.5).

Table 3.5:   **Frequency of Computer Use Outside School: Percentage of respondents answering 'Yes' for each level of usage**

	Never	Once a month	Once a week	A few times weekly	Daily	N
Girls	41.7	35.0	10.2	08.7	04.4	206
Boys	14.9	19.8	13.1	29.3	23.0	222
Total	27.8	27.1	11.7	19.4	14.0	428

Chi-square=87.18; df=4; $p_.0001$.

An unexpected result was that girls were found to report nearly as much games playing as boys at school, with 16% of girls and 22% of boys saying that they use a wordprocessor at home (the difference was not statistically significant).

Turning to the results on the aggregated scores of home computer use, the analysis of variance indicated that, for all three year groups in the selected subset, boys made significantly more use of computers, and computer use declined significantly with age (Table 3.6). Further, the decline was significantly more marked for girls.

Table 3.6:   **Means of Scores on Aggregated Scale of Computer Use at Home (homeUSE) by Gender and School Year**

	First	Third	Sixth
Girls	1.19	1.49	0.22
Boys	2.86	2.13	1.80

N=197. Analysis of variance for Gender was significant, $p<.001$. Year: difference significant , $p<.012$. Interaction between Gender and Year was significant, $p<.01$.

The analysis of computer use can be summarised as confirming the gender gap, as boys report significantly greater use of computers both in and out of school. For both genders there is a trend for school computer use to increase with age and home computer use to decrease with age.

(B)   **Attitudes to computers**

A comparison of the scores on the attitudinal scale showed that boys were relatively more positive or enthusiastic about computers. Thus Table 3.7 shows the scores on the computed scale measuring attitudes to computers for girls and boys at each stage.

Table 3.7:   **Mean Scores on Computed Positive Attitude to Computers Scale (possATT) by Gender and Year at School**

	First	Third	Sixth
Girls	2.92	2.32	1.57
Boys	4.11	2.62	2.48

N=197. Analysis of variance for Gender was significant, $p<.001$. Year: difference significant , $p<.012$. Interaction between Gender and Year was significant, $p<.01$.

The age related results that both girls and boys became less enthusiastic about computers with age paralleled the previous finding that the use of computers outside school declines with age.

DISCUSSION

In line with previous research, gender related differences in computer experience and frequency of use were found in a number of areas both at school and at home. Boys were more likely to own computers, more likely to have a wider range of experience with computers and use them more frequently. Unexpectedly it was also found that girls report as much games playing as boys at school and make as much use of wordprocessing software as boys in the home situation. Considering previous research and because games playing outside the school was more frequent amongst boys, it is likely that the amount of games playing in school is primarily teacher determined, though it is also possible that games found in schools are more appealing to girls because there are more practical reasons for using such games. The latter hypothesis is certainly congruent with the proposition that girls are more utilitarian or pragmatically disposed towards computers.

We regard the finding that girls use wordprocessors as frequently as boys as supporting the hypothesis that girls and women are prepared to use computers when they see a practical reason for it (Durndell 1990; Siann et al. 1990). We would argue that the use of wordprocessing, and perhaps other open ended software, offers obvious pragmatic advantages resulting in a reduction of gender differences in this area of technology.

Though girls were found to respond in comparatively less positive terms than boys, it is important - particularly in terms of public perception of gender related differences - to bear in mind that this doesn't necessarily mean that girls have a negative view of computers. Rather we would stress that they simply have a *comparatively* less positive view. Moreover, it could be the case that girls have a more sober or mature attitude to computers and it is the boys who hold overly positive views about computers and are too optimistic about the benefits of computers.

The present findings of a decline in positive regard of computers as pupils get older, particularly pronounced amongst girls, offers support to Lage's (1991) findings that as girls grow older their attitudes to technology become less positive relative to the attitudes of boys. In line with this finding we have previously found that the gender gap increases with age, particularly in a mixed gender (co-educational) situation. Because of the dynamic nature of this phenomenon, with its associated interaction between environment and age related factors it has been argued that 'polarisation' could be considered as part of an underlying process of gender formation (Glissov 1991).

It has also been suggested that a shift in the respondents' understanding of what is meant by 'computer' occurs with age (Wilder et al. 1988). Considering this suggestion in the light of the findings from a previous study of primary school children (Siann et al. 1990), it seems equally plausible that the change could be due to what might be called a 'sobering' effect - which comes with experience and the realisation that computers cannot match earlier (unrealistically optimistic) expectations. The 'sobering' and 'polarisation' effects deal with qualitatively different aspects of the gender gap, but there is no a priori reason why these and other factors could not be involved simultaneously. As yet these hypotheses remain untested.

Finally we turn to the educational policy implications of the present findings. Our earlier research showed that computing and information technology, as a discipline, have images that are not attractive to girls and women. For example, potential female students of computing in tertiary education appeared to be put off by the prospect of harassment in predominantly male groups, and too much time spent in front of VDUs (Durndell et al. 1990). Culley (1988) demonstrated that option choices in secondary school are often arranged so that they restrict the choices of girls. As Lightbody & Durndell (1993) pointed out subject and option choices are normally made in the mid teens, and it is such choices that have the greatest impact on career choice. It is therefore important that computer related subjects should be made more interesting and attractive to girls in the middle and latter years of secondary school. As mentioned earlier, the present findings would suggest that the use of open ended software like wordprocessors and projects with a useful goal may go some way in achieving higher interest levels amongst girls.

As previous research indicates that courses with a 'heavy' computer content may be associated with images unacceptable to girls, another step could be to 'feminise' computer based subjects in schools (and higher education for that matter). This could, for example, mean the abandonment, as far as possible, of the terms 'information technology' (IT) and 'computer science' , and the adoption of a term like 'informatics', thereby stressing the information and knowledge base as opposed to the technology base, and highlighting the traditionally more feminine aspects such as problem solving and the communicative skills needed (Glissov 1992; Buckner 1991). In support of this argument, one could mention that the continental Europeans use the term informatics in this way and 'over there' the gender gap is not as striking as it is here.

References

Bear G.G., Richards H.C. & Lancaster P. (1987) Attitudes Towards Computers: Validation of a Computer Attitude Scale. *Journal of Educational Computing Research*, 26, 9: 207-218.

Buckner K. (1991) Information Technology - Art or Science? In *Women into Computing: Selected papers, 1988-1990*. Edited by G. Lovegrove & B. Segal.

Collis B. & Ollila L.. (1990) Effects of Computer Use on Grade 1 Children's Gender Stereotypes about Reading, Writing and Computer Use. *Journal of Research and Development in Education*, 24: 14-20.

Collis B. (1985) Psychological Implications of Sex Differences in Attitudes Toward Computers: Results of a survey. *International Journal of Women's Studies*, 8, 3: 207-13.

Culley L.A. (1988) Option Choice and Careers Guidance: Gender and computing in secondary schools. *British Journal of Guidance and Counselling*, 16, 1: 73-81.

Dain J. (1991) Women and Computing: Some responses to falling numbers in higher education. *Women's Studies International Forum*, 14: 217-225.

Durndell A. (1990) Why Do Female Students Tend to Avoid Computer Studies? *Research in Science and Technological Education*, 8, 2: 163-170.

Durndell A.J., Siann G. & Glissov P. (1990) Gender Differences and Computing in Course Choice at Entry Into Higher Education. *British Educational Research Journal*, **16**, 2: 149-162.

Durndell A., Glissov P. & Siann G. (in press) Gender and Computing: Persisting differences. To appear in *Educational Research*.

Fisher G. (1984) Access to Computers. *The Computing Teacher*, 11, 8: 24-27.

Ford D.H. & Ford M.E. (1987) Humans as Self-Constructing Living Systems: An overview. *Humans as Self-Constructing Living Systems: Putting the framework to work*. Edited by D.H. Ford & M.E. Ford. Hillsdale, NJ: Lawrence Erlbaum Associates.

Glissov P. (1991) The Gender Gap in Secondary School Computer Use. In *Women into Computing: Selected Papers, 1988-1990, pp 130-144*. Edited by Gillian Lovegrove and Barbara Segal. 'Workshops in Computing' Series. London: Springer Verlag and the British Computer Society.

Glissov P. (1992) *Social and Motivational Aspects of Secondary School Pupils' Computer Use, with Particular Reference to the Gender Issue*. Unpublished PhD Thesis, Glasgow Caledonian University (formerly Glasgow Polytechnic/CNAA).

Levin T. & Gordon C. (1989) Effect of Gender and Computer Experience on Attitudes Toward Computers. *Journal of Educational Computing Research*, 5, 1: 69-88.

Lightbody P. & Durndell A. (1993) *Senior School Pupils' Career Aspirations: Is gender an issue?* Paper presented at the British Psychological Society Annual London Conference, December 1993.

Lovegrove G. & Segal B. (eds)(1991) *Women into Computing: Selected Papers, 1988-1990*, pp 130-144. London: Springer Verlag and the British Computer Society.

Loyd B.H., Loyd D.E. & Gressard C.P. (1987) Gender and Computer Experience as Factors in the Computer Attitudes of Middle School Students. *Journal of Early Adolescence*, 7, 1: 13-19.

Macleod H.A., Siann G. & Glissov P. (1988) *Cognitive and Motivational Factors in Primary School Computer Use*. Edinburgh: Scottish Education Department.

Miura I.T (1987) A Multivariate Study of School-Aged Children's Computer Interest and Use. *Humans as Self-Constructing Living Systems: Putting the framework to work.* Edited by M.E. Ford & D.H. Ford.

Siann G., Glissov P. & Macleod H.A. (1990) Cognitive and Motivational Factors in Primary School Computer Use. *Proceedings of First National Women Into Computing Conference.* University of Lancaster, 20-22 July 1988: Women Into Computing.

Wilder G., Mackie D. & Cooper J. (1985) Gender and Computers: Two surveys of computer-related attitudes. *Sex Roles*, 13, 3/4: 215-228.

4. The Development of a Computer-Based Teaching System Based on the Toolbook Programming Software

Keith Firman, *University of Portsmouth*

Summary
A full lecture course in the field of Genetic Engineering (approximately 36 hours of lectures) has been produced in the form of a hypertext teaching system which can be used for revision by undergraduate students. Throughout the main text of this book important phrases and words are emboldened and are set-up as "hot-words". These "hot-words" can be activated by clicking the mouse button, when the cursor is placed over the word, this activation will then either move the user to another part of the book, show further text, a diagram, or display an animation. To accommodate the large amount of information the book is organised into chapters, where each chapter is a separate ToolBook book. To allow seamless transfer between books, the software writes the previous location to another file, and can then read this information when navigating through the various chapters. To accompany the lectures there is an additional hypertext practical book, the pages of which can be printed and distributed for class practicals. The recipes for methods and other materials used in the practicals, can be obtained by activating the "hot-words"; the user may then, if he so wishes, easily return to the main genetic engineering hypertext, to read the theory which accompanies each practical. The practical book is arranged such, that each practical is associated with a particular part of the main genetic engineering text. Finally, we are developing a tutorial system, which will use multi-choice questions, to test the students' understanding of the subject; this tutorial system will also permit new questions to be entered.

INTRODUCTION

The successful introduction of the Windows operating system on PC-based computers, used in teaching at the University of Portsmouth, prompted me to consider the possibility of developing a windows-based teaching aid. The concept I had, was one of incorporating a full lecture course and associated practical classes, into a computer-based hypertext environment. This would allow students, when the normal lectures were finished, to use the hypertext book as a revision aid. I also wanted to use a very simple programming system, which would not require a knowledge of high-level computer language. Realistically, there were only two development tools I could use -Asymmetrix's ToolBook or Microsoft's Visual Basic. I decided on ToolBook, as this was available earlier.

TOOLBOOK
ToolBook uses a very simple English-like language titled, 'OpenScript'. This language can be used to carry out very complex processes, including dynamic data exchange between applications etc. However, I wanted to develop a very simple system, using commands that were very easy to understand and which could readily be adapted to different systems. In particular, I intended to use the "Hide" and "Show" commands to allow the user to access extra information, regarding specific topics, on demand. Other important commands used, to develop simple animations, are "move", "set" and "position".

GENETIC ENGINEERING
This subject was used, not only because it is the course I teach as part of the 'Molecular Biology' degree, at the University of Portsmouth, but also because it lends itself to the use of animation for simple explanations of the subject matter. We also intend to develop this teaching system commercially, and the popularity of genetic engineering was thought to be a "good selling point". The book was also designed to accompany an open course (workshop)

on DNA Cloning/Sequencing, and to provide the theoretical background for this particular practical workshop.

INITIAL DEVELOPMENT OF THE MULTI-CHAPTER BOOK

The first stage of production was to provide simple scripts that hide, or show, additional textual information upon activation of a "hot-word". A typical script is shown in Figure 4.1 which also illustrates the result of activating the hotword **"Bacteria"**. The only problem that was apparent from this type of script was observed when operating slower computers, such as an 80386SX @ 20mhz, where the users seemed to be unsure that a script had been activated and were inclined, therefore, to produce a multiple activation of one "hotword".

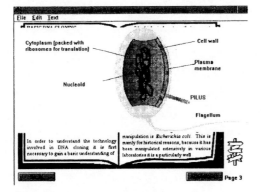

The script associated with the hotword Bacteria is:

```
To handle ButtonDown
set sysCursor to 4
set sysLockScreen to true
show group "bacteria"
show rectangle "border"
set sysLockScreen to false
set sysCursor to 1
End
```

The result of activating the hotword is to display a hidden figure:

Figure 4.1: A simple script to display a hidden diagram

To overcome this problem it was necessary to include the "Set sysCursor to 4...set sysCursor to 1" combination of commands, which resulted in the mouse pointer displaying as an hourglass, indicating that the computer was "busy".

The other major problem observed with these simple scripts was how to write to a file, in such a way that the information saved in that file could be used to store variables, when changing from one ToolBook book to another. OpenScript only remembers variables during a single instance of ToolBook, which means that when activation of a "hot-word" moves the user to another chapter, in order to be able to move back to the original page, its location must be permanently stored (e.g. in a file). After several attempts to accomplish this with text files, we discovered that reading and writing could only be guaranteed with a ToolBook book open on the desktop (although it is possible to use executeRemote to access un-opened books). A text field in the book caries a list of all previous pages visited and this is continuously updated when the "return" button is used (Figure 4.2).

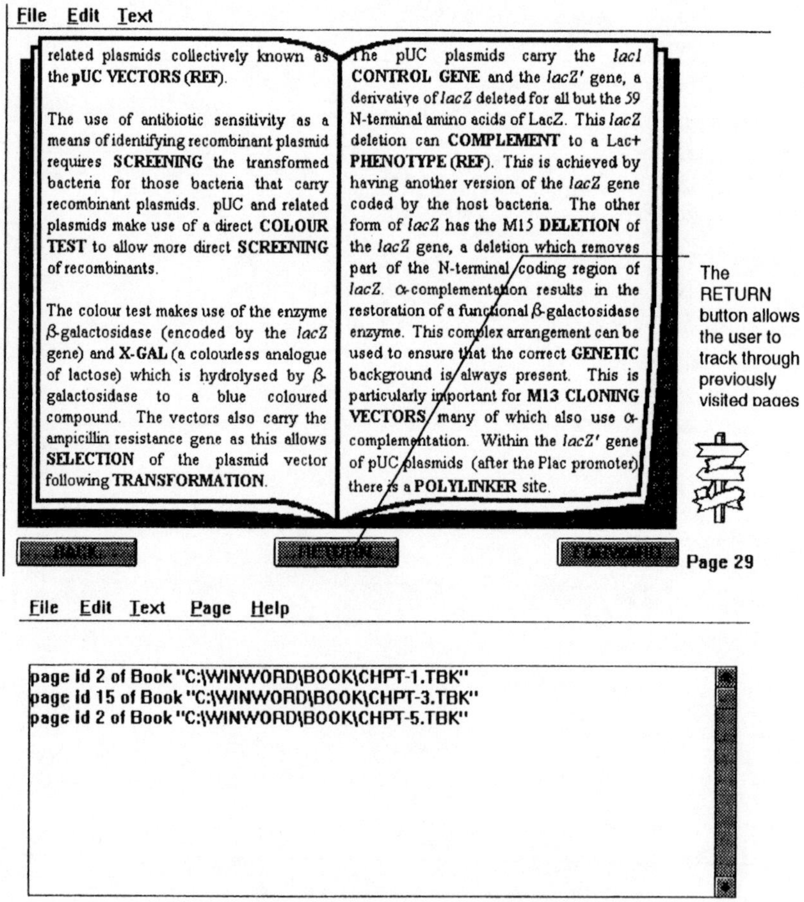

The previously visited pages are stored in another ToolBook book, within a text field.

Figure 4.2 The return button allows navigation through the chapters of the book.

ANIMATIONS USING OPENSCRIPT

The ToolBook object orientated programming language allows easy production of animations based on a macro-recorder. This recorder allows small movements of an object to be stored within a script, and then replayed on demand. However, this results in an almost unreadable script which is difficult to manipulate later (Figure 4.3). To overcome this problem, the macro recorder was used to store only the start position and the final position. The script was then written using "step i from 0 to 10...end step" to move the object by 10 (or more) steps. This type of programming is also more readable, and allowed us to incorporate an "interrupt" into the script which is activated by the escape key (Figure 4.4). This "interrupt" is extremely important, as users can often activate an animation which they have seen before and, rather than wait until the full animation is illustrated, the escape key can be pressed to re-set the page.

Figure 4.3: **An animation produced using the recorder of ToolBook.**
The script below results from using the macro recorder to record the movements of an object on the screen. As can be seen this makes alterations to the animation difficult and the script is very difficult to understand.

```
To handle buttonUp
select ellipse "Circle1"
move the selection to 1065, 1740
move the selection to 1260, 1740
move the selection to 1515, 1890
move the selection to 1695, 2055
move the selection to 1860, 2115
move the selection to 2055, 2280
move the selection to 2325, 2415
move the selection to 2490, 2565
set bounds of selection to 2490, 2190, 3435, 3060
set bounds of selection to 2490, 1845, 3840, 3060
set bounds of selection to 2490, 1575, 4140, 3060
set bounds of selection to 2490, 1395, 4575, 3060
set bounds of selection to 2490, 1185, 4838, 3060
set bounds of selection to 2490, 870, 5003, 3060
end buttonUp
```

Figure 4.4: A script that produces a simple animation.

The script below illustrates the use of a simple stepping algorithm to move an object around the screen, and also illustrates the use of the escape key to break from the animation:

```
step i from 0 to 2780 by 100
    if keyState(keyEscape) is "down"
        send enterPage to this page
        break
    end if
    set position of picture "Klenow" to 3990-(i*1.6),4335-i
end step
```

ACCESSIBILITY AND MONITORING USAGE

One of the most important aspects of writing to another ToolBook book, as a means of storing variables between instances of ToolBook, is that this also allows us to record who has used the book, when and for how long.

This information is combined with a number, that is linked to the last page the user read. The information can then be recorded by the lecturer to monitor the students progress and also enable the user to return to the page he was last reading.

ADDITIONAL FEATURES AND ASSOCIATED BOOKS

In addition to the six chapters (the final version will have ten chapters) the Genetic Engineering teaching system also includes a hypertext practical book and a tutorial system, although this is still under development. The practical book is designed in such a way that the pages can be printed for use as handouts for practical classes, and the practical details are presented in a format suited to such classes. The hypertext consists of additional text boxes, which are activated by "hot-words", that give details of materials required in each practical. This information can be used by technical staff to prepare the media for the classes. The practical book also has easy access back to the Genetic Engineering hypertext book, linked in such a way that the entry point to the Genetic Engineering book is closely linked to the practical (i.e. the theory behind the practical class is available). This form of linkage also functions in the reverse direction.

The tutorial system consists of questions, with multiple choice answers, activated by buttons. The user is informed why their choice is incorrect if the wrong answer is selected, and a mark is added or deducted based on the answer chosen. The total mark and the number of attempts made, is then stored under each user's name in a ToolBook book and is easily accessed by the lecturer. We are currently developing a question/answer generator, which will allow other people to develop their own questions, answers and marking scheme. We also intend to allow users to answer certain questions with text entered at the keyboard; which can then be printed out for marking by the lecturer.

FUTURE DEVELOPMENTS

One of the most important developments for this system will be to incorporate video images into the practical book (thus making it a multimedia, hypertext environment). This part of the project has not yet been initiated, and we are currently investigating potential MPEG video compression-decompression software. These video clips would be used to demonstrate to students various simple techniques, which are common to many different practicals. Although the clips will be relatively short, 1 - 5 minutes, the storage space required will inevitably mean that the system will be distributed on CD-ROM.

Another important development we are about to initiate is the use of a sound card, together with associated (freely available) speech recognition software, to allow handicapped persons to activate the "hot-words" in the hypertext books. Such a system will require "training" of the software to allow recognition of each individual's voice, but such software is already in common use (Creative Labs SoundBlaster 16). At this time, the use of sound in the book is not thought to be particularly advantageous.

Acknowledgements

I am grateful to the EHE Enterprise scheme for their help in developing this system and to the University of Portsmouth Enterprises Limited, for their funding of the computer hardware and software.

5. Developing Employment-based Access to Learning: The DEAL Project

Ray Land and Val Edgar Nevill, *Napier University, Edinburgh UK*

Summary
The DEAL Project (Developing Employment-based Access to Learning) was established in June 1992 with funding from Scottish Enterprise. This two year initiative has progressed on a cross-institutional basis, being jointly undertaken by Glasgow Caledonian University, Stirling University and Napier University. The fundamental aim of the DEAL Project is to enable people to benefit from higher education and gain credit towards qualifications without leaving employment, even though they may lack the traditional qualifications for entry to higher education. The project aims to analyse the potential for workplace learning, assessment and accreditation in a range of subject areas in specific companies, together with the potential scope for more flexible delivery of qualifications which are relevant to employer and employee needs. In the achievement of this aim the project is developing a model for HEIs and employers which will allow employment-based learning opportunities leading to recognised qualifications to be negotiated between the learner, the employer, the professional body, and the educational institution(s).

INTRODUCTION: WORK-BASED LEARNING AND HIGHER EDUCATION

The development of a model for work-based learning in a higher education context poses important and difficult challenges for both employers and universities. As Pierce (1993) has argued 'Work-based learning needs satisfactory ways of exposing, assessing and accrediting learning and a shift in the attitude of universities, professional bodies, employers and individual learners themselves if it is to be regarded as equal to full-time education'. These challenges need to be met in a context where the quality of the learning experience can be assured in a way transparent to the individual learner, the employer, the professional body and the higher education institution. Fitness for purpose must be able to be demonstrated to all partners in these different contexts. It is helpful briefly to examine these contexts.

THE EMPLOYER CONTEXT

The employer requires a model which, in a resource-efficient manner maintains and develops employee efficiency, effectiveness and flexibility in changing operational contexts. Our employer partners argue that this is important not only directly in terms of the impact on operational effectiveness, but also indirectly through increased motivation, enhanced self-image and the subsequent impact on staff retention. Two obvious implications of this are related to the importance of employer and employee involvement in the identification of target competencies and the adoption of learning and assessment processes that are congruent with the circumstances, needs and learning style of the employee.

THE HIGHER EDUCATION INSTITUTION CONTEXT

It is clear from the above that the model for employment-based learning must be client-centred rather than institution-centred. All of the institutions involved in the current project have already undertaken considerable developments in this area and are each leading institutions within the Scottish Credit Accumulation and Transfer (SCOTCAT) network. Thus the focus of development has to be the learning needs of the individual employer and employee. The pace of learning has to be suited to the individual's work and personal context (although probably within defined parameters) rather than the predetermined pace of a course. The location of learning has to be related to the objectives and processes of learning and the contexts of the individual rather than assuming that learning is 'located' within education institutions. This of course does not deny the considerable importance of the educational resources contained within institutions. We need however to define carefully the role of these resources and how they may be accessed. Additionally, employee learning needs do not come labelled 'further' or 'higher' education. The model should not therefore be constrained by these divisions, although clearly qualifications awarded should correspond to existing award structures.

There are a number of implications that follow from these contexts. The model for employment-based access to learning should be based on a model of credit accumulation rather than a course-based structure. The model should reward appropriate learning wherever it has taken place provided it can be appropriately evidenced. It should integrate appropriate in-house provision within the accredited framework. It should allow for the planned development of experiential learning in the workplace and it should allow for the accreditation of appropriate prior learning. In Reeve's terms (1993), the model must be open in relation to barriers to access, in relation to 'course' participation. For these reasons it is important that the model is located within the Access level together with the SCOTCAT framework, including undergraduate levels SDI through SD4, and the postgraduate level M. It is also important that the model for employment-based access to learning should build on the important features of the SCOTCAT framework which facilitates credit transfer between Universities and between Universities and Colleges of Further Education.

One further implication for the model, which is important in this context, is mainstreaming. It is easy for employment-based provision in particular, and experiential learning in general, to remain at the margins of institutional provision for which 'special' arrangements have to be made in a variety of ways. Such arrangements are often under-resourced, heavily dependent on the goodwill and commitment of groups of staff and effectively beyond the mainstream of the institution's provision. It is important for the model to address the issue of mainstreaming to support effective resourcing, quality assurance and successful long-term development of employment-based learning.

THE PROFESSIONAL BODY CONTEXT

Where a professional body has a significant locus, it is important that the employment-based learning model should address the requirements of that body. It is clearly important that the learning of the individual employee wins appropriate professional recognition. The model must therefore be developed to take into account relevant professional body requirements. It is interesting to note in this context that some professional bodies are currently reviewing their policies and procedures in relation to continuing professional development and have found interaction with members of the development team useful.

THE EMPLOYEE CONTEXT

The model is designed to fit the circumstances of clients who are in full-time employment. Currently, in the vast majority of cases, if such individuals wish to access higher education provision at undergraduate level they will often have to undertake full-time study. This involves either an extremely intensive investment of training resources from the employer (at the expense of a more extensive provision affording opportunities to a much wider range of employees) or the extremely heavy opportunity cost associated with giving up full-time work.

Part-time course-based provision within higher education is growing but is still extremely limited. In general employees are faced with very significant barriers to access which severely limit their scope for professional and personal development in relation to higher education.

It is also vitally important to reflect on the nature of adult learning in this context. There is a growing body of evidence (Marton, Hounsell & Entwistle 1984, Entwistle 1992, Gibbs 1990,) that many traditional, course-based approaches to learning within higher education lead to 'surface' approaches to learning which emphasise memorisation and a reproductive approach and fail to engage the learner in criticaly reflective activities which emphasise the need for understanding, the transformation of knowledge and its relation to prior learning. To support the development of 'deep' approaches to learning (Marton & Saljo: 1976) requires that the individual learner explicitly takes more responsibility for and ownership of the whole learning process through structures requiring negotiation, interaction and active learning approaches. One important objective of the model is therefore to support the effective development of the reflective practitioner. (Kolb 1984, Schon 1987).

The model of employment-based learning has therefore to address the full involvement of the learner in these processes of negotiation and relate them to the working and professional context of the full-time employee. This clearly has significant implications for the role and importance of work-based learning support and the pivotal advisory and support role of educational institutions. Additionally there are significant issues raised for quality assurance processes that the model will have to address.

THE DEAL MODEL

The model has been developed in relation to four main groups; employers, employee (learners), institutions of higher and further education and professional bodies. Clearly in any particular employment context the scope and role of each group will vary. In general however we may picture the learner at the centre of these interacting groups (Figure 5.1):

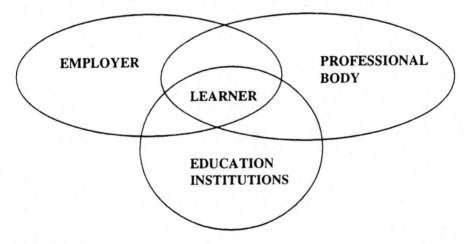

Figure 5.1

Thus, within this complex environment the model has to address the needs of the individual learner. However, this has to be achieved in a manner that is resource-efficient, is focused around the employment context and embraces the impact of learning on enhanced productivity and service delivery.

KEY ELEMENTS AND BENEFITS OF THE DEAL MODEL

The essential features of the DEAL model can best be summarised in terms of design, implementation and assessment.

The design of the model stems from the identification of the training needs of the organisation. The identified needs are subsequently translated into clusters of learning outcomes which are located at the appropriate higher education level. During the implementation of the model employees undertake the programme by drawing upon a range of work-based and other learning resources. In negotiation with the employer and the academic institution they develop individual action plans which take account of their current areas of work, their prior learning from experience and appropriate in-house training provision. The work of the employees is assessed through the compilation of portfolios of evidence of their learning as they proceed through the programme. These portfolios are assessed for academic credit by the higher education institution and, where appropriate, for professional credit by the professional body.

There are various benefits in this approach. The model not only meets staff development goals for improved business performance and service delivery but offers a learning programme located mainly in the workplace, with no replacement costs. Both the motivation and the retention of employees can be increased. Skills are updated and credit can be gained for existing skills. The model is adaptable to large or small businesses (though with certain provisos regarding very small organisations) and it widens access to further and higher education.

This model of employment-based access to learning is being developed and tested by working in partnership with specific companies and their employees to meet their particular training and development needs. The next section describes the industrial collaboration undertaken at Napier University in the area of information technology.

A WORK-BASED LEARNING PROGRAMME FOR INFORMATION TECHNOLOGY EMPLOYEES

Aims and objectives

The aim of the DEAL Project (East) at Napier University has been to develop a work-based learning programme to increase access opportunities for a potential client group who are employed in the area of Information Technology but are not currently involved in higher education. These clients are employees and managers unable to attend taught programmes on a regular basis owing to full-time work commitments. The project has continually addressed the issue of ensuring that proper control of academic standards could be maintained and demonstrated whilst providing the flexibility required by the target group.

Methodology

A learning agreement is negotiated through which clients' work-based learning, both prior and ongoing, can be accredited in accordance with university-approved learning outcomes. The redesigning of Napier University's existing Certificate, Diploma and Degree programmes in Computing and Business Information Management into a modular form based on learning outcomes has facilitated the achievement of such awards from the workplace. Approval by the University's Credit Accumulation and Transfer (CAT) Scheme of procedures for accrediting prior experiential learning (APEL) has also been a significant feature of the model.

The two companies established as partners in the project were Coopers & Lybrand and Hewlett Packard. Individual employees were selected from each company to form a pilot group and subsequently enrolled as students within the University's CAT Scheme. The pilot project originally focused on modules at SCOTCAT Levels SD1, SD2 and SD3 and is currently addressing awards at M level.

Appropriate flexible learning and training materials produced within the partner companies and within Napier were identified and matched against the approved learning outcomes of modules within the HNC/HND and degree programmes. Where necessary such materials were adapted and where no appropriate existing materials were available, for example in Mathematics for Computing Contexts, arrangements were set in train for the production of new open learning support materials to suit the work-based learning context. APL Checklists suitable for use in partner companies were developed in consultation with employees. These could be used by work-based learners to construct portfolios or undertake assessments to build up a credit profile.

In the light of this credit profile a learning agreement is negotiated with each employee, establishing a plan for attaining the learning outcomes and credits necessary to obtain the desired qualification. The learner (employee) discusses the module learning outcomes with Napier staff and agrees the manner in which the outcomes might best be achieved. The resources of the partner company are utilised wherever possible. Where shortcomings are revealed in the learner's ability to achieve the required learning outcomes directly from the work environment, then the nature and extent of the required Napier-based support is identified. The plan may incorporate any combination of learning experiences which arise through routine work activities, flexible learning materials for use in the workplace, provision of in-company training, part-time attendance at Napier University or other post-compulsory educational institutions, and the accreditation of prior experiential learning (APEL).

The programme is designed as an articulated route with multiple exit points. Regarding the point of entry, if the learner already has a qualification or learning from experience which is appropriate for a programme of study, they may be eligible for significant credit towards an award. A set of academic and administrative standards for quality assurance in the award of such credit has been established. Regarding points of exit or progression the learner decides how far to go with the programme - a certificate, diploma, degree, degree with honours, or a postgraduate qualification. Alternatively the learner may take only one or two units as an Associate Student and be awarded a Certificate of Achievement.

The feature which distinguishes this project from other forms of delivery is its capacity to concentrate on identified learner needs and the employment-based context.

The accreditation of learning is greatly simplified for candidates when they are provided with a framework of learning outcomes against which their learning can be matched. The provision of a programme defined in terms of outcomes both allows the learner to focus on specified goals and provides the accrediting body with a specific set of qualitative and quantitative criteria against which the learning can be judged.

Our experience to date would lead us to conclude that work-based learning is most effectively undertaken when it is characterised by the following factors:

- it is located firmly in the full context of the workplace;
- it is linked to improved productivity and service delivery;
- it is related to the career development of employees;

- it identifies opportunities for prior and planned future learning within the context of the everyday work of the candidate and accessible extension of that context;
- it is linked, where possible, to formal in-house training support;
- assessment is purposefully related to the workplace;
- it operates within a modular framework based on learning outcomes, supported by the CAT framework of the University.

Negotiation

The Napier team have found that for a programme of learning to meet both these needs systematic liaison with the employer is required to reconcile any differences in priorities or emphasis in the design of the learner's programme. This may take place through the workplace mentor or identified person within the Training or HRD section. With adult learners operating in organisational settings such contractual arrangements call for sensitive discussion and management.

It is essential that during the development of a work-based learning programme negotiation takes place with representatives at an appropriate level within the employment organisation, as only in this way can the necessary continuing commitment and support for the individuals involved be obtained. This is clearly demonstrated with our two pilot organisations. While there has been substantial progress with one of the pilot groups, difficulties have been encountered with the other. Although time constraints appear to have been a major problem for all participants the need for greater involvement at senior management level was deemed a critical factor.

Credit accumulation

At Napier a significant factor in the establishing of appropriate learning programmes was the approval of an open learning route for CATS students who are now eligible to be enrolled on a Combined Studies Degree in Computing and Business Information management. In early discussion with the participants at Coopers & Lybrand, it became clear that not all modules within a Computer Science degree were appropriate. The Project Team made the decision to test sample modules from within the new Business Information management degree and a package of Level 1 learning outcome modules was offered to Cooper & Lybrand participants. Individual learners found that a combination of modules from two named awards was more appropriate. Working within the SCOTCAT framework allowed individuals to overcome the limitations of a `named route' and to tailor their study programme much more closely to their work place environment.

The project team have sought to utilise the employer's training programmes as a means of achieving the outcomes of the accredited work-based learning programmes rather than undertake the accreditation of each of the training courses. This process is greatly enhanced by the recasting of such training courses to support candidates more positively in the collection of evidence. The amendment of training programmes in the light of the DEAL outcomes can potentially strengthen the employer's normal provision by more specifically targeting their identified training needs and through he incorporation of assessment. The entire workforce can thereby benefit from the improved provision.

The DEAL project recognises that there is an important distinction to be drawn between work-based learning and distance learning. Candidates are encouraged to demonstrate their achievement of the competencies because of and not in spite of the workplace context. With this aim in mind the programmes will include reference to structured work experience, training support available within the employer organisation, appropriate lists of reading and other workplace supervision or mentoring.

Future development

The funding body is keen to expand the client group reached by the project beyond those employed either by local authorities or large organisations. With this decision to re-direct the project towards small and medium sized enterprises, an in-depth appraisal and review process has taken place. Some of the key issues raised were as follows.

The BSc/HND undergraduate programmes were inappropriate. Both are broad-based courses providing an education for graduates taking up employment across a wide spectrum of employers. In contrast, our work-based learners had by their career choice and employment specialised computing skills and educational requirements. For example a systems designer developing an aircraft simulation system needs and uses quite different skills than someone developing information systems for an insurance company.

We needed to modify the original CATS framework. Initially, the intention was to accredit any prior learning before devising a learning program. For those work-based students with substantial experience, this meant getting bogged down in a lot of portfolio building before any of the 'new learning' they had signed up for could begin. We also identified a need for flexibility within learning programmes, due to the very fast-changing technology within the working environments of our pilot students. Both these issues have been catered for within our revised CATS MSc, in which study programmes have been identified as appropriate for an information technology environment. These courses are modular in nature and offer a wide variety of subject material directly tailored to specific workplace settings. Fortunately, we have been able to transfer existing DEAL students on to suitable study programs without any loss of credit already gained.

The DEAL project has recruited an external facilitator to work across all the individual projects, helping them identify industrial and commercial partners for future collaboration. The lessons learnt have been many, and the successes clearly measurable. It is with much enthusiasm and continued optimism that we embark on the further development of the project.

References

Entwistle N 1992 *The Impact of Teaching on Learning Outcomes in Higher Education*, CVCP USDU Sheffield

Gibbs G 1990 *Improving Student Learning*, CNAA

Kolb D A 1984 *Experiential Learning: Experience as the Source of Learning and Development*, Prentice Hall, New Jersey

Marton F & Saljo R 1976 On Qualitative Differences in Learning: Outcome and Process, *British Journal of Educ.* Psychology 46 (4-11)

Marton F, Hounsell D & Entwistle N 1984 *The Experience of Learning*, Scottish Academic Press

Pierce D 1993 *The Times Higher Education Supplement* 3.9.93

Reeve S 1993 Some Implications of Open Learning on Curriculum Strategy within Further Education in Graves N(Ed) *Learner Managed Learning: Practice Theory and Policy,* Higher Education for Capability

Schon D 1987 *Educating the Reflective Practitioner* Jossey-Bass, San Francisco

6. Achieving Efficiency Gains in Courseware Development

Simon Price, Phil Hobbs and Li Lin Cheah, *Centre for Computing in Economics, Department of Economics, University of Bristol*

Summary
The Teaching and Learning Technology Programme (TLTP) is the largest ever injection of public funds into learning technology in UK higher education. Much emphasis has been placed, quite rightly, on the educational goals and eventual efficiency gains of the courseware produced by the development teams. However, the extent to which these objectives will be met depends largely on the efficiency of the courseware development process itself. Strategies adopted by the Economics Consortium improve the likelihood of these objectives being met by improving the efficiency of the courseware development process. This paper describes these strategies. In particular it focuses on the separation of the academic's content authoring skills from the technical skills of the courseware programmer to attain an increase in quality and quantity of courseware with no increase in cost.

INTRODUCTION

The Teaching and Learning Technology Programme (TLTP) is the largest ever injection of public funds into learning technology in UK higher education (Darby 1993). Under Phase 1 of TLTP the UK Higher Education Funding Councils allocated £22.5m between 43 projects; under Phase 2 they committed a further £8.5m to fund an additional 33 projects; in total, £31m has been allocated to 76 projects over a four year period. As part of the TLTP initiative a consortium of eight economics departments, the TLTP Economics Consortium, receives direct grant funding of £640,000 to develop a range of computer-based teaching materials for introductory courses in economics (Hobbs 1993a). In addition to this direct funding, all member institutions have waived the overhead normally levied on grant funded projects. As a consequence, the effective funding of the Economics Consortium alone is approximately £1m over a two year period. The extent of this funding is not only indicative of the strategic importance of learning technology within higher education but also of the high cost and complexity of the courseware development process.

Significant emphasis has been placed, quite rightly, on the educational goals and eventual efficiency gains of the resultant courseware produced by development teams (UFC ISC 1992). However, the extent to which these targets will be met depends largely on the efficiency of the courseware development process itself: an efficient development process will maximise the likelihood of these objectives being met (Brooks 1975).

If the TLTP initiative as a whole is to stand a chance of meeting these objectives then the courseware development process adopted within individual consortia must deliver courseware of sufficient quality, to budget and on time (Hobbs 1993b). In order for this to happen, the adopted process must be efficient since the risk of failure increases as efficiency decreases. Therefore, it is reasonable to assume that efficiency improvements in a consortiums' development process reduces the risk to both the individual project and, as a result, to TLTP in general. In terms of this risk minimisation alone, there is a sufficiently strong case for optimising the efficiency of a project's courseware development process.

However, an equally strong case for an efficient development process can be made on the grounds of improving the quality and quantity of courseware delivered within the same budget and duration. Even though the budget and duration of TLTP projects is fixed, there is still scope for increasing the quality of deliverables through efficiency improvements in the courseware development process. Such efficiency gains are highly desirable in that they make better use of existing resources and at the same time reduce the risk of the project failing to meet quality objectives.

This paper describes strategies adopted by the Economics Consortium to improve the efficiency of the courseware development process. In particular, it focuses on the separation of the academic's content authoring skills from the technical skills of the courseware programmer to attain an increase in quality and quantity of courseware with no increase in cost.

CONTROLLING QUALITY THROUGH EFFICIENCY

In TLTP courseware development projects, as with most software projects, both time and budget are fixed; the grant funding of projects is of a fixed amount over a fixed period of time. In many cases, resources such as office space, lecturer time and programmer time are also for that same fixed period. Projects face a very real deadline for their completion in the true sense of the word; if development targets are not met then the project will fail. Indeed, if the development period slips into the time allocated for promotion and dissemination of the product then the project may deliver its product but still fail to meet its overall objectives.

Given that time and budget of a project are fixed, the only variable in the equation open to courseware developers is quality. However, quality in this context is a complex variable with two components:

- Quality of the courseware product

- Quality of the courseware development process

The quality of the courseware product depends on the quality of the courseware development process. The quality of the product is unlikely to increase without a corresponding increase in the quality of the process. That said, a high quality, efficient development process does not guarantee a high quality product; it does, however, make it far more likely.

EFFICIENCY THROUGH A PROJECT DEVELOPMENT MODEL

The Project Development Model is a document which describes the structure adopted by the Economics Consortium for the entire development process. It imposes software development control and quality assurance on the process of courseware development under the following headings and bears some resemblance to the PRINCE method.

1.   *Product Definition Phase*

   1.1. User Requirement Specification
   1.2. Functional Specification
   1.2.1. System Functional Specification
   1.2.2. Software Functional Specification
   1.2.3. Hardware Functional Specification
   1.3. Software Development Plan

2.   *Design Phase*

   2.1. System Architecture
   2.2. Software Subsystem Functional Specifications

2.3. Software Design Documents
2.4. Software Test Plan
2.5. Software Module and Integration Test Specifications

3.   *Implementation Phase*

3.1. Software Development Methodology
3.2. Usability and Instructional Design
3.3. Developer Co-ordination Strategy
3.4. Software Documentation Standards
3.5. Data Security Plan

4.   *Software Integration*

4.1. System Test Plan and Specification
4.2. System Test Results

5.   *Support Phase*

6.   *Iterations of the Development Phases*

The Project Development Model is essentially, an annotated list of documents; it is the top level of a hierarchy of documentation which serves as the Consortium's common, agreed, view of the project as a whole. Under the Developer Co-ordination Strategy, and of key importance, are the Developer Agreements between the Economics Consortium and each of its development teams. The Developer Agreements commission teams to produce a module to the project standards within a specified time and with the balance of payment to the developer only being paid on acceptance of the module by the Consortium.

Vital as these structures are to the efficient running of a large, multi-site, multi-developer courseware development project, they fall within the wider domain of software engineering and project management and as such are well documented elsewhere. They are included here only to portray a balanced picture of the development process as a whole. The focus of this paper, however, is on increasing the efficiency of a part of the courseware development process which is specific to courseware development: namely the authoring process - the transfer of subject expertise into computer-based learning materials.

EFFICIENCY OF THE AUTHORING PROCESS

Central to the efficiency of the courseware authoring process is the drawing together of the skills of the subject expert with the separate skills of the computer programmer. Traditionally, this problem has been addressed through skill acquisition. Often, the solution has been to attempt to train subject experts to programme. To date, time constraints, competing interests and a lack of professional reward have made this approach of only limited success. All too frequently, academic staff have only been able to reproduce lecture notes on the computer rather than exploiting the computational and interactive capabilities of the medium (ICBL 1993).

Another traditional approach to the separate skills problem has been to attempt to train programmers to be subject experts. Courseware developed in this way usually evolves through an interative process of written or oral specification from the subject expert and repeated modification of a prototype until, finally, an acceptable product is reached. Whilst this technique has been used to produce high quality material, it is expensive on account of the subject expert having to repeatedly convey ideas to the programmer.

A more efficient solution to the "separate skills problem" is the strategy adopted by the TLTP Economics Consortium. This strategy aims to separate the programming skills from the authoring skills and thereby remove the need for individuals who are both subject expert and programming expert. This is achieved through the encapsulation of all the advanced programming skills in a "template" developed in Asymetrix ToolBook and custom extensions written in C. The template, which is now on version 7.02, has been produced through an interative process of refinement led by the subject experts of the Economics Consortium and implemented by a small team of experienced programmers based at the Centre for Computing in Economics. The process of creating the template itself incurs many of the time penalties associated with training programmers to become subject experts, although at a less detailed level. However, having invested the time in creating this template, it then becomes practical for the subject experts to author courseware under the template without having to acquire a full set of programming skills. In effect, the skills of programming and economics courseware authoring have been separated. Authors can work in the sheltered environment of the template; programmers can continue to work on the template without having to become deeply involved in the courseware material. Consequently, both programer and subject expert can work efficiently in their respective areas of expertise rather than working inefficiently in each other's.

THE WinEcon AUTHORING TEMPLATE

The TLTP Economics Consortium has, over the course of the last 14 months created the WinEcon Authoring Template and used it to author 24 modules of courseware covering the whole of first year undergraduate introductory economics. Collectively these modules and a set of globally available resources (e.g. glossary, references, testing, help) form the WinEcon teaching software. Each WinEcon module will eventually deliver something of the order of 3-5 hours student contact time. To the student, the package will appear as a single, consistent and integrated programme. To the lecturer, the package will provide a selection of topics from which a course specific programme can be constructed to suit the course being taught; service teaching will require fewer and less advanced topics than a specialist economics degree course. Consequently, it is essential to have a common look and feel across all 24 modules to meet the needs of both educators and learners. This problem is also dealt with more efficiently through the template rather than manually trying to match styles across developers and modules.

The WinEcon Authoring Template provides an extra layer of functionality on top of the PC-based, Asymetrix ToolBook authoring tool (Ayres 1993). This layer helps to impose a common look and feel across all modules through the use of a standard page background, standard typography, standard icons, artwork, buttons and popups. In certain cases it has removed some of the feature richness of ToolBook and limited the range of options available in ToolBook: for instance, only a subset of the normal range of fonts are available.

Through the addition of extra menu items to those of ToolBook, the template allows authors to turn ordinary ToolBook objects, such as text fields and buttons, into spreadsheets, graphs, multiple choice questions, popups. All of these items impose the project standard look and feel without continual reference to paper-based style guides. At the same time they significantly reduce the complexity and quantity of programming required by the author by inheriting inbuilt functionality appropriate to that object.

The template also allows WinEcon modules to automatically support both standard 16 colour VGA graphics drivers and 256 colour Super-VGA drivers without having to adopt the lowest common format (i.e. 16 colour) or maintain two versions of each module. All the graphics are held in a ToolBook resource, or library, book (Price 1993). There is one resource book to hold 16 colour graphics and one to hold 256 colour graphics. The template then pulls graphics in from the appropriate book depending on whether the student is running WinEcon on a 16 or 256 colour machine. If, in the future, 24-bit colour graphics become the standard then WinEcon can be upgraded to take full advantage of this by simply providing a 24-bit version of the resource book; no changes to courseware are required. No extra effort is required by courseware authors to take advantage of this gain in performance and future proofing.

In addition to holding graphics, the template also holds a number of commonly used WinEcon objects within the resource books. As with the graphics, the template pulls these objects out of the resource book as the book is run by the student. This avoids embedding hundreds of identical copies of these objects into the courseware modules themselves as the courseware is authored. Consequently, a global change to the courseware may be made by changing the object in the resource book; every instance of this object will automatically be updated in every module of courseware. This increases the reliability of the courseware authored and reduced the effort required to debug and test the courseware. In particular, it is far less expensive to respond to feedback from students and lecturers during the later stages of the project. Again, no extra effort is required by the courseware author to take advantage of this time saving mechanism.

There is, however, a significant cost in terms of time and effort in creating a template in the first place. Although the WinEcon template was programmed by a small team based at the Centre for Computing in Economics, much dialogue and discussion with academics and programmers of the Consortium's eight development teams was involved in arriving at a suitable template. This in itself does not directly contribute to the production of courseware content and yet, as the following statistics collected by the Centre show, is a sizeable overhead.

Statistics for Centre of Computing in Economics
(Oct. 92 - Jan. 94)

No. documents	89
No. pages	471
No. photocopies (in-house)	43,000
No. visitors to Centre	51
No. visits to other institutions	50
No. telephone messages	1150
Cost of postage	£1165
No. mailings to Consortium	52

CONCLUSION

The template-based approach to courseware authoring adopted by the Economics Consortium is an effective method of increasing the efficiency of the courseware authoring process. It offers efficiency gains in the areas of content authoring, programme reliability, interface consistency, responding to user trials and technology future-proofing.

References

Ayres M (1993) Computers in Higher Education Economics Review, *Don't you just love being in control? Interactive features of the WinEcon courseware*, 27-32, Centre for Computing in Economics and CALECO Research Group, Bristol.

Brooks F P (1975) The Mythical Man-month - Essays on Software Engineering, *The Mythical Man-month*, 13-26, Addison-Wesley, London

Darby J (1993) Teaching and Learning Technology, *The CTISS File*, 15, Oxford.

Hobbs P J (1993a) TLTP Economics Consortium Briefing, *Economics Briefing*. Centre for Computing in Economics, Bristol.

Hobbs PJ (1993b) Learning Technology in Higher Education, *Project Management*, CTISS, Oxford.

ICBL (1993) Evaluation of the Initial Training Programme for the IMPACT Initiative (003/93), Heriot-Watt.

Price S.(1993) 1993 ToolBook User Conference, *Runtime Resource Books - Reducing Book Size and Complexity, 40-42,* Glasgow.

UFC ISC (1992)   Universities Funding Council Information Systems Committee, *Beyond Lectures: The Report of the Information Systems Committee Courseware Development Working Party*, CTISS Publications, Oxford.

7. Teaching/Learning Methods for Increasing Student Participation

R W Hind and J A Lynch, *East London Business School, University of East London*

Summary
Experiences with two methods of increasing student participation.
    In the subject areas of computing in general and programming specifically students benefit from being involved ie "doing". The saying: "Tell me and I shall forget, show me and I will understand, involve me and I will remember." is worth considering.
    Traditionally, students have been cossetted in a fairly rigid lecture - tutorial - coursework environment, numbers were not excessive and the range of ability manageable. Now the changing nature of HE has widened the access to students of vastly different ability/experiences and intake size has increased dramatically. How can we possibly manage to "deliver the goods"? Two attempts at managing the new environment at UEL are described below.

FLEXIBLE LEARNING ENVIRONMENT.

The teaching of a second programming language has always had its problems with the variety of abilities in the group. In this particular care we have students computer related BTEC backgrounds through to A level and mature student entry who will only have one year exposure to computing. This diversity of student and the variation in learning styles requires a wide variation in their learning needs and provide flexibility to resource weak subject areas.

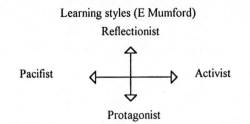

Learning styles (E Mumford)

If we are to improve over traditional lecture methods then the learning environment needs to be flexible in terms of study modes meeting the different needs yet improve motivation quality and encourage responsibility for learning. Additionally, it must be cost efficient improving results (if possible) and cope with the ever increasing class size.

    In our target group (HND Computing 2nd Year) it was easy to identify specific groups typically good programmers capable of self directed learning at one end to weak programmers who need all the help they can get. In the centre of these extremes are capable students who just lack confidence/direction.

    To support these groups overall objectives were provided with full supporting material and full lectures, tutorials and practicals. Students were then allowed to choose their mode of study which could range from working at home to attending all lectures or any combination they want.

    To support this flexibility lectures and tutorials were optional with lecture schedules, notes, work books/exercises and assignments provided in advance. Practical sessions were compulsory and used for assessment/feedback purposes.

    The tutorials and practicals became highly student driven. This requires tutorial staff to be well versed in the subject material, flexible and adaptable. Quite often they will not know (in advance) the specific content of the tutorial as it will reflect the students immediate needs not just reflect the last lecture.

There were many perceived advantages of this approach. Students are able to take responsibility for their learning. The mode of study becomes very flexible relating to where, when and how long as well as allowing students to plan research, attend lectures on a needs basis or resource other weak subject areas. Support improves for weaker students as class and tutorial attendance reduces, leaving a more even ability set. Motivation should be improved as students are not restricted by structure and work at their own pace, making the choice of study as they feel best fits their needs.

COMPARISON OF RESULTS

Two cohorts of 2nd Year HND students were considered.

Group 1   HND 2 class with traditional lecture/tutorial (1992/3 cohort)

Group 2   HND 2 class with flexible lecture/tutorials/practicals (1993/4 cohort)

Assessment Grades	Group 1	Group 2
Pass	64%	28%
Merit	14%	45%
Distinction	16%	22%
Others	6	5

Whilst these figures show a significant improvement it is difficult to determine if
- it is due to the delivery method
- it is due to different cohorts
- effects of semesterisation
but it is a significant change and worth noting.

Other statistics

30% of students found smaller lecturing size to be helpful.
20% of students used time saved to resource other areas.
30% of students felt they covered more than the usual lectures system.
15% of students flet the flexibility of study/access was beneficial.

This tends to indicate that there was a perceived improvement in the learning environment but not without room for improvement.

FUTURE DEVELOPMENT (IF FUNDING IS AVAILABLE)

There are several areas for investigation and development. Basically under the following areas:

Student profiling: Software is available to profile the student learning needs (P Woolliams UEL). This will provide a better insight into special subgroups needs.

Computer Based Auto Assessment:	To investigate computer marking of software in the area identified by developments at Nottingham Trent University (P Fazackerley, Peter Halstead and MIke Ward). This would provide faster feedback and reduce staff work load.
Work Books:	Develop a more user friendly/professional set of working notes and examples/questions... improve structre. This would provide better direction for some students.
Multi media Teaching:	Investigate the production of a multi-media learning package to support the teaching.
Video of lectures:	To be made available.

If the above areas can be resourced then significant improvements in the flexible learning environment will be achieved.

LEARNING CONTRACTS

The second activity has been introduced in an attempt to help students cope with both a gradual change in terms of the growth of class size, resulting in a less personal atmosphere, and also the reduction in assimilation time brought about by semesterisation and modularisation. The traditional concept of reading for a qualification seems to have disappeared especially in technical subjects such as computing where competencies and practical skills are demanded by first destination employers. This change has tended to move teaching towards the acquisition of practical skills. To some extent, the first activity described has helped achieve this in spite of the growth in group size. What we have perceived is a gradual reduction in the time spent by students reading round the subject they are studying. To us all, time is precious and maximising the utilisation of our time is paramount. Students concentrate their efforts into learning sufficient to complete assignments and to prepare for end of unit assessments if these are part of the assessment strategy. The learning contract activity and its method of implementation help to redress the balance and provide an opportunity for broadening the students knowledge base.

THE TRADITIONAL APPROACH

Almost all unit specifications include a reading list which is presented as essential, recommended and background material. The essential text tends to be the one and only one that students refer to. In fact many tutors deliberately tailor there presentation of the unit to more or less fit the chosen text. This has the opposite effect to that desired but is 'encouraged' because it allows students to learn about their unit material with backing from a single source. The other items on the reading list are virtually forgotten. The chance to see material presented from another authors viewpoint is lost as are the opportunities to study material that these authors consider to be associated with the topic area. The traditional solution would be to recommend that all texts on the reading list are read. With present day timescales this is impossible.

SHARING THE TASK

The learning contract is a mechanism which helps to distribute the task of reading the whole reading list. In our implementation, it consists of four phases.

Phase 1. The first lecture the students experience for a unit must be a thorough explanation of the topic areas that the unit is to cover and the topics that the tutor considers to be closely allied to the unit material. A topic timetable must also be given. This sets the scene for the unit. It is essential that the atmosphere created is one where students are anxious to find out more about this subject area. During this phase, students are told about the learning contract and how it plays an essential role in an individuals learning, the learning process of the class and that it is part of the assessment for the unit.

Phase 2. Assuming a 15 week semester, this will take place in week 3.

Each student will be required to formulate and submit for one to one discussion and agreement, a learning contract which will consist of a topic the student will investigate and how the student wishes to be assessed on the work done.

The approving tutor must ensure that the topic is relevant, is not too wide, can be investigated at reasonable depth preferably by the use of the material in the reading list and that undesirable duplication is prevented.

Most students, in our experience, wish to produce a written report and choose to be assessed on this. However, this method of assessment is only one of many and students should be encouraged to choose what is most appropriate for both themselves and the topic material.

Phase 3. Normally starting at week 6 and continuing to the end of the semester.

Each student will make a brief presentation of their work to an audience of their peers. In a class of 60 this could be one third or half of the class. The presentation need only be 10 minutes if a paper has been written or a little longer if a demonstration of the work done is to be the method of assessment.

The essential aspect of this phase is that the class as a whole is made aware of some interesting aspects of the work of the student. This is one of the two occasions when a student shares his/her efforts with colleagues.

Phase 4. No later than week 10. Each student produces a written report which is either lodged as a file in a networked computer system or in a college library. This then produces a reading resource for all students. The reports are very specific by their very nature and together provide a wide area of coverage in a fraction of the volume of the text material from which they were generated.

ASSESSMENT

As expressed earlier, our experience is that approximately 75% of the students choose to be assessed by written report and that no assessment of the presentation to their peers takes place. Grading therefore takes place off-line. Demonstrations and exhibitions of work need an on-line approach.

RESULTS

To date our experience is with a group of 26 final year degree students studying a unit entitled co-operative operating systems. Their view was unanimous in that they enjoyed the activity and that it helped to broaden their area of knowledge in an efficient and effective way. The presentations gave us, as their tutors, an opportunity to add our views and to express ways in which the student gathered material fitted in with lecture presentation topics. We made no attempt to restrict areas which students wished to cover because we would be covering them in lectures, but rather adapted lectures to utilise their material. We also made certain that we would not steal a students thunder if their presentation was scheduled after a lecture on the students chosen topic area. If necessary we could augment the students material at presentation time.

It is difficult to ascertain the affect of the activity on the end of unit examinations as this cohort of students was the first through a new unit. However, the coverage of topics the students were exposed to was far greater than we could have achieved by lecture alone. The breadth of discussion at tutorials reflected the diversity of topics covered and this must be a benefit when attending interviews for employment and future work involvement.

REFLECTION

There are a number of issues that need to be considered.

It might be the case that the activity does not directly help students achieve a higher grade in their final examinations and that the students time would be better spent pursuing more directly applicable material. This may be so, however, the intention was to provide a substitute for reading round the subject. There is no reason why students could not be more constrained in the topics they are allowed to pursue, although this defeats some of what is being attempted and can dampen some of the enthusiasm.

With a variety of assessment mechanisms being involved, the question of consistency of grading becomes an issue. Again our view, bearing in mind the intentions of the activity, is that this is not very important.

Good metrics are:
Has the student learnt?
Have the student's peers been presented with information in a suitable form for them to broaden their coverage of the unit material?
Has the participative action enhanced the learning experience?
Have scarce resources been utilised efficiently and effectively?

The activity puts high demands on the tutors in terms of a need for a dynamic approach and the ability to react to material introduced by students. We see no problem with this. For lower level courses our knowledge as tutors is such that we can easily cope, for higher level courses we can all learn together.

There is no progressive monitoring of the learning activities of students. This is a matter that will be addressed during the next run through. An interim progress report is to be a requirement, giving details of work done so far.

What if a student presents rubbish? This is an interesting problem. Obviously, if small errors are made, these can be corrected by the tutor. If the whole is nonsense the most expedient action is to watch the reaction of the presenter's peers. Do they realise? More important still, has the tutor realised? A skilful tutor can turn this into something positive. It is difficult to deal with this situation if it happens more than once. The interim report should reduce the likelihood of this happening.

8. Designing Interactive Learning Support Environments

Philip Barker, *School of Computing and Mathematics, University of Teesside*

Summary
There is a growing need to use computer technology successfully in education. Unfortunately, many conventional approaches to computer-assisted learning suffer from a number of serious drawbacks. For this reason this paper therefore proposes that lectures ('chalk and talk') will continue to be the primary mechanism of teaching in the majority of universities, colleges and schools for many decades to come. Taking this situation as a base-line, the concept of an interactive learning support environment (ILSE) is introduced. It is proposed that the ILSE approach can lead to the effective use of computer technology in education - particularly, in situations where financial resources are scarce. The design and fabrication of such facilities are discussed and a case study is then presented.

INTRODUCTION

During the last three decades many people have advocated the more extensive use of technology in education (Barker and Yeates, 1985; Benest and Hague, 1993). Indeed, in many quarters, educational technology has often been heralded as the 'saviour of education'. Laurillard (1993), for example, suggests:

'The academic system must change. It works to some extent, but not well enough. And as higher education expands we cannot always rely on human ingenuity to overcome its inadequacies.'

In a similar vein, Stevens (1993), writing in Bass and Dewan (p. 180), claims:

'It is hard to imagine an area in greater need of technological tools than education and training. The nation's schools and industry together spend ... billion per year on the business of education and training. Ninety-three percent of this expense is labour intensive, ... with no increase in teacher productivity since the 1800s'.

Computer-based technology has been seen as a possible way of addressing the above problems. Therefore, in many areas of academia, particularly universities, there are great expectations from the use of computer-based technology for educational purposes. Within the United Kingdom, for example, the recent Teaching and Learning Technology Programme (TLTP) has made available substantial financial resources for the development of instructional software for use in university teaching (HEFCE, 1993). Unfortunately, within the majority of educational establishments (including universities), the use of computers as a teaching and learning resource is marred by three major factors. First, the high cost of developing computer courseware (this will undoubtedly be an inhibiting factor for decades to come). Second, the financial and logistical problems of making available as many computers as there are seats in a large lecture theatre or library. Third, the rapidity with which computer equipment becomes obsolescent is often deemed to be an unattractive way of investing scarce financial resources.

There is no doubt that computer-based learning has many attractive pedagogic features. However, due to the factors listed above, we believe that within most universities (for some time to come) lectures will continue to be the primary vehicle by which information will be presented to students. Given this situation, it is important to realise the inadequacies and limitations of this approach to knowledge and skill transfer. Computer-based technology can then be employed to overcome these shortcomings using methods that enhance and augment student learning in the most beneficial ways.

We believe that in situations of this sort described above, the use of an Interactive Learning Support Environment (ILSE) can offer substantial benefits. The remainder of this paper therefore discusses the nature of such environments and outlines some of the important design considerations relevant to their creation. A case study is then presented which describes the development of a prototype ILSE to support the teaching of human-computer interaction (HCI) within a university context.

DESIGN CONSIDERATIONS

Much of the rationale for the use of support environments of the type described in this paper comes from the area of electronic performance support (Banerji, 1994; Gery, 1991). Like an electronic performance support system (EPSS), an interactive learning support environment is an integrated (and, probably, distributed) hardware and software toolset that has been designed for a particular pedagogic purpose.

Typically, a system of this sort is able to provide access to the electronic forms of the learning, training and information resources associated with a given course of instruction. The courses that are supported may be of a conventional nature (based on lectures or self-study material) or they may be technology-based. In the work that we have been undertaking the ILSEs have been designed to support conventional lecture courses (Lim, 1994).

The systems that we have been designing and developing offer an integrated facility to enable the creation of (and ancillary support for) 'electronic lectures' that are delivered in a conventional lecture theatre (Benest and Hague, 1993). In addition, facilities exist to enable students to access these lectures (and related course material) through the use of computer terminals that are attached to a campus-wide Ethernet communication network. These resources can also be accessed remotely by means of modem facilities or interactive terminals that are attached to the JANET network.

In the remainder of this section an outline is given of some of the major design issues that need to be considered when constructing systems such as those which we have been creating. Four aspects of design are briefly touched upon: top-level design; low-level design; building blocks; and major processes.

Top-level design

The important top-level design issues relate to:

(1) the basic way in which lecture material is prepared;

(2) how it is stored and delivered to particular points of need;

(3) how it can be accessed; and the type of software environment(s) that is/are used to support the creation of learning and training resources.

In our system an electronic 'OHP metaphor' is used to liken the lecture preparation process to one which lecturers will already be familiar with. When a lecturer has created a series of electronic OHP transparencies they can be stored in a central data base (for global access) and subsequently delivered as a normal 'online' lecture in a conventional lecture theatre using standard projection techniques. Students can also access any electronic transparency collection that has been used in a lecture by means of interactive workstations connected to a local area network. These workstations can be sited in the university library, resource centres or anywhere else where it is convenient to locate them.

Low-level design

The major low-level design considerations in an ILSE project deal with the more fundamental issues relating to pedagogic content, strategies for information presentation, the basic learning support techniques that are employed and the nature of the human-computer interfaces that are used to facilitate communication at different levels within the system. A range of different information presentation paradigms can be embedded within an ILSE facility in order to foster learning and training activities. As we suggested above, the primary information dissemination mechanism remains the conventional lecture - augmented by 'electronic transparencies'. This can, of course, be supported with other forms of electronic presentation based on the use of video lectures, video tutorials, various sorts of audio-graphic presentation and access to electronic libraries of material (which is either commercially available or which has been produced in-house).

Basic building blocks

As was suggested above, the primary 'basic' building block for the ILSE that we have been creating is a collection of 'electronic transparencies' that forms the basis of a lecture course that some staff member has given. Each transparency used in a particular lecture is indexed and can be made available to a student - either in electronic or paper form. In addition to the transparency collection a number of other important generic building blocks can be incorporated into a particular ILSE - such as electronic books (Barker, 1993; Tan, 1994), surrogations based upon the use of virtual reality packages (Kalawsky, 1993) and access to interactive modules taken from various EPSS facilities that are relevant to a particular course of instruction (Banerji, 1994).

Major processes involved

The major processes involved in developing and maintaining an ILSE fall into four basic categories: materials production; storage and/or publication; delivery; and student monitoring. Basically, materials production refers to the processes involved in creating electronic transparencies and any other ancillary resources that are needed to support student learning. Subsequently, materials can be stored in electronic form within any of a range of host nodes within a local area network; they can also be 'published' on compact disc (CD-ROM) for distribution to resource centres or dissemination to students. Another important aspect of the ILSE is the provision of facilities for student monitoring - through the administration of periodic tests and exercises that are delivered online at appropriate intervals.

CASE STUDY - AN ILSE FOR HCI

As a means of testing some of the design and development ideas described in the previous section, we decided to create a prototype interactive learning support environment for the subject of human-computer interaction. The background to this work, its current status and some possible future directions of development are briefly summarised below.

Background

For some time, the School of Computing and Mathematics at the University of Teesside has operated an 'Open Access Student Information Service' (OASIS). The OASIS system encourages lecturers to place photocopies of their (conventional) OHP transparencies (and other resources related to the courses that they run) into a centralised document repository. This is then used to provide students with access to the teaching and learning materials for the purpose of consultation, copying and/or self-study.

Recently, students studying a final year BSc HCI module were surveyed in order to solicit their views on the OASIS system (in general) and on the HCI material it contained (in particular). They were also asked about their willingness to use information in other forms - particularly, electronic information. The results of the survey are described in detail elsewhere (Barker and Tan, 1994). Basically, although students thought the OASIS was useful (in the absence of anything else), the survey did reveal a number of inadequacies and limitations with respect to flexibility of access and the availability of mechanisms for monitoring individual progress.

A prototype ILSE facility for HCI was therefore implemented with a view to using it in order to overcome the shortcomings of the OASIS system as it presently exists.

Current status

It was decided that the prototype ILSE should be implemented using a hardware and software platform that conformed to the Level-2 multimedia personal computer (MPC) standard. Detailed specifications of the various MPC standards are given elsewhere (MPCMC, 1993). The basic requirements for an MPC Level-2 system are: an Intel 80386SX CPU running at 25 MHz; a double-speed multi-session CD-ROM drive; a 16-bit digital sound card; and Microsoft's Windows (Version 3.1) graphical user interface (Jamsa, 1993). In actual fact, the machines that were finally used for developing and (subsequently) accessing the prototype ILSE far exceeded the minimum requirements of MPC Level-2. Currently, for student access, workstations based on the Intel 80486SX CPU (running at 33 MHz) are used while the development environment is provided by an Intel Pentium-based MPC system (running at 60 MHz) having 16 Mbytes of RAM and a 430 Mbyte hard disc drive. This workstation has been enhanced by the addition of a VideoLogic 'Captivator' digital video board for capturing digital motion video; this material can subsequently be played back using Microsoft's 'Video for Windows' (Barker et al, 1993).

The basic ILSE shell was created using Asymetrix's Multimedia ToolBook (Version 1.53). ToolBook is an easy-to-use, object oriented programming language that allows very high levels of author productivity to be achieved. Most elementary tasks in ToolBook (such as book, page and object creation) can be accomplished by simple mouse-based (point-and-click and point-and-drag) dialogues. Obviously, in situations where their use is appropriate, more sophisticated operations can be conducted through the use of ToolBook's scripting language (called OpenScript). ToolBook implements an 'electronic book' metaphor. It can therefore be used to facilitate the creation of reactive pages containing text, audio-visual material (pictures, digital sound and motion video) and reactive 'buttons'. Textual and graphical objects can be made reactive through the incorporation of reactive areas that can embed links to other system resources. It is therefore extremely easy to use this system to create hypertext and hypermedia structures.

A detailed description of the prototype ILSE for HCI is given elsewhere (Lim, 1994). Naturally, the system implements only a subset of the total resources available. This is reasonable since the prototype was primarily intended to act as a 'proof of principle' implementation and as an evaluation tool to assess students' reactions to providing this type of support for learning.

Future developments

The exploratory work that has been undertaken with the prototypical ILSE suggests that this approach to the provision of multimedia learning support can be very effective. This is particularly so in terms of creating more flexible ways for allowing access to learning materials. Obviously, because of resource limitations our future exploration of these systems will continue to be based on prototype development rather than on large-scale production. Three important immediate goals for the future will be: the development of hardware and software tools to facilitate the easy creation of electronic transparencies; the creation of hypermedia electronic books containing course support materials; and the production of responsive self-administered testing (and feedback) facilities to enable students to gauge the progress they are making on a weekly or monthly basis.

CONCLUSION

We are convinced that within most universitiy, college and school settings 'the lecture' will continue to be the primary mechanism of teaching for many decades to come. Bearing this in mind, it is imperative that the resources available for computer-based support are used in the most appropriate ways possible. We believe that the creation of interactive learning support environments to accompany conventional approaches to teaching and learning offer one plausible way of realising the optimal deployment of scarce development resources

References

Banerji, A.K., (1994). *Designing Electronic Performance Support Systems,* Draft PhD Thesis, Human-Computer Interaction Laboratory, University of Teesside, Cleveland,UK.

Barker, P.G., (1993). *Exploring Hypermedia,* Kogan Page, London, UK.

Barker, P.G., Banerji, A., Lamont, C.W. and Richards, S.R., (1993). *Digital Video in a PC Environment,* 583-592 in *Proceedings of Online Information '93 - 17th International Online Meeting,* 7th-9th December, 1993, Olympia, London, edited by D. Raitt and B. Jeapes, Learned Information, Oxford, UK.

Barker, P.G. and Tan, C.M., (1994). *Evaluating an OASIS,* Working Paper, Interactive Systems Research Group, Human-Computer Interaction Laboratory, University of Teesside, Cleveland, UK.

Barker, P.G. and Yeates, H., (1985). *Introducing Computer Assisted Learning,* Prentice-Hall, London.

Benest, I.D. and Hague, A.C., (1993). *The On-Line Lecture Concept,* 440-448 in *Computer-Based Learning in Science,* Proceedings of the International Conference on Computer-Based Learning in Science (CBLIS '93), Technical University of Vienna, Austria, 18-21 December, 1993, edited by P.M. Nobar and W. Kainz, ISBN: 80-7040-082-X.

Gery, G.J., (1991). *Electronic Performance Support Systems - How and Why to Remake the Workplace Through the Strategic Application of Technology,* Weingarten Publications, Boston, MA, USA.

HEFCE, (1993). *The Teaching and Learning Technology Programme: Phase 2,* Circular 30/93, Higher Education Funding Council for England, Northavon House, Coldharbour Lane, Bristol, BS16 1QD, UK.

Jamsa, K.A., (1993). *Instant Multimedia for Windows 3.1,* John Wiley & Sons, New York, NY, USA.

Kalawsky, R.S., (1993). *The Science of Virtual Reality and Virtual Environments,* Addison-Wesley, Wokingham, England, UK.

Laurillard, D., (1993). *Rethinking University Teaching - A Framework for the Effective Use of Educational Technology,* Routledge, London.

Lim, J.J., (1994). *Design of an Interactive Learning Support Environment for HCI,* Final Year BSc Computer Science Dissertation, University of Teesside, Cleveland, UK.

MPCMC, (1993). *Multimedia Personal Computer Marketing Council,* 1730 M Street, NW, Suite 707, Washington, DC 200030-4510, USA.

Stevens, S.M., (1993). *Multimedia Computing: Applications, Designs and Human Factors,* 175-193 (chapter 9) in *'User Interface Software',* edited by L. Bass and P. Dewan, John Wiley & Sons, Chichester, UK.

Tan, C.M., (1994). *Hypermedia Electronic Books,* Outline PhD Research Specification, Human-Computer Interaction Laboratory, University of Teesside, Cleveland, UK.

9. Analysis of Learning Design - A Retrospective Approach

Philip Barker and Stephen Richards, *University of Teesside*

Summary
Learning design is often a complex and time consuming activity that must normally precede the creation of an interactive product for pedagogic use. Few models exist to facilitate this activity. This paper describes the design and evaluation of a model of learning design that has been developed within the framework of a European DELTA project.

INTRODUCTION

In many computer-based learning applications relatively little emphasis has been given to the underlying pedagogic strategies that are needed to support successful learning. All too often, learning product development is oriented towards what can be achieved with the technology rather than the learning needs of users. In order to address this problem a model of learning design has been developed specifically for the creation of interactive learning materials that are to be published on compact disc. This model has been used as a basis for the implementation of a number of prototypical learning and training products. The learning products that were produced have been evaluated in order to find out how effectively the model of learning design has been embedded within them and also to discover the impact of using this model on the pedagogic uses of the resulting applications. In order to undertake these evaluations a suitable evaluation tool was developed. This allowed various attributes of the quality of the learning software to be compared with the learning strategies that they contained. It also enabled weaknesses in the implementation of the learning software to be isolated and areas of potential improvement identified.

This paper outlines the learning design model that has been developed within the framework of a European Commission DELTA project (DELTA, 1992). The model is called 'ILDIC' - an acronym for Integrating Learning Design in Interactive Compact Disc. The paper then goes on to describe the evaluation tool that was produced and the results that were obtained as a result of applying it to the evaluation of an interactive learning product that has been published on compact disc in CD-I format.

THE LEARNING DESIGN MODEL

Within the ILDIC project a broad concept of learning design has been applied to the development of interactive computer-based learning (CBL) applications based on compact disc. This has involved the identification of important factors which can effect the quality of learning products. Factors specific to multimedia learning and training technologies have been combined with general learning design principles. As a result, a model was developed consisting of ten basic perspectives. These perspectives are discussed in detail elsewhere (Good et al, 1993) but are summarised below in order to provide the context for what is to be said later in the paper.

Perspective 1: Learning theory

The learning theory perspective centres on three basic approaches: behaviourism (focusing on stimulus/response); cognitivism (focusing on thinking); and constructivism (learner involvement).

Perspective 2: Instructional position

The focus of instructional position mix is on teaching techniques rather than learning strategies - recognising the value of providing a number of different approaches depending upon the nature of teaching tasks.

Perspective 3: Machine character mix

Machine character mix refers to an element of anthropomorphism concerned with ascribing character or 'personality' to learning applications.

Perspective 4: Environment

Environmental factors include a consideration of physical, intellectual and emotional space (Holt, 1984).

Perspective 5: Use

This perspective considers the wide variety of ways in which learning software can be used - some of which can be determined in advance, whilst others will be unexpected.

Perspective 6: Control

The balance between freedom and control is extremely important, particularly where excessive control can be seen as coercive by some learners.

Perspective 7: Intervention

Intervention is one of the mechanisms by which designers are able to produce active relationships between learning applications and their users (usually in the form of feedback and/or help).

Perspective 8: Aesthetics

The aesthetic qualities of learning software can be extremely important particularly in the visual and aural dimensions.

Perspective 9: Content

This refers to the choice of material to include (or exclude), and the media used to present it.

Perspective 10: Technology

A platform should be chosen that best delivers media forms appropriate to the subject matter while considering the delivery platforms already in use by target populations.

THE EVALUATIVE STUDY

The overall evaluation strategy involved developing an effective evaluation tool that could be applied indirectly to the ILDIC model. This tool was required to assess the effectiveness of the model by looking at learning products which it had been used to produce. In addition, the evaluation tool had to address all the learning perspectives described in the previous section. The learning product itself also had to be evaluated and profiles of the users obtained.

The general aims of the tool were three-fold:

(1) to measure the degree to which learning software embeds the
       values of the ILDIC development model;
(2) to assess the quality of the learning software in question; and
(3) to provide indicators to areas of potential improvement in the
       ILDIC development model.

Since users had to undertake evaluations unaided it was necessary to simplify the evaluation tool (a questionnaire) as far as possible. For this reason, the number of questions it contained was kept as low as possible (resulting in a total of 50). The first 12 addressed product evaluation while the remaining 38 addressed the learning model.

Analysis

The data was analysed on three dimensions: product and model ratings; individual perspectives; and observations.

Product and learning model ratings were analysed statistically on: product ratings obtained from educationalists and non-educationalists; and learning model ratings obtained from educationalists and non-educationalists. These tests were designed to identify the reaction of expert educationalists to the learning product and the learning model. When more applications are evaluated it will also be possible to see if significant differences are produced in product ratings and to identify differences in the overall levels to which the learning model is embedded. It will also be possible to explore if any interaction exists between the degree to which the model is embedded and the rating given to a particular product.

Individual perspectives were analysed through comparisons between product rating and ratings on the ten perspectives contained within the model. The object of this was to try to identify which aspects of the learning product development model had the greatest impact upon the quality of the end-product.

Finally, an analysis of the experimental observations and subject comments was conducted. This took the form of reporting the more common observations which were pertinent to the effectiveness of the learning model.

Method

Twenty volunteers acted as subjects, most of which had considerable computing experience. This meant that the results of these evaluations would not have to take into consideration the problems associated with a steep learning curve for the technology itself. Of the twenty subjects, eleven were also educationalists while the remaining nine were not. The learning product that was investigated was a CD-I title (called the 'Greenland Disc') that had been produced in-house.

The evaluations took place in a screened-off section of the Human-Computer Interaction Laboratory at the University of Teesside. A CD-I unit linked to a fourteen inch portable colour television was provided. The Greenland CD-I disc was pre-loaded in the device and the opening CD-I screen was displayed. Subjects were also provided with a paper-based manual for the learning product, the evaluation tool guidelines, and the evaluation tool itself.

Subjects were asked to use the learning application for as long as they wanted. No learning objectives were provided which meant that users decided themselves how they wished to make use of the software. They were permitted to come back and use the learning product as many times as they wished before completing the evaluation questionnaire.

Results

The reactions of expert educationalists were compared with non-educationalists. In this way, the value of both the learning product and the learning model could be analysed from an educational perspective.

The t-test on product rating scores did not produce significant results ($t=1.11$; $df=18$; pNS). In other words, educationalists and non-educationalists rated the learning product equally. The t-test on learning model rating scores, however, did produce significant results ($t=3.43$; $df=18$; $p<0.01$). The educationalists and non-educationalists therefore rated the levels to which the learning perspectives were embedded differently. The mean ratings produced by non-educationalists were above the expected mean of 1.5 with a mean rating of 1.63. The scores produced by the educationalists, however, were below average with a mean rating of 1.23.

The expected mean score of 1.5 for the ten perspectives was only exceeded in four cases: instructional position (1.76); control (1.65); aesthetics (2.16); and technology (2.13). Two of the learning perspectives obtained reasonable ratings which were only slightly below the expected average: learning theory mix (1.41); and machine character (1.38). The remaining four perspectives all obtained low mean ratings: environment (0.98); use (0.8); intervention (0.75); and content (1.06).

The observations gathered through subject self-reports, interviews and free-flow questionnaire responses resulted in a large list of comments. These covered most aspects of the control interface, comments on general usability, reports of bugs and inconsistencies, and comments about the evaluation tool. Almost all of the comments were aimed directly at problems encountered in the control and use of the learning application. Very few observations were concerned with the underlying learning strategies or problems encountered while using the evaluation tool.

Implications

The differences between the educationalist and non-educationalist subject groups illustrate the value of using appropriate target groups. Educationalists rated the degree of learning model embedding significantly lower than did non-educationalists. This could be the result of the fact that educationalists generally rate learning issues more rigorously since it is an issue with which they are highly concerned. If this is the case, the evaluation tool has performed extremely well in illuminating these differences.

When the ratings obtained from the individual learning perspectives were analysed some deficiencies of the prototype Greenland CD-I disc emerged. By far the most highly rated perspectives were technology and aesthetics. This does not seem surprising since the underlying technology was specifically designed for home education and entertainment. In addition, CD-I is designed to deliver high quality multimedia information. This is likely to have considerable impact upon the aesthetic qualities of end-products designed for delivery on this platform.

In the Greenland CD-I evaluations four perspectives were rated particularly poorly: environment; use; intervention; and content.

Environment and use are the two factors within the learning model which are furthest from a designers control. In this case, the environment used was a computing laboratory which had been partitioned to provide a secluded working area. Such an environment may seem harsh and unsuited to the subject matter being delivered - particularly, to educationalists. Expert teacher support was not provided which meant that users did not have guidance towards a more rewarding learning experience.

The poor ratings obtained for intervention were expected since neither of the two primary forms of intervention (help and feedback) were employed by the Greenland CD-I disc. This was surprising since it was designed using the ILDIC learning model which stresses the importance of on-line help and relevant feedback.

The low rating of the content may be the result of the fact that this was a prototype disc. As such, the information content was incomplete. In many cases, users experienced missing or partial information. This situation should improve when the product is completed and the full scope of the final information content can be subjected to evaluation.

The observations that were made generally supported the questionnaire data. This was particularly striking with regard to intervention. Almost every subject made a comment about the poor levels of intervention. Many specifically reported that help had not been available. Further, users felt that on-line help would have been useful even if only to provide an explanation of the icons used in the interface. The fact that no performance feedback was provided was also commented on.

The other area of frequent comment was with regard to content. Content was reported by some subjects to be inconsistent, incomplete and of limited use. A feature that was found to be particularly annoying to some users was the fact that many pictures used the same caption. This had a negative impact upon users' reaction to the information content.

CONCLUSION

These evaluations have shown the potential usefulness of both the ILDIC model of learning design and the evaluation tool. Through the use of this tool, shortcomings in the implementation of the Greenland CD-I disc have been identified. These concern features which are directly addressed in the ILDIC model but which were inadequately implemented within the learning software. It is interesting to note that observations and users' comments also supported these findings.

As a result a number of suggestions can be advanced for the improvement of the Greenland CD-I disc. Perhaps the primary issues to be addressed by the designers are those of intervention and content. It is in these two poorly rated areas that designers could probably produce the most effective impact upon the quality of the learning software.

Help is an essential tool in modern software. The implementation of help facilities within the Greenland disc would have undoubtedly produced higher evaluation ratings. In addition, this would also have addressed many of the critical oral comments made by the evaluators.

Obviously, information content is already an issue which is being addressed since the prototype is an incomplete version of the final product. Even so, these evaluations suggest that unique captions should be provided for each illustration. This will then allow captions to be directly related to the content of the graphical information being presented.

Two areas for improvement which are largely outside the designers' control are environment and use. This stresses the importance for educationalists to provide suitable learning environments. In most cases the learning environment in which the product is used would probably be far better than the computing laboratory within which our evaluations took place.

Finally, the evaluation tool developed for the ILDIC project can be applied to any learning software. Such products need not have been designed using the ILDIC model. In this sense, the evaluation tool is generic; it should therefore be able to identify areas of potential weakness within any learning product. It is thus able to provide highly specific guidance to designers of pedagogic materials which should result in a substantial improvement in their quality.

References

DELTA, (1992). ILDIC - *Integrating Learning Design in Interactive Compact Disc*, Project D2012, European Community DG-XIII DELTA Programme, Brussels, Belgium.

Good, M., Shanahan, L. and Shaw, S., (1993). *Final Specification for the ILDIC Demonstrator Model*, DELTA Project D2012, Deliverable 4, Workpackage 1, Cambridge Training and Development Ltd, Cambridge, UK.

Holt, J., (1984). *Why Children Fail*, Penguin Books, London, UK.

10.   Let Me Edutain You!

Lynn Morgan and John Sinclair, *Organisational Change Research Unit, Napier University*

Summary
With the growing need to change the way in which we approach education and the facilitation of the learning environment the 'cultures' which exist in higher education institutions could mitigate against the effective exploitation of new technologies.

If these cultures are ignored, inappropriate learning tools will be developed and used. The application of these to the student learning experience may therefore devalue rather than enhance the potential of the technologies to facilitate learning.

This paper will focus on:

- the role and function of culture and how they impact on the transformation of the learning environment
- the realities which impinge on the exploitation of new learning technologies
- the factors which require consideration when attempting to bring about culture change of a transformational nature.
- the changing role of the educator and the potential resistance in 'edutaining' a mass student audience.

 The paper will conclude with a critical look at the way forward if computer technologies in education are to be used as vehicles for transforming the learning experience.

How often have you had to sit through a lecture or tutorial (as both a student and lecturer) wondering what the benefit of the experience was? Controlled in ways that may be inappropriate to your learning needs, such experiences can be counter-productive to effective learning.

This is especially true when we look at the changing nature of higher education and the make up of the student population. The growth of interest in non-traditional approaches to fostering a learning environment and the construction of materials that 'empower' the learner have brought about a major need to change our views and ways of managing the learning environment. Yet, the move (or perhaps push) into the use of new technologies can conflict with established 'cultures' in higher education institutions.

CHANGING BACKGROUNDS

Higher education has seen a great change in the background of those involved in it and the context within which it operates. Such changes have proved to be the driving force behind the move towards student-centred learning in order to facilitate the learning environment. The advances in technology have made interactive learning possible through the use of hypermedia products. Entertainment has began to be seen as a format that offers the key to stimulate both interest and motivation in students who may come into higher education poorly equipped to deal with a mass education diet!

WHY A HYPERMEDIA PLATFORM?

Hypermedia has the potential to engage and reinforce multiple senses and human facilities. For example, sight is engaged with images, hearing with sound, the rational faculty with words and emotions with colour and music. Interest can also be aroused with varying tone, tempo and movement. Hypermedia is therefore able to transcend the inadequacies of a single medium because it makes use of three modes of representation:

- enactive: concrete representation through the actions involved
- iconic: through visual or diagrammatic representation symbolic: through verbal conceptualisations

As a communication format, it is therefore better able to define experiences, ideas and emotions. (Gillette 1992)

WHAT IS EDUTAINMENT?

Edutainment is where information meets entertainment in an educational context. The information is presented in such a way that it is stimulating, motivating and entertaining and so enables the creative engagement of the user. (Geigenberger 1991) Traditionally, understanding is inclined to be viewed in rational and intellectual terms, and the role played by emotion and imagination tends to be ignored. (Reynolds and Skillbeck 1976) The development of an edutainment tool that combines all of these factors together should therefore lead to a more rewarding experience.

THE CULTURAL IMPACT AND THE TRANSFORMATION OF THE LEARNING ENVIRONMENT

Higher education institutions have a wide range of cultures within them. These cultures and the members of cultural groups exhibit beliefs, attitudes, values and behaviours which can enhance or mitigate against the use of technology aided learning environments.

CULTURAL COMPONENTS

We can see culture in terms of three levels (Schein 1985):

- Visible artefacts: lectures, seminars, tutorials, practicals, assignments
- Beliefs/values: as regards the value of learning and the input that should go into learning from all those involved (eg students, academic and non-academic support staff)
- Basic assumptions: about the meaning and purpose of higher education, eg some people may see the lecturer as the key component of any interaction who is in full control of knowledge structuring and its dissemination.

Our membership of cultural groups, be they sub-groups of students, staff, support and administrative, affects how we view the learning environment reality within higher education. Therefore, if we see all our efforts being geared towards releasing academic staff from direct contact with students, we will focus our attention to how this can be achieved in the easiest manner. Alternatively, concern with the amount of time and effort expended on assessment (rather than looking at the purpose of the assessment from both the staff and student perspective) could lead us to use technology to both 'set' and 'assess'. This lack of concern about the actual learning experience and the provision of meaningful feedback may lead some people to fear and resist the use of technology. The technology could be seen as usurping the 'expert lecturer' position or used in ways that detract rather than promote an effective learning environment.

In looking at the artefacts that are commonly used by educators:

- Traditional forms of teaching tend to over-emphasise the symbolic mode of representation to the detriment of the other two modes ie enactive and iconic. Classroom teaching and the traditional lecture situation are highly ritualised in their format. Any change from the accepted norms of lecturer behaviour that form part of these formats, may be resisted.

- Educators beliefs regarding higher education generally involve placing critical thinking and the conceptual understanding of key issues at the heart of degree courses. While pedagogics stresses the importance of interest in learning, it is only as a kind of additional psychological condition for effective learning rather than as a tool to stimulate a more effective learning environment.

Educators assumptions are often based on their preconceived ideas of what is best for 'their' students and their assumptions about how the learning environment should be constructed. Where educators assume that they are fully in control of this environment, it could lead to frustration and inflexibility when considering the design and development of more student-centred   methods of learning.

EDUCATION VERSUS ENTERTAINMENT

On the surface, education and entertainment are poles apart, to the extent that their value systems conflict. For example, information deals with reality and represents a way of contending with reality, while entertainment is considered to be a means of evading reality, either through a reduction of cognitive activity or through the reconstruction of reality in a form of fantasy.(Tannenbaum 1980) In academia this conflict is likely to be a source of resistance against edutainment as it could be seen to lower academic standards. However, a more in-depth consideration of entertainment when viewed through the theatre metaphor proves otherwise. Not only do they not conflict, they are, in fact, compatible.

THE THEATRE METAPHOR

When both systems are examined it becomes apparent that theatre seeks to achieve the same things that education does and in similar ways.

For example, they have related artefacts as shown in figure 10.1

Actors	Audience	Script	Workshop	Stage	Props
Lecturers	Student cohort	Lectures	Tutorials	Classroom, Lecture theatre	OHPs, articles etc

Figure 10.1

The objective of theatre is to portray reality through stage performances. (Mangham and Overington 1987) The same could be said for education. It attempts to portray reality through the transmission of knowledge with the stage being the classroom and the performance the process of delivery. However, ideally education does not just seek to deliver knowledge purely for assimilation, but to provide an opportunity to search for meaning and understanding. (Baume and Baume 1992) So too does the art form of theatre. Art it is suggested is "more about an experimental and exploratory approach to the world than finished objects. It is an eagerness to challenge common perspectives with fresh eyes and to create new synthesises." (Ferris 1992)

Art it is suggested is the creation of expressive forms, and a work of art in dramatic form is "an expressive form created for our perception through a sense of imagination" and what it expresses is emotion.(Mangham and Overington 1987) This link between emotion and the arts is important. For example the impact of theatre depends a great deal on the successful manipulation of the emotional reactions of the audience.(Strongman 1978) As emotion is always present in consciousness it is seen to provide the principle experiential-motivational conditions and cues for   cognitive-interpretative processes and action.(Howe 1979) This concept therefore essentially disproves the belief that entertainment evades reality through a reduction of cognitive activity.

HOW EDUTAINMENT CAN TRANSFORM THE EDUCATIONAL EXPERIENCE

Research shows that there are qualitative cognitive differences in the nature of the learning process.(Richardson et al 1987) These differences manifest themselves in two distinct approaches - deep or surface. A deep approach is when there is an intention to develop an understanding of the material presented and so the student takes an active role by interacting critically with the content, relating it to previous knowledge and experience. A surface approach on the other hand is much more passive and essentially reproductive in that the student's goal is to merely to satisfy the perceived requirements of the lecturer when doing assessments. Research shows that what many students learn in higher education does not match the ideals of a deep approach to learning. Edutainment provides the potential to help reverse this. This format gives the opportunity for the creative engagement of the user with tools that facilitate the process of association and exploration, features critical to meaningful learning and the maintenance of the user's attention.

However, care must be taken. Despite the opportunities it offers, edutainment is a difficult media to work with. Without a proper understanding of the ideology that underpins it, inappropriate tools could be developed.

INAPPROPRIATE TOOLS

Hypermedia's applicability as an effective learning tool depends to a great extent on how its interface s designed and able to present information to the student. It defines the extent of the experience. When designing the interface, the lecturer faces a dilemma. On the one hand they must retain subject coherence, and yet on the other they must give the students' the freedom to navigate through the material as they see fit so that they can participate in the edutainment experience. If this dilemma is not skilfully managed, it is likely to lead to the 'lost in hyperspace' phenomenon (Kommer et al 1992). Poor associative links mean that the students' may have difficulty in finding the information they wish. This leads to the use of ineffective navigation strategies, which disorientates them further. The end result is a fragmented view of the knowledge base, and an overwhelming desire to give up. Most lecturers do not have the knowledge or skills to help them overcome these problems and will therefore have to pursue research in areas such as interface design, useability, cognition and the visual arts, as well as appreciating that hypermedia application development is a creative venture.

Just determining a route through the material is not engaging enough for meaningful learning to take place. Instead students have to be encouraged to be active thinkers and to take up the challenge of inquiry and the construction their own ideas. However, many students don't have the desire or the training to engage in such processes. They after all have their own deep-rooted assumptions about learning, developed from school, and unless these are taken into account little advancement will be made.

If these problems are not overcome then the applications developed will achieve nothing.

The development of an edutainment approach also requires us to restructure and redefine our roles and that of the student. In trying to create a learning environment that deals with and encourages diversity of approaches to the accumulation of knowledge and its application, a partnership between learner and facilitator of the learning environment has to be struck. This may well prove difficult in a mass educational environment which has increasing become impersonal.

THE NEED FOR CULTURE CHANGE

While the main 'corporate cultures' of higher education institutions could be said to have changed in terms of how they view their customers, attention needs to be focused on the cultures that exist which provide the climate for learning.(See figure 10.2) Attention therefore requires to be given to the following key issues in respect of the cultural components that will impact on the effective use of new technologies (Schein 1985):

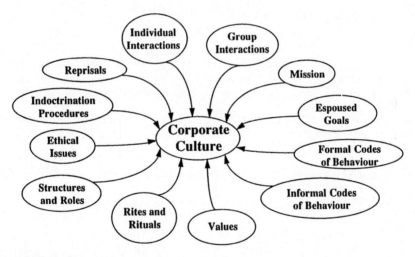

Figure 10.2

We have to be clear about why we want to make use of new technologies, the advantages and disadvantages that they possess and the need to see that their use will require a change in the structure and processes by which higher education is delivered. Without paying regard to these, we are in danger of only seeing a marginal use of new technology learning products which do little more than provide a novelty factor in a student's learning experience.

CHANGING ROLES FOR EDUCATORS AND LEARNERS

The use of new technologies is not enough in itself to create new learning environments which allow learners to exploit their own strengths and develop their own learning strategies. We need to realise that new roles for ourselves as educators are required and a more proactive and responsibility oriented role derived for learners if we are to achieve real and lasting benefits from new learning platforms such as multimedia and hypermedia.

References

Baume C and Baume D (1992), *Course Design for Active Learning*, CVCP University Staff Development and Training Unit

Farris S, (1992), Art Direction in Multimedia, *Multimedia Review* Vol 3 No 4

Geigenberger T (1991), *Infotainment and Presentainment*, Proceedings of Multimedia 91 Conference

Gillette J (1992), Observations on Computer Multimedia Form, *Multimedia Review* Vol13 No 2

Howe H (1978), *Nebraska Symposium on Motivation*, University of Nebraska Press

Kommers, Jonassan and Mayes (1992), *Cognitive Tools for Learning*, Springer-Verlag, Berlin:London

Mangham I and Overington M (1987), *Organisations as Theatre*, John Wiley and Sons Ltd

Reynolds J and Skillbeck M (1976), *Culture and the Classroom*, Open Books Publishing Ltd

Richardson J, Eysenck M and Piper D (1987) *Student Learning*, Open University Press

Schein E (1985), *Organisational Culture and Leadership*, Jossey-Bass, London

Strongman K (1978), *The Psychology of Emotion*, John Wiley and Sons Ltd

Tannenbaum P (1980), *The Entertainment Functions of Television*, Lawerence Erlbaum Inc Publishers

11.   Supporting Partnership in Education Through Technology

David G Gibson, *St Andrews College, Bearsden*

Summary

The concept of partnership
Education at all levels is undergoing a series of fundamental changes. As a recent working party of the Committee of Scottish University Principals chaired by Professor A.G.J. Macfarlane (1992) reported, Institutions of Higher Education are no exception. In addition, the institutions for teacher education are also experiencing the effects of significant shifts of emphasis in the Primary and Secondary sectors, which, in turn, have implications for the content and methodology in College courses. The effects of local government reorganisation are also apparent, and result in changes in the way the institutions view their client base.

A key result of these changes is the emerging philosophy of partnership between the Colleges and their clients. Not only do the Colleges provide services to the education system through inservice training and consultancy, and the provision of newly trained teachers, but the education system also provides services to the Colleges through the placement of student teachers for teaching practice, and assisting with research. In Scotland, the partnership extends into the first two years of employment during which the teacher serves a probationary period, monitored and reviewed by the General Teaching Council for Scotland, and continues to develop skills and competences. This partnership is therefore the means whereby student teachers are able to perceive a continuum in training, from the time of admission to College to the end of their probationary period.

The complexity of the partnership involving the Colleges, the Education Authorities and the schools is recognised. Other links in the network of relationships have assumed growing importance, notably those between parents and schools on the one hand, and universities and colleges on the other. A series of shared understandings needs to be achieved regarding the roles and responsibilities of the organisations and individuals involved and the nature of partnership itself. This project, funded by SHEFC's Flexibility in Teaching and Learning Scheme, seeks to assist this process through the development of a flexibly–delivered learning pack for student and probationer teachers, and for staff in colleges, schools and Authorities.

EVIDENCE OF NEED

A good deal of research has been conducted on the development of expertise in classroom teaching during initial training and the first years of teaching.For example, Kyriacou (1993) conducted a survey of such research but concluded by highlighting three important questions that still needed to be addressed:

- What is the relationship between the training experiences offered and the development of expertise?
- What types of training experience are most effective, and why?
- How can initial training and induction into the first year of teaching best take account of differences in needs amongst individuals?

The General Teaching Council for Scotland (1992) has expressed concern about the quality of support for probationer teachers, while the Scottish Office Education Department's guidelines for initial teacher training courses(1993) places emphasis on the clarification of the roles of the partners in this partnership, in order that the required set of teacher competencies can be developed.

In a study of partnership in initial teacher training, Elder and Kwiatkowski (1993) concluded that

- all parties have to understand the course model adopted;

- each has to understand and accept his/her role and responsibilities;
- individuals have to have confidence that the others are carrying out their role;
- the enabling strucure must facilitate the delivery of these mutually dependent roles;
- the progression of development of the student and the implications for the support and assessment roles must be clearly understood by all;
- quality assurance with regard to placement requires to be developed.

Again, in a survey of probationers, Draper et al (1992) identified three major areas for action:

- the improvement of continuity between the training of student teachers and their early experiences in teaching;
- the clarification of the roles and responsibilities of probationer teachers, staff in schools, and Authority staff;
- a need for timely information and feedback to the probationer about progress.

Since the quality of teaching and teacher training seems likely to be on the political agenda in the UK throughout the decade, the need for evidence to increase our understanding not only of how to improve this quality, but how to manage and sustain it will be paramount. Clearly, there is much work still to be done in identifying the factors most affecting the management of the partnership process and the quality of this developing relationship.

OBJECTIVES AND CONTENT OF THE PACKAGE

All of the above supports the intention to develop a flexible learning pack to encourage and support partnership between Colleges, their students and their schools. This pack would seek to:

- strengthen the Colleges' partnerships with schools and Authorities;
- improve quality and effectiveness through the achievement of continuity of experience of student teachers from initial entry to college to the end of the probationary teaching period;
- clarify the roles and functions of all involved from colleges, schools and local authorities.

The individuals for whom this pack would be developed include:

- student teachers;
- probationary teachers;
- College tutors;
- school mentors and senior school staff;
- Regional advisers.

The contents of the Package would include material covering the following:

- a shared understanding of Partnership;
- a clarification of the roles and responsibilities of college, school and LA personnel; assessment and effective feedback;
- managing the partnership process.

Gibson (1984) highlighted the key role that video could play in promoting staff development. Elsewhere, Gibson (1981) argued that developing technoloy was enabling a significant shift in emphasis from teacher control to learner control. Given the range of subject matter in the present study and the disparate audience, it was felt that a greater degree of interactivity would allow a more flexible approach to be adopted.The package contents will thus contain interactive individual and group study materials appropriate to the various facets of partnership, to be used by staff and students in Colleges, by teachers and advisers in Authority inservice sessions, and by teachers and senior staff in schools. It would include:

- a CD–ROM disc;
- video covering case studies related to the probationary period and initial training teaching experience (with cross–references to the CD–ROM);
- supporting documentation.

FLEXIBLE METHODOLOGY

The video will illustrate issues of partnership in the different contexts of the case studies and will serve as a stimulus for discussion and for setting agendas for further exploration through the CD-ROM.The CD-ROM disc will feature a number of key extracts taken from the video, assisting users to place the issues in context. It will enable users to examine issues and themes by accessing the materials on the disc in a number of ways, for example by looking at one particular issue as it is exemplified in a range of different case sudies. Users will be able to decide themselves what specific theme or focus they wish to examine: navigation through the material will not be prescriptive and facilities will be provided to enable users to access the material in a flexible user-driven way.The text resources will comprise a guide to the package and suggestions for ways in which it may be used.

MULTI-MEDIA TECHNOLOGY

The development environment comprises a Macintosh Quadra 800 running Macromedia Director with a range of multi-media packages including Adobe Premiere, Adobe Photoshop and various Quicktime tools. A large volume Optical Disk Drive is used for resource back-up. For the end-user, however, a CD-ROM drive allied to a standard macintosh computer is all that is required.

TIMESCALE

The development of the pack will involve three phases over a period of fifteen months:
    Phase One will comprise initial research over three months into examples of good practice, and the identification and collection of materials. Phase Two will involve the production of the package, which will consist of a video and CD–ROM with supporting documentation designed for individual access. This Phase will last nine months. Phase Three will consist of the piloting and evaluation of the materials.This will last three months.

EVALUATION

The success of the package will be measured in two ways. In a pilot stage, evidence will be obtained from users about its effectiveness from the point of view of the institutions and individuals making use of the materials. This piloting will result in appropriate modifications to the materials before final release.

A longer term evaluation will be made of the final package The criteria to be used in assessing the level of success of the package will involve eliciting responses from tutors, mentors and probationers regarding their satisfaction with the materials.

References

Draper J, Fraser H & Taylor W *A Study of Probationer Teachers* Scottish (1992) Council for Research in Education, Edinburgh

Elder R & Kwiatkowski H (1993) *Partnership in Initial Teacher Education* Northern College Dundee.

General Teaching Council (1992)*The Management of Probation* GTC Edinburgh

Gibson D G (1981) Resource centres in Scottish secondary schools *British Journal of Educational Technology 12 (1)*

Gibson D G (1984) The use of video in a national training programme for teachers in Shaw KE (Ed) Aspects of Educational Technology XVII *Staff Development and Career Updating.*

Kyriacou C (1993) Research on the development of expertise in classroom teaching during initial training and the first year of teaching *Educational Review 45 (1)*

MacFarlane AGJ (1992) (Chair) *Teaching and Learning in an Expanding Higher Education System.* Report of a working party of the Committee of Scottish University Principals.

Scottish Office Education (1993) *Guidelines for Teacher Training Courses* Department (1993) HMSO.

12a   Getting the Wording Right

Phil Race, *University of Glamorgan* **and Sally Brown** *University of Northumbria at Newcastle.*

Summary
A common factor governing the success of computer-assisted learning programs and open access education, is the optimum use of words. Whether on-screen, or in print, words are the primary medium of communication to learners, and the quality of these words governs the quality of the intended learning experience. A second common factor of computer-assisted learning programs and open access education is that there is usually **not** the opportunity for the intended meaning of words to be elaborated by use of tone of voice, emphasis, body language, and other 'human' qualities.

It is proposed that to accommodate the ways in which people learn best (in other words in the four processes of (1) cultivating the 'want' to learn, (2) providing abundant opportunity for learning by doing, (3) providing learners with relevant feedback, and (4) helping learners to make sense of their learning experiences), additional care needs to be taken in the ways that words are used in computer-assisted learning programmes and in open access education. There is increased danger that the developing sophistication of computer-assisted learning media and desktop publishing blinds educational designers to the need for clear communication of messages to learners.

We will give examples of the sort of 'wordsmithing' which militates against successful learning, and explore ways of making optimum use of words to give learners a feeling of ownership of their learning achievements.

The workshop activities will explore the use of words both for on-screen use, and in-print use. The workshop will aim to produce a set of recommendations for the optimum tone and style suitable for computer-based learning programmes, and for open access education programmes.

WHY SO MUCH COMPUTER-BASED TRAINING?

Computer-based training in all its many forms has been the focus of exponential growth in the last ten years. There are many reasons for the proliferation of computer-based learning some of which are listed below.

Costs and prices

- costs of hardware have fallen dramatically, and will continue to fall.
- the sophistication and speed of hardware has risen beyond all expectations, and seem set to continue to increase.
- the costs of software packages have fallen dramatically in real terms, a trend enhanced by the unit costs benefits accompanying mass production.
- the sophistication of software packages has increased tremendously, making computer-based learning increasingly attractive to users.

Attitudes and familiarity

- the younger generations are now already familiar with the use of computer-based systems for games, home entertainment and uses for schoolwork.
- people's keyboarding skills are much more developed than in past times, with a wide range of devices from crossword solvers, electronic diaries and word games using familiar 'qwerty' keyboard.
- 'technofear' is diminished - most people are no longer afraid that they will break the computer if they do something wrong.

- most young people have at least some computerised equipment of their own, and consequently are much more willing to try out any similar equipment they come across.
- there is increasing recognition nowadays that it is almost impossible to lose permanently large sections of work on computer programmes (barring electrical disasters), and people are more willing to commit first-stage draft text to screen rather than to paper when writing.

Impact and visual pleasure

- with high-resolution graphics and the use of bright colours for computer games, people increasingly expect that computer screens will be pleasing and stimulating visually.
- for many people, visual imagery contributes strongly to learning and thinking, and computer-based packages offer a range of images and stimuli exceeding that which printed media normally deliver.

However, although the factors listed above contribute to the growth of computer-based media for home entertainment and for learning, probably the most important factors relate to the links between computer-based training and the processes whereby people learn.

LEARNING PROCESSES AND COMPUTER-BASED TRAINING

It is increasingly being accepted that the success of any training programme or learning resource depends on the extent to which learning-centredness is achieved. It is useful to adopt a model of learning based on the everyday experiences of how ordinary people learn. Race (1994) proposes that there are four key processes which accompany successful learning.

- *wanting* to learn (or good motivation)
- *learning by doing* (practice, trail and error, experimentation)
- *feedback from other people* (trainers, teachers, colleagues, anyone!)
- *digesting* (making sense of what has been learned, and feedback received).

This model of learning is based on the replies of thousands of people of all ages, disciplines and professions, asked straightforward questions about how they learned things successfully (and about what sorts of things went wrong when their learning was not successful). Race has already explored the conflicts between this model of learning and traditional assessment, and the much better links which can be achieved by using self-assessment and peer-assessment (Race, 1992). Since then, Brown and Knight (1994) have produced a challenging review of the design and use of assessment instruments and processes, with many instances of the importance of 'getting the wording right' in designing assessed tasks and assessment criteria.

The 'wanting, doing, feedback digesting' model of learning has very powerful links with computer-based learning, as outlined below.

Wanting

- stimulating visual imagery and colour does much to make learning attractive and interesting.
- with computer-based systems increasingly used for games and home entertainment, the boundaries between study and relaxation are less sharply defined, increasing the attraction to 'play' and learn at the same time.

- many people are attracted by computer-based learning but alienated by traditional text-based learning.

Learning by doing

- computer-based learning is essentially interactive, and depends entirely on learners making choices, making decisions, entering commands or data, and so on.
- it is not usually possible just to 'read' or scan the content of computer-based packages; to move further requires some 'doing' of one kind or another.
- with many universities offering 24-hour access to IT resources, it is possible for learners to make wider choices about when they do their studying with computer-based learning materials.

Learning from feedback

- computer-based learning systems can provide the most immediate feedback that is possible - usually virtually instantaneously
- feedback delivered in relatively small amounts, and often. This helps the feedback to be directly relevant to the tasks learners have just done or the decisions they have just entered into the programme.

Digesting

- Because learners on computer-based learning programmes can go at their own pace, and can repeat things that they have not yet fully grasped, their opportunities to 'digest' and make sense of what they learn are increased.
- Computer-based programmes can tackle the need for digesting directly. For example, review episodes can be built into learning programmes to help learners consolidate what they have learned (the equivalent in print-based materials - summaries or reviews - are only too readily skipped by learners wanting to push ahead).

USER-FRIENDLINESS

It is hard to imagine now that not long ago, anyone who interacted with computers had to learn complex languages to become able to instruct the machines what they should compute. Entering a program into a machine required patience, precision and a lot of time. Then, most people who used computers needed to know at least something about computer programming.

Now, relatively few computer users need to know anything about computer programming or about how computers work. The skills which are needed are now 'doing' skills. The manuals which come with new computers are as thick as they ever were, but fewer people read anything more than how to set the machine up in the first place - if that. People nowadays are comfortable with the fact that they only work with quite tiny proportions of the data available to them on a computer programme. They work on a need-to-know basis and don't feel that they have to master the whole package.

Most software is now designed to be learned by interacting directly with it, through pull-down or on-screen menus. Packages are designed for 'learning by doing' and feedback is readily given whenever users attempt to do something which they may not really wish to do (for example lose data or change existing files).

'Learning by making mistakes' is turned into one of the most productive ways of learning - except that it is now 'learning by finding out what would have happened if I really had made that mistake' with the help of in-built feedback responses to all eventualities. For people who still prefer not to make 'mistakes' and learn from feedback, most computer packages have built-in 'help' menus which provide all of the information which once would only have been found in an unfriendly manual.

Computer-based packages also seem much more user-friendly because of the attractively-laid-out and often colourful screen designs, yet whatever the user-friendliness of the machines themselves and the software packages they run, words are still important.

GETTING THE WORDING RIGHT

From our comments so far in this paper, we hope you will feel that computer-based learning has many advantages over learning from printed resources or from trainers and teachers, although there are still many learners who prefer paper-based packages. It is not a very good idea to use your laptop in the bath!). Learners using computer-based packages have many of the benefits of open learners - learning at their own pace, learning by doing (and making mistakes in the comfort of privacy), getting feedback on an individual basis, and having opportunities to 'digest' what they have learned. However, it all still depends on language.

There are several cautionary factors to be taken into account when we consider how best to employ words in computer-based learning packages:

Only a small amount of information at a time

Even a monitor screen completely filled with words contains less information than a typical page of a book or printed package. Besides, a screen with too many words on it looks considerably more intimidating than a full printed page. Therefore, condensing information into succinct, precise statements or questions becomes an essential art for computer-based learning designers.

Now you see it, now you don't

With printed materials, it is very easy for users to glance back to remind themselves of something they're just beginning to understand. It's also easy for them to glance forward to see what is coming next, helping them gain a sense of 'where they are' in the grand scheme of things. With computer-based packages, once a decision to a question or task is entered, the original words are likely to disappear temporarily as the screen becomes filled with the next phase - feedback. It can be quite hard for learners to navigate themselves back to a sequence they wish to go through again for consolidation. However, as CD-I and hypermedia technology develops, this problem will be progressively eradicated. At the moment, it is possible to move around within learning packages in these media, but it is not always as straightforward as flicking through a text. Furthermore, printed materials can usually be carried around and used for 'quick revision' at almost any time; with computer-based packages the opportunity to revise may only occur in a particular location and at particular times.

The words are more important anyway

Most of the words used in computer-based learning materials are there for definite purposes. These include:

- setting tasks of questions for 'learning by doing';
- giving feedback to what learners have just done;
- providing just enough information to lead to the next task or question.

In printed materials, it matters less when some words are important and others are only of passing interest - indeed it is usually not too hard to tell which words are which in this respect. With computer-based materials, learners may well need additional guidance to alert them to those screens of information which are the most important things for them to address with keen concentration.

Getting the tone right

Consider your audience and try to fit the vocabulary and structure to the people who will be using the material. Using language with an inappropriate register alienates users.

WORDS WHICH HELP LEARNING TO HAPPEN SUCCESSFULLY

We have already suggested that successful learning needs attention to four factors: 'wanting, doing, feedback and digesting'. We would like now to make some recommendations regarding on-screen use of words under each of these four headings.

Wanting

- Avoid patronising learners by 'over-the-top' informality. Such informality is alright when it is *known* that the target group of learners likes such an approach, but can be counter productive when several different types of learner use a package.
- Most people warm to a relatively informal approach (remembering the reservations expressed above). It is useful to address learners as 'you', and to build this personal pronoun into task instructions and feedback responses.
- Many packages allow learners to enter their names (or nicknames) early on in the programme, so that feedback responses can address learners directly by name.

Doing

- The task instructions are probably the most important words in computer-based learning packages. It is therefore crucial to make instructions as short, clear and unambiguous as possible. For complex tasks, several short sentences work better than one long sentence with lots of commas.
- Wherever possible, use bullet-points or icons to help learners to find their way around material and to recognise listed items.
- Make tasks and questions as 'visual' as possible. For example, if an option is to be selected by learners from a set of possibilities, it is useful to make each option stand out 'visually' for example by 'boxing' each option, or by using different colours for each option (but being careful not to let the 'best' or correct options become recognisable just from the layout or colours used).
- Give learners every chance to find out about possible mistakes. For example, learners who choose a 'correct' or 'best' option in a multiple choice question may indeed have done so because they understood the question and knew the answer, but they may also have simply guessed.

'Decide which is the best option, and work out what is wrong with each of the other alternatives' is a much more useful type of question than just 'Pick the best option'. That said, it is of course necessary to build in to the programme a way back to the question from each feedback response, so that learners can check whether their thinking about respective options is correct.

Feedback

- Learners who have just made a choice of option, or entered data in response to a question need to find out two things a quickly as possible:
  'Was I right?'
  'If not, *why* not?'
  The first few words of feedback responses need to let learners know where they are. It can get rather boring for learners if the same positive words (such as 'well done') are used every time they make a good choice or get a task right. There are countless ways of saying 'well done', and many 'levels' of 'well done' depending on whether the task was a really difficult one, or one which most people should have done correctly. It would be patronising to reply 'splendid' if the task was easy, but perfectly acceptable if it was a really tricky task.

- For learners who did not choose the correct (or best) option, or who entered incorrect data, even though they may be working in the comfort of privacy, it is important that they are not led to feel that they must be the only people on the planet to get things wrong. Better still, it helps greatly if they are reminded positively about the value of learning by mistakes. Responses to incorrect choices can usefully 'defuse' the situation with words along the following lines:

    - 'Don't worry, many people think this is the case, but...'
    - 'The question was tricky, and catches most people out.'
    - 'You probably chose this option because you thought that....'

- It is very useful to keep the tasks or questions in sight while responding with feedback. Sometimes there is room on the feedback screen for the whole of the original question (maybe in smaller lettering than on the question screen). However, even when this is not the case, there are ways of reminding learners of the questions as they read the feedback comments. For example, when replying to a true-false question it is more useful to reply that:
  'it is *false* to say that electrical current is measured in kilowatt-hours; current is measured in amperes (amps), while *energy* is measured in kilowatt-hours'
  than simply to reply:
  'false': current is measured in amperes'.

- It is important to avoid unproductive interaction. For example, there is little point including questions or activities which no-one would get wrong. Posing the tasks or questions orally to groups of live students is probably the quickest way of finding out whether what seems like a wonderful question is going to serve useful purposes in practice.

Digesting

- It is all-too-easy to assume that because learners have got something right half-an-hour ago, they can still do it. It is therefore useful to pause now and then, and include tasks and activities which give learners the chance to find out whether they really have mastered an idea, or whether it was just a fluke first time round.
- Digesting (in the physiological sense) involves taking from our food that which we need. With learning experiences, it is useful to help learners do something very similar - in other words to identify the main ideas that they will need to take forward as they continue through the package.
- Digesting (in the physiological sense) is also about discarding in due course what we do not need (the roughage). It is very useful to help learners see which parts of the information they have been thinking about were only for 'noting in passing' or 'a means to an end'.

At the workshop associated with this paper at the AETT 1994 International Conference in Edinburgh we intend to harness the skills and experience of participants to develop a set of further recommendations to add to the above discussion - or indeed to replace it altogether.

CONCLUSIONS

Many features of computer-based learning are already close to the ways that people learn naturally. We need, however, to be careful not to get carried away with the impact and gloss of the presentation of computer-based learning packages at the expense of making sure that the words themselves used within the packages work towards successful learning. We assert that using appropriate language is a key feature in ensuring that learners are turned on rather than turned off when using computer-based learning, and that the skills necessary to get the wording right are ones which need careful honing and development to ensure the best results.

References

Brown S, and Knight, P (1994) *Assessing Learners in Higher Education* Kogan Page London

Race P (1992) *Quality of Assessment; Aspects of Educational and Training Technology XXVI* Eds Roper and Shaw, Kogan Page, London

Race P (1994) *The Open Learning Handbook* (2nd Edition) Kogan Page, London.

Rowntree D (1994) *Preparing Materials for Open, Distance and Flexible Learning* Kogan Page, London.

12b   Getting the Wording Even More Right!

Sally Brown, *University of Northumbria at Newcastle* and Phil Race, *University of Glamorgan*

This article forms a companion piece to the paper "Getting the wording right" (Chapter 12a) which was presented to the AETT conference 11- 13 April 1994, and develops further some of the ideas therein, in the light of the comments and reactions of the participants at the linked workshop. It also describes some of the workshop processes, so that these can be made available for use by others.

We thank   Mike Cook, University of Humberside, Silvia Scott, Nottingham Trent University, Heather Powell, Nottingham Trent University, Eric Foxley, University of Nottingham, Catherine Scott, University of North London , Joyce Warmsley, Employment Department, Sheffield, Dominic Palmer Brown, Nottingham Trent University, Stewart Houston, Grange Loan,Edinburgh and Margaret Mill, Napier University for their contributions.

Expressed aims of the participants who attended the workshop included:

* To learn something more about effective 'wording' for teaching.
* How to convey the message: I'm looking for the experts view.
* How to avoid some of the obvious pitfalls in designing open-learning materials.Some principles to follow.
* Insights and practice into clear and effective writing of explanation and instruction.
* **Fresh** ideas about effectively using Computer Based Teaching as a "learning tool" Re-enthusing myself.
* Accurate, precise, helpful use of English.
* Get some insight into what I do right and what I could do better in my teaching materials.

Following an introductory exercise, the key ideas of the companion paper were summarised using overhead projection transparencies, and this was followed by a writing exercise. The participants were asked to undertake a brief writing task, the completion of which modelled many of the processes engaged in when writing open learning packages and computer-based learning materials.

The task was based on the Japanese poetry form, Haiku, which being extremely short, enables a complete poem to be written in a fairly brief period of time. Haiku consist of three lines only, the first consisting of five syllables, the second with seven syllables and the last having five. Classically, the last line refers to the changing of the seasons, the transitory nature of life, the passage of time or another similarly philosophical theme.

Examples of Haikus were demonstrated, for example:

> The horse stands foursquare,
> Stalwart, resolute, resigned,
> He longs for spring time.

Once the form had been fully explained, individuals were then asked to write one each of their own, before going into pairs to share and critique each other's. Each pair was then asked to select one of their two products to work on and polish, then they presented these using the overhead projector to the group as a whole.

EXAMPLES OF HAIKU FROM THE GROUP:

Watching spring move north /seems I'm trav'ling to keep pace/ still the lambs will grow.

Old Edinburgh's walls/ took many years to build./The hills are forever.

The plane leaves the runway/Lift a hand and wipe a tear/Lift-off - Story ends

Salt spray in the beach/Children splash and run around/Kicking summer sand

Let me throw a pot/Feel the soft clay in your hands/The pot knows its time

Henry the biker/Riding across England in sleet/Reviles endless Winter

Cold and fresh alone/sweet smell of sea salt and weed/Winter approaches

People wushing Evewywhewe/Twanspowt is now all awound/Newev the Twain shall meet

(All Haikus are copyright to the authors)

The second half of the workshop involved unpacking the learning from the exercise and translating that learning into guidelines for good practice, which then could be used in the writing of sample elements of learning packages relevant to the participants' own work.

The Haiku exercise demonstrated that the art of writing effectively incorporates, typically:

> task analysis
> drafting
> precision
> piloting
> getting and giving feedback
> revision
> completion.

Whether the writing activitity is a Haiku, an article, an element of an open learning package, a screen in a computer-based learning package or a book, it is necessary to start by analysing the task carefully and making sure the requirements and parameters are known. This can be done individually or collectively but ,especially where work is commissioned, it is essential that the author has a clear vision of what is required

However small the writing task, probably the most difficult part is getting the first draft started. For many people, the idea that this first draft can be very rough is liberating, and allows an early begining to be made. It is usually disastrous to attempt anything too polished in the first instance, but it is a much easier task to work on and re-edit an existing document than it is to attempt perfection too early.

In writing Haikus, getting the syllable count exactly right, while still being grammatical and making sense requires a great deal of precision: making it beautiful, meaningful and/or funny is another challenge! This is equally the case with writing any kind of learning materials, when accuracy and correctness are important, but so are immediacy, appeal and authenticity. Open learning materials can be very dull and dry if they are not enlivened by the author's individual voice.

Our Haiku writers got feedback from each other and were able to make improvements in their writing as a result of this. Open Learning materials should always be piloted with naive as well as experienced learners to ensure that all likely "glitches" are eliminated as far as possible, by trying them out in practice with people as close as possible to the likely end users.

Getting and giving constructive feedback are essential elements of any kind of public writing. The co-authors of this article are convinced of the benefits of co-authoring, especially when co-authors are comfortable enough with each other to give hard feedback without fear of giving offence, as well as giving credit where credit is due in cases of excellence. Often a second (or third or fifth) view can help the writer see possibilities that were not originally apparent and can provide a fresh view to the writer who is often so close to the subject that objectivity becomes difficult. Piloting is therefore an unmissable opportunity to get to know how our writing is perceived by others.

Revisions can then be made in the light of these insights, leading to a better finished product than can be achieved by an individual writing in isolation. Completion of the task is perhaps the most satisfying element, but authors can also find it difficult to let go of a cherished project. An open learning package, like a poem, is never finished but simply abandoned at the least damaging point!

Our workshop participants were able to provide guidelines on writing open learning materials following their experience of writing in action. These included:

- Include only material that will be used /is needed.
- Orientate students properly in order to get them working well.
- Ensure logical progression of material
- Make sure that the content hits nail on head
- Organise material so that its readily to hand.
- Plan and design packages considering everything that might go wrong and take account of this in writing materials.
- Don't agree to unrealistic deadlines.
- Plan the aims of teaching package so that they are realistic - don't be over ambitious

FINAL THOUGHTS

Getting the words right when writing open learning materials requires a combination of innate ability to work with words, hard graft in terms of writing and rewriting, the ability to take account of constructive feedback and to modify materials accordingly and the energy and stamina to finish the task, ideally hitting deadlines too! The educational and theoretical content of the packages must be entirely sound and appropriate, but getting the shape, tone and register of the language right often means the difference between success and failure in terms of package appeal.

Section 2 : **Computer Assisted Learning (CAL) and Computer-Based Training (CBT)**

13. The Design and Use of Computer-Based Tutorials for Teaching, Learning and Assessment of Quantitative Research Methods

Bryan Scotney and Sally McClean, *University of Ulster*

Summary

In recent years it has become possible to introduce elementary classes to statistical packages at an increasingly early stage in their undergraduate studies, due largely to the increasing availability of user-friendly packages, and to the increasing capability of micro-computers at an affordable price. Such packages are largely self-contained and require the students to know very little about the machine or its operating system. Teaching takes place in a computer laboratory giving the students immediate hands-on experience.

This teaching method both encourages and enables the student to adopt a more exploratory and research-oriented approach, with attention focused on method selection rather than simply calculation. Through the analysis of real data the student gains experience of problems as they arise in practice, and develops both a more critical approach to the use of statistics and an awareness of the capability of computers.

This paper describes the design, production and implementation of a suite of hypertext CBT's concerned with Descriptive Statistics, Introductory Data Analysis, Questionnaire Coding and Analysis, and using *Minitab*, developed under the funding of the Enterprise in Higher Education (EHE) Initiative. The development tool, is the authoring language *Guide*, and implementation is on a *Novell* network. The tutorials are structured to meet three primary objectives: the introduction of concepts, the facilitation of revision,and the acquisition of skills for project work. Concepts are introduced through directed learning and assessment, whilst student-centred learning is used for revision and project skills. Objective testing is also incorporated into the tutorials which may be used for either self-assessment or formal examination. The statistical methods are discussed with reference to the statistical computer package *Minitab*, and the flexibility of the hypertext medium is exploited to simulate the carrying out of statistical analysis using *Minitab*.

INTRODUCTION

Due to both the continuing rapid expansion of Higher Education and improving technology, the use of computers in teaching and learning has dramatically increased in recent years. This has been accompanied by a rapid development of hypermedia software for educational applications, including computer-based tutorials (CBT's). As increasing attention is centred on the teaching role of universities, so there is a search for greater efficiency in teaching. Associated with this is the current attention being paid to teaching quality, as highlighted in a recent paper from the Committee of Vice-Chancellors and Principals (Partington and Elton 1991).

CBT's offer the potential for improved learning efficiency, teaching efficiency, and flexibility. Computer Based Learning (CBL) can significantly enhance students' learning capabilities (Darby 1992), with increased learning efficiency having important consequences in allowing for an expansion in course content. This is particularly attractive in subjects where topics such as research methods are being introduced without any corresponding reduction of content in other areas. In terms of teaching efficiency, CBL is most cost effective in Higher Education institutions in situations where large numbers of students study courses which have elements such as research methods in common. Investment in CBT production for quantitative research methods is justified by the numbers of students now being introduced to this topic from a variety of disciplines. This diversity of disciplines, together with the increasing range of students' entry qualifications, demands a flexibility in teaching and learning quantitative research methods which CBT's can facilitate. By the use of 'buttons' or 'hotspots' embedded within the information presented, the user can have considerable influence over the order in which information is delivered (Richards *et al* 1991). In this way the student is given the tools to control his or her learning (Isaacs 1990) within an individual working pattern.

CBL can be considerably more interactive than passive participation in a lecture, providing prompt individual feedback, and CBT's are particularly suitable for providing revision or consolidation of basic principles (Bishop *et al* 1992). Additionally CBT's can benefit the teacher in terms of immediate feedback on the students' performance, which can be recorded for later reference (James 1986). Hence the students' individual difficulties may be identified for later personal attention. Finally, CBT software can grow and develop, and it should not be seen as a fixed product (De Diana 1991).

DESIGN CONSIDERATIONS FOR THE CBT'S

The effectiveness of the CBT's is very dependent upon their design (Stanton and Stammers 1990). Gagné *et al* (1986) have suggested a number of events which enhance learning when included in a learning situation:
- gaining attention
- informing the learner of the objectives
- presenting stimulus material
- providing 'learner guidance'
- providing feedback
- assessing performance

These provide a basis for identifying the design considerations for the CBTs, which can be generalised into three groups:
- aims of the CBT's
- content of the CBT's
- the most effective style of presentation and delivery

In considering the aims of the CBT's it is important to provide meaningful interactivity for the learner. Repetition of tasks is avoided, as this does not involve meaningful participation. It is also necessary for the CBT's to demonstrate ease of use, an important factor pin-pointed particularly by non-computer science students (Whiting 1989). It is essential that the tutorial environment is user-friendly and self-explanatory. The content of the CBT's is organised clearly and systematically with consideration for the most effective method of instruction. The presentation and delivery strategies incorporate text, graphics, and animation. (As the CBT's are installed in multi-user laboratories, the use of audio presentation has been avoided.) The material being presented has been alleviated of too many distractions, thus enabling the user to focus on reading and assimilating the information (Smeaton 1991).

STRUCTURE OF THE CBT'S

The CBT's are stored as a non-linear sequence of frames within a set of documents, arranged initially as nodes in a tree, but allowing for structured access to any node from any other (James 1986). The CBT structure adopted is a combination of hierarchical and network hypertext organisation, which allows both simple browsing and searching for specific information. The inclusion of a hierarchical aspect in the CBT design derives partly from the fact that the material presented originates largely from existing teaching material, but is also to support navigation between the screens of the CBT's (Smeaton 1991). Hence the learner can browse to related or associated screens without worrying about where to go next.

An overlay screen layout is used throughout the CBT's to facilitate the simultaneous presentation of different types of information (text, pictures, simulated output from other computer applications, additional information and explanation). For navigation within the

CBT's a standard control panel has been devised consisting of a number of icons or buttons for accessing other locations in the CBT's. The control panel partially overlays the information screen so that it is always available and each icon retains a unique and fixed position on the screen (Megarry 1991). The frame navigation buttons are self-explanatory, such as 'MENU', 'PREVIOUS', 'NEXT', 'MAIN MENU', etc. Scrolled text (with the finger pressed continuously on a 'browse' button) has been avoided, as it results both in there being no part of the information which is static (Benest 1991), and in some information becoming temporarily hidden behind items such as control panels.

Text and graphics are used in a variety of different ways in the design of the CBT's in order to achieve efficient and effective communication. The text styles and colours adopted are used globally, in order to unify themes and to assist the user to readily identify different types of information and the different options available at any time in terms of interaction and navigation (De Diana 1991). For graphics, construction, destruction and highlighting of diagrams are all ways which are used to convey important features. The temporary highlighting (for example, by a change of colour) of the section being discussed is particularly effective.

One of the most important features of the hypertext CBT's is the presence of 'buttons' or 'hotspots' (not just for navigation) which, when 'clicked on', carry out an event. The buttons are usually defined globally, so that the user becomes familiar with the facilities which they provide, and different button types are identified by the mouse pointer changing to a specific shape when moved over a particular type of 'hotspot'. In the CBT's, both types of objects (textual and graphical) exist as buttons, where only part of, or all of, the object is made into a 'hotspot' (Richards *et al* 1991). For example, the 'hotspots' within a menu screen are reference buttons which enable the user to jump to more specific sub-menus or directly to specific topics in the CBT's (an example is shown in Figure 13.1); other 'hotspots' such as note buttons provide extended information on the related text or graphic in a 'pop-up' window opened temporarily on the current screen.

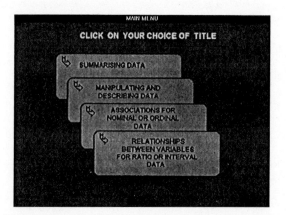

Figure 13.1: Main menu consisting of 'hotspots' which link to sub-menus for each topic

Animation is frequently used in the CBT's for a variety of purposes, especially in simulating the use of the statistical package *Minitab*. Control buttons are used to activate events such as the character-by-character appearance of *Minitab* commands, to simulate their entry by a keyboard user. Correspondingly, Minitab output screens are subsequently revealed, featuring 'hotspots' which initiate the provision of further explanation or interpretation of results. Figure 13.2 illustrates this facility used to interpret a hypothesis test.

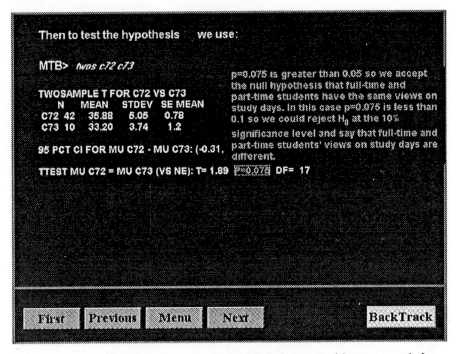

Figure 13.2: An information screen displaying Minitab output with a pop-up window offering explanotry interpretation.

The CBTs incorporate sections which aim to test the user's understanding of the information delivered by the tutorials in earlier frames. The strategies employed include multiple-choice questions, true/false techniques, and simple open-ended questions requiring short textual or numerical answers. Question styles which require the user to examine presentations of data or to interpret the output from statistical tests have been developed. Figure 15.3 shows a multiple response question which requires the student to interpret information presented in a contingency table as output by *Minitab*. The user's responses are evaluated by the software, which then provides feedback on the correct answers and on the user's performance (Whiting 1989).

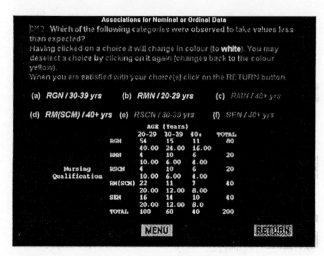

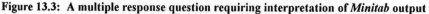

Figure 13.3: A multiple response question requiring interpretation of *Minitab* output

CONTENT OF THE CBT'S

The first set of CBT's introduces the basic ideas and applications of descriptive statistics, namely summarising data; manipulating and describing data; associations for nominal or ordinal data; relationships between ratio or interval data. It aims to provide students with an intuitive understanding of statistical concepts and a variety of relevant examples are used to illustrate the techniques. A knowledge of mathematics beyond basic numeracy is not required. The statistical methods are discussed with reference to the statistical computer package *Minitab*, and the flexibility of the hypertext medium is exploited to simulate the carrying out of statistical analysis using *Minitab*. The CBT's are designed to develop the student's ability to organise, present and interpret data in a number of ways. In addition, the concept of statistical inference is introduced in order to enable the student to carry out and interpret simple hypothesis tests. Each tutorial concludes with a test with feedback which the student may use to appraise their understanding.

The second set of CBT's is centred on questionnaire analysis. The tutorials cover all of the stages of coding data, forming variables and scales, structuring the analysis, formulating hypotheses, describing and presenting variables and their relationships, and testing hypotheses involving one and two samples. Again the hypertext medium is exploited to simulate the carrying out of statistical analysis using *Minitab*. The data demonstrated in these CBT's are those collected from a 1992/93 module cohort of Health Science students. A particular feature of these tutorials is the facility to refer to the appropriate section of the questionnaire at any point to re-establish the link between the questions and the analysis of the responses to them.

USE OF THE CBT'S

The CBT's have been developed under the funding of the Enterprise in Higher Education (EHE) Initiative. The tutorials are targeted specifically at Health Science students and use data sets relevant to their subject of study. It is also important however that the CBT's have a structure which permits additions and modifications in content to take account of future use with extended student groups.

The hypertext tutorials have been developed using version 3.1 of the *Guide* hypermedia system running under *MS-Windows* version 3.1 on an IBM compatible PC with a hard disk. A high-resolution enhanced graphics adapter (EGA) or VGA display or better and a colour display is highly recommended. For use with a class in a computer laboratory the system was run under the management of a *Novell* Network. This facilitates the maintenance and updating of the tutorials and also allows the possibility of the network manager collecting individual student answers from the respective work-stations for inspection by the class instructor.

For teaching which is focused on the computer and the use of packages, as is increasingly the case with quantitative research methods, the student is already familiar with the environment and is timetabled to spend a large proportion of the course in a computer laboratory. No additional resources are therefore required for CBT delivery.

The tutorials are structured to meet three primary objectives : the introduction of concepts, the facilitation of revision, and the acquisition of skills for undertaking and assessing research work. Concepts are introduced through directed learning and assessment, whilst student-centred learning is used for revision. Research skills are gained and developed in both modes of learning. Objective testing is used for student self-assessment. Prior to using the CBT, the lecturer introduced the students to the system, initially in a lecture theatre, and subsequently in a computer laboratory. This gave the lecturer the opportunity to introduce each topic verbally to the student group before they used the appropriate section of the tutorial. In order to facilitate independent learning, the CBT's were accompanied by a paper-based booklet which explained the essential features of the system. The students were permitted to work through the tutorials both during class and in their own time, and both individual and group use of the system was encouraged.

EVALUATION OF THE CBT'S

At the end of the 1992/93 academic year, a confidential evaluation questionnaire was completed by the cohort of 70 students. 67% completed all of the tutorials and 84% completed at least three-quarters, with 56% usually completing the CBT's in class. 66% of the students found the hypertext CBT's either very or fairly helpful, with 67% reporting that they either enjoyed, or at least did not mind, using them. This has to be considered in the context of most of the students having had no previous experience of *MS-Windows* applications, and hence having to develop new computer skills associated with use and control of the mouse. It is therefore encouraging that over 80% of the students found the CBT's satisfactory or better in terms of organisation of material, screen presentation, ease of following instructions, and use as a revision aid. Virtually all of the students found the end-of-tutorial tests to be of value as a means of self-appraisal.

ACKNOWLEDGEMENTS

We would like to thank the Enterprise in Higher Education (EHE) Initiative for supporting this project, Nuala Colgan for developing the software, and Computing Officers Andrew Gregg, Ian Cantley and Michael Docherty for their assistance throughout the project.

References

Benest I (1991) An alternative approach to hypertext, *Educational and Training Technology International, 28* (4), 341-346.
Bishop P, Beilby M and Bowman A (1992) Computer-based learning in mathematics and statistics. *Computers and Education, 19* (1/2), 131-143.

Darby, J (1992) Computers in teaching and learning in U.K. higher education, *Computers and Education, 19* (1/2), 1-8.

De Diana I (1991) Electronic Study Book Platforms, *Educational and Training Technology International, 28* (4), 347-354.

Gagné R *et al* (1988) *The Outcomes of Instruction in Principles of Instruction Design*, Holt, Rinehart & Winston, New York.

Issacs G (1990) Course and tutorial CAL lesson design: helping students take control of their learning, *Educational and Training Technology International, 27* (1), 85-91.

James E (1986) Computer-based teaching for undergraduates: old problems and new possibilities, *Computers and Education, 10* (2), 267-272.

Megarry J (1991) 'Europe in the round': principles and practice of screen design, *Educational and Training Technology International, 28* (4), 306-315.

Partington, O and Elton, L (1991) Teaching standards and excellence in higher education: developing a culture for quality, *Committee for Vice-Chancellors and Principals*, Universities Staff Development and Training Unit, University of Sheffield.

Richards S, Barker P, Giller S, Lemont C, and Manji K (1991) Page Structure for Electronic Books, *Educational and Training Technology International, 28* (4), 291-301.

Smeaton A (1991) Using hypertext for computer based learning, *Computers and Education*, 17 (3), 173-179.

Stanton N and Stammers R (1990) A comparison of structured and unstructured navigation through a CBT package, *Computers and Education, 15* (1-3), 159-163.

Whiting J (1989) An evaluation of some common CAL and CBT authoring styles, *Educational and Training Technology International, 26* (3), 186-200.

14. Learning by Designing: A CAL Option for Final Year Undergraduates in German

Felicitas Rühlmann, *University of the West of England, Bristol*

Summary
As recent academic surveys and reports have shown, Higher Education establishments are currently facing an increasing demand for more open access and flexible learning, together with the need for quality assurance of teaching and learning. As far as commercially available courseware is concerned, there is still a lack of suitable materials that could be used or easily customised to accompany or replace lectures and/or certain tutorials. The needs of undergraduates can often only be met by tailor-made materials which are fully integrated into their studies.

Traditionally, there have been considerable efforts in providing students of Languages and European Studies at the University of the West of England with tailor-made textbooks, printed dossiers and self-study materials for their respective degree courses. Accompanying audio tapes, computerised grammar exercises in foreign languages and translations using hypertext techniques have also been produced by academic staff in order to enhance independent student learning.

However, most academic staff in our Faculty still regard the in-house production of integrated multimedia courseware as costly and cumbersome. To address this problem I have designed, developed and piloted a final year option for multimedia CAL design. This was meant to enhance students' understanding of education and training technology, improve their knowledge about certain subject areas and lead to the production of computer delivered courseware that could be integrated into subsequent undergraduate teaching and learning in various disciplines.

COURSE OUTLINE

The main aims and objectives of this CAL option are outlined below:

1. to integrate self-study CAL materials development into mainstream teaching within our Faculty of Languages and European Studies;

2. to improve students' language skills in German;

3. to introduce students to new concepts and principles for the design of CAL tutorials which are being used in business and commerce and which are based on the latest academic research;

4. to acquaint students with criteria for courseware evaluation;

5. to improve students' transferable skills by adopting a teamwork approach for the production of courseware design documents;

6. to encourage students to work on their own initiative through project planning and adopting different responsibilities;

7. to encourage students to reflect on teaching methods and the content of their own undergraduate studies, and apply improved methods and contents in their own design projects;

8. to set up an in-house resource bank of multimedia CAL tutorials for student-centred learning.

The course stretched over eleven weeks and concentrated on:

a) forms and functions of CAL, CAL versus CBT, historical background;
b) the evaluation of CAL courseware;
c) the exploration of criteria and new principles for courseware design;
d) the introduction to an authoring system;
e) the production of CAL design documents.

Subject areas for CAL design projects included:

a) German language acquisition;
b) German life and culture;
c) German economy;
d) business administration (in German);
e) information systems (in German).

All subject areas are closely related to degree courses currently offered at the University of the West of England, i.e. undergraduate courses in Modern Languages, Modern Languages with Information Systems and a postgraduate course in European Business Administration.

Within the given framework, students were free to choose their own topics. At the end of the course, students handed in their group projects in the form of design specifications and programmable-ready material for the development of CAL modules. This material could now be implemented with a view to it being offered to first and second year undergraduates through stand-alone or networked multimedia PCs.

In order to assess the success of the teaching and learning, students were given anonymous evaluation forms at the end of the course. Nine out of eleven students returned the questionnaire. One third of the students said that the course had met their initial expectations and two thirds said that it had exceeded them.

DESIGN ISSUES AND THEIR REFLECTION IN STUDENTS' PROJECTS

For students to learn from and contribute to academic research in CAL, the prototype multimedia template which I had developed to facilitate the speedy production of tutorials was integrated in the course. It played a major part in the introduction to the principles of quality courseware design. Students' comments were continually being fed back into my current research on template design in order to enhance design standards and the user friendliness of the prototype.

Three design documents were produced. Group one compared British and German driving regulations, group two explained the German political system, group three designed a game on European monuments. All projects entailed an introduction, learning objectives, screen templates and routing, a complete storyboard including graphics design sheets and flow diagrams for interactive tasks.

LEARNING OBJECTIVES AND TARGET AUDIENCE

Only after giving an accurate account of what learners are supposed to be able to achieve, (i.e. name, locate, describe, identify, define, operate etc., rather than "know", "understand" or "appreciate") after completion of the program can the success of the learning process be measured in interactive tasks and questions.

In all projects, students had encountered difficulties with the definition of detailed learning objectives. Neither were learners informed of the main objectives before entering the module for the first time, nor were they allowed to access objectives at any time during the course in order to check their own progress. Moreover, the lack of clearly stated objectives had a restrictive influence on students' design of interactive tasks. Where learners could have been encouraged to carry out a variety of activities in any one task, interaction in students' projects was generally restricted to multiple choice and gap filling exercises.

In order to pitch both language and content at the right level, it was crucial to map out the profile of the target audience from the outset. As regards the use of the target language, students had considerable problems trying to restrict the complexity of lexis and grammar constructions in their designs. In one project, students had devised a glossary to provide an on-line lexical help system. However, in order to ensure effective learning for non-native speakers of the target language, all projects should have included both on-line glossaries and grammatical help systems. Another possibility would have been the introduction of a choice between two language levels per program.

SCREEN FORMATS AND USER INTERFACE DESIGN

In all design projects, a number of fixed screen formats were applied (Figure 14.1).

Generally, icon design and navigation toolbars followed conventions for applications in a Windows environment. Problems arose with the definition of foregrounds and backgrounds. For instance one project deviated from ergonomic principles by introducing a brilliant white background instead of a moderated light colour, assuming that brightness might contribute to the clarity of instruction screens, but neglecting the fatigue brought about by very high contrast and brightness.

Another design feature that tended to be overlooked was the distinction between objects placed on either the foreground or the background of a particular frame. If the authoring system used for the implementation of the project allows overlays, it is advisable to indicate that objects such as pointers, arrows or frames highlighting certain parts of a graphic or even text objects be placed on the front screen, whereas larger pictures or objects that remain on screen for several frames may be located on the back screen.

In project one, areas allocated for text in information and question screens were not given enough space for the amount of text included in the storyboard. The text area in project two covered a quarter of the screen and in project three it was designed vertically to cover one third of the screen space. This allowed only up to six words to be entered per line. In project two students used layered text in sequences of information screens in order to split information into self-contained units. In project three text units were displayed in different colours in relation to factual statements. To avoid problems with text areas, it is advisable to specify the exact number of lines and characters per line that may be used in each text area, provided that fixed screen types are employed. With setups such as in projects two and three it is particularly important to split up blocks of text into small meaningful units in order to enable text intake at a glance.

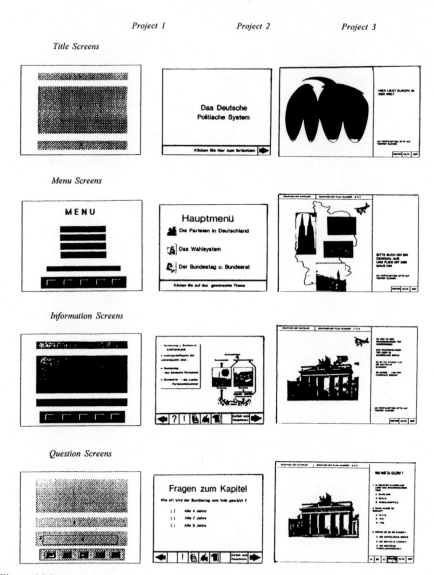

Figure 14.1

In all projects thought was given to the location of text areas on screen, but problems occurred with the more complex designs of multiple choice screens. Hardly any space was allocated to feedback text after learner input which was judged to be wrong. In project one, the strip allocated for graphics displays across the top third of the screen could have created difficulties when tall graphic objects needed to be included to illustrate a question. In project two no screen space was allocated for feedback text, and in project three feedback text was displayed when question and choices were no longer on screen. The problem in project one could be addressed by either placing the icon banner vertically along the right screen margin throughout the program or by splitting graphics and text areas vertically in interactive tasks. The relevant screens in projects two and three would have to be re-designed.

Problems occurred mainly in terms of the number, consistency, availability, conventions and positioning of icons. Students were advised to give the user a maximum of control and choice. In projects one and three, students restricted the number of icons available on each screen to five and six respectively. In project two space was allocated for nine icons to be available simultaneously. The availability of icons was indicated in projects two and three by either displaying or not displaying them in the icon banner. In project two the user was not allowed to exit the program on the first two screens.

In order to avoid cognitive overload for the user, more than seven icons could have been either grouped together, reduced in number or combined into pull down menus. For reasons of consistency, all icons in one tutorial should adhere to the same standards. They should be of the same size and colours, pictograms should be either used on their own, provided they are clear and simple, or together with text, but an icon banner should avoid mixing pure pictograms with pure text icons. If pictograms are used, they should be self-explanatory and in line with established software conventions, such as a question mark representing a help function, a pen or hand holding a pen indicating a note-taking facility. In project two such conventions were ignored. The availability of icons could have been brought in line with current conventions of de-highlighting icons when they are unavailable. In order not to restrict the user's control, exit must be available on all screens. In project one the exit and backwards icons were positioned on the left and the icon for advancing on the far right of the icon banner. This cannot be regarded as a convention in standard courseware design as yet: Cates *et al* (1993) appear to have placed icons on the navigation column in a random order, with "go on" in the middle of the icon banner and "exit" on the very right. Yazdani (1993) has placed exit in the lower left and advance in the upper left corner of the screen. Chaski and Mehlenbacher (1993) have arranged "Quit "to the left and "Next" to the right end of their icon banner. Although in text-based CAL tutorials this order may have to be reversed to pay tribute to certain cultural conventions, such as writing and reading from right to left in Arabic (Brockett *et al* 1992) or top down in Japanese (Nara 1993), it is well in line with conventional control panels in hifi systems, where backwards arrows are located and point to the left and forward arrows point to the right. Moreover, scroll bars in most software applications are conveniently placed at the lower and right margins of the screen, with the arrows indicating advance placed in the lower right corner of the screen and pointing to the right or downwards. Also, this setup is most user-friendly, because advance is clearly the most frequently used icon in a tutorial, and having to search for it in the middle of an icon banner each time the user wants to progress in the course may lead to frustration. To be consistent, the least frequently used icon, i.e. exit, ought to be placed on the ultimate left of the icon banner, as applied in project one (figure 14.2).

Figure 14.2

Learner orientation was only given on information screens in project one. Here, a title line was reserved to indicate the chapter which the learner is accessing. Generally, this information ought to be available on all screens in order to prevent the learner from becoming disoriented.

INTERACTIVE TASKS

The design of interaction screens with hot spots and the structuring of flow charts for interactive tasks proved to be a particularly weak spot in all projects. I believe that these problems need particular attention which would lead beyond the framework of this paper. I am planning to discuss these problems in detail in a future paper.

MEDIA

Students restricted the use of audio to a minimum and decided not to use video facilities at all in their projects. In project two, which dealt with the German political system, an audio facility would have been particularly useful. The content of this tutorial was lecture-based with added interactivity, and the possibility of listening to the explanations given in the foreign language would have enhanced the learning process. In projects one and three sounds indicated positive or negative feedback, and in project three countries could be identified via their respective national anthems. In project one the use of video clips or animation would have been appropriate, particularly for the section on driving instructions.

Programmable-ready graphics design sheets were included in projects two and three, whereas group one had decided merely to define screen types and graphics areas and number all graphic objects individually on separate graphics design sheets, so that graphics arrangements on screen could be referred to by names and numbers in the storyboard. Some problems occurred with the number of different graphics used and their relation to the subject matter presented on any one screen. Too often, general pictures were used, with text being the only variable through a number of information screens. One team attached a colour chart to their design. The separation of graphics sheets from the storyboard is necessary for a graphics artist and a developer to work simultaneously when implementing the program. The use of few graphics may be a cost effective solution, but it could make the program boring and monotonous. The inclusion of colour charts can be most useful for the consistency of implementation and for the limited range of colours usable with graphics cards below super-VGA standard.

All projects are of sufficient quality to be implemented, with only few amendments to be carried out. Problems with courseware design mainly occurred in the following areas:

a) learning objectives in connection with terminology;
b) lack of multimedia and the use of graphics in relation to content;
c) flow charts, interactivity and feedback for learners;
d) screen formats and navigation metaphors.

Particularly where interactivity and screen design are concerned, further research in this field is needed to enhance the quality of CAL tutorials.

CONCLUSION

Involving students in the production of flexible CAL tutorials as outlined above can be a challenging step on the way to in-house courseware production. It can help change students' perception of flexible learning by encouraging them to play an active part in providing it. Furthermore, the process of learning by designing can enhance student motivation and generate quality learning. As a consequence of the positive response to this design option, I am now planning to offer a new module for CAL courseware design and development in two stages, in which the design is followed by the implementation of students' projects.

References

Ambron S and Hooper K (eds) (1990) *Learning with Interactive Multimedia: Developing and Using Multimedia Tools in Education* Microsoft, Redmond WA

Brockett A, Clark I and Taylor O (1992) Development of a Human-Computer Interface *ReCALL* 7 (11/92) 17-27

Cates W, Fontana L and White C (1993) Designing an interactive multimedia instructional environment: The Civil War Interactive *ALT-J* 1 (2) 5-16

Chaski C and Mehlenbacher B (1993) LINGO: Software for Representing, Teaching and Gathering Information about Metalinguistic Knowledge-Construction *Computers and Texts* 6 (11/93) 10-12

Clarke A (1989) *The Principles of Screen Design for Computer Based Learning Materials* The Training Agency, Sheffield

Götz K and Häfner P (1991) *Computerunterstütztes Lernen in der Aus- und Weiterbildung* DSV, Weinheim

Harrison N (1990) *How to Design Effective Computer Based Training: A Modular Course*

Miller G (1956) The magical number seven, plus or minus two: some limits on our capacity for processing information *The Psychological Review* 63 81-97

Nara H (1992) Visual Salience as a Search Category in a Kanji Dictionary in Interactive Japanese: Understanding written Japanese *System* 20 (1) 75-91

Yazdani M (ed) (1993) *Multilingual Multimedia: Bridging the Language Barrier with Intelligent Systems* Intellect, Oxford

15. Utilisation of Computers for Teachers' and Students' Use at School

Takashi Ikuta *Niigata University,* **Mitsuhiro Inoue** *Tokyo Gkugei University* **and Yasusi Gotoh** *Warino Elementary School, Japan*

Summary

This section outlines the distribution and utilisation of computers for teachers' and students' use at lower and upper secondary level. In 1985, the Japanese Ministry of Education, Science and Culture established the Task Force on Elementary and Secondary Education an Information-oriented Society. In 1989 the Ministry of Education, Science and Culture announced the new Course of Study, in which objectives and standard content of each national guidelines for the curriculum for each of the four school levels: kindergarten, elementary school, lower secondary school and upper secondary school.

The purposes of introducing computers in school are as follows:

1. Elementary schools
   (a) To improve and enrich the method of teaching
   (b) To familiarize pupils with computers through their utilisation as learning tools

2. Lower Secondary schools
      To make greater use of computers functions such as simulation and information retrieval so as to help students acquire computer awareness and literacy

3. Upper Secondary schools
      In computer education special attention should be given to the progress of information-oriented society and the effect of computers on the individual and society.
      To devise an effective way of using computers according to the condition of students as well as the type and characteristics of subject matter, for specific purposes such a motivation, acquisition of educational content and application of newly acquired knowledge.

In this section, an example of computer utilisation in elementary school on the study of *tuishu*, a traditional Japanese craft, will be presented on video.

BACKGROUND OF COMPUTER INTRODUCTION IN SCHOOLS

In 1985, the Japanese Ministry of Education, Science and Culture, recognizing the need to modernize the nation's public school curriculum, established the Task Force on Elementary and Secondary Education in an Information-oriented Society. In 1989, the Ministry announced the new Course of Study, containing the specific objectives and standard content of each subject or each area of school activity, and national curriculum guidelines for each of the four school levels: kindergarten, elementary school (grades 1-6), lower secondary school (grades 1-3), and upper secondary school (grades 1-3).

The purposes of introducing computers in school are as follows:

1. Elementary schools
   (a) To improve and enrich the teaching
   (b) To familiarize students with computers through their utilization as learning tools

2. Lower Secondary schools
   To make greater use of computer functions including simulation and information retrieval so as to help students acquire computer awareness and literacy
3. Upper Secondary school

To devise effective ways of using computers according to the condition of students as well as the type and characteristics of subject matter.

In computer education special consideration should be given to the progress of an information-oriented society and the effect of computers on society and on individual lives. Attention must be paid to devising effective ways of using computers in accordance with the students' capabilities and motivation, the type and characteristics of the educational content to be acquired, and appropriate application of newly-acquired knowledge.

The 1993 Course of Study emphasizes the importance of informatics for all students at every school level in content and method. In the lower secondary school. "Basic Informatics" has been added to the elective core of requirements in Industrial Arts/Home Economics, and focuses on developing students' computer literacy. This one-year course of 35 periods for lower secondary third grade students will be taught by computer trained teachers. The four major content areas are (1) Computers and society, (2) Familiarity with computer hardware and systems, (3) Use of computer software, and (4) Application of computer systems.

COMPUTER DIFFUSION IN SCHOOLS

In 1983, the Ministry of Education, Science and Culture initiated an annual survey of computer diffusion and use in public schools; these results are informative to the overview of computers in Japanese education.

The 1983 diffusion of computers in elementary, lower secondary, and upper secondary schools is 0.6%, 3.1% and 56.4% respectively, as compared to the rate of 57.7%, 94.7%, and 99.7%, recorded in the latest 1993 survey (Table 15.1). The greatest rate of increase came after the 1989 announcement of the new Course of Study which emphasized the introduction of in formatics education in all schools from elementary to upper secondary.

The frequency of computer use in schools was surveyed in 1991 by the Ministry, as shown in Table 15.2. This reveals the small number of schools taking advantage of the computers on hand. The conditions which contribute to the infrequency of use are, first, the small number of computers installed, and second, the relatively few teachers with training for educational operation of computers.

The results of this survey point up the critical issue of training teachers so they are enabled to prepare students to function optimally in a new information-oriented society. Unless such training is properly planned and implemented, the children born into an information-rich society will be nurtured by teachers illiterate of the new information technology.

Table 15.1: Computer Diffusion Rates

Type of School	Percentage(%)				Average number per school with computers			
	1990	1991	1992	1993	1990	1991	1992	1993
Elementary	30.9	41.0	50.2	57.7	3.1	3.3	3.8	4.3
Low sec.	58.9	74.7	86.1	94.7	5.5	8.3	12.8	19.2
Upper Sec.	97.8	98.9	99.4	99.7	29.8	34.3	40.6	46.5
Average	62.5	75.5	79.5	84.0	12.8	15.3	19.1	23.3

Table 15.2:Frequency of Computer Use (%)

Type of School	Several times/yr.	One or two times/mth	About one time/wk.	More than 2 times/wk.	NO ans
Elementary	25.3	22.9	19.6	29.1	3.1
Low sec.	18.9	19.9	20.1	38.7	2.4
Upper Sec.	6.8	8.0	14.7	68.5	1.9

MULTIMEDIA USE IN SCHOOL; AN EXAMPLE OF THE DEVELOPMENT OF MULTIMEDIA SOFTWARE AND ITS USE IN THE SOCIAL STUDY CLASS

The "Report for the Promoting Audiovisual Education Utilizing New Education Media," issued by the Ministry in 1992, expressed government policy for promotion, development, and distribution of systems and software related to multimedia and high definition television sets, in schools, as well as in the wider society.

As a result of the intensive research and development of several technologies in recent years, these different kinds of media have become integrated, or unified, into one media, now widely referred to as "multimedia." This paper describes the use of instructional multimedia in a Japanese elementary school social studies class.

PURPOSE

The two purposes of this study are

1. To develop the hypermaterials which help students to learn Tuishu, a Japanese traditional craft.
2. To identify how the hypermaterial affects student interest and attitude in learning.

MATERIALS

Three kinds of materials were employed to construct the hypermaterial:

1. printed school materials prepared by the school district for the study of Tuishu, many of which were collected from the *Tuishu Kumiai* Association,
2. movie films and videotapes about Tuishu obtained from the Murakami City audio-visual centre,
3. still photographs and paintings.

A scanner, Adobe Premier, and a word processor were used to input the materials int he process of developing and designing the color interactive software program. The hypermedia program was composed of seven information stacks; tools for production, materials, production process, statistical data, interview with the craftsman, the history of Tuishu, and the introduction of products. The interlinking of the information stacks enabled students, by inputting a key word, to bring up the desired information, and read, listen and view the material.

Subjects

The thirty-four students of a public school fifth-grade (age 11) class with no previous educational computer use history were selected to participate in the classroom introduction of the hypermedia.

Procedure

Computer introduction

Although many of the students were likely familiar, through their playing with home television computer games, with electronic media, none had used computers for an instructional purpose. Eight Macintosh II VX computers from Niigata University were brought into the classroom. The classroom teacher, a long-time computer user and programmer, began the students familiarization with the computers and mice by 45 minutes of play time with two programs, Uno and Kid Pix. One is a card game and the other a drawing programme. The keyboard was not introduced since the hypermedia did not require it.

Instruction

Immediately following, the lesson was introduced by the teacher showing two similar-appearing two bowls to the children. Guesses were solicited from the children about the probably price of each. Since one of the bowls was an inexpensive plastic copy of the authentic hand-carved wooden bowl, the children's interest was aroused wondering why one of the bowls was 40 times more expensive than the other.

The students' suggestions of possible reasons for the cost differential formed their learning plan, and were the basis of their investigation to discover why Murakami *Tuishu* is so expensive. They identified the following 10 points:

1. Time taken to make one bowl
2. Number of *Tuishu* craftsmen
3. It is made from natural wood?
4. Cost of lacquer.
5. Are all steps done by hand?
6. How many production steps are there?
7. Is lacquer produced in Japan or imported?
8. History of Murakami Tuishu
9. The most difficult process of production.
10. How many coats of lacquer are applied?

At this stage of the lesson, small groups of five students each were formed to facilitate the cooperative learning process. Each group operated one computer containing the hypermedia program, "Study of Murikami *Tuisi*." Students took turns locating different points and identifying the answers. The entire class session was video-recorded for subsequent protocol development, and analysis. After participating in these learning activities, the students created a newspaper displaying much of their new knowledge about the traditional craft, *Tuishu*.

Results

An image map instrument and a Semantic Differential scale were administered before and after the students' negotiation of the hypermedia.   Figure 15.1 is one student's image map of Murakami *Tuishu* made before using the hypermedia and Figure 15.2 is the same student's image map after. The pre-hypermedia image describes the traditional craft in much greater detail. The details included by the student range from concrete facts to abstract concepts. The SD scale was developed to identify the items on a 5 point scale. This scale was also administered before and after. The aggregate average score for each item was calculated and then plotted, as shown in Figure 15.3. Every post-SD score was significantly higher than the pre-SD score.

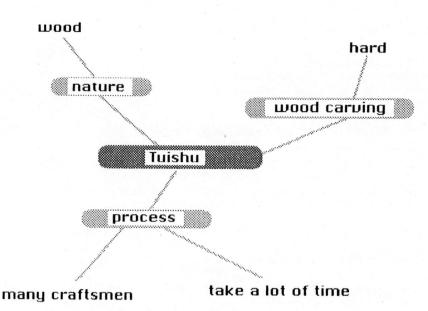

Figure 15.1 Pre-hypermedia Image map of child A

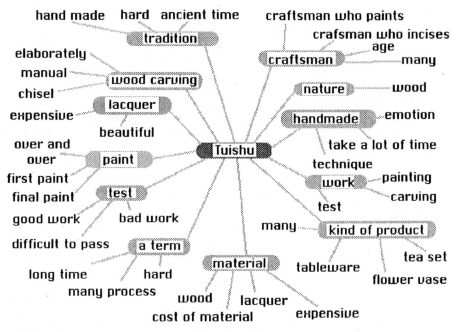

Figure 15.2 Post-hypermedia Image map of child A

CONCLUSION

The image maps displayed in Figures 34.1 and 34.2 shows the student grasped the central points of the lesson in his understanding that natural materials were used traditionally for a long time, a product must be tested heartily, as well as his appreciation of the craft and the art that has now earned his affection.

Using hypermedia, the students felt their social studies class to be more enjoyable and interesting, and indicated greater willingness to do the necessary work. They described the class as easier to understand, and as being better liked. It has not been demonstrated that students lose interest and attitude improvement over those for subjects presented by traditional methods.

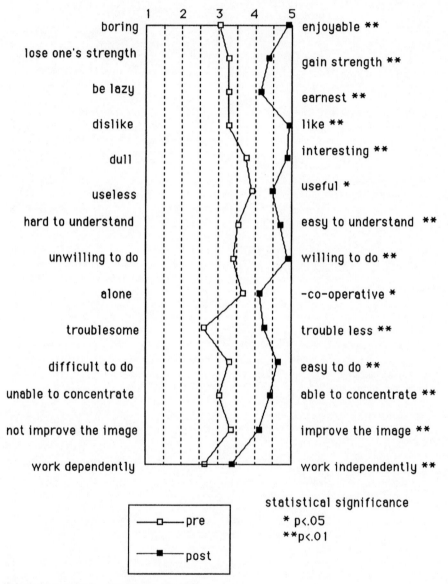

Figure 15.3   Profile of Social Study Class

16.   A New Educational Tool: Modules and Parameters

Grace Stewart, *Glasgow Caledonian University*

Summary
This educational package is intended to assist students' understanding of the concepts associated with the implementation of modules, and in particular with the use of parameters. It is designed to involve the student interactively, and so differs from traditional text-based CAL delivery material. The product was developed in Asymetrix's TOOLBOOK. Students can easily become confused by the volume and complexity of information to be assimilated when learning about modules and parameters - formal/actual parameters, parameter passing mechanisms, local/global variables, procedures vs functions, etc. The package supports the lecturer's teaching by using a mixture of visual demonstrations, textual explanation, and interaction from the student. Animation is used where appropriate, eg to show the flow of logic through code as modules are accessed, the use of memory in storing values for parameters and variables, the effect upon parameters of different supporting mechanisms. On quitting the product, the user is required to 'log out' so that student access to the material can be monitored, and to provide the user with the opportunity to feedback suggestions/problems to the support programmer.

INTRODUCTION

The potential benefit of Computer Based Education (CBE) has been recognised for a number of years, and yet the amount of successful software available to support effective learning at University and Higher Education level is still very limited. Until relatively recently, the time required to produce a comprehensive CBE package often ran into man-years, and this constraint meant that the development of CBE material was based largely on textual media and formatted as tutorial text together with question and answer routines. As a consequence, CBE was in danger of becoming nothing more than electronic page turning, with no real advantage over conventional book-based learning other than a facility to monitor students' progress remotely.

The recent advent of sophisticated authoring software such as HyperCard™ and Toolbook™ has dramatically reduced software development time, and the author is of the opinion that there has been a consequent resurgence of interest and activity in the production of 'bespoke' CBE in the higher education sector.

The support for visualisation available in Toolbook is of particular interest. Observations made some eight years ago, on the relevance and importance of the human visual system in enabling and improving information processing, still hold true (Bocker et al 1986). Moreover it is still the case that graphical representations of complex structures are under-utilised in training software, although the past two or three years have seen a flowering of simulation software produced as CBE tools, and in general CBE has begun to encompass images and animation.

The advent of object-oriented programming, multimedia software and affordable hardware on which to run it has produced a considerable expansion of interest and output in the CBE area, and this expansion seems likely to continue over the next few years.

APPLICABILITY OF CBE IN COMPUTER STUDIES

It seems ironic that while CBE is used in teaching a wide variety of topics such as mathematics, engineering, economics, history, it is relatively rare to find CBE software which has been developed specifically to support the teaching of computing itself. Some products are starting to emerge, and these can be categorised into three areas.

- simulation of hardware equipment
- support for software development skills
- visualisation of the operation of hardware and software

Simulation is commonly used to illustrate topics which in 'real life' would be difficult or dangerous to experience in a learning capacity due to some constraint(s) inherent to the nature of the subject being studied. Perhaps the best known use of simulation is that of the flight-simulator on which aircraft pilots are trained. Recent work for British Rail has achieved mixed success from projects on a much more modest scale (Novak 1993). In computing simulation can enhance and enable understanding of hardware concepts, which would otherwise require students to dismantle equipment (Douglas 1993) or would render laboratories of computers unusable while students were given training, for example on systems configuration.

Support for software development skills is an area in which a lot of work is ongoing. A number of authors, often actively involved in the day-to-day delivery of programming courses, are beginning to produce and use CBE software which will enhance traditional approaches to the teaching of software development. One drawback in this area is the tendency of such projects to explode in size as their ambitious nature tends to be to try to replace the traditional mix of lecture/tutorial/practical/assessment with one all-encompassing CBE package (Hauntaniemi et al 1993). The resultant package is often so cumbersome that it becomes an electronic language manual rather than an innovative advance in learning techniques. Moreover the very size of the project may be such that a number of authors will work on it, with a number of personal styles (Siviter 1993). This would seem to run counter to the fundamentals of the design of such software, which amongst other key points stress consistency in the user interface and presentation style (Henno 1993). The multi-authoring approach can of course be very productive and can lead to an interchange of ideas which enriches the final product, but extra care must be taken over the design of the product, perhaps with a standardised protocol being imposed on all authors (Prior and Beresford 1993).

Visualisation of the operation of hardware and software is an area which, in the author's opinion, offers a significant improvement in a student's ability to learn certain key concepts which repeatedly seem to cause difficulty. These concepts often involve dynamic interaction, and the traditional teaching approaches provide only a modestly successful support environment for students encountering them for the first time. One difficulty would appear to lie in the inability of static teaching media to demonstrate certain key areas which are best dealt with through dynamic means such as animation.

The rapid prototyping afforded by Toolbook, together principally with its support for animation and user interaction, made it an ideal choice of product with which to develop CBE software in support of these complex but fundamental concepts.

THE MODULES AND PARAMETERS PRODUCT

The approach of using program visualisation and computer based animation in order to illustrate the inner workings of dynamic structures and concepts was first utilised within the Department of Computer Studies in 1986. Within the severe limitations imposed by the equipment of the era, several successful products were developed and used within the department to enhance the students' learning experience. These early products were marketed to the FE and HE sector, and presented at several conferences where they received a modest degree of acclaim.

The project which is the basis of this paper was intended to enable the development of an innovative teaching/learning product, which utilised program visualisation and animation techniques to enhance students' knowledge and understanding of the concepts which underlie the use of modules in software engineering. The product was also intended to assist students' understanding in all of the concepts associated with the implementation of modules, and in particular with the use of parameters. It is designed to involve the student interactively, and so differs from traditional text-based CAL delivery material.

The formal objectives were to

- develop a prototype product to enhance the lecturer's delivery of software engineering concepts associated with modularity
- create a student-centred, interactive interface
- develop the product in such a way that it could be used as a distance-learning aid, with pace and access controlled by the student

Work began on the project in November 1992, with some 350 hours of programming support funded. The first version of the package was evaluated towards the end of June 1993 by staff and volunteer students in the Department of Computer Studies at Glasgow Caledonian University. The feedback provided from this evaluation was used to improve the product and enhance its operability, and version two was used in December 1993 as the main vehicle for the teaching of modules and parameters in the Programming Principles module of a postgraduate conversion course in Computer Studies. The students' comments, as captured by the logout process built into the product, were evaluated and further enhancements took place. The version discussed in this paper was finalised in March 1994.

The perceived benefits of using the Modules and Parameters package are

- an improvement in comprehension of the concepts addressed by the package, through the use of visualisation
- students are enabled to control their own learning pace
- constant accessibility of material provides support for student learning at times when staff would not normally be available

CONTENT

The package has a hierarchical menu structure, with an options map which illustrates the structure graphically and permits free navigation around the options without accessing the menus.

The user can choose to work through a short introductory session which explains the use of buttons, hotwords etc throughout the package. No written user manual is necessary.
The main areas supported by the product are

- concepts of modularity
- concepts of parameters
- mechanisms of parameter passing
- functions vs procedures

Throughout, simple illustrations are used to symbolise key concepts and as the student progresses through the package these are gradually replaced with examples of code and simulations which show the execution of the code.

The main topic areas were selected for development because over the years, successive cohorts of students had had problems with these areas. Students can easily become confused by the volume and complexity of information to be assimilated when learning about modules and parameters - formal/actual parameters, parameter passing mechanisms, local/global variables, procedures vs functions, etc. The package uses a mixture of visual demonstrations, textual explanation, and interaction from the student. Animation is used where appropriate, eg to show the flow of logic through code as modules are accessed, the use of memory in storing values for parameters and variables, the effect upon parameters of different supporting mechanisms.

Although the sections of code provided to support the package's simulations were written in Pascal, the product is **not** attempting to teach the implementation of modules in Pascal. Rather it has a general information base, enhancing a student's understanding of the underlying principles of the use of modules in **any** language.

Figures 16.1 to 16.3 show snapshots from key areas in the package

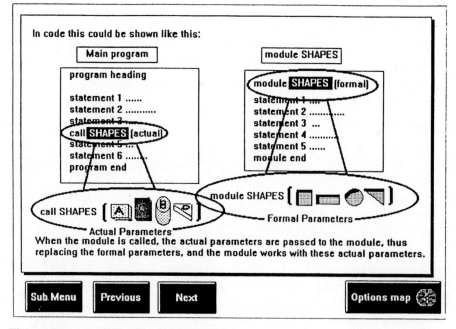

Figure 16.1: A page from the Parameters Concepts section

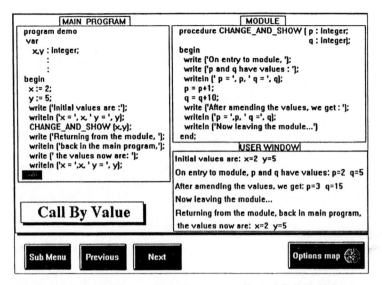

Figure 16.2: The end state of a demonstration on the effect of Call by Value

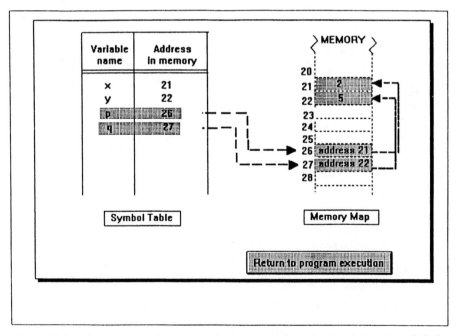

Figure 16.3: A snapshot of memory during execution of a module using Call by Reference

When the user exits from the product, a comments page is presented and the personal details identifying the user are solicited, together with any comments, suggestions, criticisms etc. These remarks provide useful feedback to the lecturers using the product as course material, and also influence the product's future development.

One interesting comment which was made by some students was that the illustrations seemed too trivial. One student felt that they were insultingly childish. This reaction was totally unexpected and perhaps suggests a hitherto unsuspected (by the author) pitfall of CBE - if it succeeds in its aims by simplifying the problem, it runs the risk of creating the impression that the topic was not difficult in the first place. On the other hand, it may simply highlight that the author's choice of illustrations was inappropriate. Perhaps a future development might be to carry out an in-depth study of people's differing learning styles and how to accommodate these styles in one product.

CONCLUSION

The Modules and Parameters product has been in use during session 1993/94 as a learning and teaching aid. Student uptake has varied, with some students logging several sessions of two or three hours' duration, while others logged minimal sessions of ten or twenty minutes. Students who used the product seriously, in sustained sessions, performed at least as well in written examinations as students taught traditionally the previous session. The lecturer felt that the answers written demonstrated either a clear understanding **or** no understanding and no 'memory dump' either. Further study of the students' utilisation patterns should prove interesting and worthwhile, and will influence the development of new products in the area of visualisation of programming concepts.

ACKNOWLEDGEMENTS

The author gratefully acknowledges the work of the support staff who implemented the project in Toolbook : Marianne Farrell and Fiona Neilson.

References

Bocker H, Fischer G, Neiper H (1986) The enhancement of understanding through visual representation In : Proceedings of CHI'86 : *Human Factors in Computing Systems,* Boston, April 1986

Douglas I (1993) Training on complex equipment using graphical simulations in a hypermedia environment In : *Proceedings of Hypermedia in Vaasa '93, Finland,* May 1993, pp 71-76

Hautaniemi J, Ramo E, Malmi L (1993) *CALPAS :* A CAL environment for Pascal programming In : *Proceedings of Hypermedia in Vaasa '93, Finland,* May 1993, pp 116-120

Henno J (1993) Some guidelines for PC hypertext authorings In : *Proceedings of Hypermedia in Vaasa '93*

Novak S (1993) Multimedia in simulation and training In : *Proceedings of Multimedia Finland,* May 1993, pp 121-126
Systems and Applications Leeds, December 1993

Prior M and Beresford R (1993) Methodology for representation of Toolbook screen designs In : *Proceedings of First UK Toolbook Users' Conference,* Glasgow, September 1993. pp 24-31

Siviter P (1993) The CAL for computing project In : *Proceedings of Hypermedia in Vaasa '93,* Finland, May 1993, pp 261-265

17. Computer-Assisted Learning Architecture of Computers

James Williamson, *Bolton Institute*

Summary
The three programs written to support teaching address these specific topics:

The first has options to convert data to binary and two positive integers, or carry out subtraction based on the conversion to two's complement. Each uses small numbers, selection at random, and checks the accuracy and the amount of time that it takes the student to answer.

The second program allows the user to design logic circuits and test them. The testing uses colour to indicate the state of each wire; the input can consist of a bit-stream and the user can specify a delay chip in the circuitry.

The third program was initially written to support the topic of micro-code implementation. This allows students to define and to test their own micro-code. This has been used with the first year students to allow them to key in pre-defined programs in machine-code and to run them. The execution includes animation of movements of data along buses, both within the CPU and between CPU and memory.

This paper will give theoretical background to the development of the systems, comment on student experience, describe the future potential of the systems and draw some conclusions.

BACKGROUND

Bolton Institute have recently introduced a new HND course in Business Information Technology. There has been a course in HND Computer Studies for ten years. To enable students to change from one course to the other, it was decided to offer a common first semester. One subject where problems were foreseen was in Computer Architecture. Computer Studies students had commented in surveys that they found the subject matter difficult to understand and rather 'dry'.

The subject matter of the module includes data representation and manipulation, logic circuitry with truth tables and the relationship between computer hardware and machine code language. It was therefore decided to attempt to alleviate the 'dryness' by writing specific software to help maintain the students' interest and allow them to develop a better understanding of the subject.

SOFTWARE DEVELOPMENT

Three programs were written in the Clipper language. The reasons for using this language included:-

a) Programmer familiarity- the favourite language is the best
b) Generate machine code programs for DOS- students can be given copies which will work on any DOS machine
c) Facilities of language for both high speed development and complete control

The first program requires students to carry out conversions from decimal to binary, adding binary and subtracting binary using two's complement, derived from one's complement. The conversion is based on successive subtraction of the decreasing powers of two; if the student enters a one for a specific bit the computer calculates the subtraction and displays the result alongside the next power of two for which the user will enter a one or a zero. The student is not expected to carry out the subtraction, as we are not attempting to develop or test numeracy skills. The technique of successive subtraction emphasises the concept of bit value, which would not be as visible using repeated division by two. With addition and subtraction, the student must first convert a decimal number, less than sixtyfour, and then specifies the sum and carry bits starting from the least significant bit. Their entry for the carry bit is automatically re-displayed above the next for the next position. Subtraction involves the student in converting the second value to binary, converting to one's complement, adding one for two's complement, converting the first number and then adding the results.

The users can select which of the tests they want to do from a menu; the program will repeat the chosen exercise five times and display their mark and the time it took the student when they return to the menu.

The second program allowed the student to enter a design of a logic circuit and test it. Rather than depend on any specific graphics standard, the software uses rectangular boxes for all gates and uses a symbol to indicate the logic function. The program was designed about simplicity of use and did not include concepts like optimisation. The results of testing were displayed by using the colours red (one/true) and blue (zero/false). One specific circuit was shown to the students (using the blackboard); this circuit used gates to implement a two-bit decoder which caused the output from one of four different function gates to be selected. This indicates the concept of program (function selection) and data (function inputs) interacting with all inputs being binary data.

The third program is a (pseudo) machine code emulator. This allows a student to load and execute a machine code program for a pre-defined machine code-language. The program animates a variable length instruction being loaded from RAM into the CPU and shows the program counter register (PC) being incremented. The computer then executes the instruction while displaying a comment which explains what the instruction does. The student can then change the program in RAM and watch their program execute. There is also an assembler so the student can enter the assembler language, convert it to machine code and run it. The selection of the computer instruction is done via a pick list; the student only enters text for labels and values.

Another facility provided by the program is to explore the relationship between the machine code and its micro-code implementation. This is achieved by animating a diagrammatic representation of the registers and buses of the CPU and the interface between the CPU and RAM. Each step of the microcode activates one or two registers to output their contents onto their output bus; one more register can be opened to receive data on its input bus. The ALU can take data from two different buses. The student can then see that when the machine code instruction is to load the accumulator from the RAM contents of an address, the following sequence is needed:-

a) move the address from part of the IR to the MAR
b) move the contents of the MAR via the address bus to RAM
c) move the contents of the address to the MRB via the data bus
d) move the contents of the MRB to the ACC

IR Instruction Register
MAR Memory Address Register
MRB Memory Read Buffer
ACC Accumulator

In comparison, a JMP instruction requires only one microcode step

a) Move the address from part of the IR to the PC

Another facility exists for the student to define their own microcode and implement a machine code instruction. The microcode can itself call subroutines of microcode, and another screen display shows this happening as the machine code is executed. Thus a student can define a machine code language and test it by writing a program in machine code which uses it. Once a set of machine code instructions has been defined then the user may create their own assembler mnemonics and work in assembler language.

The pseudo-CPU has several registers available for any use and an ALU which has arange of instructions including shift and rotate. These actions put values flags for conditions such as Acc=Zero, Carry Set etc. These can then be recognised from within microcode to implement machine code instructions such as JZ (Jump if Acc equals Zero).

STUDENT EXPERIENCE OF SOFTWARE

The software was welcomed by most students, though the lack of help screens and documentation was a problem for some less experienced students. The first program caused the able students to compete for the fastest time for a perfect score, whilst the less able students concentrated on achieving a perfect score.

The use of the second program was not as successful due to some errors in the software, and the manner in which it ran. The software automatically allocated reference letters to the Input Nodes. This meant that if a student was attempting to implement a design for   A and (B or C) then the first input node would automatically be A. If the student created the B or C first, then
the input identification would be wrong. The software was also capable of accepting variable length sequences which was not needed.

The third program was too complex for the BIT students to fully understand but the Computing students spent quite a long time using the options available. The system has also been used by students of Electronic Engineering and the reports have been favourable - from staff and students. The problem that the BIT students had was that the animations were not capable of individual selection. This meant that the fetch-cycle animation included the CPU/register animation and the micro-code debug screens. The software has since been modified to control the duration/speed of the screens. A zero value suppresses the display.

ANALYSIS OF RESULTS

There was no attempt at formal evaluation of the student experience but the students always fill in an end-of-unit questionnaire. From these it seems that the complaints about 'dryness' have disappeared, but complaints now suggest that we need to ensure the software is more closely integrated into the module, and more closely link the subject areas to each other. Other improvements were suggested to make the software more user-friendly, and capable of being used without tuition.

THEORETICAL PERSPECTIVES

Hammond et al (1992) analysed reasons why IT is not used widely as a teaching tool in Higher Education. They write that

> "those who use such phrases as the 'not-invented-here syndrome' are under-estimating and under-valuing the conventional process by which lecturers prepare and update their materials. They refer to textbooks, monographs, reseach literature and their own research and experience for sources of factual material, ideas, representations and organisation during the preparation of lecture notes, seminars and tutorials. What emerges is that the lecturer's interpretation of the topic is to be taught."

The nature of elementary computer architecture is not in the same domain as the subject areas being described above. The content is new to most of the students, but the use of binary may easily have been taught some years previously. The use of microcode is new to nearly all the students, and provides a means of allowing quicker students to develop skills to a higher level than is needed for the course. This development can take place without the lecturer having to provide anything extra; it takes place by self-motivated students exploring the potential of the software.

The ability of students to understand computer operations as deterministic requires an understanding of the scientific view of phenomena. R Millar (1991) wrote a paper entitled 'Why Science Is Hard To Learn' which included the following

> "For most people, the ability to predict the consequences of everyday events and hence achieve some feeling of security and order in events is much more important than the possession of a theoretical framework for these predictions and regularities."

Students who have problems with computer programming often blame the machine for not working 'correctly' - ie. not the way they think the machine should work. Many students fail to connect the principles of internal architecture as taught, with the language with which they program. The use of software in the simulator is designed to allow students to see that the inner workings of a CPU are in fact simple, and that complexity is derived from the structure of the software:- ie it is something the student can control. By allowing the student to 'see' the code execute, they develop an awareness of the basis of its predictability. Faults in programs can then blamed on specific components of the solution, and not on gremlins.

JCAL recently re-printed an article by R. Hooper (1990) entitled "Computers and Sacred Cows". He states

> "The real issue is not one-way versus two-way, but the need for a clever balance in the design of an educational system between both kinds of communication. The point is that one-way methods tend to be cheaper than two-way, just as mass instruction is cheaper than individual instruction."

Everybody in education knows that money is in short supply and we must maximise the use of whatever we have. In Higher Education it is the norm to have one computer per student for the duration of practical lessons. At Bolton Institute we have such a level, but some of the machines are too slow to run Windows effectively. There is always a shortage of the highest specification machine and a tendency for lecturers to want to use the 'latest' software. By writing the software for DOS machines, the students have a very good chance of being able to use the software when they want. The article compared the use of 16mm film with a room of graphic work-stations. The animations could certainly have been done on film, but the developer would have still had to use software to generate the animations. This is partly because the screen displays were not designed, but evolved on a trial-and-error basis along with the software functionality.

The understanding of student learning and its relationship to various activities is very complex. Anderson (1985) wrote

> "The learning process itself is automatic and unintentional but the quality of what is being learned depends on the quality of the generative process that yields the information for the automatic learning mechanisms to operate upon."

The fact that the students no longer complain about the 'dryness' of the subject matter suggests that the quality of the generative process has been improved. The software has certainly motivated some students to spend more time working in this area than they would have done otherwise. It is always difficult to know how much students are benefiting from their hands on experience, but is is easy to observe their preference for machine utilisation over attending lectures.

In an article entitled 'Problems With Classroom Teaching' Thomas (1992) pointed out the following

> "Moreover, keeping pupils in task requires managerial skills rather than pedagogical ones and only works to the extent that the pupils will be spending more time doing something, albeit at a low cognitive level"

In Higher Education students are expected to be self-disciplined and have a mature approach to self-development. However the idea of having students spending minutes on end doing binary arithmetic in a classroom environment is not advisable. The difference in speed performance, the early finishers compare results, the problem of the lecturer seeing individual performance make this impractical. In the computer environment these problems were overcome.

An analytical framework to consider the nature of computer software to support learning was suggested (McDonald et al,1977). They suggested four paradigms as follows:-the instructional, the conjectural, the revelatory and the emancipatory. The three programs can be seen as functioning in different paradigms. Although the binary program did not do the basic instruction it developed student ability in an instructional manner. The other two programs use both the conjectural and the revelatory paradigms, according to whether the student is animating existing work or developing their own work. It is the ability for the software to cross the boundaries that should hopefully lead to the same software being used by students from BIT as well as those from Electronic Engineering.

Finally, from Pappert (1980)

> "In many schools today the phrase 'computer-aided instruction' means making the computer teach the child. One might say the computer is being used to program the child. In my vision, the child programs the computer and, in doing so, both acquires a sense of mastery over a piece of the most modern and powerful technology and establishes an intimate contact with some of the deepest ideas from science, from mathematics, and from the art of intellectual model building."

If the student can develop an internal model which relates data representation, data manipulation, microcode and machine code then they can pass the unit. The software appears to be helping but the need for further development and integration into the taught syllabus is recognised.

References

Anderson J R (1985) *Cognitive Psychology And Its Implications,* Freeman

Hammond et al (1992) Blocks to the Effective Use of Information Technology in Higher Education, *Computers and Education,* Jan/Apr

Hooper R (1990) Computers and Sacred Cows, *Journal of Computer Assisted Learning,* March

MacDonald, Atkin, Jenkins and Kemmis (1977) *National Development Program in Computer Assisted Learning,* Council for Educational Technology

Millar R (1991) Why Is Science Hard To Learn, *Journal Computer Assisted Learning,* June

Pappert S (1980) *Mindstorms,* Harvester Press Ltd

Thomas A J (1992) Individualised Teaching, *Oxford Review Of Education,* Vol 18

18. Utopia: A Software & Video Package to Teach Basic Windows and Unix Skills

Trevor Fixter, *University College, Stockton*

Summary
The difficulties of teaching Windows and Unix basic skills to non-computer literate students is discussed in the context of the "platform specific" problems which are encountered in the transition from the use of PC-based Windows software to that which is installed on the average workstation operating under some form of Unix. It is suggested that the confusion lies in two areas. One is the multi-tasking capability of Unix workstations, the second is the students need to understand more fully than is the case with PCs, both the use of the operating system command language (Unix) and the way in which files are structured within the Unix environment.

A CAL tutorial will be demonstrated - currently being developed by University College - which attempts to address these problems in the form of interactive software, the use of integrated video sequences and the incorporation of an "on-line" assessment mechanism.

INTRODUCTION

There are very few academic courses today, which do not expose the student to Computers and hence, some form of computer software.

Students taking non-computer related courses often experience difficulty in attaining the basic computer skills which, once gained, will enable progress to be made in the use of software which is of specific relevance to their subject areas..

It is true that ever increasing numbers of the incoming students population have had some contact with PCs and often also, related Windows software. However, the transition from a PC based Windows system to that of a Unix Workstation seems nevertheless fraught with difficulty.

The main sources of confusion for the student are arguably threefold:

- First: the multitasking capability of UNIX which allows for the creation of multiple Windows within which separate processes can run. - is very different from the "single window/one process" PC based system.
- Second: is the ability - and sometimes the need - to access and make use of the Unix command language from "within" the Window environment.
- Third: even the most basic of Unix commands, often require some familiarity with the way information is stored and therefore accessed or added to. Thus the student should have a basic grasp of how data is structured and how it relates to the use of many Unix commands.

UTOPIA

The development of a CAL/CBT system to address these issues effectively, has required the construction of three conceptually though not practically, distinct modules.

The first, is an interactive software tutorial system. The second is that of an on-line assessment mechanism to monitor student/software performance. The third, is integrated video sequences with a primary role of explaining in every day though conceptually relevant terms, the nature and structure of the Unix file system.

Tutorial Content

Windows
The Windows emulation's cover many of the basic operations which are common to many XWindow systems but which are specifically relevant to users of Sun's OpenWindows..
These are as follows:

- The properties of the Mouse.
  Moving
  Pointing
  Select Button
  Adjust Button
  Menu Button
- The use of the Workspace Menu.
  Selecting an Item.
  Sub-Menus
- The Properties of Windows.
  Re-sizing
  Iconosing
  Quitting
- The basic usage of a File Manager.
  Opening a File
  Drag & Drop Operations to Text Editor

Unix
The Unix section provides essential background information as well as emulation's which cover basic commands common to all versions of Unix
These are as follows:

- Unix Typing Conventions
- Changing a Password
- File Copying
- Viewing the Contents of a File
- Creating a Directory
- Moving to Another Directory
- Printing the Date on the screen
- Determine Your Location within the File System
- Outputting Files to the Printer.

Software: Method of Construction
The creation of this has been in two parts. The use of an Authoring tool has provided the quickest way of constructing the basic instructional element of our package. This has been linked to emulation's of both Windows and Unix operations, which must run at the appropriate stage in the tutorial "document".
The Authoring tool chosen was Mediawrite, from Paradise Software. This was considered the most suitable in terms of cost and flexibility, from a limited number of packages available for this platform. Mediawrite consists of three separate applications; a multi-media document-composition system with a limited hypertext facility; HyperCmedia, a

programmatic interface to Mediawrite's multi-media capabilities which are "transportable" to "C" programs and Uniflix, a Video manager. We have utilised the first two of these capabilities whilst the use of "on-line" video though desirable, is impractical given the playing time restrictions imposed by the limitations of memory vis-à-vis data compression techniques. The emulation's have been constructed through the use of "C"(for the Unix Emulation's), Xview - a tool kit of C Libraries which accesses Xlib for the creation of a suitable Xwindow environment and Window emulation's - and some Xlib.

THE CREATION OF A TUTORIAL ENVIRONMENT

A major problem with any Windows environment in the context of the construction of software which actually "uses Windows to teach Windows", is the nature of that environment. Windows can normally be created or destroyed, menus can be invoked in various ways which provide options such as "Quit", "Close" or "Back". Uninstructed use of any of these, would render what is supposed to be a well structured, organised introduction to basic Windows concepts, into a session of unacceptable confusion. It would of course also be difficult to incorporate any sort of monitoring/marking facility into software of such an "anarchist" nature.

An obvious answer to this problem would be to code from scratch, a custom made Window Manager. However, given the limitations on time, funding and programming expertise, this was not a realistic option. This problem has been partially solved by creating a Root Window "overlay" to the normal Root Window.as created by OLWM(Open Look Window Manager). Within this environment a compromise solution was reached in terms of what Windows functionality has been retained or omitted within any given exercise, without "misrepresenting" the nature of Windows totally and thus impairing the software's usefulness as a teaching aid.

In this respect, it was necessary where possible to tailor the tutorial environment to suit whatever aspect of Windows or Unix was being taught at that stage. This means for example, that Window utilities such as Text Editors or File Managers - and their accompanying menus, are configured to perform those actions which are relevant for a particular exercise. Unix exercises are similarly carried out in a Command Tool(or Terminal Emulator) without the various "escape" menu options - such as "Quit", "Close" and "Back" - normally associated with that structure. Whilst all options are still available as menu choices, they have been disabled with attempts to access them resulting in an appropriate "pop-up" message being generated.(Figure 18.1).

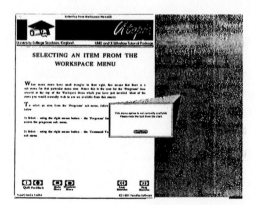

Figure 18.1

TUTORIAL STRUCTURE

Access to the exercises is by a menu system; there is a Main Menu from which either Windows or Unix exercises are accessible. From the sub menu which is displayed from the choice of either of these two options, a choice of several basic Windows or Unix exercises is available. Although the user can decide in what order exercises are completed, there is nevertheless a requirement to complete all exercises successfully. This requirement is enforced by access to the final exercise being "refused" until all exercises are completed. Visually the result of this is the appearance of a pop-up message which informs the user of the exercises still not attempted.(fig 18.2)

Figure 18.2
The following figures show a selection of exercises which are broadly indicative of the way in which the entire tutorial is structured. Please note that "boxed" words are hypertext links to information on that particular concept or topic.

Figures 18.3a/18.3b/18.3c illustrate the sequence of instructions, Windows and information notices which appear during the course of the "Iconise/Re-open a Window" exercise.

Figure 18.3a

Figure 18.3b

Figure 18.3c

Figures 18.4a/18.4b/18.4c is taken from the Unix section and illustrate the sequence of instructions, Windows and information notices which appear during the "Changing Your Password".exercise

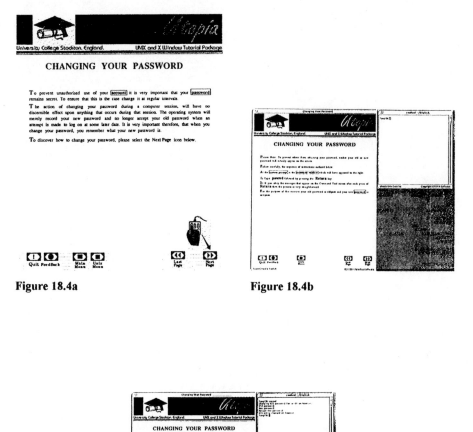

Figure 18.4a   **Figure 18.4b**

Figure 18.4c

Experience has shown, that students may repeatedly make syntactical errors when attempting to input Unix commands. Thus for the sake of progress, Utopia allows five attempts at any given Unix exercise before a pop up notice is generated indicating a suitable course of action(Figure N.5)

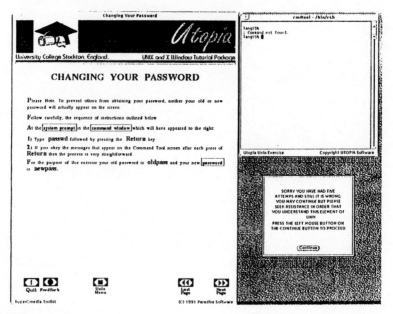

Figure 18.5

USE OF HYPERTEXT

Hypertext links, using Mediawrite, are easily constructed as are most of the elements required in the construction of a Multi-media document. The hypertext facility has been used to provide further information on Windows and Unix concepts which the knowledge of, although not critical to student progress, will provide useful additional knowledge.   The Hypertext facility has been kept deliberately limited as a more complex system would seriously compromise any attempts to test or evaluate student performance.(Smeaton, 1991: Using Hypertext for CB learning)

MONITORING/ASSESSMENT MECHANISM

The data collected from each users session with Utopia, is recorded in a temporary "User File" situated in the user's own account.   On termination of Utopia, the File is automatically destroyed after it's contents have been transferred to a main "User File" which would normally be situated in a Supervisors/Lecturers account.
At University College, this file is structured as an S.P.S.S. data file to allow various statistical analyses to be conducted on the complete data set.   However, this is a matter of personal preference; the File's structure can easily be changed.
    The information collected is in four parts:

- General User Information : which consists of the users computer ID and name
- Information regarding the use of Hypertext. Each "link" access results in the fact being recorded
- Information regarding the time taken for each exercise to the nearest minute.

- The score achieved for each exercise within the final exercise block plus the overall score which as well as being recorded, is also output to the user on exercise completion.

The final version in terms of what information is worth storing, is still being considered. In practical terms, the programming techniques required to store most data regarding software/student performance, are fairly straightforward.

SUPPORTIVE DOCUMENTATION

An on-line information document has been created in addition to the tutorial described above. This was created using Mediawrite. The students are instructed to invoke this document in iconised form for their perusal, if (a) they forget some of the material in the tutorial or (b) they need additional information.which is not covered in the tutorial.

VIDEO

The video sequences, three, with a total playing time of 17 minutes, do not attempt to address the subject matter already covered by the software. The manner of presentation is informal and is intended in the opening sequence to provide early reassurance(in the manner of "Computing for the Terrified") leading on later, to variations of a library analogy to describe both Windows(the second sequence) and the Unix File structure which appears within the third sequence along with material which stresses the importance of correct syntax. The final sequence also provides reinforcement in the form of a summary of those items covered during the course of the entire two hour session...

The average time taken to complete Utopia, is approximately 1 hour 20 minutes. Obviously, this varies but the bulk of students are usually finished within this period. This allows around 40 minutes within a typical 2 hour session for the playing of the Video segments at the appropriate time. This method of presenting Video is suspect in theory at least, as it would appear impossible to synchronise the group's progression through the software to coincide with the ideal "time slot" within which the Video should be played. (the ideal solution to this problem would be the use of CD-ROM.). In practice, however, the system works quite well as the opening and closing sequences are obviously at beginning and end with a "playing window" usually appearing for the middle sequence which caters adequately, for both ends of the ability spectrum.

PORTABILITY

To run Utopia the following hardware and software requirements would need to be met:

- A Sun Microsystems desktop SPARCstation.
- SunOS 4.1 or greater
- A Paradise Software(Mediawrite) HyperCmedia Library

Utopia should also run within a Motif Windows environment, providing the above requirements are met.

CONCLUSION

Utopia assumes a basic familiarity with computers. For example, no reference to the layout of a computer keyboard.is made. Furthermore, it does not attempt to address the full complexity of either a modern Graphical User Interface. or Unix. In this respect it cannot at present, replace totally, those traditional methods of course delivery which cover the subject area in greater depth. However, the material covered in Utopia, is delivered in less time and with less "hassle"(a subjective observation) than similar material delivered in the traditional way.

Even allowing for these limitations, the results have been encouraging. Student response has been very positive and, providing that it links successfully with more in-depth material as is the case at University College, it proves to be an excellent introduction to both Xwindows and Unix.

19. CBT's - On-Screen Simplicity Hides off-Screen Complexity

David Hughes and Povl C. Larsen, *School of Computing, University of Plymouth*

Summary

A recent research project (Hughes and Larsen, 1993) undertaken by the authors has highlighted the value of methodologies, which whilst improving the performance of companies, also serve to educate and develop company staff in the tools, techniques and technologies required for success. A particular problem in small and medium sized companies is lack of skills, or the financial resources to acquire such skills, to cost justifying investments in their businesses. (Hughes et al 1994). To address this problem the authors have developed an approach, supported by a computer based tool, to take companies through a structured process of identification of suitable investments and justifying their cost.

The principles underlining the development of computer based training (CBT) Tools is that they should be easy to use and simple to understand - no matter how complex the subject matter being dealt with. An analogy of the swan may be appropriate, its calm, peaceful appearance on the surface of the water as it floats gently along the river often belies the frenzied activity below water as it swims amongst currents and tides. In the early development phase of the CBT, the computer screens were laden with information to assist the user in completing the required tasks. Far from simplifying the use of the tool, the busy screens added to the apparent complexity.

Users who tested the software, were overwhelmed by the amount of data required and became quickly disenchanted.

In developing a CBT for the cost justification of new manufacturing investments, the authors realised that it was vital to identify, *not how much data* was required on each screen, but *how little.*

The CBT concerned, utilised a modified Profit and Loss Account. Instead of entering data directly on to the main Profit and Loss Account, under the headings of sales revenue, raw material costs, WIP, direct labour, production overheads and expenses, data entry screens were constructed to enable the user to enter the data in its constituent parts, that is, Sales Revenue as volume of goods sold multiplied by the average unit price, raw materials as raw material unit cost multiplied by volume produced, etc. This 'focusing down' enabled the construction of simple, effective screens and laid the foundations for future changes to occur.

A similar 'focusing down' approach was adopted throughout the CBT, for selecting business needs, identifying the potential to change the business processes necessary to implement possible technologies and in the entering of cost and benefit data resulting from technologies identified as suitable for investment.

The paper describes the processes adopted in 'focusing down' and how the approach was used to identify, *not how much data,* but *how little* was required on each screen. The paper concludes by discussing the difficulties encountered and how they were resolved.

FOCUSING DOWN

'Focusing Down' relates to the process of breaking down main factors into their most basic structure. In the development of a new approach to cost justification of manufacturing investments, the authors utilised an adaptation of the Profit and Loss Account. Through 'focusing down' the authors were able to display the sales product and company wide effect, new investment could have on a business.

Focusing down, also enables future changes to be made. For example, if a user wanted to know the effect that a 25% increase in sales revenue would have on the net profit of the company, then the user needs to know how the increase in sales revenue was brought about. If the increase was due to an increase in unit price then the cost factors in the Profit and Loss Account would remain unchanged. However, should the increase be the result of increased volume, then the cost of raw materials would increase, as would, WIP, direct labour and production overheads.

In the analysis of a business's financial status, as represented by a Production, Profit and Loss Account, the first 'focusing down' required breaking the 'company wide' financial status into sales products.

The second 'focusing down' reveals Sales Revenue, Cost of Sales and Expenses.

The third 'focusing down' breaks Sales Revenue into volume of products sold and average unit price, Cost of Sales 'focuses down' to raw materials, bought out parts, work in progress (WIP), direct labour and production overheads and Expenses into salaries, depreciation, rent and rates, finance costs and inventory holding costs

The fourth 'focusing down' concentrated on the Cost of Sales section, by breaking down both the raw materials and bought out parts into opening stock, purchases, closing stock, volume produced (which may be different from the volume sold), percentage scrap and average unit cost. WIP was broken down into opening and closing stock and percentage scrap. It was found that Direct labour and production overheads could not usefully be 'focused down' any further.

DIFFICULTIES ENCOUNTERED

Two main types of difficulties were encountered. The first related to the amount and style of data displayed on the screens coupled to the familiarity of the target audience, the management teams of small and medium sized manufacturing enterprises - the usability. The second to the content of the CBT screens themselves, the functionality.

In developing the CBT, the authors were aware that the CBT would be used by users of varying computer literacy. As such, in designing the original screens, it was thought that users would appreciate immediate 'on-screen' advice on the tasks required of them. However, in tests it was found that far from instilling a sense of confidence and ease of use, these screens overwhelmed the novice user. Conversely, users with some experience found the 'on-screen' assistance helpful, whilst those with the most computer experience demanded that it be 'turned off'.

From these initial tests a further version was developed which provided a brief description on screen plus a menu bar, placed at the top of the screen, offering a help facility that could be selected by clicking on with the mouse. This 'help' facility explained in greater detail the tasks that had to be completed before progressing to the next stage of the methodology.

In subsequent testing users, with at least some experience of working with computers, reported improved usability and their critique of the CBT had progressed to the actual functionality of the software. However, among those users who were not familiar with computers, dissatisfaction was still evident.

To ensure the CBT was acceptable to as wide an audience as possible it was agreed that the inclusion of a tutorial explaining the underlying rationale, structure and terminology would greatly enhance the CBT. Two of the new screens used in PRO£IT version 1.0 are shown in Figures 19.1 and 19.2.

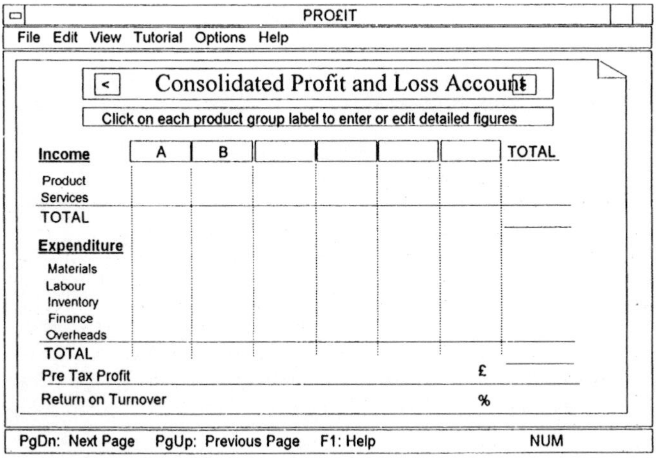

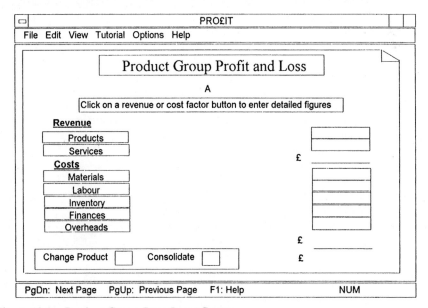

Figure 19.1: Consolidated Profit & Loss Account

To allow for future changes to occur in the Profit and Loss Account screen, as depicted by Figure 19.1, the data had to be broken down into its sub factors. To enable this to occur the user selects one of the boxes above each column which results in the screen shown in Figure 19.2 to appear.

Data cannot be entered directly to this screen either. The user must select one of the buttons, such as under Revenue, Products, whereupon another screen appears requesting data on market share, percentage market share for users company and average unit price. Each of the other buttons request similar data 'focused down' to the basic requirements.

Figure 19.2:   Product Group Data Input Screen

Under the heading of functionality, direct labour and production overheads presented the main problem. From discussions with industrialists and from literature surveys it became evident that a number of differing methods were currently employed in assigning these two factors to sales products.

CONCLUSIONS

The methodology was tested initially as a paper document, in the form of a workbook detailing a user led process methodology, prior to the building of the CBT. The development of the methodology and use of successive CBT prototypes have been reported elsewhere.

This paper concentrates on the basic method adopted for 'focusing down' such that both the presentation of data is improved by better screen designs and the functionality improved by the ability to uncover successive levels of detail - to understand the base data behind the figures. Further work is aimed at developing the tutorial aspects of the CBT to provide instruction on the rationale, content and structure of the methodology and training users in various tools and techniques of financial appraisal.

References

1 Development of a User Led Methodology for SME's to Assist in Identifying CIM Technologies for Specific Business Performance Improvement Requirements, Larsen, P. V., and Hughes, D.R., *8th World Productivity Congress*, Stockholm, Sweden, Stockholm: Royal Swedish Academy of Engineering Sciences, 4:1-7- 1-9, 1993.

2 Benchmarking Manufacturing Performance - The Results of the UK Manufacturing Survey 1993", Hughes, D.R., Smart, P.A. and White,S., *Operations Strategy and Performance, European Operations Management Association, Ninth International Conference*, Cambridge, UK., June 1994.

20. Computer-Based Training - Lessons from the Retail Industry

Andrew J. Stanley, *University of Greenwich* and Marios C. Angelides, *London School of Economics and Political Science*

Summary
The past few years have seen a rapid development in small, powerful and relatively low cost technology that has once more lead to serious consideration of computer based training (CBT) for high volume educational requirements. However, it is not only the world of education that is reassessing and redefining its attitude to CBT. Recent developments have not gone unnoticed in the world of industry and commerce. Although CBT, in one form or another, has been used by a number of major companies throughout the U.K. for over 20 years, the uncertain economic benefits and the initial cost of the equipment has resulted in relatively few organisations being able, or willing, to pursue this form of training. However, as recent developments have compelled the world of education to re-examine its attitude to CBT, so the world of business has also been similarly constrained. The purpose of this seminar is to present the results of some recent research on the use of CBT training methods in three leading companies in the retail industry of the U.K. All three companies place a high priority on the quality of their training function at all levels, and have mature and established computing functions. This research revealed three distinct approaches in the companies use of CBT which may well cause a modification to some conventional models regarding the feasibility of introducing CBT methods in both business and education. This parallel development in the worlds of education and business raises the possibilities of joint co-operation in future projects so that both may learn from each other's experiences, not only to avoid treading the same paths and making the same mistakes but also to share insights and applications. The goal for all interested parties must be to maximise the use of technology to provide a more effective education and training experience.
Keywords: Computer Based Training, Learning, Retail Industry.

INTRODUCTION

The expression "computer based training" is now generally used to describe the use of the computer as a teaching and administrative tool within a learning situation. This situation comprises not only the dynamic act of imparting information and skills but also to the more mundane acts of organisation and management of the event. The extent to which the computer can be used to assist in these circumstances ranges from the simple compilation of participants names and the training modules they are undertaking to a sophisticated, wholly computerized, interactive learning environment.

The purpose of this paper is to examine the effect that new technological developments in CBT have had on three major companies in the U.K. retail sector and the assumptions that may be drawn from the research. The second section of the paper outlines the important technological advances relevant to CBT, the third section then examines the use of CBT by three leading U.K. companies in the retail sector. The paper concludes with discussions of the implications of these studies regarding the assessment of CBT applications.

THE CHANGING FACE OF CBT

CBT has been in operation for some twenty years now and its use documented in a wide range of companies including British Aerospace, British Telecom, Barclaycard and American Express. At first the CBT courses were about the new technology itself but gradually the field of CBT training has widened and now includes tasks such as business operations, clerical procedures, engineering and maintenance operations, instructional simulations and management training.

Presentational processes have also changed as technological developments in computer systems, graphics and video techniques have lead to innovative means of delivering computer based training. Early methods of presenting material were based upon the ideas used within programmed text. They were little more than electronic books, that is, a series of text-based frames for the participant to work sequentially through, interspersed with questions to test understanding of the concepts covered. However, current advancements in chip design, high capacity storage, and programming techniques together with the use of artificial intelligence and expert systems have seen the development of virtual reality and interactive media systems which have the capability of changing dramatically the presentation of computer material. However, it must be stressed that although computers offer many advantages such as instant feedback and dynamic graphics they will not turn poor training materials into good ones. Careless consideration of the objectives and purposes of the training process will not produce a successful programme irrespective of whether it is implemented using computers or any other form of delivery.

It is perhaps surprising that CBT has not made an even greater impact, after twenty years, on the world of commerce and industry especially given the accepted benefits that CBT offers. However, this must be viewed in the light of expensive hardware costs that new entrants were faced with in the early years of development which have only recently fallen to a level acceptable for wider implementation.

A VIEW FROM THE RETAIL TRADE

Retailing is a major sector of the U.K. economy with aggregate retail sales of over £13 billion for 1993 employing some two million people in approximately 350,000 retail outlets in a dynamic and volatile environment. Unlike other sectors of the economy the nature of retailing requires a high degree of interaction with the public. Selling techniques, customer relations and maintaining quality standards must rank high in training priorities. The requirement for efficient and cost effective training to large numbers of employees is evident and certain companies such as supermarket groups and multiple department stores, would appear to be prime candidates for CBT.

The organisations chosen represent three of the most successful companies in the industry, particularly within the food retailing sector. Each of them place great emphasis on the quality and standards of the training function and are enthusiastic in their implementation of new technology to improve the effectiveness of their personnel.

Company No. 1

CBT is a method that has gained a high profile in certain areas within this company during the past six or seven years. It is not considered economical for general sales training at store level for two main reasons. Firstly, 'on the job' training is considered to be the most effective method of training, and secondly, the cost of providing the necessary hardware for all retail and distribution units is considered prohibitive. Using existing equipment is not possible as it is fully occupied controlling current operations.

CBT has had the biggest impact at the supervisory and managerial levels coordinated at Head Office. The prevailing method regarding CBT is to seek out opportunities for its application to particular situations. This method involves a training advisory officer who has a special remit concerning CBT. The advisor acts as an intrapreneur searching, company-wide, for relevant CBT opportunities to exploit.

One particular CBT application was developed for in-store food supervisors and replaced a three day training seminar previously held in a hotel. The course was devised in conjunction with an external supplier, and uses a combination of workbooks, CBT and follow-up workshops. The objective was to make the supervisors more responsive to potential commercial opportunities within the store.

The programme consists of three modules which represent three phases of training. Accompanying each module is a number of workbooks followed by a CBT session. Each workbook and CBT session is expected to take between 45 and 60 minutes to finish, with a recommended module completion time of one week.

The CBT element of each module is designed to test trainees understanding of the workbook material by applying it to a particular situation. For example, a computer simulation of a food store layout requires trainees to correctly place different categories of food within large display cabinets (known as gondolas). They have to consider variables such as required temperature conditions, storage capacity of the gondolas and strategic positioning of the items. Prior testing of workbook material is required before attempting the simulation exercise.

Other applications concerning management training have been developed involving the analysis of sales data to recognise business opportunities and a module that enables trainees to determine the optimum mix of goods for sale in different store locations.

Company No. 2
CBT is provided in this company from two main sources: the computer centre based at the Head Office and individual study centres, which exist in each of the six areas into which the country has been divided.

The computer centre provides a mainframe based distributed system linking the head office to retail outlets and distribution depots. The centre has been involved with CBT for about seven years and in conjunction with the Retail Training Department, provides CBT training packages for both the retail outlets and the depots. These packages are designed and written in-house primarily for training in computing and financial procedures but also for stock ordering, scanning and personnel systems.

CBT courses are constructed as individual learning packages, mainly text based and used with an accompanying workbook. Course material is designed to be worked through as a sequential series of modules but nevertheless with a degree of autonomy to allow for individual routing through the material.

The courses contain testing procedures for assessment of trainees understanding of material together with on-line management facilities for monitoring store usage of the courses. The packages are written for both the introduction of new systems and as a result of modifications to existing systems. The centre believes that although initial investment in equipment and training for CBT can be expensive it represents a good return on that investment. They feel that CBT is the quickest and most effective solution to systems training compared to more traditional methods, even though a full cost and benefits evaluation does not appear to have been carried out.

A particular interest in the use of interactive video systems has lead to the development of a warehouse training package being used at a major warehouse depot which the centre feels could be extended to systems and sales training.

The individual study centres are open learning centres established for use by all grades of employees. The provision of training differs from that provided by the computer centre in that the training packages are bought in from external vendors rather than being designed and written in-house. The study centres provide a range of material including CBT, video and audio cassettes, for courses such as language learning, computer applications and management theories. The centres are showing an increasing interest in CBT methods, especially interactive multimedia systems.

Company No. 3
The third company have a central training division which coordinates retail training from the Head Office. However, CBT is now directed by the technical training group whose original function was to provide computer systems training and support for end users throughout the company. The company's involvement with CBT began around 10 years ago with the introduction of an interactive system called Phoenix. This is an American system designed to run on IBM mainframe systems and has various authoring and student management facilities as built in features. Phoenix was used for generic technical training of computer staff, using 'offthe shelf' packages. The desire was for controlled, consistent and cost effective training, which Phoenix was able to provide.

Direct experience in the design and maintenance of CBT courses came about as a result of the second project which concerned the introduction of an electronic mail scheme for the Head Office and distribution depots. An external consultancy was engaged to design and implement a CBT course for users. The result was a 12 hour instructional course, mainframe based, for eight people at a time. The system had to be fine tuned by the internal technical training team, giving them their first experience with authoring languages. The system has proved successful and has been used to train around three hundred people so far. The larger retail outlets are now using the system.

Further experience in maintaining CBT systems arose when a new on-line stock management system was introduced to the company about four years ago. However, the event which lead to the technical training group finally deciding to design and write their own CBT software was the introduction of a new on-line personnel system for the stores. A new external consultant group provided CBT software which was considered inadequate and had to be greatly modified. As a result, a current project involving the installation of new computer systems for stores will be accompanied by a CBT system which will be PC based, designed, and written in-house. The only external input has been the feasibility study carried out by consultants. It has been estimated by the company that around £200,000 will be saved by adopting this approach.

It is clear from these studies that the three companies have adopted their own individual approaches to the use of CBT. Company one continue to implement their intrapreneurial management philosophy and outsource CBT operational developments wherever possible. Company three, after experiencing disenchantment with external consultants, have developed their own skills and now produce their own packages. Company two has adopted a mixed approach using in-house skills for systems training and also purchasing externally produced packages for use in their learning centres.

CONCLUSIONS

Traditional CBT theory seems to suggest that organisations who benefit most from CBT are those requiring high volume, low cost, standardized training. An exception to this is the use of simulators in, for example, the training of pilots, where only the standardized training function is required. This particular application has always been viewed as an exception to the rule primarily because of the high costs involved in the traditional training methods.

However, the research above indicates that high volume training throughput is no longer a necessary prerequisite for the introduction of CBT, the targeting of small, specialized, high cost (but high value added) groups for CBT, has now become economically feasible, neither is the requirement of unchanging training procedures. Both of these notions compel providers of training to reassess their thoughts concerning CBT.

Although advances in technology, both hardware and software, have made available the use of multimedia facilities at a cost within reach of all organisations, there is still the expensive overhead of labour effort to consider. The worlds of business and education are treading similar paths. If costs and expertise can be shared then CBT can move into a new dimension taking full advantage of the new technology and providing more effective training programmes to meet the ever changing needs of the society in which we live and work.

References

Kearsley, G. (1987) *Computer Based Training: A guide to Selection and Implementation*, Addison-Wesley.

Beech, G. (1984) *Computer Based Learning: Practical Microcomputer Methods*, Sigma Technical Press.

National Computing Centre (1989) *A Review of the Cost Benefits of Computer Training (CBT)*.

Central Statistical Office (1993) *Business Monitor - Retailing 1990*.

Central Statistical Office (1994) *Economic Trends*, February 1994.

21. Designing CBT - Focusing on the Issues

Andy Hamilton, Jon Silverside, Andy Torrance, and Helen Hann, *University College Salford.*

Summary
CBT techniques and technology have developed rapidly in recent years. This has necessitated the formulation of new design methods. In the HESTOR project to educate housing staff we are creating a highly interactive simulation of a housing estate, enhanced with multimedia to add realism. Housing staff will have to run the estate and face the type of problems they would meet in real life. Our design for this project considers the environmental model, the educational model, interfaces, and narrative. These four elements of design are integrated by the development of a story which then becomes the plot for a video. The video promotes formative evaluation by all concerned with the project.

INTRODUCTION

In the 1970's computer based training was mostly text based, typically offering the trainee a multiple choice of answers. As our understanding of CBT has developed, and as technical advances have offered more facilities, the sophistication of CBT systems has increased. In conjunction with the increasing complexity of CBT systems, design methods have been developed in order to maximise the effectiveness of the CBT produced. As CBT design is a new and developing area of study, theories of CBT design have been based on work carried out in other disciplines, particularly learning theory and psychology (Gagne & Briggs, 1979; Alessi & Trollip, 1990). Whilst this work has given us useful conceptual models of CBT and students interaction with CBT, it is our contention that it is time to enrich these models so that we are better able to make use of interactivity and multimedia presently available; thus enabling us to build more effective educational systems

The need for a new approach to CBT was recognised when we began the HESTOR project at University College Salford, to design a Housing Estate Simulator for the education of housing staff. Our vision of HESTOR is of a CBT system that will put the user in the position of managing a housing estate. They will be put into the types of situation they would have to deal with in practice, and will meet with life like responses from the system. To give this realism we are using graphics, sound, animation and video, and we wanted to combine these media in an effective way. Hence our search for new multimedia design methodologies. Multimedia enhanced simulations for education or "realistic simulations" have been produced, notably ICCARUS (Powell, 1992) and Simhealth (Mace, 1993) and we have built on their experience.

Realistic simulations are difficult to construct. Successful design requires the application of a wide variety of skills not normally found in one person. It would seem that a team approach is more likely to be successful, as it was for ICCARUS and Simhealth. There is no proven formula for design, let alone a proven methodology for the implementation of the design. What follows is an overview of the design approach that we developed for HESTOR.

The design of a realistic simulation can be broken into the following elements:

- A model of the Environment
- An educational model
- Interfaces: Text, Icon, Graphical and Video
- Narrative and continuity

A MODEL OF THE ENVIRONMENT

Housing staff are primarily concerned with the effective maintenance and development of social rented housing. The vast majority of this housing is in housing estates of several hundred properties. Therefore the representation of such estates is the central concern in building the model of the environment. Constructing this model is not an easy task. Changes in government policy, and the continued increase of homeless, unemployed, and low income families over the last two decades (Malpass, 1990 & 1993; Wilcox, 1993; Page, 1993; HMSO, 1993) has added to the difficulty of understanding the working of housing estates.

In order to establish a framework to our understanding, the primary task in building the model is the identification of key parameters. These parameters would both give feedback to those using the simulation and also be part of the dynamic that drives it. Such a key parameter for a housing estate is the number of empty houses, expressed as the "voids rate". The government has determined that the accepted level for voids is 2%. Thus this would be a target for students using the simulation to aim for. The voids rate will effect the housing model in a number of ways. In particular empty houses generate no revenue and are liable to vandalism. This drain on resources would have to be represented by algorithms of the estates financial parameters. A high voids rate would also have a negative effect on tenant satisfaction about living conditions in the estate. The tenant satisfaction parameter would be quite complex in that it is dependent on a variety of other factors such as the location and other characteristics of the estate and the expectations of tenants. Ways of calculating the effect of these influences would need researching. From the above considerations it is clear that a coherent model could only be produced in close co operation with those working and researching in the housing area.

It should be noted that the primary function of the housing model is to support the educational model. As such the housing model is to be realistic rather than predictive. The essence of this subtle distinction is addressed in the discussion of the educational model.

AN EDUCATIONAL MODEL

In the design of an educational simulation it is necessary to have a picture of how it will promote the learning process. Learning will take place as a result of the students interaction with the simulation, with other students, and with their tutor. The nature of this interaction is the educational model. The design of the educational model is intended to promote skills development rather than rote learning. In particular we want to promote decision making skills. Decision making is strongly influenced by the environment, (Eiser & Van der Pligt, 1988), hence the emphasis on realism in the simulation.

Before constructing the educational model we need to consider:

- What do we want to teach?
- What is the most effective way to teach it?

Precisely what we want to teach will be revealed by a full training needs analysis, although it is clear that housing staff require new educational approaches to prepare them for an increasingly difficult job.

Students react in different ways to particular types of learning experiences. For instance some students may prefer learning through theoretical exercises. As Housing Officers have chosen jobs that involve them going out into the community and assessing a situation for themselves, it can be expected that they are suited to the experiential learning gained from realistic simulations such as HESTOR. A thorough analysis of the most appropriate learning style for Housing Officers can be done using the learning styles classification procedure developed by Kolb, (Kolb, 1984).

In order to construct an educational model it is necessary to understand how our students learn. We all learn in our own way and fit the perceptions we gain from experience into our model of the world we live in. These perceptions or "Personal Constructs" not only give us our understanding of the world but also affect our attitudes, (Kelly, 1955). Making sense of the real world is very individual and haphazard. Over a limited timescale or in a hostile environment our experiences can induce misunderstandings and negative attitudes, (Eiser & Van der Pligt, 1988). A simulation has the advantage that the experience can be controlled, either to give a balanced view or to provide learning experiences to promote specific skills. HESTOR is being built up with reference to the educational model that we are creating. The particular techniques we are using for creating the necessary interactivity between student and simulation are discussed below.

Many students like to reflect on their experiences and to learn from them. It may seem that this type of learning is not promoted by a simulation based educational model. However it depends how the simulation is set up. In HESTOR students will work in pairs as this will increase beneficial interactivity, (Issroff, 1993), and, in particular, the discussion that takes place will enable reflection on the possible decisions they could take. Further to this, students will be encouraged to enter reasons for their decisions, and their predictions of outcomes, into HESTOR. HESTOR will store these comments, as well as automatically recording all decisions, and simulation outcomes, in a personal log. At the end of the session students will get a print out of their log. They can study this themselves and discuss it with their tutors.

One of the criticisms of reflective learning is that it does not motivate the learner. With the use of HESTOR there is a strong motivation to "succeed"; for instance to reduce the voids rate to 2% in an estate. Those who only meet with partial success in their task may feel frustrated, However this frustration is turned to good advantage as it promotes study and discussion of the log.

Housing officers have to handle a lot of information in their job. The handling of all types of textual information would be incorporated into HESTOR, using Hypertext facilities. For instance, when considering the installation of security devices on an estate, a housing officer could obtain product information and cost by phoning round. In HESTOR such information would be available, but just as in the real world, the student would have to know what to ask for. Also students would refer to standard texts that they would normally have in the office, in the same way as in real life, apart from the Hypertext facilities giving faster access. Not only will this add greater realism to the simulation, but it will broaden the spectrum of learning modes available to the student.

After students have used HESTOR on several occasions they might begin to question the working of the housing estate model. This would be welcomed as a sign that they had now built up a good enough conceptual model of their own to want to explore the one they are presented with. Such students would be shown how to interpret HESTOR's parameters, and change their values. They could then have the satisfaction of running their own model of a housing estate and observing the changed behaviour that different assumptions produce. Such use of the model would promote in depth studies of aspects of housing estates, and could assist research projects.

We defined our educational model as being the nature of the interaction promoted by the simulation. We recognise that this interaction is significantly affected by the way the information is presented on the screen, and the flow of information as the screen changes,

(Booth, 1989). Thus interface design and the narrative and continuity of the simulation are seen as critical to the effectiveness of the educational model.

INTERFACES: TEXT, ICON, GRAPHICAL AND VIDEO

Interfaces have to be designed with close regard to the working of the simulation as a whole. In HESTOR the ways in which features can be accessed is of primary importance. As far as possible the housing officer should feel that they are in their working environment. For instance information that is normally held in a filing cabinet would be accessed through an icon of a filing cabinet.

HESTOR is being developed so that anyone with an interest in housing will be able to access it. In particular we are designing the interface for tenants to be able to run the simulation. Not only will this widen the scope of HESTOR, but it would promote understanding about estate problems and tenant participation in the management process.

It has been found that sticking pictures on the front of software that has already been designed is not effective (Booth, 1989). A skilled graphic designer was a member of our design team from the HESTOR's inception. This informed early debates about the way students would react to the system and appropriate methods of representing information: a valuable learning process for the design team. Also the HESTOR interface gained a distinctive "look and feel". (Figure 21.1)The main picture represents a housing estate. The small squares are houses that are colour coded to signify condition and occupancy.

NARRATIVE AND CONTINUITY

In the HESTOR project we used the production of a storyline to drive the design process. The aim was to describe how housing staff would interact with HESTOR when used as a finished product. Describing the whole of HESTOR would have been difficult and thus we choose the voids issue as being an easy place to start. Also it is representative of HESTOR as a whole, in that it combines "hard" facts such as property conditions and "soft" facts such as tenants reactions to their physical environment.

When the first draft of the story was produced, this was discussed with the members of the design team. The story was criticised in respect of the educational and housing model, as well as realism and flow. This initiated a prototyping cycle in which a new draft was produced in response to criticisms. This prototyping continued for 4 drafts of the story.

It had been our intention from the outset of the project to make a video of our vision of HESTOR. Thus, as the story developed, we also developed the interface to reflect other design changes. In editing the video we used cut away shots from students discussing the voids problem, to the graphical interface. In early versions of the video this caused some confusion as some viewers assumed that HESTOR already existed. Whilst this proved the effectiveness of the video, it was necessary to add an introduction to it to anticipate any confusion.

When the story had been finalised on the 4th. draft we shot the video. Subsequently we went into a prototyping cycle for the video. To date we have produced the 3rd. edit of the video prototype. In showing this video we have enlisted the support of the North West branch of the Institute of Housing amongst others.

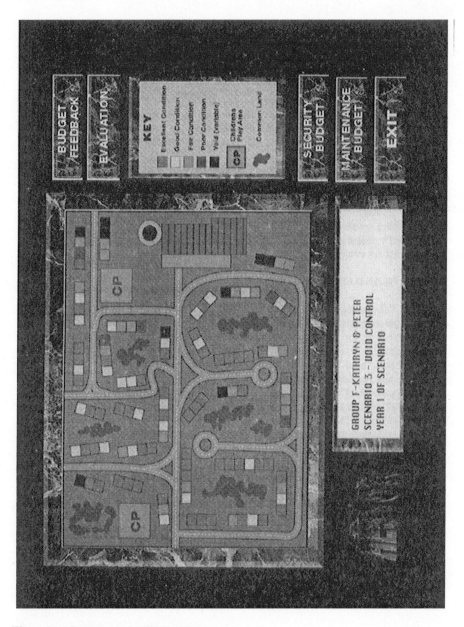

Figure 21.1 Prototype of a HESTOR screen.

The whole process of producing the story and the video, which we call video prototyping has satisfied the two aims of the design process:

- to provide focus for formative evaluation of the design by the design team and others, and, through this dialectic, to combine the elements of the design in a dynamic way.
- to provide a narrative path that would engage, and thus motivate, the user (Lepper & Malone 1987).

CONCLUSION

We suggest that members of the design team should have in depth practical experience in their particular design area. Furthermore, knowledge is no substitute for skill. The fusion of the design elements into a seamless whole has been a key concern of the project. We have employed video to enhance the design process as it is the only way of representing HESTOR in action. The video has provided an effective focus for our design activity, and it conveys to others our vision of HESTOR.

References

Alessi, S. & Trollip S. (1990) *Computer Based instruction: Methods and Development* Prentice Hall

Booth, Paul, A. (1989) *An introduction to Human Computer Interaction,* Lawrence Erlbaum

Eiser, R. & Van der Pligt, J. (1988) *Attitudes and Decisions,* Routledge

Gagne, R. & Briggs M. (1979) *Principles of Instructional design,* Holt reinhart and Winston,

HMSO (1993) *Social Trends ,* central statistical office, HMSO

Issroff, K. (1993) *Motivation and CAL in different Learning Situations,* in proceedings of AI-ED 93, World Conference on Artificial Intelligence in Education, University of Edinburgh.

Kelly, G. (1955) *The Psychology of Personal constructs,* W.W. Horton

Kolb, D. A. (1984) *Experiential Learning,* Prentice Hall

Lepper, M. R. & Malone, T.W. (1987) *Intrinsic Motivation and Instructional Effectiveness* in Computer Based Education in Snow R.E. & Marshall, M.J. (Eds) *Aptitude, Learning and Instruction: conative and affective process Analysis,* Lawrence Erlbaum Associates

Mace, S. (1993)*Simulator explores health care funding* in Info World 22/11/93, page 24

Malpass, P. (1990) *Reshaping Housing Policy,* Routledge

Malpass, P. (1993) *Housing Management and Residualisation,* in Housing review, 42, 4, pp 58–61, Housing Centre Trust

Page, D. (1993) *Building for Communities: A study of new housing association estates,*
Joseph Rowntree Foundation

Powell, (1992) J. A. *Fireplay, ICCARUS, Intelligent Command and Control Acquisition and
Review Using Simulation,* in Interactive learning International 8, 2, pp.109-126, April/June
92

Wilcox, S. (1993) *Housing Finance review 1993,*   Joseph Rowntree Foundation

22. Computer-Based Learning of Discrete Mathematics with Mathwise

Diana Mackie, *Napier University*

Summary
Three mathematics lectuers at Napier University are members of the UK Mathematics Courseware Consortium which has received substantial funding under the TLTP programme to develop computer-based materials for foundation and service mathematics. Mathwise, comprising 25 modules designed for independent study, is currently being developed at universitites throught the UK. it is hoped that a preliminary system will be available at Napier later this year. At Napier a Level 1 mathematics applications module for Software Engineering and Computing students is being developed using the PC-based multi-media authoring sytem Toolbook.

THE UKMCC AND MATHWISE

In 1992, the United Kingdom Mathematics Courseware Consortium (UKMCC) was awarded funding under the Technology in Learning and Teaching Programme (TLTP) for the development of computer-based mathematics courseware for students of science and engineering (Darby 1993). The UKMCC comprises academics from more than 30 UK universities with principal sites located at Birmingham, Cambridge, Coventry, Heriot-Watt, Keele, Liverpool and Southampton (Beilby, 1992). By drawing on the experience and expertise of practising lecturers from this wide range of universities, the suitability of the materials being developed is assured.

The computer-based modules currently being developed by members of the consortium are specifically aimed at

- bridging the gap between school or college and university by providing flexible courseware suitable for students from widely varying mathematical backgrounds.
- convincing students of the relevance of mathematics to their particular application areas in science and engineering.

The complete system, known as Mathwise, consists of course modules, reference 'leaflets', computational tools and assessment exercises. A total of 30 modules in areas of foundation mathematics and applications is currently being developed, each module containing the equivalent of 5 hours of lectures. Members of the UKMCC believe that the learning materials produced will enable the changing pattern of first year undergraduate teaching to be managed in an efficient and effective manner (Beilby, 1993).

DESIGN OF THE MODULES

The highly structured, self-study nature of the courseware provides a powerful new learning environment for students of mathematics. It offers students flexible study patterns giving them the opportunity to bring themselves to the level they require.

In many cases, a module will be used to replace conventional lectures but the nature of the learning experience being offered will change. Use of Mathwise encourages students to take responsibility for their own learning. It promotes active learning, enables application areas to be presented in a lively and relevant manner and encourages further exploration.

Although the range of authors involved in producing the modules inevitably results in a diversity of approach and style, Mathwise presents a consistent graphical user interface, including the basic screen layout, icons and navigational buttons.   Global resources that can be accessed from all points in the system include

- a glossary of terms used
- reference leaflets summarising topics required in modules or units in a module
- a bibliography
- the Beta Handbook containing mathematical formulae, rules and information
- computational tools such as a graph plotter

Many features of the system can be adapted to suit the local needs of individual institutions. For example, details of assessments attempted and the results may be logged centrally.

TECHNICAL DETAILS

The minimum computing requirements for running Mathwise are a PC with 386sx processor, 4MB memory and Microsoft Windows 3.1 or, an Apple Macintosh with System 7.

One of the development platforms being used is the PC-based Toolbook authoring system, described as a software construction set for building Windows applications (Asymetrix, 1991).   Toolbook is an object-oriented development environment incorporating graphical drawing tools for creating objects on the screen and a language used to program the behaviour of the objects in response to system or user-generated events.   The built-in features of Toolbook reduce the amount of work ordinarily involved in creating educational software whilst automatically including all the benefits of the Windows environment.

THE DISCRETE MATHEMATICS MODULE

At Napier University in Edinburgh, a discrete mathematics module is being developed on a PC-based system using Toolbook.   This module is designed for teaching mathematics to first year students on computing or software engineering courses.   Typically, students entering these courses not only have diverse mathematical backgrounds but also very little idea of why they should be studying mathematics at all.   A primary aim of the module is, therefore, a motivational one.

The importance of formal methods within software engineering has become increasingly apparent in recent years, particularly in the context of safety - critical systems.   The language of discrete mathematics enables a formal specification to model the behaviour of a software system in a powerful, concise and unambiguous manner.   This allows both the developer and the customer to understand and reason precisely about the system.   The use of mathematics also facilitates formal reasoning and provides the possibility of proving that a particular program is correct in the sense that it meets its specification.

The mathematics is introduced through a series of case studies, each of which presents a situation for which a software specification is required.   A mathematical model of each system is constructed using the notation of the formal specification language Z (Diller, 1991), which is fast becoming an industry standard.   For example, one case study examines a system for making and checking seat reservations on an aircraft whilst another investigates a mail-order system for the sale of compact discs.   The mathematical content of the module and the applications oriented approach have been used in Computing and Software Engineering courses at Napier for several years.

The module is divided into 6 units, each of which introduces one or more mathematical topics within the context of a case study.   Although there is a natural order of progression through the units, a student may choose to omit a unit or vary the order of study if that seems to be more appropriate. Each unit is further divided into sections that can vary in length from one page (i.e. screen full) of material to seven or eight such pages. Again the order in which these should be tackled is recommended but not fixed. At appropriate points within a case-study, when a new mathematical idea is required, the student is directed to a section that introduces the new concept, explores related topics and provides an opportunity for interactive exercises.

At each level within the multi-layered hierarchy, a menu of choices available to the student is listed together with explanatory titles. This enables him to skim through material with which he is reasonably familiar in order to identify less familiar topics or, alternatively, to look back over previous units and repeat a section. From all points within the structure there is access to common reference materials and software tools such as a graph plotter and a calculator.

The mathematical topics introduced include sets, propositional logic, relations and functions. Each unit contains exercises with worked solutions that enable a student to practise newly learned skills or test his understanding of a concept. The module also includes a bank of self - assessment questions.

The software is highly interactive and flexible in use to cater for the differing needs of the users. Illustrative examples of a new topic or a fuller description of a solution are frequently accessed by clicking on the appropriate buttton. This supplementary information is usually displayed in a pop-up window so that it does not interrupt the flow of the lesson. Careful use of colour enlivens the presentation and helps to emphasize particular sections. Graphical illustrations are included wherever possible and animation is used to demonstrate some concepts. These techniques together with interactive exercises all contribute towards a stimulating and active learning approach.

DEVELOPMENT PLANS

The Napier module is scheduled to be complete by June, 1994 and to be available within the first version of Mathwise later this year. A partially complete version of the discrete mathematics module is currently undergoing evaluative trials at Napier. It is hoped that a preliminary Mathwise system will be available for students at Napier University for the 1994/95 academic year.

References

Asymetrix Corporation(1991) Using Toolbook, Asymetrix Corporation, Washington

Beilby M (1992) UK Mathematics Courseware Consortium, Maths & Stats newsletter, CTI Centre for Mathematics and Statistics, 3 (2) 15-19
Beilby M (1993) Mathwise: A Learning Environment (part 1), Maths & Stats newsletter, CTI Centre for Mathematics and Statistics, 4 (4) 2-5

Darby J (ed.) (1992)Teaching and learning technology projects: TLTP, The CTISS File 15 27-70

Diller A (1991) An Introduction to Formal Methods John Wiley & Sons Ltd, Chichester

Section 3 : Multimedia and Hypermedia

23.   Paradoxes in Hypermedia: Design, Support and Training

Jacquetta Megarry, *Educational Consultant, Scotland*

Summary

Experience of large real-world hypermedia systems suggests that their design and maintenance presents various paradoxes not apparent with small demonstrators. Drawing on two large hypertexts with European content – *Europe in the Round* (a mature commercial product) and *Cities 400* (an advanced, more multimedia prototype) – the author illustrates some design challenges including

* vertical versus lateral, linear versus random-access: hypermedia reinvents the role of print
* read-only versus read-write: what users want differs from what designers imagine
* 'lost in hyperspace': myth or reality?
* moving video may be the most popular medium, but is it the least useful?

The spread of advanced hypermedia also poses paradoxes for training users. In an age when technological advance and convergence far outstrips the capacity of teacher education to keep up by traditional means, we need a fresh approach: why not use the competence and confidence of children to train their teachers?

INTRODUCTION

This paper draws on my involvement in the design and development of two hypermedia systems: *Europe in the Round* and *Cities 400*. Both use colour, graphics and some animation, and *Cities 400* features photographs and multilingual sound as well.

Europe in the Round is a mature point-and-click hypertext released annually since 1991 on both CD-ROM and floppy disc for both Macintosh and Windows 3 PCs, and widely used in the UK, especially in education: in Scotland alone over 600,000 pupils were licensed by 1993, in addition to many colleges and universities. It offers around 15,000 screens of information about the twelve countries of the European Community (as of 1994), especially about studying and working in them. Despite its massive size, it has been found very easy to use. An important reason for this is its simple and consistent graphic user interface. In particular, navigation is by three standard icons:

* *Go back* – retrace your last step
* *Help* – context-sensitive, including interpretation of icons
* *Start* – back to base

Two powerful features – *Custom* and *Collections* –allow users to add their own data and make their own presentations. In the Macintosh environment, users create new *stacks*, on PCs they make ToolBook *books*, but the process does not require awareness of which software (or even which computer) they are using, let alone the use of commands or reference to manuals. *Custom* is a stack/book which allows users to enter their own addresses and/or notes and have them connected seamlessly with the rest of the system; each entry is indexed automatically on its front screen, which can be reached by a single jump from anywhere in the 'public' system. *Collections* is a feature that enables users to collect (make copies of) any number of screens from any part of the system and present them as a slide show or printout. The user has the option to have 'Comment' screens interleaved between each *EitR* screen; these are filled in later, by typing into a simplified word processor and/or by recording comments through a microphone.

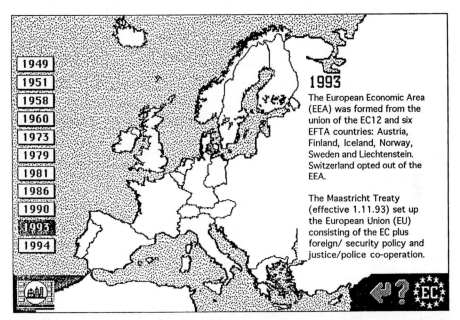

1949
1951
1958
1960
1973
1979
1981
1986
1990
1993
1994

1993
The European Economic Area
(EEA) was formed from the
union of the EC12 and six
EFTA countries: Austria,
Finland, Iceland, Norway,
Sweden and Liechtenstein.
Switzerland opted out of the
EEA.

The Maastricht Treaty
(effective 1.11.93) set up
the European Union (EU)
consisting of the EC plus
foreign/ security policy and
justice/police co-operation.

Figure 23.1: a sample screen from *Europe in the Round* showing the three standard icons at bottom right

Cities 400 is a multimedia prototype (for both Mac and multimedia PC) developed during 1993; it builds on the *EitR* experience and aims to help students to find out about where to study in the EC, with an emphasis on the 400 or so university cities of Western Europe. Because it was created by the same team, augmented by partners in Italy and the Netherlands, its user interface is broadly similar. However, it adds the important feature of a *User screen*, in which the user makes such choices as:

- language on screen (three languages were built into the prototype, nine were planned)
- which currency is the basis for conversion rates
- from which country telephone numbers are shown as dialled
- volume level (speech is used for authentic pronunciation of cities and places of interest)

A notable feature of *Cities 400* is its use of colour photographs: each city has a nodal screen with text and a characteristic photograph, linked to other screens by buttons on left and right; the leftmost buttons lead to regional and national data (maps, statistics, currency and travel) while the right buttons give access to more information about the city – universities, history, recreation, business, and images. The images are of places of interest, arranged in sixes, each city having one or two screens ie there is a bank of 7 or 13 photographs for each city. Each set of six photos are shown initially at 'thumbnail' size, but the user can click on any thumbnail to make it 'grow'. Landscape photographs then nearly fill the screen, whereas portrait photos are magnified to a lesser extent. Either way, the caption remains visible (with irrelevant captions hidden) and buttons are available to take the user to the spoken version of the captions and/or a city map with the place of interest highlighted.

VERTICAL AND LATERAL, LINEAR AND RANDOM ACCESS

It is in the nature of hypertext that it concerns and demands lateral thinking. This seems directly opposed to the linear, vertical structure of a book. However, the situation is more complicated. While our eyes may follow a roughly linear track in the process of decoding print, meaningful reading depends on lateral, cyclical activity in our brains. To make sense of the book, we must read *actively*, making nonlinear links between the authors' thoughts and our existing mental structures, testing their notions against our experiences, perhaps finding counter-instances or extensions.

Whalley (1993) advocates an 'alternative rhetoric for hypertext'. He exposes the myth of book linearity, following de Beaugrande in presenting readers' paths graphically. Nevertheless, expository text is structured and organised to assist a dialogue with the reader. It has a coherence that lends itself to study. By contrast 'hypertext is a *fragmented* text form, and hence fundamentally flawed as an expository medium' (Whalley 1993, page 7). It has unlimited malleability – for example offering multiple perspectives on a domain or text. An example of this is the way in which *Cities 400* allows you to follow a trail from a photograph of Napier University's Merchiston Tower to its map location, to information about Edinburgh that might help potential students to know whether they wish to study there, to searchable information about subjects offered at Napier, to a searchable screen of history which documents the links between John Napier, logarithms and the naming of Napier College, then Napier University. Here readers are invited to imagine 'in their mind's eye' what conference delegates were shown in a flash: the software lets you do all this, and more, in less time than it takes to read this sentence. Contrast the flat, linear information in the *Edinburgh: most beautiful city in Britain* booklet which delegates received in their joining instructions with that in *Cities 400* and you see another aspect of Whalley's multiple perspectives.

However, books and booklets have an important and continuing role. Kommers found that 'students need extra guidance before they know how to utilise hypertext facilities'; hypertext is perceived as 'too open to be effective while studying in the traditional school context', and especially so by less able students (Kommers 1990). They need structured help – and print is an ideal medium for providing such support. This is precisely the rationale of our follow-up project in which we developed printed support materials to help both students and teachers to use *Europe in the Round* as part of the secondary and college curriculum (Megarry 1993a).

Before 'back to basics' is used as an anti-hypertext slogan, let us remember how little classroom experience we have of mature, supported hypertext. Rather than despair of the approach, we should note the concern and try to implement hypertext support properly. After all, more able students are better at learning *whatever* the teaching method. They tend to know more, possessing more mental hooks upon which to hang things, so they learn better from browsing than their less able peers.

My perspective on all this is that hypermedia does not – and will never – replace books and print: it invites a new relationship, in which print is reinvented and celebrated afresh.

READ-ONLY VERSUS READ-WRITE: HYPERMEDIA AND BOOKS

An *intrinsic* feature of hypertext, often forgotten by those who promote point-and-click multimedia databases, is that it blurs the distinction between user, author and editor. Users should be free to forge their own pathways, add their own data, record their own reactions, and so on. In computer jargon, hypertext is read/write, not read-only. This flexibility sounds wonderful in theory, but requires careful management in practice if authoritative data is not to be carelessly wiped out , or deliberately rearranged, by users who may be inexperienced, playful or downright mischievous.

I have argued before that CD-ROM is an ideal medium for mass storage of rich hypertexts (Megarry 1988). One of the main attractions of CD-ROMs in schools, especially schools with inventive pupils, is their robust, read-only nature. Teachers need not fear mass deletion, electronic graffiti or virus epidemics on their CD-ROMs. But if hypertext is read/write, how can it survive on CD-ROM which is read-only? In *Europe in the Round* we use a combination of mass data on the CD-ROM with interactive read-write data (including *Custom* and *Collections*) on the user's hard disc. We put considerable ingenuity into a variety of read/write features, ranging from our currency update mechanism (which allows the user to update values from a daily newspaper without quitting) to the unlimited scope built into *Custom* and *Collections*. We have paid a price in the effort needed to make installation as simple as possible, especially in for read/write networking in the Windows environment.

While users are extremely enthusiastic about the system, our impression is that what they really want is a robust point-and-click database ie they mainly use it in read-only mode. Perhaps three years is too short a time to justify such a sweeping generalisation. However, maybe we have been carried away by our own enthusiasm for user input. To find out which, we need systematic data, not impression and anecdote. We are now debating offering software which, with the users' permissions, could record usage both discreetly and systematically so as to understand better which parts of the system people actually visit, and for how long.

Administrative problems can arise in a multi-user hypertext if anyone can change the data and/or structure. It can make for a range of difficulties from embarrassment over graffiti, to seriously misleading information, to impossible issues of maintenance. Someone, somewhere, must store a 'clean copy' in a safe place in case there is a need to start from scratch. In the context of *Europe in the Round*, as suppliers we can provide seamless links with *Custom* but we warn users that they are responsible for its content, maintenance and protection in the event of a renewal. Although *Custom* is closely linked into the system, in the context of data renewal it is completely isolated. If users were to modify substantial parts of the system, they would preclude the option of benefiting from our renewals.

There is, after all, a closer analogy between hypertext and books than at first appears. As part of the process of active reading, we may reach for our pencils. But books are read-only. Annotating a library book would be an act of vandalism; even if the book is your personal property, your notes may distract you, or another reader, later. So, for a body of professional writing with which one wants to interact, hypertext has many attractions over paper. Not only can one make unlimited annotations using electronic "Post-it"s, but you can also link the citations into your personal database of references, articles and notes. You can choose to compare your comments with those of others or to conceal them.

'LOST IN HYPERSPACE': MYTH OR REALITY?

There is a well-known cliché about the dangers of being *lost in hyperspace*. Dillon et al (page 169 in McKnight) provide a detailed and coherent criticism of whether this problem actually exists, or whether it means what it seems to. Evidence for it turns out to be 'distressingly thin'; could the navigation problem be a methodological myth?

Users who find unexpected results from a menu tend to return to the start, rather than to the menu at which they took a wrong turning. Such behaviour is consistent with the progressive model of acquiring a cognitive map of electronic space which Dillon et al put forward. It also chimes with my experience of watching hundreds of users working with *Europe in the Round*. Users do not, in fact, get 'lost' at all: obviously some people find things slowly at first, and after experience they find short-cuts; their search patterns become more efficient as they gain competence and confidence with the system. However, when they have trouble finding something, they do not talk as if *they* are lost, but as if the *data* is lost within the system. The distinction is fundamental.

Perhaps some of the confusion or aimlessness that users experience is simply the product of a browsing state of mind. As an early *Europe in the Round* field-tester said, poignantly, "The system could be intimidating because the user has to decide 'what next?'." Quite so.

MULTIMEDIA HYPE: MOST POPULAR, LEAST USEFUL

The fact that the different media types – text, diagrams, photographs, sounds, animation and video – can all be delivered on a desktop computer should not blind us to the inherent differences between them. Moving video is often considered the most attractive: on first acquaintance with a multimedia package, many users view the video snippets first. This should not influence designers unduly, especially in view of the effort and budget required to secure relevant and high-quality footage – an effort which may have to be renewed frequently, since video is prone to date and expensive to update. I say 'secure' since it is sometimes cheaper to shoot afresh than to pay for usage rights, especially when developers wish to keep open the option of new markets; the administrative effort of fresh negotiations, and the design cost of risking failure, may be prohibitive. These problems are naturally not at the forefront of users' minds when they say they 'like video'. What the users want, or think they want, may not be what they need.

Exactly what does moving video contribute? In the context of how the package is used, how often is the video viewed? In many cases, I suspect, the answer is once only. Video has to be watched in real time, and can sensibly be interrupted only in certain places. It cannot be printed, and can be cumbersome to edit. Yet many designers act as if it is the Holy Grail of true multimedia.

I am not against the use of video *per se*. There are subjects – for example the teaching of practical skills in physical education – where full-screen, full-motion video is obviously the best medium available; the Scottish Higher Grade Physical Education videodisc is a superb example of its use (Megarry 1994). What I am attacking is the indiscriminate use of video. It is difficult for designers to resist the pressure of users' expectations and preferences, but sometimes they should stand firm. We have so far resisted the temptation to include video in *Europe in the Round* or *Cities 400* partly because of the appeal of near-instant access to information, and partly because it would have diverted resources from more useful facilities.

ARE CHILDREN FIT TO TRAIN TEACHERS?

We live at a time of accelerating progress in hardware and software. The convergence of technologies that used to be distinct – such as video, telecommunications, photography, publishing and computing – challenges the most creative of educationists. The sheer pace of development makes it impossible for teachers to keep up by means of traditional routes such as pre-service or in-service training. Finding a solution to the mismatch in pace demands that we indulge in what Charles Handy calls 'upside-down thinking' (Handy 1994). Children are untroubled by rapid change, and more efficient as learners than adults. Why not enlist them to train teachers?

The two arguments for using children to train teachers are economic and pedagogic. The economic one is obvious: the teacher's time is a scarcer, more expensive resource than that of the pupils. Why, then, do we not follow the economic logic and harness the considerable teaching potential locked up in our young people? Anderson et al (1993), for example, found that teachers do not learn to create HyperCard stacks efficiently despite the use of a 'minimal manual' created with outside funding and needing regular updating to keep up with new versions of HyperCard and system software. Yet children who have unrestricted access to a Macintosh can learn to design stacks without any training at all (Megarry 1993b).

The pedagogic argument is less obvious. Children may not only be more efficient at learning – especially learning about information technology – than adults, they also may need the opportunity to discover for themselves anyway. 'Rather than pushing children to think like adults, we might do better to remember that they are great learners and try harder to be more like them' (Papert 1994, p 155). The epithet attributed to Piaget puts it more strongly: 'every act of teaching deprives the child of an opportunity of discovery'.

What children need is access to the hardware and some monitoring and channelling of their progress. It is educational, as well as satisfying, for the child who has acquired hypertext expertise to pass it on. It builds communication skills and confidence, though not complacency, since another child will always have a different need, a difficult question, perhaps a better method. Creating a climate in which skills are shared and problems solved co-operatively requires effort, but it is a better use of the teacher's skills and it teaches children a vitally important life skill.

Must it challenge the teacher's role or dilute the quality of education to acknowledge that some children learn some things faster and better than their teachers? It is not a question of intelligence, but one of attitude and lack of experience (partly self-inflicted). Anderson et al's teachers were handicapped by 'a lack of self-confidence' and 'injured professional pride'. Children are altogether more matter-of-fact about computers, less worried about making 'mistakes' or looking foolish. If suitably encouraged, they make many more key-presses and mouse-clicks per minute, so they learn faster from their explorations. Yet in many schools, their progress is inhibited because teachers effectively act as gate-keepers. If teachers believe a software feature to be 'advanced' or 'difficult', they never discover how easily children could have mastered it. Those who are terrified of technology learn its use neither quickly nor easily. Teachers have many other priorities and pressures, and their expectations of mediating children's access to knowledge is so deeply ingrained that it takes a real effort to question it.

Papert paints a vivid picture of Joe, a fifth grade elementary teacher, afraid that he might undermine his own authority as a teacher by admitting his limitations with computing, emerging into the sunny relief of promoting student collaboration (Papert 1994, p 65-6). Librarians seem to have less difficulty with this model, and take readily to the idea of fostering pupil autonomy. Writing about the use of *Europe in the Round*, the Fortrose Academy school librarian said:

> 'I am constantly coming across new screens which I have never discovered before, usually when I look over the shoulder of a student who is finding his way around the disc ...The students ... are often seen explaining how it works to others ... They truly become more independent as a result of the experience.'
> (MacKenzie 1994)

I do not underestimate the mental and organisational energy needed to set up collaborative learning within the classroom. However, organising children is within the expertise of teachers, and children's time is 'cheap'; by contrast, teachers' time is expensive, and creating (for example) HyperCard stacks is not within their normal repertoire.

Are learners fit to train teachers, then? Not yet, perhaps, but I believe they could become so. As a test of this bold hypothesis, I encouraged my son to offer a workshop on *Training beginners to create multimedia* at this conference. A participant's account suggests that the session was successful, if unorthodox (Budgett 1994); Bloomer and Stevens provide their report elsewhere in this volume. The workshop – my offspring in both a literal and metaphorical sense – broke new ground by showing that this fresh approach does work.

CREDITS AND ACKNOWLEDGMENTS

Europe in the Round is published by Vocational Technologies Ltd of 32 Castle Street, Guildford, GU1 3UW, UK. Its design and maintenance is a team effort, including John and Nick Twining of VT Ltd, Ian Clydesdale (graphics), Bob Tennent (technical consultant) and myself (Product Manager). I directed its development project (1989-91), which was funded by the UK Employment Department. *Cities 400* (as of April 1994) was an advanced prototype seeking investment and publication. The prototype was developed with some EC funding (under IMPACT) by a team which augmented the above team with Dick Tucker of SVB, Amsterdam and Pier Giacomo Sola of Scienter, Bologna.

I acknowledge gratefully the talents of the above teams; David Hawkridge for stimulating my recent reading; and valuable editorial comments on this paper in draft by Robin Budgett.

References

Anderson A et al (1993) Teaching teachers to use HyperCard: a minimal manual approach *British Journal of Educational Technology* 24 (2) 92-101

Budgett R (1994) Beginners Pluck *Times Educational Supplement* 5 August 1994

Dillon A et al (1993) Space – the final chapter pp 169-191 in McKnight et al

Handy Charles (1994) *The Empty Raincoat: Making Sense of the Future* Hutchinson, London

Kommers P A M (1990) Hypertext and the acquisition of knowledge (unpublished PhD thesis) Universiteit Twente, Netherlands

Mackenzie F (1994) *Europe in the Round:* a cross-curricular resource *Eurofios* (newsletter circulated by Grampian Region) Issue 2, January

McKnight C et al (1993) *Hypertext: a Psychological Perspective* Ellis Horwood, Hemel Hempstead

Megarry J (1988) Hypertext and compact discs: the challenge of multi-media learning *British Journal of Educational Technology* 172-183

Megarry J (1991) *Europe in the Round:* principles and practice of screen design *Educational and Training Technology International* 28, 4, 306-315

Megarry J (1993a) Support materials for *Europe in the Round* (series of six packs: published by J Megarry, Landrick Lodge, Dunblane, FK15 0HY, UK)

Megarry J (1993b) Editorial *British Journal of Educational Technology* 24 (2) 83

Megarry J (1994) Games in freeze frames *Times Educational Supplement* 25 March 1994 p 28

Papert, S (1994) *The Children's Machine: Rethinking School in the Age of the Computer* Harvester Wheatsheaf, Hemel Hempstead

Whalley P (1993) An alternative rhetoric for hypertext pp 7-17 in McKnight et al (1993)

24.   Media Studies: The Virtual Workshop

Peter Dean and Luke Hockley, *University of Luton, UK*

Summary
Digital technologies have implications for the curriculum of media studies, its delivery and the support of student practical work. This paper is an introduction to how these factors have influenced the formation and development of the school of Media Arts at the University of Luton.

INTRODUCTION

Rather than report on empirical research findings this paper attempts to crystallise some of the experience of teaching media studies in an environment where digital technologies are prevalent. For convenience, and accepting a high degree of overlap, the influence of these technologies on media studies can be grouped into three sections: course delivery, production/curriculum issues (the necessity of grouping these together will be explored below) and support of student practical work.

MEDIA STUDIES: AN OVERVIEW

Typically media studies is concerned with the analysis of media artefacts, generally referred to as 'texts'. The analysis includes studying the production of texts, the working practices of the media industries and their impact on society. It may also involve a detailed textual reading, or interpretation of a text or series of texts. Thus questions of institutional and legislative control over production, the consumer's access to the media, "reading" a text and the social significance of media activity are central issues in the curriculum.

Consequently much of media studies aims to be a detached analysis of media institutions and practices and their social consequences and some university departments adopt this approach almost exclusively. However media studies has increasingly promoted 'active' learning (Alverado et al 1987) and sought to engage students in meaningful practical activity in seminars. The intention is to provide the opportunity for students to reflect on issues in a practical context rather than to develop overtly vocational craft oriented skills. The hope is that practice will reveal what theory may have obscured (Masterman 1985).

MEDIA ARTS AT THE UNIVERSITY OF LUTON

The School of Media Arts at the University of Luton is a new department only three years old, yet it has fifteen full time members of staff and over four hundred students. From its inception it regarded theory and practice as interdependent elements to the study of the media, while noting that this division is not always practical or sensible (Fleming 1993). The school found in new digital technologies the possibilities of extending this pedagogic approach through using digital photography, digital video and multimedia.

Personal computers gave students a new way to explore the construction and meaning of images and with the simple actions of cut and paste examine how images are constructed and convey meanings. Similarly desktop digital video made it possible to analyse moving images and soundtracks in a way that previously needed a video editing suite.

It was also evident that the emergence of new technologies in both domestic and industrial spheres could be studied in much the same way as other more traditional media. New media texts in forms as diverse as computer games and QVC (a home television shopping channel) gave rise to familiar questions of ownership, access, control and impact. There was also the additional debate over the status of the digital text and to what extent a digital image created using a package such as Adobe Photoshop is different to a chemical photograph of a similar subject.

Given this context is was clear that photography and video production should play a central part in the student experience. Additionally as computers become capable of displaying digital video, playing back audio CDs and displaying photographic images from Photo CD it became apparent that media studies was going to have to come to terms with digital media and the ever increasing role of digital communications (Feldman 1994).

For example it was decided that in media sociology lectures students should be as likely to study Microsoft as the British Broadcasting Corporation. The subject of textual analysis might be a Hollywood film or a multimedia CD ROM. Practical work should involve both digital and traditional technologies.

In teaching practical work digital technology was not to be separated out as something special or problematic. Instead a photography class could be held in either a darkroom or a multimedia suite. Likewise video workshop might involve videotape or digital video. The aim was to encourage students to adopt the best production process for their communication needs.

The inclusion of substantial amounts of practical work in an undergraduate degree caused more than a sideways glance of suspicion from colleagues used to a more traditional lecture, essay and examination approach to teaching and assessment. From such circles two fears were prevalent; that the degree was a thinly disguised industrial training school and that vocational skills were being developed at the expense of more important academic skills.

However the Media Arts team felt it was important to give students the opportunity to show a grasp of their subject area in a variety of ways and for this to be examined with an equally diverse pattern of assessment. While essays and examinations were retained for written assignments it was felt that audio-visual work would give students the chance to demonstrate an academic understanding of their subject through the media that they were studying. In this context it became apparent that assessment should not evaluate students' craft skills but test the thoroughness with which the students had engaged with the issues of this study. In practice this does not stop students striving for high production values but it does place the academic nature of their work firmly centre stage.

EXAMPLES OF STUDENT WORK

One of the first pieces of digital work within the school was a five minute piece of digital video called Signing Times. This presentation explored the difficulties that a hearing impaired person can experience. Intended for a hearing audience it positions the viewer alternately as hearing and hearing impaired.

More recently the school has undertaken a large project with the British Film Institute to provide a multimedia guide to the facilities of the BFI library. Initially students were supplied with a brief from the library staff from which the students had to distil the essential facts, structure the relevant information, and present the complex cataloguing systems in a simple manner.

Figure 24.1: An example screen from the BFI Library Guide

COURSE DELIVERY

As the school has expanded so too has the role of digital media in the delivery of degree programmes. Students have access to a range of packages, mostly on CD ROM, which enable them to pursue academic research. For example the CD ROM of the British Film Institute's SIFT (Schecter 1967) library data base and The Times on CD ROM.

More recently the school has started to author its own multimedia courseware which falls into two categories; open learning courseware and material to stimulate class discussion. The division however is not straightforward as the same courseware may be used as the subject of a lecture, to start a discussion and for students to use as open learning material.

OPEN LEARNING

One of the first pieces of courseware developed by the school was "Rough Cut" The program utilises digital video and sound to introduce students to some of the fundamental processes of video editing and the construction of film narrative. The program runs as a HyperCard (Apple (Apple 1991) stack, with a colour interface and utilises the QuickTime (Apple 1993) extension to the Macintosh operating system.

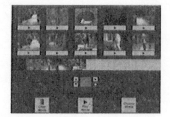

Figure 24.2: The construction screen from Rough Cut

Students are given a window from which the can play any one of eight clips of digital video. By clicking on the clip it can be added to the construction bar across the middle of the screen. Clips may be added in any order together with one of five soundtracks. On opting to "Make movie" the student's choice of clips and soundtrack is played back as a continuous sequence or movie. When used in a seminar lecturers are able to work with the students to explore possible combinations of clips and the effect of changing soundtracks.

On a practical level the program alleviates some pressure on video editing facilities. More significantly it gives students access to a creative tool. Previously a typical seminar exercise would have been to sequence still images while this package enables a much fuller examination of the issues of film narrative.

DISCUSSION STARTERS

The package, On Narrative introduces some of the key concepts of narrative in terms of film theory and how they can be applied to narrative in multimedia. Authored with Macromedia Director (Macromedia 1993) it uses sound commentaries, digital video and hot text to encourage students to interactively examine how narratives are constructed and what expectations they bring to films and multimedia programmes.

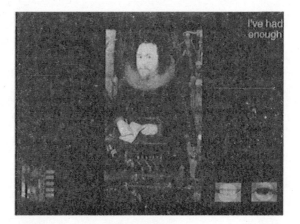

Figure 24.3: An example screen from On Narrative

Courseware is used in a variety of contexts. Some students use On Narrative to examine some of the concerns of narrative theory while others will concentrate on the construction of the packages and examine issues such as interface design, user control and navigation.

Another discussion starter This is a Man's World, is designed to stimulate discussion around gender and technology. It encourages students to examine why men are represented as controllers of technology while women are depicted as technophobic.

Figure 24.4: The opening screen from It's a Mans World

SUPPORT

As practical exercises and production work have been introduced into the curriculum a number of practical issues concerning the support of such work have been identified. In keeping with the integration of digital media work into the curriculum the digital media production facilities are located centrally with the other production facilities. Staff accommodation is at another campus within the town. Timetabled workshops and seminars are used to introduce students to the production tools available but much of the student's time is spent on personal production work carried out independently. This can leave the student feeling isolated from the available support and minor problems can escalate into a major disruption of the production and the learning experience.

Initial experiences offering telephone support to students clearly showed that it is very difficult for staff to diagnose and solve difficulties from the description given over the telephone. Obviously some topics such as colour matching are impossible to discuss effectively without common visual information. An alternative solution (Taylor et al 1991) was sought that would enable the staff and students to communicate more effectively and for both parties to be able see the work under discussion

The student digital production facilities are based on a suite of Macintosh Quadra 840AV computers. These are linked to each other and to the University network using twisted-pair Ethernet. Each of the staff responsible for teaching and supporting digital production work also has a Quadra 840AV on their desk. These computers are similarly connected to the University network. This hardware base together with the network infrastructure provides scope for the sharing of digital texts in production and enhanced communication between sites. The AV Macintosh models are equipped with PAL video digitising in addition to the audio digitising capabilities of any Macintosh. Combined with the standard Ethernet connection this allows video conferencing (Feldman 1994) to be integrated into the production environment. To promote the use of these features Apple include ES•F2F_ (ESoF2F '92), video conferencing software produced by The Electronic Studio_. As supplied this software supports two-way video conferencing using cameras connected to any QuickTime_ compatible video digitiser and connected via any AppleTalk_ network. At additional cost, ES•F2F_ can be upgraded to support the sharing of application windows. With this additional feature, it appeared ES•F2F_ offered a highly cost effective way of integrating a support mechanism with the production facilities.

Trials commenced using this approach to support new users learning simple still image manipulation techniques using Adobe Photoshop_. ES•F2F_ does not provide any support for audio communication so various shareware 'chat' utilities were tried but these were found to be very awkward to use so conventional telephone calls were made in parallel. As set up the users could see each other face-to-face over the video link, talk to each other over the telephone and share the window displaying the work in progress. The student could work on the window using the applications tools. The supporter was able to make coloured marks on the window using a 'pencil' tool. These marks lie over the top of the window but do not change the contents.

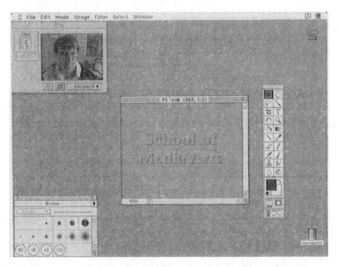

Figure 24.5: ES•F2F_ working in conjunction with Adobe Photoshop

Superficially, it would appear that adding a face-to-face video link would greatly enrich the communication but this did not prove to be the case. The video link was almost superfluous with most of the exchange taking place over the telephone with the shared window as the focal point of the discussion. Observing that conventional tutorials involving computer-based work usually take place with both parties facing the screen and not each other makes this less surprising.

Whilst the video performance, particularly over Ethernet, was very impressive, the rate at which the shared window updated was very slow. This meant that the participants always had to verify that they are both looking at the latest view of the window. In addition, the window sharing module of the supplied version of ES•F2F_, 2.05 was rather unreliable. Whilst video and window sharing function over slow network connections such as LocalTalk_ a faster network such as Ethernet is required for acceptable performance levels.

Following this pilot work a number of conclusions have been drawn:

- The use of standard hardware and software components greatly reduces the cost and complexity. The support mechanism can become an integral part of the production facilities.

- When supporting computer-based production work it would be better to concentrate on fast, reliable sharing of screens, rather than use network bandwidth for a video link. We intend to look at packages such as Timbuktu Remote for this purpose.
- The video link is easy to use and reliable. It may be that in other support situations, such as essay tutorials, the face-to-face communication may be more important. Trials of this will be included in the next phase of the project.
- The supporter needs more powerful and intuitive annotation tools. There is no rubber to accompany the pencil tool in ES•F2F_. After making six marks the first mark disappears when another mark is made. This can be very confusing!
- Remote support opens up many possibilities for a more flexible approach to the learning process. Staff can support students according to their need, not according to their physical location. Potentially, staff and/or students could be at home. If remote support becomes the norm, staff can have far greater control over when they are available to help by making themselves visible on the network or not.
- There are implications for centrally provided technical support services. These can be integrated into such a network service. Three way conversations involving the student, lecturer and technical support staff could quickly resolve problems that would otherwise seriously disrupt the student's work. This would also promote close co–operation between academic and support staff.

CONCLUSION

A number of further activities are planned as a result of the experiences gained. The remote support of the digital production process is to be further investigated using tools more directly concerned with window sharing such as Timbuktu Remote. This will take precedence over the video conferencing. The range of courseware is to be further developed. Existing programs are to be extended into study packs for more independent study in addition to broadening the range of materials. The role of video conferencing in the remote support of student work is to be developed into areas where face-to-face communication is more important. The existing practice of discussing the first draft of essays with students is to be extended so that students can share the word processor window with staff and discuss the essay over the video link.

The experience of teaching media studies in the School of Media Arts at the University of Luton suggests that there is considerable value in studying the development of digital media. The production equipment that is needed for students can also be used by staff to produce courseware and provide distance workshop support. However given the current state of desktop video and networking provision there remain a number of questions over how satisfactory this type of support is for students. Nonetheless media studies appears to offer a series of critical strategies which can be used to track and analyse the adoption of digital production technologies by the broadcast industries and in the growing range of digital media in the home.

Acknowledgements

Signing Times was produced by Anita Turvey, second year student, BA(Hons) Media Studies, University of Luton.
The BFI Library Guide was produced by Luke Hockley, designed by 2nd year students, BA(Hons) Media Studies, University of Luton with artwork by Kavita Hayton and technical direction by Peter Dean.
Rough Cut was produced by Luke Hockley with technical direction by Peter Dean.

On Narrative and This is a Man's World were produced by Kavita Hayton

Bibliography

Manuel Alvarado, Robin Gutch, Tana Wollen. *Learning the media: an introduction to media teaching* 1987 Macmillan, London 1987 p28-35

Len Masterman, *Teaching the Media Comedia* London 1985 p27

Dan Fleming, *Media Teaching* Blackwell, Oxford 1993

Tony Feldman, *Multimedia,* Blueprint, 1994, p128

Film Index International, Chadwyk-Healey Ltd, Cambridge, 1993

Hypercard 2.1, apple Computer Inc, Cupertino, 1991

Quicktime Multimedia Architecture, Apple Computer Inc, Clupertino, 1989-93

Macromedia Inc, San Francisco, '93

Taylor J. et al, *Discourse and Harmony:* Preliminary findings in a case-study of multimedia collaborative problem solving, 00C 1990 International Award Winning Paper presented at the conference Problems of Support, Survival and Culture, April 1991

Tony Feldman, *Multimedia,* Blueprint, 1994, p88

ESoF2F, The Electronic Studio, a division of McBain, Noel-Johnson & Co Ltd., London, 1992

25.   Resource-Based Learning Using an Open Hypermedia System

G.A. Hutchings, W. Hall and S. White, *University of Southampton*

Summary
In the future, the working environment of the undergraduate student will become more and more computer-based, as the availability of word processing, spreadsheets, and data analysis tools such as statistics packages increases. The most effective learning systems will be those which enhance the existing working environment, rather than trying to hide, isolate or simplify it. The ability to integrate the student's own work and ideas into the corpus of materials available will be essential if learners are to be able to carry out the constructional activities which many argue lead to effective learning. In addition, those directing the learning of others will require an environment which enables existing resources to be integrated with new material, tailored to suit a variety of different users with different aims, goals or background knowledge (Hutchings, 1993).

INTRODUCTION

For as long as the personal computer has been available to the educational establishment, it has been proposed as a potentially powerful tool to facilitate the learning process. However, developments in the field of CAL have not lived up to the expectations of its enthusiastic proponents, and the large-scale uptake of computer-based techniques for teaching and learning has yet to occur.

Hypermedia techniques have been proposed as the solution to the problems of traditional CAL. The network structure of nodes and links means that a variety of routes is provided through the same body of information, thus providing access to introductory material for naïve learners, while at the same time allowing more advanced learners to by-pass this and access advanced, detailed material rapidly. There is no need to build models of either the learner or the subject domain (Hammond 1991), and there is the advantage that browsing through a large corpus of information by following links and relationships encourages implicit as well as explicit learning (Duchastel 1990). For these and other reasons, hypermedia has been embraced by that section of the education community interested in exploring the use of computers for teaching and learning, and it is clear that, for better or for worse, hypermedia functionality will be a constituent of a significant proportion of learning systems produced in the future.

There is a growing body of evidence in support of the fact that simple browsing systems are insufficient to provide a suitable, engaging environment in which learning may occur. Hammond (1991) argues that the freedom of movement available in hypermedia systems is not necessarily a sound basis for learning, since learners are liable to ramble through the information in an instructionally inefficient way, their choices being dictated more by spur of the moment decisions than by any plan or strategy. In addition, Hammond argues that such browsing is passive rather than active, and does not engage the student sufficiently. Similarly, Mayes (1991) describes deep learning as a by-product of using cognitive tools, which he defines as follows:

> *The concept of a cognitive tool....is easy to describe. It is simply a device, or technique, for focusing the learners analytical processes. A cognitive tool can be regarded as an instructional technique in so far as it involves a task, the explicit purpose of which is to lead to active and durable learning of the information manipulated or organised in some way by the task.*

One of the most important features of Intermedia, which is widely accepted as the most successful educational hypermedia system to date, was the fact that the distinction between author and reader was removed, so that any user could add information and create links (Yankelovich *et al* 1988). Those people who authored the Intermedia webs were the ones who benefited most. This gives support to those who say that learning technologies should be based on a constructivist approach, rather than the objectivist approach typified by traditional CAL materials (Jonassen 1991). The intention of objectivistic techniques is primarily to convey objective knowledge, whereas constructivists argue that knowledge is neither an exact copy, nor a mirror of reality, but the forms of it are constructed by the person who experiences it (Pieters & de Bruijn 1991).

In this paper we describe an information management system, Microcosm, which has been used in the development of learning materials for a number of different subject areas. We argue that Microcosm provides an environment in which the student is able to engage and interact with the subject material, rather than simply observe the material by browsing, as is the case with many other 'hypertext' systems. Examples of these applications are described, and finally we describe how the basic model can be extended to provide access to distributed resources without bothering the student with the physical locality of the material they are accessing.

MICROCOSM

Microcosm is a hypermedia system which allows users to browse and query large multimedia collections (Davis *et al* 1992). However, Microcosm is fundamentally different from most hypermedia systems because of its ability to integrate information produced using a variety of third-party applications. The system consists of a number of autonomous processes which communicate with each other by a message-passing system. No information about links is held in the document data files in the form of mark-up. Instead, all data files remain in the native format of the application that created them. All link information is held in link databases (linkbases), that hold details of the source anchor (if there is one), the destination anchor and any other attributes such as the link description. This model has the advantage that it is possible to have different sets of links for the same data, and also it is possible to make link anchors in documents that are held on read only media such as CD-ROM and videodisc.

An important feature of Microcosm is the ability to generalise source anchors. A spectrum of link possibilities exists, from explicitly defined anchors to dynamically generated anchors:

Specific Links

The user is able to follow the link only after selecting the anchor at a specific location in the current document. Specific links may be made into buttons.

Local Links

The user is able to follow the link after selecting the given anchor at any point in the current document.

Generic Links

The user is able to follow the link after selecting the given anchor at any point in any document. Generic links are of considerable benefit to the author in that a new document may be created and immediately have access to all the generic links that have previously been defined.

Dynamic Links (e.g. Computed Links)

Not all links need to be created by an author. For example, relationships between pieces of information can be computed, based on statistical analysis of the content (e.g. Computed Links), or related information can be retrieved based on attribute coding of documents.

The ability to make third-party applications 'Microcosm aware' or to use the clipboard to communicate means that Microcosm is more than just another hypermedia system. Instead, it can be seen as a means of integrating the applications which constitute the existing working environment, rather than just adding to the clutter of the desktop.

MICROCOSM AS A COGNITIVE TOOL

The Scholar Project at the University of Southampton is funded by the Teaching and Learning Technology Programme (TLTP). Its aim is to provide a campus wide structure for multimedia learning, and Microcosm is the system chosen to provide that structure. A number of applications currently under development with The Scholar Project make use of Microcosm's various features to provide cognitive tools for learning.

Spanish materials for engineers and scientists transfers a topic box presentation of learning resources onto the computer desktop. Learners are able to access authentic texts which have been scanned into the system at the same time as exploring the corresponding text transcripts. Learners are able to select any text which they wish to examine and from there to Follow, Show or Compute Links in order to discover relationships with other documents in the application. The requirement for the student to make a selection and then to choose an action to perform on that selection means that the interaction with the system is an active one, with the student having to think and make decisions about the direction of the exploration all the time, rather than simply clicking on buttons and following pre-authored links in a passive way.

The Department of Human Morphology is producing a number of applications on the joints of the human body—so far applications covering the shoulder and wrist have been completed, but others are under development. Each application comprises a number of text documents, anatomical diagrams and video sequences which illustrate the movements of the joints. Linking all this material together is a single linkbase containing a variety of specific, local and generic links between the information resources.

A general resource which is applicable to all of the Human Morphology applications is a glossary of anatomical terms. Associated with this glossary is a linkbase containing a generic link for each glossary entry. This glossary and its asociated linkbase is made availbale to users of all the applications, and demonstrates well the principles of the resource-based approach to the production of learning materials.

Another important feature of the Human Morphology applications is the Multiple Choice Question (MCQ) shell which has been produced using Toolbook. In isolation MCQs have limited potential as an educational tool. However, in this case the student has the ability to select any part of the question or any of the answers and interrogate the resource-base by following or computing links. This provides access to potentially explanatory material, and because this access is via generic links, this explanatory material is available to the student at no extra cost to the author. In addition, for each answer to the MCQs, the author is able to specify a short response. The student has the option to "Explain..." each of the responses.

When this is done, the MCQ shell sends a Show Links message to Microcosm, which retrieves any generic links in the linkbase based on words and phrases in the response.

Another application developed for Engineering students has been designed to to replace a laboratory class on Phase Diagrams. In this case the design team wanted to present the information in a more controlled manner than was the case with the Human Morphology applications for example, where each piece of information is presented initially in a new window. Here, parts of the content are inherently sequential—the material explains how to construct and interpret a Phase Diagram—and as a result Toolbook was selected as the primary delivery tool.

However, a glossary has been developed, and students have access to all the terms in the glossary via a set of Microcosm generic links. Microcosm is heavily used to manage the resources used 'behind the scenes'. None of the graphical resources are stored internally in the Toolbook books, as this would make them inaccessible in any other context. Instead, the images are imported into the books dynamically, so that the Toolbook books act essentially as document viewers rather than documents themselves. Again, this approach means that resources are available to other authors, or to the same author in different contexts, thereby reducing the authoring effort over time.

Another application which demonstrates the advantages of separating structure (i.e. hypertext links) from content (individual information resources) is Cell Motility, which has been used in various stages of development in the Department of Biology at the University of Southampton for a number of years. Although it has not been developed under the Scholar Project, it nevertheless typifies the resource-based approach which the Scholar Project is trying to foster. This application has two different linkbases available to the students. The first contains primarily specific links, many of which are buttons. Each document has on average two or three links, thus providing flexible but still reasonably well structured access to all of the most important information resources.

The second linkbase contains entirely generic links. This important distinction means that the student receives no visual clues as to the presence of link anchors, imposing a very different feel on the same information. In the former case, the presence of the buttons tells the student "there is more information on subject X", whereas in the latter case, as is also the case with the Spanish for Engineers and Scientists material, the onus is on the student to interrogate the system: "What information do you have on subject X?".

EXTENDING THE RESOURCE-BASE TO GLOBALLY DISTRIBUTED INFORMATION

As was described above, Microcosm has been implemented as a set of autonomous interacting processes (viewers and filters), each of which performs a specific task. Messages generated by Microcosm are passed along a chain of filters and each examines the message and determines whether it should perform any actions based upon this message, or alternatively ignore the message entirely and pass it to the next process in the chain. The extension of this model to provide access to distributed resources therefore simply involves the inclusion of a filter which understands Follow Link messages and is also capable of comunicating with services such as Wide Area Information Servers (WAIS) and World Wide Web (WWW) (Hollom and Hall 1993). Microcosm builds a message which incorporates the selection, for example a text string, and the action Follow Link. In the case of WWW, the extra filter looks this string up in a table similar to a linkbase and retrieves a Universal Resource Locator (URL) associated with that string, which can then be used to retrieve the appropriate HTML document.

Because access to distributed information is provided in exactly the same way as locally stored information, the student does not need to worry about where that information is physically located, and can instead concentrate on analysing the data when it is presented, rather than worrying about whether to use http or FTP, Mosaic or Gopher.

CONCLUSIONS

In the future, the working environment of the undergraduate student will become more and more computer-based, as the availability of word processors, spreadsheets, and data analysis tools, such as statistics packages, increases. The most effective systems will be those which enhance the existing working environment, rather than trying to hide, isolate or simplify it. The ability to integrate the students own work and ideas into the corpus of materials available will be essential if learners are to be able to carry out constructional activities as described above. In addition, those directing the learning of others will require an environment which enables existing resources to be integrated with new material, tailored to suit a variety of different users with different aims, goals, or background knowledge.

Microcosm is an example of such a system. In one sense, its strongest feature is simply the fact that it provides a link service for any MS-Windows program. The fact that these links are kept totally separate from the information itself means that the same content can be presented with different link sets for different groups of users, thus reducing the burden of creating and updating materials. Using Microcosm, traditional techniques such as question and answer sessions and guided tutorials can be combined with other materials such as research papers, bibliographic databases and access to bulletin board services to provide a heterogeneous information environment with which the learner can engage and which can become an integral part of the overall learning environment.

This distinction between the information environment and the learning environment is an important one, as it marks a departure from traditional thinking, in which the computer was the learning environment. Instead, Microcosm can be thought of as providing computer supported learning rather than computer based or computer assisted learning. As Hammond (1993) states, learning is not the same as information retrieval. Learning is the result of a subtle interaction of the learning environment, the materials and tools, and of course, the learner.

What the computer can do is provide easier and perhaps better access to the resources and information required for learning to occur, whether this access is in the form of Wide Area Information Server queries or simply pointers to the appropriate sections of books and journals in the library. However, the decisions about which parts of the information retrieved as a result of this service are important or relevant, and the responsibility for whether any learning occurs or not must ultimately lie with the learner and not the computer system. Support for this comes from Ess (1991) who describes how one student used Intermedia materials to produce a particularly well written essay, stating that it is tempting to understand this event as confirming the success of Intermedia's original design to serve as a supplement to, not replacement for, class lecture, discussion, and reading.

References

Davis H, Hall W, Heath I, Hill G and Wilkins R (1992) Towards an Integrated Information Environment with Open Hypermedia Systems In *ECHT '92: Proceedings of the Fourth ACM Conference on Hypertext* Milan Italy November 30th–December 4th (1992) 181–190

Duchastel PC (1990) Discussion: Formal and Informal Learning with Hypermedia In *Designing Hypermedia for Learning* Jonassen DH and Mandl H Eds Springer Verlag Berlin 135–146

Ess C (1991) The Pedagogy of Computing: Hypermedia in the Classroom In *Hypertext '91: Proceedings of Third ACM Conference on Hypertext* San Antonio, TX December 15–18 (1991) 277–289

Hammond N (1991) Tailoring Hypertext for the Learner In *Cognitive Tools for Learning*

Kommers P A M Jonassen D H and Mayes J T Eds Springer Verlag Berlin 149–160

Hollom RJ and Hall W (1993) Integrating Internet Resource Discovery Services with Open Hypermedia Systems *Department of Electronics & Computer Science,* University of Southampton, U.K. CSTR 93-14

Jonassen DH (1991) Semantic Networking as Cognitive Tools In *Cognitive Tools for Learning* Kommers P A M Jonassen D H and Mayes J T Eds Springer Verlag Berlin 19–21

Mayes JT (1991) Cognitive Tools: A Suitable Case for Learning In *Cognitive Tools for Learning* Kommers P A M Jonassen D H and Mayes J T Eds Springer Verlag Berlin 7–18

Pieters JM and de Bruijn HFM (1991) Learning Environments for Cognitive Apprenticeship: From Experience to Expertise In *Designing Hypermedia for Learning* Jonassen DH and Mandl H Eds Springer Verlag Berlin 241–248

Yankelovich N, Haan BJ, Meyrowitz NK and Drucker SM (1988) Intermedia: The Concept and the Construction of a Seamless Information Environment *IEEE Computer* 21(1) 81–96

26. Hypertext in the Classroom: Changing the Roles of Teacher and Student

David Bateman and Vicki Simpson, *University of Kent, Canterbury*

Summary
Learnfortran is a self-paced hypertext course which teaches the fundamentals of computer programming in the Fortran 77 programming language. The material is authored in Guide and runs under Unix on an X-terminal. We report on the philosophy of learnfortran and of our experiences in using it with a group of first year undergraduates.

INTRODUCTION

We describe a pilot project, undertaken at the University of Kent, which has involved developing a hypertext version of a well-established lecture course from the existing course material. Section 2 outlines the course as it has been traditionally taught and the material which has been developed to support it. In Section 3 we describe the philosophy and structure of the hypertext version of the course. Section 4 explains how we ran both versions of the course with a group of undergraduates and describes the results which we obtained. In Section 5 we present our conclusions and give an indication of the work that is continuing.

THE COURSE - AS IT WAS

Fortran has been taught as a first computer programming language to both Mathematics and Physics students at the University of Kent for many years. The course has generally consisted of 20 lectures + 10 practical classes and is taken by students in the first term of their first year.

Over the years a lot of courseware has been developed to support the course. The courseware is stored as separate computer files, which can be read on-line from a computer terminal or printed out. The files are organised into the following groups

- NOTES ... what is said in each lecture
- DEMOs ... the illustrative example programs used in each lecture
- SAQEXs ... skeleton program specification for each programming exercise
- ANSWERs ... the lecturer's sample solution to each SAQEX

The typical Fortran lecture involves explaining one or two features of the Fortran language, and then illustrating the use of each language feature via an example DEMO program. Students are encouraged to read these 'good' DEMOs in the hope that they will learn to emulate a similarly good programming style. However, programming is a skill that can only be acquired through practice, and for many students, the more programs they can write at a level that matches their knowledge level and programming ability the faster their programming skills will develop. Each SAQEX exercise is designed to test the students' ability to use a particular language feature, as well as to reinforce the knowledge and skills which have so far been acquired. Each SAQEX usually has a DEMO file which can provide the student with a potential source of 'help' with the SAQEX. The primary source of assistance is, however, provided by supervisors at the weekly practical class. Here students can obtain tutorial guidance on SAQEXs they cannot do, and others they cannot get to run correctly on the computer. Students are not expected to attempt all the SAQEXs; some are 'recommended', some are 'optional', others provide additional reinforcement for those students that need it. The SAQEXs are not used for assessment purposes (one assignment is set for this purpose) and students have access to an ANSWER file for each SAQEX which they can read at any time, either to show them how to do the exercise, or to enable them to draw comparisons with their own attempt.

THE PHILOSOPHY AND STRUCTURE OF LEARNFORTRAN

Although the existing courseware was felt to be complete and self-contained (it had not changed for two years), students often failed to make the most effective use of it. This is not surprising. Each document (a NOTES file, a DEMO file etc) is stored as a 'stand-alone' computer file. While documents often contained explicit (and sometimes implicit) textual cross-references to other documents, it was left to the students to find a way of using the two documents together. This typically involved having a hard-copy printout of one document, while reading the other document at a computer terminal.

Hypertext systems offer a mechanism for organising and linking documents in a flexible way. The aim of learnfortran was to provide a working environment for students which was easy to use and would facilitate the use of existing courseware documents together.

The courseware had to run under the unix operating system. This was dictated by the compiler which had to be used for the course. Guide was chosen as the hypertext authoring language because of extensive local knowledge and support. The end product, learnfortran, provides a multiple window environment, the layout of which is shown in Figure 26.1.

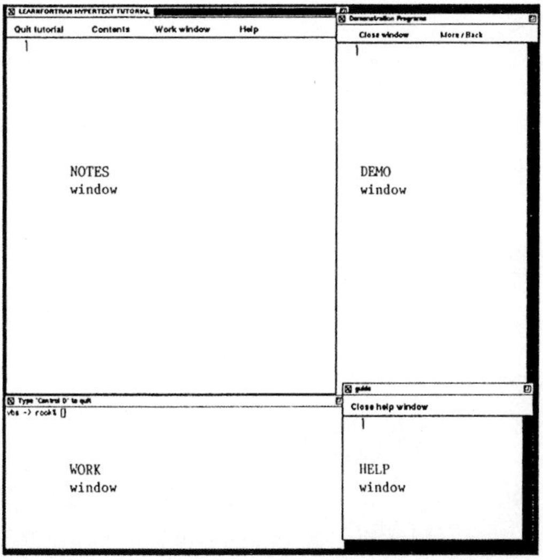

Figure 26.1 :Hypertext in the Classroom: illustrates the overall structure of learnfortran

The NOTES window displays a page of the course lecture notes; these are still divided into separate lectures (or hypertext sessions). A Contents page enables the user to select whichever session he wishes to study, and to move rapidly between sessions. Each session has its own Contents page providing rapid access to a topic of interest. References within the notes to a

DEMO, SAQEX or ANSWER document can be activated to display the selected document in the DEMO window. If the user wishes to run a program or attempt an SAQEXercise the WORK window can be opened and used. This is a conventional unix window. A HELP window can also be opened to remind the student of the commands he may need to use when working in the WORK window. The environment therefore enables the student to carry out his own work while being able to see simultaneously the page of course notes and the demo program that will help him.

It has been noted elsewhere (Stanton and Baber 1992) that "motivation of learners may be impaired if they become overwhelmed by freedom in the learning environment". We have tried to keep the teaching environment simple, and learnfortran merely combines the flexibility of hypertext with the structured approach required to teach a programming language. Figure 26.2 shows the multiple window environment from a typically active learning situation in the course. The student is about to write his own program to the exercise displayed in the WORK window. The page of notes and the demo program which will help him to start the exercise are also open.

Figure 26.2 : Hypertext in the Classroom showing a typical learnfortran screen

TESTING AND EVALUATING LEARNFORTRAN

By the beginning of the academic year 1993/94 learnfortran courseware had been produced for the first half of the Fortran course. Preliminary testing by volunteers had provided encouraging feedback, and suggested that it was ready to use in a teaching situation. The first year Mathematics undergraduates were selected to trial learnfortran on X terminals. Students are normally taught in practical class group sizes of 15-18 students. The 62 students were divided at random into four groups as follows:

Group A   Did not attend lectures. Were allocated THREE timetabled hours of learnfortran classes per week; ONE hour was supervised.

Group B   Attended lectures + a ONE hour supervised learnfortran class per week.

Groups C & D   Attended lectures + a ONE hour supervised terminal class per week. Had no access to learnfortran.

Students in Groups A and B had unrestricted access to learnfortran outside the timetabled hours. Groups C and D also had unrestricted access to computer terminals. 16 students were assigned to Groups A and B; 15 students to each of Groups C and D. Group A was seen as the 'pure' learnfortran group; Group B provided the best education that the course could offer; Groups C and D followed the course in the 'old format' of lectures + practical classes. All groups reverted to this format in the second half of the course.

Students in Groups A and B were required to complete a weekly progress questionnaire about their experiences and progress with learnfortran. Comments were generally extremely favourable. Most students experienced little difficulty in using learnfortran. Most felt they benefitted from the self-paced nature of the course, although two students from Group A did not complete learnfortran before starting the second half of the course. Most of Group A enjoyed taking responsibility for their own learning, and did not feel that they had suffered by not attending lectures. Several students from Group B reported, however, that lectures often contained alternative explanations of difficult concepts which learnfortran did not offer. This problem has been identified by (Mott 1993) when he says that "A great deal of notes on a computer, or anywhere else, is that you cannot ask them questions, and because they are rarely complete or perfect, you need to ask them questions".

We used Guide's automatic transcript facility to record details of every learnfortran session undertaken by students from Groups A and B. The transcript files provide us with a factual record of each learnfortran session, such as the number of times the HELP window is opened, the number of times each hypertext button is selected, and the amount of time spent between opening and closing buttons. This information is currently being analysed in the hope that it will provide us with an insight into any common usage patterns with learnfortran.

One week after the end of the learnfortran course all students were set a short pencil and paper test, the results of which are shown in Table 26.1.

Group	A	B	C	D
Highest Mark	76%	84%	80%	74%
Lowest Mark	28%	24%	34%	34%
Mean Mark	52%	64%	56%	58%

Table 26.1

The results at least suggest that the students from Group A, who attended learnfortran only, had not been severely disadvantaged. However, it would be dangerous to read too much into the results of this test.

CONCLUSIONS AND CONTINUING WORK

It was felt that learnfortran achieved its very limited objective of offering 'value added' education through better organisation, structure and linking of existing courseware. Students were better able to manage their own learning and could resolve many of their own problems by referring back to an earlier session or to a previous example program. The teacher in turn also found it easier to monitor each student's progress, and was therefore able to offer more focussed and individual assistance where it was needed.

While learnfortran may replace the lecturer, it does not replace the teacher. Learnfortran falls short of offering a total learning environment for students. Our experiment identified a number of places in the courseware where students could not begin a programming exercise. This is where the skilled teacher provides the right level and degree of tutorial help for the student. It is believed that much of the help and guidance required by the student already exists within the original courseware, but has not as yet been integrated into learnfortran. Work is in hand to improve the guidanceavailable to the learnfortran student by adding extra teaching functionality.

Learnfortran is not viewed as an environment that will totally replace the teacher. However, it may not be necessary for the teacher to be in the classroom providing the tutorial support. A lot of tutorial assistance is now provided via electronic mail. It is planned to add a 'mail' menu option to learnfortran so that the student can obtain classroom level tutorial support from a remote tutor.

The current version of learnfortran is closely coupled to the teaching environment at Kent. We are planning to produce a learnfortran shell which can be customised for use at other institutions using different hardware and a different compiler to those we use at Kent.

ACKNOWLEDGEMENT

We are particularly grateful to Wilma Strang for her constant encouragement, enthusiasm and support for learnfortran, and to Martin Broom and the first year Mathematics students who have tested it and and provided invaluable feedback.

References

Mott P (1993)   Principles and Architecture for a Course-Processor, *International Journal of Computers in Adult Education and Training,* Vol 3, No 3.

Stanton N and Baber C (1992)   An investigation of Styles and Strategies in Self-Directed Learning, *Journal of   Educational Multimedia and Hypermedia,* Vol 1, No 2.

27. Theoretical Aspects of Representation in Hypermedia Learning Environments

Alan P. Parkes, *Computing Department, Lancaster University*

Summary

The purpose of this paper is to promote discussion of theoretical and methodological issues that are central to representations in hypermedia learning environments. Cunningham, Duffy and Knuth (1993) define *hypermedia* as consisting of nodes of information connected by machine supported links. We call a system hyper*text* if the nodes of information are primarily textual, and hyper*media* if the nodes can consist of information in different media (text, graphics, images, sound, and so on). For us, however, one defining characteristic of a "hyper" system is that in order to follow the links in the material, the user specifies operations by interacting directly with features of the external representation of the nodes of information (for example, pointing the mouse at part of a picture and "clicking" to retrieve information related to that part).

This paper exploits theoretical aspects of research in *representation, learning,* and *human-computer interaction* (HCI) in the quest for tools to support the design, analysis and evaluation of hypermedia learning environments. Our interest is mainly in the teaching of the more mathematical aspects of computer science (specifically formal language and automata theory), though our analysis has wider application than this. We have been investigating the representation of reasoning in formal domains by simple and familiar direct manipulation operations and procedures (such as "cutting" and "pasting") on predominantly graphical procedures. In particular, the paper focuses on two concepts that describe the transfer of interface activities from a familiar system to a new domain: *operational* and *procedural correspondence.*

DOES RESEARCH IN HYPERMEDIA ADDRESS LEARNERS' REAL PROBLEMS?

Hypermedia was initially conceived as a tool for information retrieval (IR), but attention has increasingly focussed on its potential as a learning environment. One initial selling point of hypermedia was the greater freedom to explore, or to *browse,* enjoyed by its users than that provided by traditional IR systems. Researchers are now considering whether or not the same degree of freedom, leading to what Mülhäuser (1992) calls "anarchistic" computer-based learning (CBL) systems, is desirable in a learning environment. Whalley (1993) suggests that basic hypermedia presents a *fragmentation* of the domain knowledge, and the lack of an explicitly authored linear structure may result in learners being unable to appreciate the intended structure of the author's argument. Researchers such as Hammond (1991, 1992) are concerned with investigating additions to basic hypermedia that will support its use in learning environments. One approach is to impose structure by building "maps" or "guided tours" into the system. The former approach is criticised by Laurel *et al.* (1992), as they point out that a map is essentially a new interface that the user has to learn to use, while Stanton *et al.* (1992) suggest that providing maps may interfere with the processes whereby users derive a *cognitive map* for themselves. Laurel *et al.* go on to describe a hypermedia database of American history, in which guided tours are given by iconised talking period characters (e.g. an American Indian Chief).

One problem with the above approaches is that they are aimed at overcoming problems of the use of hypermedia *per se* rather than directed at the problems encountered by learners in specific domains. In other words, the problems are caused more by the *representation* than by the domain. We have been investigating the use of different representations to promote undergraduate learning in formal language and automata theory, specifically directing our efforts to determining the problems learners have in this domain. It turns out that many of the problems are specifically related to the type of representation being used at a particular time, or rather, the problems are sometimes of a general nature, but manifest themselves in different ways that are sensitive to the representation being used. It is our experience that domains such as formal computer science are considered "hard" by students because of the types of representation that are used in the teaching of those domains.

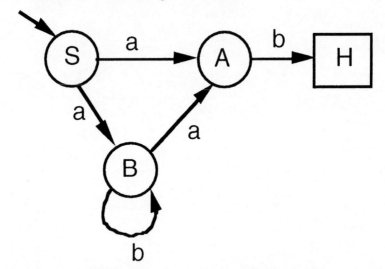

Table 27.1: "Easy" vs. "Hard" concepts (adapted from Smith et al., 1982)

In discussing the perceived "hardness" of mathematical subjects, it is interesting to use as a tool an analysis reported by Smith *et al.* (1982). The analysis in question is the production of a table representing concepts (actually relating to *interfaces*) that users find *easy* alongside antonymous concepts that users find *hard* (see Table 27.1 for some of these concepts). The Xerox Star interface, the subject of the Smith *et al.* paper, and a major influence on subsequent successful designs such as the Apple Macintosh user interface, was designed to reflect the "easy" concepts identified in the analysis. The analysis is of interest to us because on first sight it would appear that theoretical computer science is difficult for students precisely because, as usually taught, it is described by all of the concepts in the *hard* column. However, rather than the subject itself, it is the *representations* that are usually used in the teaching of computer science (the obscure and archaic notation, for example) that embody the concepts described in the *hard* column. As an example of this compare Figure 27.1, a pictorial representation of a string processing finite state machine, with Table27.2, a tabular representation of the same machine. The representation in Figure 27.1 is *concrete*, and contains *visible* links between states (links that have to be *generated* by the viewer by mentally linking repeated labels in the Table 27.2 version). To really appreciate the power of the diagram, however, one has simply to see which representation provides the most suitable tool for determining the truth of statements such as:

- "it is possible to reach the halt state from the start state"
- "the machine contains a loop"
- "all acceptable strings start with an **a** and end in a **b**"
- "the shortest string accepted by the machine is **ab**".

easy	*hard*
concrete	abstract
visible	invisible
copying	creating
choosing	filling in
recognising	generating
editing	programming

Figure 27.1: A finite state machine equivalent to the representation in Table 27.2

			State		
		S	A	B	H
Symbol	a	A, B	-	A	-
	b	-	H	B	-

Table 27.2: A tabular representation of the machine depicted in Figure 1.

It is also clear, therefore, that the usefulness of a particular representation depends on the tasks being carried out, or the questions that the user is required to answer with, or from, that representation. This is very important for the interface of CBL systems in general, and particularly for hypermedia learning environments, where many representations may be used. In the remainder of this paper, we focus in detail on the hypermedia representation issues arising from a viewpoint that sees the problem domain as a hypermedia state space, and the implications of this viewpoint for the analysis of users' specific activities and inferences in such state spaces. Our analysis will occasionally refer to the analysis of "easy" and "hard" concepts summarised in Table 27.1.

OPERATIONAL AND PROCEDURAL CORRESPONDENCE

In other papers (Parkes, 1992; Parkes, 1994), we discuss the different dimensions of representation introduced by Larkin and Simon (1987). Following Larkin and Simon, we can compare the *informational* aspects of different representations. The representations in Figure 27.1 and Table 27.2 are, in Larkin and Simon's terms *informationally equivalent*. However, we can also compare the *computational*, or information *processing* aspects of different representations. In these terms, our two example representations are radically different, in that the computational cost of answering our questions was much lower in the case of the picture than for the tabular representation.

Our previous work has focussed on the *inference* component of the computational dimension, while current research is examining design choices of representation and interaction styles for hypermedia (Parkes, 1994a). Here, we devote more attention to details of the *search* component. There is nothing new about using the notion of state space representations, as originally defined by Newell and Simon (1972), as a metaphor for user activity in a hypermedia system. Zellweger (1992) refers to the user as a "computational engine" [p40] that determines the sequence of nodes visited (i.e. a search procedure), while Thimbleby (1992) sees the user as engaged in the "...graph theoretic problem of traversal, search or optimisation" [p163]. Parkes (1991), discussing hypermedia information retrieval systems, distinguishes between hypermedia search spaces that are *serialised* (i.e. the traversal of the search space is represented by successive displays over time), and those that are *wholistic* (where single displays represent major parts of the search space). All of these approaches take a *global* view of the "hypermedia representation as search space" metaphor. We wish now to turn our attention to matters at a more local level.

In the classical view of problem solving, traversal of a state space (i.e. the transition between states) is performed by applying *operators* to one state and transforming that state into a successor state. Our introductory description of the process of following the links in hypermedia may have suggested that the operators in hypermedia are essentially simple, involving the clicking of an object. This suggestion is misleading, as in hypermedia for *learning* we may require operators to have a much greater cognitive significance than the indication of a straightforward relationship between two items of information. By way of a non-hypermedia illustration, consider a "store block" operator in a word processor. This operator is usually simple to carry out: we select, say, "Copy" from a menu when a block has been highlighted. The cognitive aspects of the operation are more complex, however, involving the user in conceptualising some kind of semi-permanent store that holds the text for a period of time.

We have been investigating the use of hypermedia links to support reasoning in theorem proving tasks in formal computer science. The motivation behind this is to represent reasoning in formal computer science so that it appears to the user to conform to the *easy* concepts in Table 27.1. For example, we wish to make proving an *editing*, rather than a *programming* exercise. Users' *physical* activities in our interfaces are restricted to the selection operator (pointing at an object or a menu item and clicking). However, the successive states in our interfaces represent steps in a proof, i.e. *reasoning* steps. For related approaches, albeit in different domains, Hammond (1991; 1992) and Thomas and Mital (1992) describe hypermedia systems where the links represent the relationships between steps in an argument.

An interesting issue is the extent to which we can represent complex reasoning processes by the use of operations that are familiar to our users by virtue of being found in other systems which they frequently use. To put it another way, we seek out *operational correspondence* between parts of systems, i.e. we adapt the description of formal reasoning so that it can be represented in terms of operations that are grounded in familiar systems. An example of operational correspondence can be found in one of our studies, where the steps of the proof were modelled by "cut and paste" operations on a graphical representation. Figure 27.2 shows an operationally corresponding point in a word processor and one of our interfaces. Following Payne's (1988) distinction between operational and *figurative* (i.e. semantic) dimensions of interface activities, we can also identify certain instances of *figurative* correspondence between operations. An example of this is the use of a "store" to hold the most recently cut part of the diagram, as demonstrated by Figure 27.3, which shows the state of both systems immediately after the corresponding operations in Figure 27.2 have been carried out.

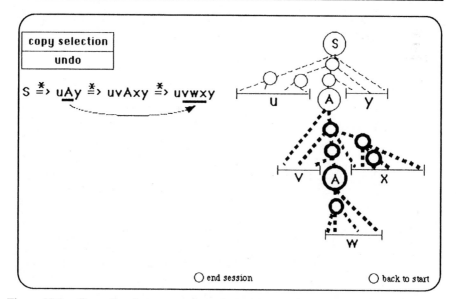

Figure 27.2: **Operational correspondence between a word processor (top), and our interface (bottom)**

seek out *operational correspondence* between parts of

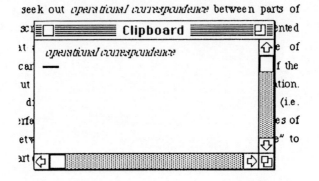

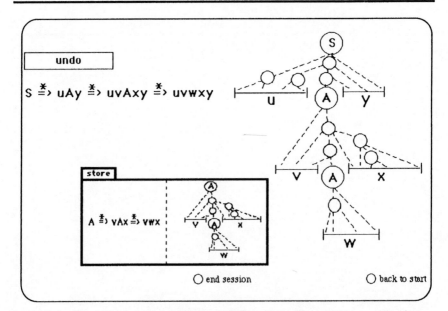

Figure 27.3: Figurative correspondence: the effect of the Figure 27.2 operation in a word processor (top) and our interface (bottom)

An influential view of user activities from the HCI literature (e.g. Card Moran and Newell, 1983), is that operators are not considered in isolation, but are combined by the user into meaningful chunks called *methods*, these being essentially *procedures* (which is what we will call them) devoted to the accomplishment of some task. For example, the "store block" operator in our word processor would be a component of a procedure to copy a block of text to another location in a document (e.g. mark block, store block, go to new location, insert block). In our interface described above, there is *procedural correspondence* (the method being select sub-diagram, store sub-diagram, select new location, insert sub-diagram - see Parkes, 1994b, for more details of the interface).

DISCUSSION

Despite our careful design of the operational and procedural correspondence between familiar systems and our interfaces, only a very small part of the semantics of an operator or procedure in the new system is explained by the user's knowledge of that operator or procedure in the familiar system. The reason for this is that the semantics in the new system are much richer. Consider, for example, the correspondence between a typical use of the "insert" operator (as in the method for copying the block of text) and the use of the same operator in the formal language interface. In the formal language interface the insertion (of the *sub-diagram*) into the existing picture has a meaning in terms of formal languages along the lines of "perform an alternative derivation from the lower A".

One problem is that there is a limit to how much a complex domain can be simplified. Put in terms of our "easy-hard" analysis, at some point the learner will be required to *create* or *generate* an explanation of the richer semantics of familiar procedures as applied in the new domain. Failure to do this will mean an inability to transfer any knowledge gained to new problems, or even an inability to apply the acquired knowledge in any situation that does not have the support of the interface in which it was acquired (c.f. Ohlsson, 1988). This may be a problem that increasingly arises with the novel representations facilitated by hypermedia and multimedia, examples being Holland's Harmony space system (Holland, 1992; Parkes, 1992, contains a related discussion of this system), and the system described by Blattner *et al.* (1992), that uses abstract sounds to represent turbulence in fluid flow, to support the learning of fluid dynamics by Physics students.

We propose the concepts of operational and procedural correspondence as useful tools for designing, analysing, and predicting the simplicity and learnability of the hypermedia interface. Designing representations for learning is concerned not only with the diagrams, or the text, or the sound, but also with the operations and procedures that learners apply to those representations. As Larkin and Simon (1987) say, a representation is a data structure along with *programs* that operate on that data structure. Our notion of correspondence provides a framework for the designer to seek out familiar procedures that can be used to represent more complex processes in a novel domain. Such an approach may be a useful tool to help in the design of future systems in which any problems encountered by the learner have their source in the domain, and not in its external representation.

References

Blattner M.M., Greenberg R.M., and Kamegi M. (1992) Listening to turbulence: an example of scientific audiolization. In M. Blattner & R. Dannenberg (eds.), *Interactive Multimedia Computing*. Reading, MA: Addison-Wesley.

Card S.K., Moran T.P., and Newell A. (1983) *The Psychology of Human-Computer Interaction*. Hillsdale, NJ: Lawrence Erlbaum.

Cunningham D.J., Duffy T.M., and Knuth R.A. (1993) The Textbook of the Future. In C. McKnight, A. Dillon and J. Richardson (Eds.), *Hypertext: A Psychological Perspective*. Chichester: Ellis Horwood.

Hammond N. (1991) Teaching with Hypermedia: Problems and Prospects. In H. Brown (Ed.) *Hypermedia/Hypertext and Object-oriented Databases*. London: Chapman and Hall.

Hammond N. (1992) Tailoring Hypertext for the Learner. In A.M. Kommers, D.H. Jonassen, and J.T. Mayes (Eds.) *Cognitive Tools For Learning*. Heidelberg: Springer-Verlag.

Holland, S. (1992). Interface design for empowerment: a case study from music. In M. Blattner and R. Dannenberg (eds.), *Interactive Multimedia Computing*. Reading, MA: Addison-Wesley.

Larkin J.H. and Simon H.A. (1987) Why a diagram is (sometimes) worth ten thousand words. *Cognitive Science*, 11, 65-99.

Laurel B., Oren T., and Don A. (1992) Issues in multimedia interface design: media integration and interface agents. In M. Blattner and R. Dannenberg (Eds.), *Interactive Multimedia Computing*. Reading, MA: Addison-Wesley.

Mühlhäuser M. (1992) Hypermedia and Navigation as a Basis for Authoring/Learning Environments. *Journal of Educational Multimedia and Hypermedia*, 1 (1), 51-64.

Newell A. and Simon H.A. (1972) *Human Problem Solving*. Englewood Cliffs, NJ: Prentice-Hall.

Ohlsson, S. (1988) Sense and reference in the design of interactive illustrations for rational numbers. *Artificial Intelligence and Education, Volume One: Learning Environments and Tutoring Systems*. Norwood, NJ: Ablex.

Parkes A.P. (1991) Manipulable Inter-Medium Encodings for Information Retrieval. *Proceedings of RIAO '91, Intelligent Text and Image Handling* (pp 300-319). Barcelona, Spain, April 2-5.

Parkes A.P. (1992) The inferential appropriateness of a manipulable inter-medium encoding. In M. Blattner and R. Dannenberg (Eds.), *Interactive Multimedia Computing*. Reading, MA: Addison-Wesley.

Parkes A.P. (1994a) Hypermedia representations for learning: formal and informal observations on designs and directions. To appear in ED-MEDIA '94: World Conference on Educational Multimedia and Hypermedia. Vancouver, Canada, June 25-29, 1994

Parkes A.P. (1994b) A study of problem solving activities in a hypermedia representation. To appear in *Journal of Educational Multimedia and Hypermedia*.

Payne S.J. (1988) Methods and mental models in theories of cognitive skill. In J.A. Self (Ed.), *Artificial Intelligence and Human Learning: Intelligent Computer-Aided Instruction.* London: Chapman and Hall.

Smith D.C., Irby C., Kimball R., Verplank B., and Harslem E. (1982) Designing the Star user interface. *Byte*, 7 (4), 242-282

Stanton N.A., Taylor R.G., and Tweedie L.A. (1992) Maps as Navigational Aids in Hypertext Environments: An Empirical Evaluation. *Journal of Educational Multimedia and Hypermedia*, 1 (4), 431-444.

Thimbleby H. (1992) Heuristics for Cognitive Tools. In P.A.M. Kommers, D.H. Jonassen, and J.T. Mayes (Eds.) *Cognitive Tools For Learning*, Heidelberg: Springer-Verlag.

Thomas P. and Mital V. (1992) Hypertext Document Retrieval and Assembly in Legal Domains. In A. Monk, D. Diaper and M.D. Harrison (Eds.), People and Computers VII, Cambridge: Cambridge University Press.

Whalley P. (1993) An Alternative Rhetoric for Hypertext. In C. McKnight, A. Dillon and J. Richardson (Eds.), *Hypertext: A Psychological Perspective*. Chichester: Ellis Horwood.

Zellweger P.T. (1992) Toward a Model for Active Multimedia Documents. In M. Blattner and R. Dannenberg (eds), *Interactive Multimedia Computing*. Reading, MA: Addison-Wesley.

28. Case Study: The Development of an Interactive Multimedia Application to Support Open Learning Engineering Students

S MacDonald and S Cairncross, *Napier University*

Summary
With the increased trend towards open access and flexible learning to satisfy the needs of students undertaking courses in a part-time mode, additional support is required for engineering students with course syllabus requirements for Laboratory work. The advent of low cost and high performance multimedia technology has made the development of course specific CAL packages feasible. Multimedia technology has been described as a "technology in search of an application". We have attempted to apply multimedia technology to the provision of support for engineering students undertaking unsupervised Laboratory practical work.

INTRODUCTION

Engineering subjects are heavily dependent on laboratory work during which the students have an opportunity to apply the theory introduced in lecture and study material. The open learning study model offers significant advantages to part-time students who have a wide range of home and work commitments. In order to resolve the need for study time scale flexibility with the requirement for engineering theory application it becomes necessary to introduce an element of unsupervised laboratory work into the timetable. Laboratories supporting a range of engineering courses offered by Department of Mechanical, Manufacturing and Software Engineering of Napier University are equipped with computing facilities which interface to a manufacturing environment. The development of a range of flexible learning delivery modules which utilise the facilities of the MMSE Control Laboratory (hereafter referred to as "the Lab") has necessitated the development of material to remotely introduce the students to the facilities of the Lab.

A staged evolutionary model for the development of the material was devised. A video was developed describing the facilities of the Lab which has equipment to support Computer Sensor and Control Engineering courses. The videotape delivery medium was selected as the most accessible format. Copies of the video were made available to students to enable them to familiarise themselves with the Laboratory equipment prior to exposure to the hardware. The video was supported by an accompanying worksheet describing the operational details. Due to the large range of facilities in the Lab and the inflexible and sequential nature of video presentation, the second stage of the development was identified and an interactive multimedia package produced.

The video was digitised and incorporated into the interactive multimedia package enabling the student to navigate and browse the information. In addition, the multimedia package was further extended to provide on-line tutorials covering background theory. This sequence in summarised in Figure 28.1. The following paper describes the background to the development of the video and interactive multimedia package, the production process and gives an account of the subsequent assessment of the package.

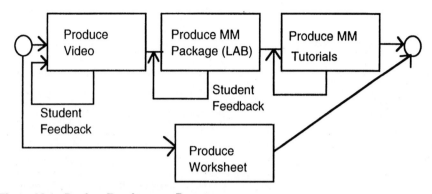

Figure 28.1 : Product Development Process

RATIONALE

Multimedia systems are systems which integrate a set of different types of information media, including both static media (text, graphics, images) and dynamic media (sound, video and animation) into a single co-ordinated output of training, education and presentation material.

Multimedia is not a new technology, rather it is the integration of the existing technologies of audio, video, animation and telecommunications with traditional computing. Advances in these different technologies (compression techniques for audio and video, high resolution graphics displays, graphics oriented user interfaces, CD-ROM applications, programming interfaces, authoring languages) have enabled this integration to take place.

Multimedia can be used to improve communications in a number of different areas. Of interest to the authors is the application of multimedia to the development of Computer Assisted Learning Materials. CAL has long been used in higher and further education and a wide range of packages can be bought off the shelf. Increasingly these packages incorporate an element of multimedia. Such packages, although useful, are by their very nature general and often do not meet all the needs of a specific course. In particular they cannot be used to provide instruction to students about laboratories, equipment and experiments specific to a particular course. However, as the cost of computing hardware has fallen and as the availability of powerful authoring packages has risen it has become feasible for individual departments, both in terms of money and time, to develop tailor- made packages. It was decided to develop such a package using Authorware Professional to introduce students to the Lab and to provide them with the necessary background material to complete the experiments.

The interactivity offered by a package such as Authorware Professional offers many advantages. Teaching materials can be prepared so as to allow individual students varying degrees of navigational freedom through the finished application. Although advice is given as to the preferred initial route to follow, students can decide which sections they wish to view and in what order. Students can control their own pace as the travel through the package, concentrating on material they are unfamiliar with and skipping over material they already know. Students can also repeat or review sections as needed, for example going over some basic theory in preparation for an assignment. The non-sequential nature of multimedia can also allow interested students to pursue areas of interest in greater depth. Empowering students, so as to give them greater control in a structured manner over their own learning, can only enhance that learning experience and make it more meaningful.

Students can also interact with the package in other ways. Provision can be made for on-line testing with instant feedback given to the students. A multiple choice quiz could be offered at the end of a section, scored instantly and the student given their mark. If need be, feedback can be given to areas which the student has not grasped. The student can be given the correct answer and be advised to repeat that section or review others. The results of these tests can be stored to file and be accessed at a later stage by the students themselves and staff, thus allowing progress to be monitored.

Students can also be asked to click on objects to reveal the outcome of some action, for example, the flicking of a switch. Such active involvement in the learning process will improve retention rates. Retention rates can be improved in other ways as a result of employing multimedia. Mastery is generally improved when more senses are engaged in the learning process. Multimedia enables us to do this. Students can read text and look at pictures, while moving images can be incorporated into the package to illustrate processes. This is particularly useful in engineering; for example, demonstrations of equipment use can be filmed and digitised providing a much more useful explanation as to how to proceed with an experiment than a text based set of instructions can offer. This is of major benefit when providing open learning material for unsupervised laboratories. Audio reinforcement can also be given, for example verbal encouragement when a student gets a question wrong.

REQUIREMENTS ANALYSIS

Each year, up to 170 students undertake an element of unsupervised work in the Lab. The students range from those enrolled on a variety of Departmental undergraduate courses to students on Degree courses offered by other University Departments who elect to study a computer sensing module. The only pre-requisite is some knowledge of a high-level programming language. The flexible learning delivery mode means that students with very diverse academic backgrounds can proceed at different rates. In addition, the students will require different levels of support. While the video offers a basic introduction to the Lab, by using the package the student can select key topics of interest or browse to gain an overall understanding of the use and background theory.

PLATFORMS AND ACCESS

The widespread availability of video players was a major factor in the initial delivery medium identified. The video format enables students to maximise the effectiveness of their on-campus time, by having prior exposure to the Lab layout and facilities. The students can access the video through the campus library's Open Learning Centre or through the Departmental booking system. In each case the video can be booked out or viewed on-location.

The multimedia package offers capabilities beyond the straightforward information presented by the video. Information, test and feedback sections were identified to allow the users to discover the theory behind the Lab Exercise work. The multimedia package is installed on a network of dedicated multimedia computers located in the Computer Assisted Learning Lab. This Lab is a departmental resource and students have open access.

The feasibility of a University wide CD production facility is currently being investigated. If this is not established in the near future a servicing company will be used to produce a CD-ROM from the hard disk version of the package. The CD-ROM will be available in both PC and Apple Macintosh formats. Student access to the CD-ROM Disks would be the same as for the video.

In each case there are no facilities for on-line access to the multimedia package in the Lab. The Lab PCs will host a reduced version of the multimedia package. Since the students would be running this package from their workbench in the Lab the level of information required would be of a more specific and navigable nature.

PRODUCT DEVELOPMENT

While making use of existing materials is an efficient means of interactive multimedia production (Kommers 1993) this can be extended beyond published materials to encompass all multimedia development resources. In the case of the development of this package, valuable resources included students enrolled on the Department's Multimedia Technology MSc / PG Dip course. These students have an element of group video production work built into the course. One of these groups developed the original video. This meant that the cost to the Department was minimal and that the students had the satisfaction of producing a meaningful piece of work. The video production process is detailed in Figure 28.2. The Edit Suite is a centralised resource supported by the Educational Development Unit (EDU).

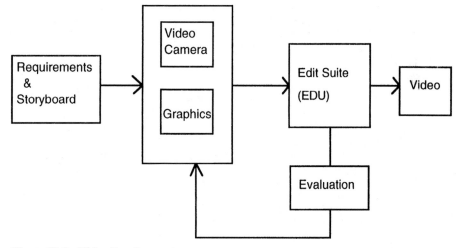

Figure 28.2 : Video Development

A written worksheet, based on supervised Lab course material, was developed to complement the video.

The package operational information and structure was based on the video and its original storyboard. The same worksheet was used to complement the informational content of the package. Additional worksheets were developed to provide written material to reinforce the theory and tutorials introduced in the package. The development process of the multimedia package is described in Figure 28.3.

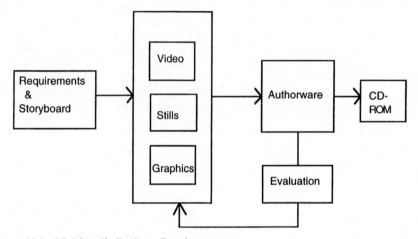

Figure 28.3 : Multimedia Package Development

In contrast with the development of the video, the development of the multimedia package reflects the trends towards production decentralisation. The development of multimedia applications has become the domain of the creative designer. Powerful development software tools are enabling the process to complete without the need for specialist technician support, or the utilisation of expensive centralised equipment.

RESOURCE AND COST BREAKDOWN

The following table gives a breakdown of the costs involved in the production of all the materials developed during the project. The costs are based on hourly rates as follows:

    Technician Support Hourly Rate   £20
    Teaching Staff Hourly Rate   £40
Student hours are displayed but not costed.

	Hours Student	Hours Technician	Hours Teaching	Materials £	Costs £
Video	60	4	2	10	170
MM Package	0	40	4	-	960
Worksheet	0	0	4	-	160
				Total Costs	1290

Table 28.1 : Resource and Cost Breakdown

PRODUCT EVALUATION

The overall evaluation model was selected to confirm that the aims and objectives of the presentation had been met:

• introduce students to the facilities of the Lab
• instruct students on the initialisation and use of the Control Panel - Switches and A/D Converters
• provide location, time tabling and safety information

These overall objectives were subsequently used as a baseline for the development of a questionnaire which was tailored to suit the video and multimedia package respectively.
    In addition to an evaluation of the video objectives, further information was required of the student's response to the additional objectives of the package:

• provide a navigable structure
• provide theory sections containing both background information and test / feedback sessions

The questionnaires were based on the Waterworth Usability Assessment (Waterworth, 1993). A group of students were identified as a representative sample for the video evaluation. The results of the questionnaire on the cross-section are detailed in Table 28.2. The columns run from very satisfied at point 5 on the scale to not satisfied at point 1, and values are given as a percentage of the cross-section.

Question	5	4	3	2	1
Level of interest	2.15	62.37	9.68	15.05	10.75
Order of information	17.07	70.73	12.20	0.00	0.00
Quantity of information	10.06	56.80	12.43	20.12	0.59
How helpful is information?	5.03	50.20	25.14	16.76	2.79
Written information easy to follow?	10.00	71.25	12.50	6.25	0.00
Was information reliable?	17.75	29.59	27.81	20.71	4.14
Appropriate to course?	34.15	65.24	0.61	0.00	0.00
Was information complete?	5.56	47.78	18.89	17.78	10.00

Table 28.2 : Student Product Evaluation

The majority of students felt that the video was of interest and very appropriate for their course. The overall satisfaction rating is shown in Figure 28.4a. The confidence the students had in the material presented shows a different spread (Figure 28.4b). Extending the multimedia package beyond the scope of the video material, and in particular the addition of background theory and tutorial sessions, attempted to address this issue. The package background theory sections were designed to be used by students to gain an awareness of the underlying concepts and thus to increase the levels of confidence in the material prior to working in the Lab.

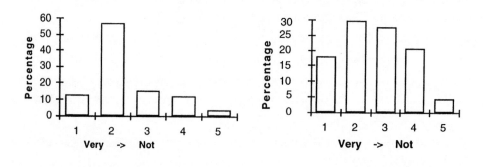

4a) Overall Satisfaction   **4b) Confidence**

Figure 4 : Student Product Evaluation

A large proportion of students were not convinced that the information would be of much help during their tutorials. This may have been due to the uncertainty of what their specific course would be covering during the tutorial sessions. To improve the student's levels of confidence the package was designed to offer "virtual lab" facilities where the student could discover exactly what was expected of them during the tutorial sessions.

Early results of the evaluation of the multimedia package indicate that the issues associated with the limitations of the video have been addressed with some success.

CONCLUSION

Interactive multimedia computer assisted learning has an important role to play in the provision of open learning materials. In general, mastery and retention rates improve when interactive multimedia is used as more senses are involved in the learning process and the process becomes more active with the learner in control. While this has long been recognised, it is only with the advent of recent technological change that its widespread provision on an individual and tailor-made basis has become possible.

There is some concern over the expense involved in developing special-purpose CAL packages (Kochar 1985), however, this case study is an example of an application which has led to the development of an economically-viable CAL package which serves the needs of a very restricted audience.

Acknowledgements

The authors would like to thank Shu-Chen Cho, Michael Dalglish, Ian White and Jon Morris for their significant contributions to the project.

References

Kochar A and McLean J (1985)   The Design and Development of Computer-Aided Learning Systems for Industrial Applications. *AET Proceedings* 1985.

Kommers P (1993)   Scenarios   for the Development of Educational Hypermedia. *Educational and Training Technology Journal* August 1993, Volume 30, Number 3. Kogan Page, UK.

Waterworth J (1992) *Multimedia Interaction with Computers* Ellis Horwood Ltd.

Floyd S (1991) *The IBM Multimedia Handbook* Brady Publishing

Appendix A : Student Questionnaire (Video)

Student Questionnaire

The following questions relate to the Control Laboratory video. Please watch the video and answer the following (using a cross on the scale to show what you think):

1. How interesting did you find the video?

Very	Quite	Don't Know	A Bit	Very
Interesting	Interesting		Boring	Boring

I_____I_____I_____I_____I

2. Did information appear to occur in the right order?

Very Well	Quite	Don't Know	Poorly	Completely
Ordered	Good		Ordered	Mixed up

I_____I_____I_____I_____I

3. Did you get a lot of information from watching the video?

A lot of	Some	Don't Know	Not	Very
Info.	Info.		Much	Little

I_____I_____I_____I_____I

4. Will watching the video help you in the tutorials?

Definiately	Probably	Don't Know	Probably	Definately
Yes			Not	Not

I_____I_____I_____I_____I

5. How easy was the written information to follow?

Very Easy	Quite Easy	Don't Know	Quite Difficult	Very Difficult

I_____I_____I_____I_____I

6. Could you rely on what you learned from the video when you are in the Laboratory?

Yes	Sometimes	Don't Know	Not Much	No

|_____|_____|_____|_____|

7. Was the video appropriate to your course?

| Very | Quite | Don't Know | Not Very | Not At All |
| Appropriate | Appropriate | | Appropriate | Appropriate |

|_____|_____|_____|_____|

8. Did the video cover everything you need to know about this Laboratory?

| Complete | Fairly | Don't Know | Fairly | Incomplete |
| | Complete | | Incomplete | |

|_____|_____|_____|_____|

Please use the space below to write any other comments you would like to make about the video:

29. Multilingual Multimedia: Meeting the Needs of Specialised Language Learners

Phillipe Delcloque, *Napier University*

INTRODUCTION

Course in basic French for hotel receptionists

At the beginning of 1994, I was asked to produce distance learning materials to teach basic French to a small group of hotel receptionists more than eighty miles away in Braemar. The course was intended to prepare them for a simulation of face to face communication at the reception desk or telephone conversations with French customers. I had to advise as to how long the course should run for and how many 'live' sessions across an ISDN line there would be between myself as the native tutor and pretend customer and the six Braemar receptionists who, I was also told to assume, would be complete beginners in French and not computer literate.

For those who are not aware of ISDN technology, it is simply the use of a telephone line, rather like a sophisticated modem, to transmit all the information from one computer screen to another. ISDN stands for 'Integrated Systems Digital Network'. It requires special cards in each of the computers concerned as well as suitable cameras at both ends. It allows the possibility of video conferencing as well as full data exchange. In this way, telephone conversations at the very least can be adequately simulated and of course some degree of real face to face interaction by virtue of seeing the person you are talking to in a window of your screen. The picture quality is slightly superior to the new 'video phones' but it deteriorates if you increase the size of the window. So, naturally, it cannot replace real face to face interaction because of presence and notably body language issues (paralinguistic features). Professionals particularly in the design industry are already benefiting from the use of this new technology by being able to share creative ideas remotely.

Parameters for the course : duration, "airtime"

It was made clear to me that the budget for production and live conversations was very limited and that I would have to concentrate on teaching the very basics. So, given the financial constraints on 'airtime' particularly, I felt that I could have only 10 live sessions of five minutes each with each of the six receptionists. This would be spread over 10 weeks with one 30 minute session per week where all six receptionists would be present and would therefore benefit from witnessing the performance of their colleagues or 'peers'. The communications would be entirely in French and each week would see a different situation set. I therefore had to select ten fundamental 'settings', each with a dialogue between the receptionist and usually just one customer. Three of those would simulate a telephone conversation and the other seven would be face to face simulations. In addition, I thought it wise to include three additional modules on the alphabet, numbers and telling the time. An interactive hypermedia document would be written to prepare the learners for those short dialogues. In addition to the live conversations in French, a short discussion in English would help to ascertain the response to the course. A final evaluation would also be carried out by the return of the learners' assessment sheets, a feedback questionnaire, a report from the Braemar ISDN base and comparisons of initial and final language tests.

Assumptions for the course

No knowledge of French

I was somewhat sceptical of this claim, naturally, as I thought that at least some of the six students would have studied some French at school which would provide 'positive transfer' in the learning process. An initial questionnaire and test was therefore designed to examine the subjects' real competence. The same test would then be used at the end of the course ten weeks later to ascertain their progress. The test would be limited to the same duration (Maximum half an hour) and would include an investigation of several basic language skills : Aural Comprehension, Speech production, Basic Grammar and Vocabulary and General Knowledge.

No knowledge of computers

Again this was likely to vary and as a result it was deemed sensible to include some questions (to be answered truthfully) in the initial questionnaire. The Braemar team would also include comments in their final report. The CALL course design had to be as 'intuitive' as possible and take nothing for granted.

PREPARING THE CORPUS

The background : linguistic studies :   'Vocabulaire fondamental, etc...'

In an ideal world, a targeted 'corpus analysis' of expressions likely to be encountered in hotel reception situations could have been undertaken but time and resource constraints prevented that from happening. We based our included lexicon on some 'Vocabulaire fondamental' principles and simply added the targeted corpus.

Adding the special corpus of the hospitality field

Given the time scale for supporting material production, the simplest way to achieve this aim was to scrutinise five relevant text books and extract the most recurrent items from the individual lexicons found at the back of each publication. A basic list of suitable situations or settings was also determined in this way.

Passive versus active knowledge

It was clear that the active lexical knowledge could and should be limited to achieve the targeted learning outcomes and that expressions should be kept to the most simple (and perhaps the closest to the English structure for added positive transfer). However, there would be a need for a wider range of expressions to be assimilated 'passively' as the customer frankly could be expected to use any wording, not necessarily making any allowance for the 'foreign' receptionist.

Analysis of users' needs: Establishing their corpus

To increase the corpus while the live sessions were taking place, it was deemed desirable to invite the receptionists themselves to add to the final list of acquired expressions. Each week, they would prepare a list of English words or phrases they wanted to learn and fax the list to me before the following session. The translations could even be incorporated in the special, very useful, 'Notes section' of the hypermedia program.

DESIGN OF THE TEACHING MATERIAL

Defining the learning outcomes

Each of the ten lessons would cover separate learning outcomes although inevitably, there would be some degree of overlap. The following is a list of the chosen outcomes   (in chronological order) :

1) Greeting customers on their arrival.
2) Alphabet and numbers (including telephone).
3) Dealing with reservations (on the telephone).
4) Describing room facilities and meeting customers' requirements.
5) Explaining meal times and hotel rules.
6) Leisure activities in the hotel and the vicinity.
7) Giving directions.
8) Dealing with complaints.
9) Taking messages on customers' behalf (telephone).
10) Settling the bill including various forms of payment.

Refining the minimal linguistic corpus

Within the context of those outcomes, care was taken to incorporate minimal units of learning gradually and at every linguistic level :

- Basic phonology: concentrating on those sounds which are most likely to cause misunderstandings.
- Basic grammar: (a typical example was the inclusion of the conditional tense although it would not normally be found in such a basic corpus). Its frequency in the 'added specialised data' is due to its function as the polite tense. By contrast but for similar reasons, the 'tu' form would not be found in conversations between receptionists and their clients. This was pointed out when basic conjugations were introduced.
- Basic vocabulary: As already explained, it was essential here to distinguish the active lexicon of only 200 items from the added list of expressions designed to increase passive knowledge (some of which did not even figure in the 3500 words of 'Français fondamental').
- Paralinguistic considerations: cultural matters as well as body language would not normally form part of such basic learning strategies, but the 'Notes pages' in the hypermedia program were particularly suitable for the inclusion of such comments which do matter in effective communication.

Centrality of the computer material

The few multimedia CALL courses on the market today are either self-contained packages or 'add-ons' to a book accompanied by audio tapes. Very few are designed 'from the computer down'. Great care was taken to provide extensive printing facilities to accommodate learners' preferences and to assist revision. Audio cassettes were also included to provide 'total immersion', so that the students could use them in their homes, cars, etc...

Design of the CALL package

Any computer language course must include a totally intuitive interface so that any learner, no matter how computer phobic acquires the linguistic content not a set of computer routines. Even the 'DOS' based products have had to incorporate such strategies in their design. The Macintosh interface is renowned for its ease of use. To further assist this process, it was decided to include a main menu program which would lead to all the lessons with only one exit route to avoid any chance of "navigation into hyperspace".

Support material : paper, audio, video

Due to the centrality of the computer material, it was easy to 'down print' the situations, dialogues, exercises and tests. Each lesson would consist of more than five pages and the total would form a useful booklet, which the students could use at home when they did not have access to the computer. In addition, one audio tape and one video tape (including situations and dialogues) was supplied.

Designing the initial (and final) test

Each lesson includes an interactive (question and answer test) which prepares students for 'live' role playing on the ISDN line. In order to further increase students' motivation, an initial test was devised to analyse the students' previous knowledge. The test was structured to include the basic units of learning already described : phonology, grammar, lexicon. A section concerning cultural knowledge was also added. The test had both an 'indicative' and an analytical function. The same test would be done by each student at the end of the course 10 weeks hence to ascertain what had been learnt. Such 'semi-objective' testing is normally done at one year intervals to target effort and indicate progress in a sort of 'Diagnostic and cure approach to language learning and teaching'.

LESSON STRUCTURE AND FACILITIES

Total immersion versus source language input

The general principle adopted here is that any **visible** item has a universal iconic value supplemented by French words, most of them being cognates or quasi-cognates (words which happen to have either the same spelling as English words or a transparent structure, e.g. 'Leçons'). Any **hidden** item such as a pop-up page would include instructions, hints or explanations in English. This would provide total immersion without the associated problems with respect to beginners using the course for autonomous learning.

The range of facilities

Many of the features found in multilingual multimedia programs are included here : translation, aural comprehension, page or field printing, many types of exercises ranging from gap-fillers, multiple choice protocols, interactive role playing, voice recording with immediate comparison with digital native. All this is accompanied by on-line help on every page, explanatory pop-up fields including grammatical, lexical, paralinguistic and cultural notes.

SEMI-INTELLIGENT ROUTINES

It is fair to say that the original version written in Hypercard suffers from the limitations of its basic string-handling facilities which forced me to program many alternative correct answers, a very time-consuming process. Future versions will hopefully incorporate some semi-intelligent parsing thus increasing the analytical power and reducing tutor preparation's time, a crucial issue in C.A.L.L. today.

A novel recording feature

A/B comparisons of students' recordings against native models have become commonplace in multimedia programs. This one goes one step further by providing a path for the user to file his/her sound recordings on a separate module which can then be copied onto a floppy disc for later check by the tutor. Naturally, this is limited to approximately 1.5 minute of sound recording at full bandwidth per floppy but it is sufficient to record an entire dialogue.

On-line help : phonological assistance

In the development of future programs designed for higher level (university language students), we intend to provide a 'phonology' button, which would display phonological transcription in a separate box. This would also be accompanied by a separate exercise section which would verify the student's own transcriptions.

DELIVERY OF MATERIAL AND ON-LINE SESSIONS

The rationale behind the specific materials delivered

Each CALL lesson will be delivered at least one week before the live session. This is due to start at the end of April 94. The entire set of paper, audio and video material will be delivered at the beginning of the course. This will allow a 'total immersion strategy' by enabling the receptionists to work on it in their spare time wherever they may be.

Preparation for the on-line sessions

Each lesson done on the computer represents two to three hours' work per student. As is now clear, all areas of language acquisition are covered : aural comprehension, oral production (including recording), vocabulary and grammatical reinforcement and cultural and usage notes. Such comprehensive learning strategies could not be accomplished without computer support. By the time the student is asked to role play the dialogue live, a confidence build-up should have occurred and the results will hopefully be impressive.

Time and frequency of on-line sessions

As explained earlier, each student will act the dialogue with the tutor and possibly enter a basic interactive conversation for five minutes each week for ten weeks. They will all witness the live sessions deriving mutual benefit from each others' performances. In addition, the audio part of the conversations will be recorded at the Edinburgh base, this may also be possible (subject to hard disc capacity) in Braemar. On that basis the recordings could be played back to the receptionists for their self (and peer) critical appraisal.

Monitoring and assessment of sessions

The tutor will give each receptionist a mark out of 10, one week after each session. At the end of the course, this will produce a mark out of 100. In addition, if the students agree, the self and peer assessment marks could be mixed with the tutor mark. Monitoring will be achieved by feedback from the students each week as well as the staff in Braemar and by a final questionnaire filled in by each student.

CONCLUSION: CALL FOR SPECIFIC PURPOSES: IS IT REALISTIC?

Languages for Specific Purposes is a relatively new field of research. Targeted pedagogic materials of any kind are few and far between. Tutors must often rely on the use of authentic materials using different media, although predominently textual.

For multimedia producers, the perceived size of the market is everything and writing a course like the above makes no sense. Any such course would have to fit on a CD-Rom which becomes a cost-effective proposition from 1000+ numbers.

But the need for specialised materials is perhaps greater for a number of reasons. Firstly, because potential learners are most likely to need to improve their linguistic skills in an autonomous learning situation, where materials using different media are essential to effective tuition. Secondly, because there are so few text-books in special fields. And finally because of student numbers and timetabling constraints in most institutions, where it is rarely cost-effective to teach students with specific needs. The market is indeed larger than people realise and combined research into C.A.L.L. and L.S.P. presents a unique challenge.

30. Hypertext Across the Disciplines: An Analysis of Readers' Approaches to a Multi-Disciplinary Hypertext Tutorial

Wilma Strang and Jill Tardivel, *Hypertext Support Unit, University of Kent*

Summary
Much has been written about the interactive and individualised nature of computer-assisted learning, in particular recently of hypertext documents. It is unusual for a hypertext document to be applicable across a wide range of disciplines. However, a long-term study at the University of Kent has monitored the use of just such a document. This paper analyses readers' approaches to the Xtutor document and presents findings in the following areas:

- patterns of use by discipline and status
- learner pacing
- interactivity
- use by non-native English speakers
- open learning.

Xtutor, a hypertext introduction to the X windows system, has been used by over 400 people at the University of Kent in the past 20 months. Over 100 of these users, working on Xtutor on an open access machine, have had their sessions recorded in fine detail for the purposes of this major study.

Analysis of data has illustrated the following points -

- wide variations in session length
- wide variations in mumber of accesses
- 'feeler' access
- comparisons of use by individuals within/between disciplines
- wide range of users by status and discipline

The implications of these findings for higher education institutions investing in the provision of hypertext materials is discussed.

INTRODUCTION

This paper reports a study monitoring the use of xtutor, an interactive hypertext tutorial designed to introduce new users to X Windows. The work done on this tutorial forms part of the 'Hypertext Techniques for Online Documentation' project begun at the University of Kent in October 1991. The project is funded by the Information Technology and Training Initiative.

THE HYPERTEXT TECHNIQUES FOR ONLINE DOCUMENTATION PROJECT

This project began at the University of Kent in October 1991. The aim of the project is to increase the effectiveness of online documentation and training materials by using hypertext techniques and to apply this specifically to provide and distribute UNIX reference and training materials.

Thanks to the pioneering work done by Professor Peter Brown in the development of Guide, the University of Kent has consistently been involved in the promotion of hypertext presentation of online documentation. The ease of selective perusal of reference documentation made possible by hypertext has long been a theme of Professor Brown's work and as early as 1987, he identified the possibilities opened up by hardware and software developments -

"The modern graphics workstation has several advantages that provide a basis for displaying online documentation that human readers will find pleasant. Among these advantages are:

- interactive control using menus (pop-up or pull-down) selected by a mouse or other pointing device.
- integrated text and graphics.
- use of different fonts.
- use of separate windows. This is especially valuable for computer documentation (ie documentation about the computer's own software or hardware), since one window can contain the documentation and another window can be running a sample session using the software that the documentation describes." (Brown, 1987)

Although these advantages may indeed be taken for granted now, in 1987 this was an extremely far-sighted view. The current project uses the UNIX implementation of Guide. The choice of UNIX was because -

1   it is non-proprietary

2   it is seen to be increasingly used by University Computing services. It was estimated at the start of the project that by 1995 well over 80% of services will be deeply involved in UNIX

3   it has - like most large operating systems - a big need for more effective online documentation.

The first deliverable from the project was to be a means of displaying the information embodied in the UNIX manual pages in a way that allows selective perusal and easier following of cross reference links. Like all user manuals, the UNIX manual must cater for a wide variety of users. The aim of a hypertext presentation of the manual is to make it easier for all users to more quickly and accurately find the information they need. The projected user base is wide and a hypertext presentation is suitable for use by any UNIX users, whether they consider themselves to be novices or experts. It is wise in any case for developers of UNIX documentation and training materials to be cautious about this often drawn distinction -

"It seems not to be the case, at least for systems like UNIX, that the experts know all that the beginners know and more . . . Rather it seems that individuals have particular local knowledge about how to do things. Therefore even experts may use documentaion when they are in circumstances outside their expertise. In this respect, they will have certain similarities with beginners in that particular domain."(Wright 1988)

INITIAL STAGES OF THE PROJECT

The advantages of working within the ITTI framework were apparent very early in the life of the Kent project as the premise upon which the Kent project was based was confirmed by work done by a complementary UNIX training materials project based in Edinburgh University. The team there undertook, as the first stage in their own project, to survey the use of Unix, X Windows and Database software in UK higher education institutions. Their report

(Smith 1991) confirmed the premise upon which the Kent project was founded. From our point of view, the findings were particularly significant in four main areas. They found that -

1   UNIX is being increasingly used by universities. It was estimated that by 1994 well over 80% of services would be deeply involved in UNIX.

2   75% of sites surveyed estimated that more than 40% of their displays would be bitmapped - a significant change from the situation current in the autumn of 1991 and one with clear implications for hypertext developers of IT training materials for UNIX.

3   Over 75% of sites reported that they provided local training for users of UNIX. The authors of the report concluded that ". . . computer service staff may be spending time producing UNIX training materials which ought to be available at cost throughout the UK academic community".

4   By 1992, over 80% of sites would be supporting X Windows.

The survey therefore confirmed the initial thrust of the Kent project - there is a need for documentation and training material on Unix and the capabilities for displaying this in hypertext will increasingly become available.

   In addition, the increase in the numbers of students being admitted to universities will undoubtedly mean an increase in the number of UNIX users. More than ever before, these will be users with a very wide range of previous computer experience, many likely to have none at all. As UNIX systems on bitmapped terminals proliferate and as student numbers increase, it is likely that many inexperienced users will encounter UNIX in the X environment and will need help not just in using UNIX but in manipulating the X environment itself since X is -

". . . rapidly becoming the de facto standard in windowing systems." (Mikes 1992)

It became clear therefore that there was a need for training material for these users simply in how to manipulate the X environment.   Again, a complementary ITTI project based in Edinburgh - a different project with a different project team to that which produced the survey referred to - was able to provide input here.   While the team were producing X Windows training materials, they were not aiming them at the non-traditional wide user base which we saw as our audience.   After discussions with them, we saw a real need for a simple introductory tutorial to X.

PROJECT DELIVERABLES - `GMAN' AND `XTUTOR'

With all this information in view, the project moved forward in two directions -
`gman'- The Unix manual in hypertext format
   The `gman' utility converts UNIX manual pages (including locally produced pages), written using the standard `man' macros, into hypertext on the fly. No extra storage is needed. The /usr/man text files themselves are pre-processed before being fed into Guide hypertext and displayed on the screen in hypertext form. The `SEE ALSO' sections of the manual pages are automatically converted into active links, allowing the reader to move easily from one page to other related pages at the click of a button.
`gman' was made available at the end of the first year of the project in September 1992.

'xtutor' - an interactive hypertext tutorial for new users of X windows

xtutor was designed and written as a result of the perceived need illustrated by the survey conducted by the Edinburgh ITTI project. If users are to derive maximum benefit from the hypertext presentation and associated active linking provided for UNIX manual pages by the 'gman' utility, they must be conversant with and confident in the use and manipulation of the X Window system. xtutor aims to give the user an opportunity to become familiar with the general facilities available in the X environment. It includes a description and demonstration of X, together with a series of activities involving the user in working with the basic features of X such as window manipulation - moving, resizing, iconizing etc - and use of the mouse menus. The tutorial is designed for users with some computer experience but who have not previously worked with X.

XTUTOR - DESIGN, DEVELOPMENT AND USE

Given the nature and remit of the project, it was obvious that the X Windows tutorial would be written in hypertext and the appropriateness of the application was clear. If users were to be able to make full use of the hypertext presentation of the UNIX manual pages, they would need to be able to use both X Windows and hypertext. xtutor would help them to do both.

xtutor was planned from the start as a structured, almost hierarchical hypertext. Descriptions of hypertext types abound and inevitably overlap but these, by Jonassen and Grabinger (1990), fit the tutorial most aptly since it was designed to enable users to achieve certain very definite, task-oriented learning objectives. Duchastel (1990) opines that hypertext is not suitable for the presentation of instructional material and suggests rather that by its nature it espouses a constructivist approach to learning. Cunningham et al (1993) argue too that hypertext seems ideally suited to supporting constructivist learning environments. In the case of xtutor however, the achievement of some of the more detailed objectives depends upon the mastery of some of the simpler features of X and therefore an 'exploratory' hypertext was not deemed suitable. This does not mean that the tutorial is rigid or that the user is constrained to pursuing only one path through the material. Such an approach would defeat the very object of presenting the material in hypertext in the first place. Rather, the user of the tutorial is presented with a 'suggested path' which s/he may choose to follow or not, as the case may be. The path is implied by advice about possible selections from menus, by numbering of items in the hypertext and by indentation and layout.

As Hammond (1993) says -

". . . the level of learner control available within hypertext systems is a two-edged sword for the learner; self-regulation may be possible, but at the risk of haphazard browsing. The problem is too often an implicit assumption that the learner's goal of understanding can be equated with the designer's goal of information provision. If learning also needs thought, then it is often the case that more explicit direction and control, to restrict the learner to realistic goals and to a sensible part of the domain knowledge, needs to be judiciously mixed with freedom of action."

User studies of xtutor show, however, that Jonassen and Grabinger may be right to insist that users' patterns of use rather than developers embedded structures contribute to the definition of hypertext type. It soon became clear as user patterns were studied that many users were calling up the tutorial, iconising it and using it only as a reference document to help them when they got into trouble with window manipulation or logging out.

PATTERNS OF USE AT KENT

Collecting the information

Xtutor was made available on networked teaching, research and general purpose UNIX computers at the University of Kent. One computer, known as `eagle' was designated a cross discipline general purpose machine, available to any member of staff or postgraduate on the campus. Xtutor was promoted as available on this machine, both by advertising it each term using the internal electronic news service and by placing posters above the terminals which supported the X windows system. These terminals were in open access computing rooms within the Computing Laboratory and in other parts of the University, principally in the Biology, Chemistry, Physics and Electronic Laboratories.

Each time xtutor was invoked by users on eagle a number of details about the session were recorded. These included the users identifier, the start and end times of the session and a complete transcript of the session with xtutor, recording each action performed by the user.

The information collected in these transcripts were collated and analysed for the period between May 1992 and February 1993, the first 21 months of availability of xtutor.

How xtutor was used

During the period between May 1992 and February 1993, xtutor was invoked on eagle 279 times by 117 individual users, almost 2.4 accesses per user. Table 30.1 shows the overall frequencies of accesses and the average total length of time per user for each frequency.

Table 30.1

No accesses	Frequency	Ave times used hh:mm:ss
1	60	00:07:06
2	31	00:13:37
3	12	00:25:44
4	5	01:00:58
5	2	00:28:40
6	2	00:37:21
7	0	
8	2	04:07:14
9	0	
10	0	
11	0	
12	1	00:58:02
-	-	-
22	1	04:23:27

Those users who invoked xtutor on one occasion only ran xtutor for an average of 7 minutes 6 seconds. However the time of a single access ranged from one second to 1 hour 39 minutes.

Sixty three people used xtutor for less than 5 minutes, just over half those who invoked xtutor. Four people used xtutor for over two hours and one person used xtutor for over six hours.

From these figures it can be seen that the patterns of use of xtutor are highly variable. Presumably some users invoke xtutor, inspect it, decide that it is not appropriate to their needs and never return to xtutor. Others work their way through the tutorial in a single session. Some users repeatedly return to xtutor, with one subject returning 22 times. It is notable that although over 90% of persons using xtutor did so between 9 am and 6 pm, almost 10% used xtutor outside these hours, including individuals who invoked xtutor between 10pm and 2am.

Several users invoked xtutor for one or more short periods of time before a longer session. This suggests that xtutor is first inspected, then used in a longer session when it is convenient.

Several short sessions indicate that xtutor is being used as reference rather than purely tutorial material. Anecdotal evidence supports this. We strongly suspect that some of the very long sessions of over one and a half hours (five in all) occur when xtutor has been kept available on screen, as reference material. Similarly from anecdotal evidence we are aware that a few of the quick visits to xtutor of less than two minutes are the result of persons using xtutor as reference material, looking up information, then leaving xtutor.

The users recorded so far are predominantly from the science disciplines, reflecting not only the more traditional use of UNIX computers, but the availability of X terminals on the campus. (see table 30.2). Within the last six months a hundred networked personal computers with X terminal emulators have been installed in interdisciplinary colleges at the University. We expect an increase in future of users from other disciplines, reflecting the greater availability of the X window system across the campus.

Table 30.2

Discipline	Under grad	Post grad	Staff	Other	Total
Biology	0	13	4	0	17
Chemistry	1	7	3	0	11
Computing	13	2	28	0	43
Electronics	8	0	6	0	14
Humanities	0	0	1	0	1
Information Technology	1	0	0	0	1
Library	0	0	1	0	1
Maths	3	1	7	0	11
Other	0	0	0	1	1
Physics	11	0	2	0	13
Social Sciences	0	3	1	0	4
TOTALS	37	26	53	1	117

This study has underlined a broad range of styles of use for xtutor. A single session covering the whole tutorial should take from half an hour to one hour. The range of times for which xtutor is invoked is much broader than this. The number of entries and the times at which xtutor is invoked suggest that users break down their sessions to suit their own work patterns and that xtutor, designed initially as a teaching tool is also being used as a work of reference.

The reality, that people will take what they require from an available computer based learning package, when they need it, and in the amounts they can accommodate, must be taken into consideration when designing computer based learning material, if that material is to be used to maximum effect.

References

Brown, P.J.(1987) On-line documentation, in *State of the art in computer graphics,* ed Earnshaw, R., Springer-Verlag.

Cunningham, D.J., Duffy, T.M. and Knuth, R.A.(1993) The Textbook of the Future in *Hypertext: a psychological perspective,* eds McKnight, C., Dillon, A. and Richardson, J.,Ellis Horwood.

Duchastel, P.C.(1990) Examining Cognitive Processing in Hypermedia Usage in *Hypermedia* Vol 2 (3).

Hammond, N.(1993) Learning with Hypertext in *Hypertext: a psychological perspective* eds McKnight, C., Dillon, A. and Richardson, J. Ellis Horwood.

Jonassen, D.H. and Grabinger, R. Scott (1990) Problems and Issues in Designing Hypertext/Hypermedia for Learning in *Designing Hypermedia for Learning,* eds Jonassen, D.H. and Mandl, H., Springer Verlag.

Mikes, S.(1992) *X Window System: Program Design and Development,* Addison Wesley.

Smith, J.(1991) *University and Polytechnic Computing Services - A questionnaire survey of the use of UNIX, X Windows and Database software,* Computing Services, The University of Edinburgh.

Wright, P.(1988) Issues of Content and Presentation in Document Design, in *Handbook of Human Computer Interaction* ed Helander, M., Elsevier Science Publishers.

Both Xtutor and gman are vailable by ftp from unix.hensa.ac.uk in the subdirectory misc/unix/unix_guide/guide_docs.

Section 4: Open and Distance Learning

31.   The Case for Flexible Learning

Roger Dobson, *Personnel Director (International), United Distillers*

Summary
Ten years' experience of delivering education and training in major retail and beverage concerns has involved major investments in new technology.   Independent evaluation indicates high learner acceptance and effectiveness and highlights factors influencing learning motivation.   Yet have managers accepted flexible learning as a legitimate alternative to the classroom?   Is technology based training an attractive strategy for international concerns and for the educational challenges of the third world?

"In Case of Fire" is a 1 hour video programme that was developed for Woolworths stores and which I adapted for video disc.   It was made available to over 10,000 employees in B&Q DIY stores at hundreds of locations around the UK.   Whenever I have shown this video sequence to audiences around the world it seems to have had a memorable affect.   Certainly, when we evaluated its impact among the B&Q workforce there was a very high level of awareness of the programme.   This was especially encouraging given that the target population had a very high proportion of part-time employees and was vulnerable to significant labour turn over.

When I addressed the 1987 AETT Conference I talked exclusively about my experience of developing open learning in B&Q.   At this, your 29th Conference I would like to explain my enthusiasm for flexible learning by drawing on ten years of working at, or close to, the "coal face" of learning in large highly commercial organisations.

In 1984 I was based in Edinburgh working for Scottish & Newcastle Breweries.   As Head of Training I was concerned with replacing a large central training function, that concentrated on residential programmes, with a more flexible delivery system that emphasised greater ownership of training by line management. Two events had a profound effect upon my interest in flexible learning.   The first was a demonstration of interactive video arranged by the MAST learning organisation.   That was my first introduction to technology-based training.   Even after ten years I can recall the visual images of a programme which was designed for the sales force of international paints, and as I recall highlighted the huge potential market in painting ships bottoms! Although this was a video tape system it seemed a very stimulating method of learning compared with my experience of the classroom.

About the same time I had the good fortune to meet the Head of Training of Jaguar cars who was then in the second year of overseeing Jaguar's open learning programme. Jaguar's problem of meeting the demand for learning packages from employees who were learning in their own time contrasted sharply with my experience in Scottish & Newcastle of reluctant trainees calling off from residential training courses.

Shortly thereafter I was able to pilot, within Scottish & Newcastle Breweries, a number of open learning packages that had been developed by the Manpower Services Commission through the Opentech Project.   At first hand I was able to observe the enthusiasm of learners for materials designed with the learner in mind, and where they had the flexibility of determining time, place and pace of learning.   I was also very attracted by the apparent cost effectiveness.   We were able to provide the equivalent of a days training with materials costing less than £10 per unit - and the materials could remain with the learner for as long as they wished.

When I worked for B&Q between 1985 and 1988 we were opening a new store every two weeks, employee numbers were growing by 2,000 a year and, together with labour turnover, we had to train 8,000 new recruits per year.   Half of the employees were part time and 25% worked less than eight hours per week. I believed that with open learning we could deliver high quality, consistent training at up to 300 locations right across the British Isles. We would also satisfy an essential requirement that training was accessible at times convenient to the trainee. Within 3 years we developed 15 self-study work books, 24 linear videos on laser disc, 7 computer based training programmes using text and graphics and 4 interactive videos. We also made use of some generic interactive videos. It appeared obvious to us that we had a powerful and very cost effective training delivery system. Using self study work books we addressed a need to improve stock-take procedures -because of the audit requirement to keep stock take sheets we were able to make a direct comparison between using this flexible approach to learning with the previous traditional instructor approach. We observed 22% improvement in performance whilst reducing training costs by 75%.

Our first interactive video programme was aimed at improving employee performance in selling credit to customers - an important feature of high ticket items. Again we were able to contrast credit sales performance in stores where staff had been trained using interactive video compared with like stores where training depended upon conventional methods. We noticed a markedly superior performance in those stores using interactive video. To better understand how employees were using our materials we commissioned Lancaster University to evaluate our open learning. Not surprisingly they found that video had the greatest impact. Lancaster looked particularly at what motivated employees to learn in the work environment of a retail store. They found there were three key motivators:

- relevance
- recognition
- and qualifications

If it was transparently clear to the learner that engaging in learning would have a personal pay back, either by improving performance or reducing anxiety then they were motivated to learn. If a supervisor or manager recognised the learners efforts just by asking how they wereä getting on, then that was very motivating. But, most significant of all was the qualification. If by engaging in learning there was the possibility of gaining a vocational qualification which had currency outside the organisation, ideally nationally, then that was the most powerfulä motivator of all.

Although United Distillers is very different from B&Q, back in 1988 I thought there was the possibility that open learning could be an effective delivery medium for training and that developing vocational qualifications would both motivate and accurately target training. At that time our Scottish operations employed over 5,000 people at about 60 sites, many in remote areas and engaged in quite complex activities. We malt barley in 7 day continuous shift operations. Our grain distilleries are large plants with sophisticated control systems. Export administration and shipping is located in Glasgow and captures orders from around the world. In Clackmannanshire alone we have millions of casks of whisky quietly maturing in over 170 acres of warehousing. The final product is prepared for the consumer in increasingly automated packaging plants where flexibility, service and quality are essential.

Over a period of five years, working with Scotvec and our colleagues in the Scotch whisky industry we have developed vocational qualifications for malt distilling, grain distilling and packaging. The motivational aspect of vocational qualifications has proved to be the same as that we found in B&Q even though the profile of the work force is quite different. Employees are predominantly full time, mature - on average about 40 years of age and with an average of about ten years service. Where we have invited employees to work for a vocational qualification about 80% have volunteered - well over a thousand are now involved.

Broad based delivery of training through open learning and technology took longer than I expected because of our concern with developing an appropriate hardware strategy. However, over the years there were isolated examples where we were able to experiment. Many of our malt distilleries have visitor centres where we encourage the general public to learn something of the processes of malting whisky. Even here we use modern technology with a video disc system that gives them some background information. To help our visitors learn about the heritage and process of making malt whisky we employ 70 Visitor Centre Guides most of whom are seasonal staff. As ambassadors of the company it is vital for them to be knowledgeable in the process of making malt whisky. They must also have good customer care skills. Training has to be consistent and because of the seasonal nature of the trainees it has to be effective over a short period of time. The Scottish Council for educational technology developed a self study workbook for us to train Visitor Centre Guides. We also adopted a workbook approach for training new staff at our grain distilleries. A £20 million investment combined with the introduction of continuous shift working meant we had to train 120 process operators within a period of 12 weeks.

The self study work book was in two parts. The first part dealt with general company matters and then discreet modules covered each part of the process. A video provided an overview of the process and then to check on knowledge we developed a computer game. We also supported each trainee with a designated mentor - who is an experienced employee.

The Scottish Development Agency commissioned Coopers & Lybrand Deloitte to evaluate our training in grain distilling. I quote from the summary of their findings:

> *"Induction and Health & Safety training was highly successful. It rapidly orientated the trainees to United Distillers' values and culture, it clearly communicated United Distillers' expectations and what the trainees could expect from United Distillers, and it provided the trainees with an awareness of the total production process and their job context. Induction produced highly motivated trainees with a very positive attitude towards their jobs and united distillers. Technical training involved working alongside an experienced employee, on-the-job. It was supported by a comprehensive technical manual and a computer game. The trainees generally attained a satisfactory (or better) level of competence within a relatively short time span. The practical nature of the training was appropriate to both the type of learning and the type of learner. The mentor system consisted of allocating an experienced employee (not their supervisor) to each trainee to oversee their smooth integration into United Distillers. Although there were some implementation problems, the concept has value as a signal of the Company's commitment to the trainee's full and timely assimilation into the productive workforce."*

Having good quality feedback on the implementation of a project or new initiative is enormously beneficial.

This was my experience in B&Q with Lancaster University and I used their specialist expertise throughout the introduction of vocational qualifications in United Distillers. More recently, Lancaster evaluated the introduction of digital video interactive technology. DVI was the format we eventually decided was right for us. The business identified that a key priority for training was to support a process of continuous improvement in our packaging plants.

Two training programmes are now in place. The first addressed problem solving and the second is concerned with quality improvement. Decisions on hardware are always very difficult and potentially risky. Technology is developing so fast it's like trying to step on to a moving elevator. Although it is early days the feedback from the Lancaster University evaluators is encouraging and I quote from their evaluation of the introduction phase.

"The implementation events which introduced the DVI material and the potential of the open learning centres in the four sites are characterised by their professionalism and clarity. There was a strong corporate message concerning investment in people through training opportunities. The machines and the material were considered to be of high quality and easy to use. The emerging benefits included the unthreatening nature of the learning environment. There did not seem to be a problem of 'technophobia'. The physical environment of the Open Learning Centres was also considered to be of a high standard, comfortable, cheery and informal. A good proportion of team leaders and managers had already begun to develop 'use' strategies. There was a concern that the momentum would be lost if a rapid expansion of materials could not be sustained. The main practical worry focused on the time management of Open Learning Centre use. Overall, the initiative had a strong endorsement by the target group of this evaluation."

My own horizons changed in 1993 when I assumed responsibility for the human resource function of our international region. This covers over 100 countries in Latin America, the Caribbean, Africa and the Middle East where we market and sell about 100 brands of whisky, gin, vodka and rum. We have in-market operations in Mexico, Venezuela, Brazil, Argentina & South Africa and operate through third party distributors in many other countries. We employ about 1500 people. We are principally a sales and marketing operation, although we do have a significant manufacturing facility in Venezuela. The effectiveness of our sales force is a major influencer on performance. Some time ago we identified the need to raise awareness of our products amongst sales personnel, particularly emphasising the advantages of heritage and quality. To meet this need we have introduced the "knowledge programme" comprising work books, video tapes and audio tapes.

You will not be surprised that I am considering the scope for using PC based technology to develop further this flexible approach to training. The challenges for us in international of geography, language (predominantly Spanish, Portuguese, French as well as English) and culture all suggest to me that there is considerable potential for the application of flexible learning. An important part of the corporate values of United Distillers is a commitment to participate fully in the communities of which we form a part. I think that this has been widely recognised in Scotland for many years. In Venezuela, where we are a significant employer, we are also active. In the capital, Caracas, acute problems of poor housing are exacerbated by inadequate education resulting from a shortage of teachers. We have recently become associated with an initiative to help to train teachers. I hope that we can draw on experience in Scotland in training teachers using interactive video and apply that experience in Venezuela. I have seen this huge problem of education in other underdeveloped countries. Surely flexible learning, applying technology where practical, has much to offer.

If I look back at my own personal journey through open learning, distance learning CBT, TBT and flexible learning my conviction that this is an effective, stimulating and powerful delivery method for learning remains. However, I am probably more cautious than I used to be. I suspect that our ability to apply training technology has not kept pace with the rate at which technology is developing. It is all too easy to be preoccupied with technology for its own sake and neglect the far more important issue - application of technology. It may be that our concern, in United Distillers, to invest wisely in hardware which led us to selecting DVI unnecessarily delayed by several years our adoption of technology in training. It might have been better to have gone with the proven format of video disc and worried about having the latest technology at the first replacement opportunity.

On occasions when I have introduced flexible learning I may have underestimated the need to establish an appropriate context. By context I mean the establishment of an environment where there is substantial commitment and understanding of training strategy within the overall business strategy.

To achieve a long term change in the delivery mechanism of training requires the whole-hearted commitment of line managers, personnel managers and training specialists probably at several levels in an organisation. This can be very difficult to achieve. Many of these important players will have been comfortable in the orthodox learning environment of the class room and are uncomfortable with an approach which empowers learners. In addition, I have found that many training professionals are resistant to adopting new methods which inevitably change their roles. Trainers often feel vulnerable when they are asked to be responsible for substantial business investment possibly of the order of hundreds of thousands or even millions of pounds. Paradoxically they will happily spend the same amounts in small tranches, from their revenue budget on training courses and accommodation.

No matter how strong the intellectual case for flexible learning, and even the emotional case for flexible learning, the main condition for long term adoption of flexible learning is the economic case. A sound economic case supporting a training or human resource strategy that is integral with the business strategy and recognised as such by line managers offers the best chance that flexible learning will deliver all that it promises.

32. A Toolset for Open Learning Development and Delivery

Keith Whiteley, Madjid Merabti and Steven Keller, *School of Computing and Mathematical Sciences, Liverpool John Moores University*

Summary

This paper describes the development of a computer aided toolset for the production and delivery of Open Learning material. The project was motivated by the increasing pressures felt in today's educational environment which are brought about by the expansion of the student population and the consequent reduction in time available for direct teacher-student contact. The tools developed during the project address a complete systems approach to Open Learning production and delivery. In particular, two major tools have been produced; a course development tool and a course delivery tool. These provide the Open Learning Developer with a complete environment for Open Learning courses.

INTRODUCTION

The increase in the availability of computers and software at affordable prices in the workplace, as well as in the home, makes the development of computer based learning material a reality. This proliferation of systems and information bases makes the challenge of open and distance learning an attractive solution. As an example, most colleges and universities are now connected to a world spanning computer network with instantaneous interchanges. This large range of directly accessible information is being increasingly exploited, both formally and informally, by the student body. The existence of such systems is even more significant if one takes into consideration the changing face of college and university education with ever growing class numbers and ever decreasing unit of resources.

To harness these changes in the working environment we need to take advantage of the technological advances presented by such systems and our effort described in this paper is aimed at building a number of tools that help lecturers and teachers prepare computer based learning material in a flexible and consistent manner.

The eventual learning material or document to be given could be considered as an unrestricted information space and therefore one can dynamically construct or re-construct paths of investigation or learning. This view of learning material, although very interesting, requires a number of complex underlying structures to be satisfactorily executed. Even in restricted environments such W3 one can see that the quality of service deteriorates rapidly with the increase in the information space and is even less deterministic when information is accessed remotely through computer networks. In some established systems such as Guide (Brown, 1992) there is a continuous visualisation space which is achieved through link markers which themselves are activated by the user. An older system (Hypercard) (Goodman, 1987) allows the user to move from one window to another in a discontinuous manner using buttons or active objects to navigate through the information space.

Our work follows the path of these two systems where, by in large, the learning document is essentially statically hardwired. However, in some instances it would more interesting for the user to have a dynamically constructed information space or learning document. To this end we a provide a mechanism whereby the student can construct his or her own pathway through the learning material in the form of a bookmark system. In our environment we provide multiple book marks which can associated with a whole document or parts of document. In addition the book marks are expanded with a facility for annotating the references. This additional features allow the user to dynamically reconfigure the information space or learning document for new accesses, make up an additional parallel information space by processing the notes on the margin that these annotations provide, and can be used by the system and thus the teacher for tracking the student's progress. The aggregation of the bookmarks information gathered from all users could also be used after analysis to identify weaknesses in the document or learning material.

LEARNING ENVIRONMENT

One of the main requirements for the delivery platform is that of a widely accessible computer system. This decision was taken despite the fact that many of the developments in these field are concerned wholly with exploiting the most expensive and latest technology. However, we believe that a development environment on a less expensive and technological intensive would better suit the mass educational market in the university environment, schools, and at home for say distance learning. Thus the ultimate platform for delivery must be commonly available and reasonably priced.

To this end, we developed the system on the PC machine running Microsoft Windows.

We decided that two tools were appropriate for the project. A Course Development Tool which provided the user with an Open Learning Development Environment, together with an Execution Engine for course delivery. Both these tools were to be developed using commonly available PC/Windows applications development tools.

THE DESIGN PHILOSOPHY FOR THE ENVIRONMENT

The basic design philosophy of the toolset is straightforward. It provides for the development of a structured Open Learning course which allows the authors to incorporate course material from existing sources in addition to newly developed work. Furthermore, the toolset should provide the student with an easily used and attractive working environment in which learning can take place in as flexible a manner as possible, yet one which maintains an aspect of rigour. Based on this philosophy, the following design criteria for the toolset have been adopted :-

a) Course Development Tool

- The ability to specify an appropriate learning model at the start of course development
- ensuring conformance with this model during subsequent course development
- incorporation of existing and newly developed course material into the course structure
- Minimum imposition on courseware developers with regard to inclusion of 'hypertext tags" in the material

b) Course Delivery Tool

- presentation of textual, visual and demonstrational material
- access to appropriate external software from within the tool student self assessment
- preparation of suitable personal revision notes inclusion of bookmark features

In addition, an important extra feature is the ability to allow the course development team to "dry run" the material at various stages of its development by use of the execution tool. This would allow the team to get early feedback on the overall structure of the course and permit aspects of the material which were felt to be particularly "difficult" to be given early user exposure. Additionally, it provides the team with an overall view of the developing content and quality of the course.

COURSE LEARNING MODEL

Based on the above criteria, the first stage in the development process was the definition of a suitable learning model. This model should provide for the features required by the design criteria and furthermore, should be capable of itself being captured in some computer compatible form, so that conformance can be checked during courseware development.

As an initial experiment, a simple conventional model (Holmberg, 1989) was adopted which consisted of the following components :-

- "aspects' (a major course theme element), "modules" (identified subject topics) and "units' (a specific learning unit)
- Self assessment questions and tests
- Demonstrations
- Aims and Objectives

These components form a hierarchic structure in which relationships (in the sense of a relational database) exist between the components. This "relational hierarchical model" has the following structure -

a) An aspect consists of a number of modules
b) A module consists of a number of units
c) Aspects and modules satisfy a number of high level objectives
d) A unit satisfies a number of low level objectives
e) A unit has a number of associated assessments, tests and demonstrations

The structure of this simple model is shown in Figure 32.1

This model has been implemented in the form of a simple relational database using Borland's Paradox.

Toolset Components

A number of development tools were evaluated as potential candidates for the software development process. Tools were required for both the development of the Course Development Tool and the Course Execution Tool. Since the two developments were, in a sense, independent (since the "communication" between the two tools was solely through the use of text files), two sets of development tools were examined

Course Development Tool

Paradox relational database for model representation
Object Vision for the initial development of the user interface

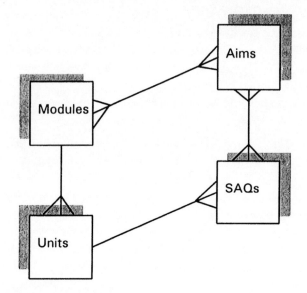

Figure 32.1: The Learning Model

Course Execution Tool

> A variety of C/C + + development systems
> Microsoft's Help Compiler
> Knowledge Pro

The use of C or C + + as a general development system was rejected. This was necessary because of the accelerated timescale required for the implementation of the system. Subsequently, however, the release of Windows-specific development systems (Microsoft's Visual C + + and Boriand's C + + for Windows) have provided developers with a route to fast Windows software development. The lack of specific hypertext features in these systems would still, however, possibly preclude their use in 'one-off' projects of this kind.

Microsoft's Help Compiler (hc) looked more promising. The major advantage of using hc is the familiar look of the execution machine, since its appearance is that of the standard Help facility found in all Windows applications. To some extent, the development of material specifically for hc conformed to our requirement for a "nonobtrusive" mechanism for specifying hypertext links, because this system uses a simple scheme of 'tags' embedded in the text files in order to provide the required structure. It has many aspects which were felt to be desirable for our system, in particular, the use of "pop-up" windows for additional and glossary type information was thought to be a good feature. However, because of its ultimate lack of flexibility and its complexity in implementing certain operations (for example its representation of browser sequences), it was rejected.

The development system which was finally decided was based on two sets of tools. For the development of the CDT, Paradox and Object Vision were adopted and for the Execution Tool, Knowledge Pro was used. These tools were felt to give a good compromise between the need for a reasonable run-time efficiency and the need to use flexible and non-complex tools.

THE COURSE DEVELOPMENT TOOL

The Course Development Tool was designed as two independent components ; namely the relational data model and the user interface. The relational data model is set up using Paradox's data tables. The entries in the tables vary depending on the entity they represented. For example, the table holding the Module elements of the course holds

> Module Identifier
> Module Text File
> Module Synopsis
> Objectives Addressed
> Assessments carried out
> Demonstrations performed

Through a suitable choice of such tables, it is possible to represent each of the elements of the model using such tables. Through Paradox's Query commands, it is also possible to extract information such as :-

> The set of modules associated with an aspect The Units which addressed a specific objective

and other relational aspects of the model. File names are also used to represent the structure of a model, within the constraints of the restricted filename length available under DOS. Text is prepared using Word for Windows with Macros being used for the inclusion of the "tags" required by Knowledge Pro's hypertext links.

The User Interface has been developed using ObjectVision. This software is particularly suited to the development of user interfaces to Paradox data models. It allows the user to view data stored in tables and to add new entries into these tables. For the user of the Course Development Tool, it provides them with the facilities to

- obtain an overview of the course structure ensure that the objectives are being satisfied in a consistent manner
- investigate the balance of User Assessment throughout the course
- make modifications to objectives, assessments and course elements

The User Interface for the Course Development Tool consists of a number of windows which show the elements which make up the Model. These windows are selectable and may be scrolled. The selected window can then be scrolled to show the aspect of interest in the window. The remaining windows then show the other elements which relate to that chosen aspect.

THE COURSE DELIVERY TOOL

The execution tool takes the files produced by the developer and presents these to the student on a PC/Windows platform. The student can work through this learning material and is also able to access a number of tool features through the interface. These features are designed to give the student feedback regarding their performance and to introduce a degree of flexibility into the learning environment. Overall, the tool features available to the student are :-

- A tool bar for selection of facility
- The course text
- Assessment questions
- Exercises
- External tool access

The execution tool also allows the user to create bookmarks and revision notes for controlling their own learning environment. An example of the user interface is shown in figure N.2 below.

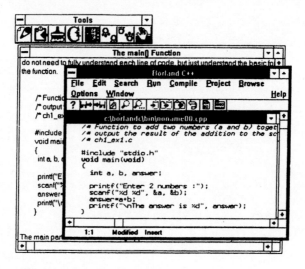

Figure 32.2: The Execution Tool

USER EXPERIENCES

The development environment has been successfully used in the implementation and delivery of a course for teaching Object Oriented programming Merabti *et al* (1994).   Another development in progress using the support environment is writing and the delivery of a course on teaching engineering design. The ability of launching new and independent processes from within the environment has been found to be particularly useful. This is because the students need to evaluate their design decisions. This task is performed by an independent tool which simulates the behaviour of the system under consideration.

There is much research in the developments of hypermedia and hypertext systems. The biggest challenge is how to separate the contents from the structural support, thus allow an interchange and portability of information from one structural representation to another and as yet there does not seem to be a universally accepted solution (Nanard 1994). The separation would increase the re-use of learning material as support environments evolve or when new systems are introduced. Our development environment also suffers from this lack of separation. However, we took a number of steps to reduce this problem. These include the minimum embedding of information within the learning material, the use of standards languages, standard interfaces, and a number of independent processes such as the simulation executive described earlier.

CONCLUSIONS AND FUTURE WORK

The toolset provides the developer and student with an environment in which production and delivery can take place in a flexible manner. The ability of the toolset to enable early feedback of the quality and content of the learning material and the incremental nature of a possible development technique lead us to conclude that this approach of an "Open Learning Support Environment" is a promising future area of investigation. Initial feedback from both developers and students indicate that this "prototyping" aspect is attractive, particularly when coupled with the toolset's ability to maintain a rigorous learning structure during this incremental development. In addition, the execution tool provides a learning environment which leads the student through the material in a manner which allows both feedback on performance and the personal development of customised notes.

Future work will concentrate on the development of the system for a range of delivery systems. To this end, current work is concentrating on the use of Mosiac as a run time engine, together with HTML as the text formatting language. Initial indications are promising, particularly with regard the Unix "flavour" of this system.

References

Brown P.J. (1992) *Unix Guide: lessons from ten years' development, Proc.* ECHT'92 , Milan, ACM Press., pp. 63-70, Dec. 1992.

Goodman D. (1987). *The Complete Hypercard Handbook*, Bantam Books, New York, 1987.

Holmberg, B., *Theory and Practice of Distance Education*, Routledge Education, 1989

Merabti, M., et. al. (1994). *OZone: Object Oriented Systems in an Open Learning Environment*. TaTTOO'94: Teaching and Training in the Technology Of Objects.

Nanard, J. (1994). *Multimedia and Hypermedia facing the concept of active document.* BIWIT'94: Information Systems Design and Hypermedia. 231-243.

33. Two Brief Case Studies of Higher Education Courses by Computer Conferencing

Anita Pincas, *Institute of Education, University of London*

Summary
The administrative and educational issues involved in teaching by computer conferencing to UK and international students are different from those involved in either traditional face to face or traditional distance education. Discussion will be based on personal experience (at the Institute of Education, London University) as course director of:

- Certificate in online Education and Training, a two term part time certificate that has run three times to a student group of 45 widely scattered people, ie in the UK and across the world.
- MA TESOL by Computer Networking, a two year part time masters degree for English teachers, started in January 1994, and offered initially only to UK students.

The implications of innovation, especially technological innovation, and the factors to be considered for good educational practice, will be highlighted.

INTRODUCTION

This paper will refer to two courses which I am currently running at the Institute of Education, London University by computer conferencing.

1.   **OET** (Certificate in Online Education and Training), a two-term part-time course entitled "Problems and Principles in the Use of Computer Networks for Course Delivery". Most of the 50 or so students are in fact lecturers and trainers in higher and continuing education, whose chief aim is to experience computer conferencing to consider using it in courses of their own. They are spread across the United Kingdom, and many countries of the world. They access the computer network via JANET or INTERNET or their own modems at home.

    The course is taught by three lecturers from the Institute, and three from the UK Open University. The conferencing system used has been CoSy, housed on the OU's host computer.

2.   **MA TESOL** (Teaching of English to Speakers of Other Languages) a two-year part-time masters degree course for working English teachers   They have chosen to study by computer networking rather than attend part-time classes in order to be able to work in their own time at home, and have rejected conventional distance teaching, because of the isolation it implies and/or because they cannot spare the time to attend the intensive residential periods that most distance MA TESOLs require.

    The course is equivalent to the well-established MA TESOL that has been taught at the Institute of Education for many years, and is taught by staff of the Institute using CoSy housed in Birkbeck College's host computer..

COMMON FEATURES OF THE TWO COURSES

Mode of communication

Both courses use computer conferencing (cc) as the main medium of communication. This uses technology very similar to that used for electronic mail (e-mail), but the software is different, as will be explained below.

Computer conferencing is not synchronous; participants log on at whatever time they choose. The conference is in fact a set of files, held on the host computer, which all registered members can access: they can read them and write in them. The files are held permanently on the host, so that people logging on can read everything that has been "said" so far, and then add their own messages.

For educational purposes one can think of what occurs in any one file of a cc as the written analogue of a live face-to-face (f2f) seminar. The computer seminar extends over any period of time that the tutor allows (in fact over the duration of the whole course). This enables students to enter and leave the seminar at times convenient to themselves, knowing that they never risk missing anything.

Cc has many advantages over e-mail, which is really just automated high-speed post. Cc is economical since a contribution intended for many recipients need only be transmitted once into one conference and all legitimate participants will have access to it. Recipients are not bombarded with an unordered set of messages from different people, which then have to be collated. Instead, several dialogues proceed within the files of the conference. In cc one can see a discussion developing, whereas e-mail loses the structure of interaction. Within cc, moreover, users are automatically brought into contact with all other participants which does not normally occur with e-mail.

The tutor can, if desirable, edit the conference to make it more coherent, summarise it, remove unacceptable input, add further comments, etc. It is possible to discover who has been into the conference, and follow through to people who have been absent. A cc becomes a database in itself, filled with information provided by the members. But it is more flexible than a database, which normally has pre-ordained formats. A cc database evolves as the users use it.

Need to learn new computing and communication skills

In both courses it is crucial for students to

i   Be able to type adequately.

ii   Be able to perform basic word-processing tasks

iii   Be connected by the telephone lines to the host computer. This means that they either have access to an inter-university communications network such as JANET, in order to log into the host, or they have a PC with a modem and appropriate comms software to drive the modem. For novices in electronic communications, it is not easy to decide which is the best modem or comms software to buy, nor is it easy to learn how to use these from the manuals alone. They contain quite esoteric terms like *text-logging, autotype, parity, baud-rate*, etc.

iv   Be able to use the conferencing system in conjunction with the comms software.   In the commercial field, organisations such as the American COMPUSERVE or the English CIX, have prepared helpful packages which make the process very much simpler. But for our educational use of CoSy such packages were not available. It is expected that in the future many of the problems that our pioneering students have had with the technology will be overcome by more user-friendly software solutions.

v   Be able to transfer the communication and interaction skills familiar to f2f environments into a totally written mode, at a distance in space and time from the interlocutors. Even when the technology becomes easy to use, learning to handle this new mode of communication takes some time, both for tutors and students.

CONTRASTING FEATURES OF THE TWO COURSES

Goals

OET attracts students who wish to experience communication by computer networking and are not very concerned about the award of the Certificate. Only about one third of the 150 or so students who have taken it over the last three years have completed the coursework requirements. This has a significant effect on the nature of the course.

The MA TESOL, on the other hand, is a normal post-graduate degree course for teachers, and has to conform to London University regulations.

The students in OET are extremely relaxed about "attendance" and participation, and do not feel under pressure to do what the tutors ask of them. They are self-motivated and quite likely to steer the course in the direction of their own interests. The MA students, by contrast, know that they have to "attend", do all set coursework, and pass exams. Because of these factors, the design for each course is radically different.

While each is divided over the period of time into sections, or modules, in the normal way, the constraints of university requirements are missing from OET, which has a much looser structure. Topics are set for discussion, readings are recommended and tasks are given. But these are springboards for the students' activities, and there is no attempt by tutors to exhort them to compliance with directions. The result is free-ranging discussion among the students, with tutors joining in and/or helping the discussion by summarising it at certain points. It is in many ways similar to the kinds of online discussions that can be found on COMPUSERVE OR CIX, even though it is slightly more organised by virtue of having a course outline.

The MA, however, is very tightly structured indeed. It is divided into strict time-blocks, with quite specific instructions to individual students telling them which tasks they have to do and when. The students know that the tutor is monitoring their participation which is compulsory even though not assessed.

Course design

1. *New technology*

Both courses address the need to learn new technology by starting with a f2f meeting in which basic hands-on instruction and practice are arranged. But this is part of a one-day general course induction, and only one hour can be devoted to actual practice. Moreover, the practice is perforce on JANET, and therefore does not include methods of using a modem and comms software. It would be impossible to deal with the great range of hardware and software in use by all the students. They were warned in advance to buy from a friendly supplier who could offer after-sales support.

In addition to managing the connections to the host, it is also necessary to learn to use the conferencing software, CoSy,.which is command-driven, and not windows-based, It is in fact easier than most wordprocessing, since a very small number of commands will suffice for basic reading and writing of messages.

Students are provided with a manual and a set of specially written exercises taking them through the main commands.. Some work their way through the exercises at the start of the course, as advised, and find them helpful. Others want what they have come to call "instructions for dummies", ie an even simpler manual that would take them through potential pitfalls, give general advice, and generally provide an online tutorial. It seems as if they merge their technical problems with the CoSy problems, and see all the difficulties as arising from one source.

Many students do experience extreme difficulty and frustration in the early weeks, and the courses have to make allowances for this. In OET it does not matter as much as in the MA, since the course is not so tightly structured. But for the MA special provisions have been made to try to ensure that students can get started and continue studying even while they have technical problems. These are partly the regular f2f meetings and the provision of courseware. (see below).

It would, of course, be highly desirable to ensure that all course members were using the same modems and comms software, but for our courses this is unrealistic at present. The Open University has launched a computer conferenced course for which students are supplied with laptops and software, and that may well be the ideal solution.

It may also be desirable for a degree course to start with a pre-sessional skills period. But experience has shown that students do not take advantage of these, and it might be necessary to make such a period compulsory. For both of our courses, the computing facilities on the host have been made available to the students more than a month before the starting date. But very few students have taken advantage of this opportunity. Some have not even set up their hardware by the time the course starts! This is partly due to the optimism of inexperience; they do not understand the advice given, and do not realise how long it will take them to get organised.

2. *Course Structure*

In both courses, the conference is divided into a number of separate areas for discussion. These are in fact separate files, which, in CoSy are called "topics" They are summarised in the tables below.

a.) OET. The 20 weeks are divided into 5 modules:

Module 1
Course Design - 7 weeks: Weeks 1-3 Introduction to issues in
                             course design, and encouragement to
                             practise CoSy.
                             Weeks 4-6 Discussion of potential of
                             computer conferencing in course
                             design.

Module 2
Collaborative Learning -   4 weeks. This consists of various
                             group tasks and opportunities to
                             discuss how group work can be
                             managed in cc.
Module 3
The Online World -   4 weeks. This period is devoted to
                             exploring the resources of world-
                             wide Internet.

Module 4
Implementations -   4 weeks. An opportunity for students
                             to investigate their special interests and
                             possible applications of cc.

The last week of each module is a "writing week" in which students write 1500 words on the topic of the module. The collection of writings forms the coursework for award of the Certificate.

There are two f2f meetings. The first day of the course is held at the Institute of Education, and consists of activities to help students get to know each other, hands-on practice in the conferencing system, and brief talks about computer conferencing. The second f2f day is about the middle of the course, is optional, and involves further practical use of computer networks, especially other conferencing software.

The following chart lists the Topics (files) which make up the course conference, called OET94. The course designer is free to create any desired structure of topics, giving them his own titles. The pattern of numbering we have used is fairly transparent. All general discussion topics end in 0. and all students read and write in them. In addition, students are allocated to one of the 4 discussion groups and remain in the same group for each module.

There are several topics alongside the course itself. One is an essential Noticeboard for administrative announcements. Students are not allowed to use this. They have their own area for non-course discussion, namely Cafe which is for social chat, and Projects which is for discussion of their own reasons for wanting to learn cc. In zfiles the tutors and students can post readings of special interest.

TOPICS	DESCRIPTION
000	Noticeboard.
100 -	Module 1 general discussion
101 -	Discussion group 1
102 -	Discussion group 2
103-	Discussion group 3
104	Discussion group 4

This pattern is repeated for each module, ie 200, 201, 202, 203, 204, etc.

cswk -	discussion of coursework
projects	description of individual s' future cc plans
cafe -	chat and socialising
zfiles -	documents, papers, articles.

All students receive a detailed course guide which sets out the aims of the course, the above course structure and assessment provisions, brief summaries of the goals of each module together with a reading list for each, and information about the tutors. There is no specially prepared course material. Passwords and identification names to enter the CoSy system, and directions for attendance at the f2f meetings are sent well in advance. Later, students also receive an address list, and a collage of photos of all the students and tutors so that they can relate faces to names on the computer.

The entire course is conducted online, by reference to set readings in textbooks which students are expected to buy. The tutor starts discussion and activity at the start of each module and allows students to handle the discussions their own way in the groups. The tutor may join the discussion within a group if necessary, but will most likely make overall comments in the general discussion area (100, 200, etc) from time to time. These comments pick up interesting points made in all four student groups, and give all participants an overview of what is going on. This is roughly equivalent to a f2f situation in which a number of workshop groups are set up in the room, the tutor moves from one to another, and at the end chairs a plenary session where the work of all groups is brought together.

Every time a student logs onto the conference, s/he will have to look at at least 4 files, namely 000 to see if there are new announcements, 100 (later 200, 300, 400) to see what the tutor is saying about this module, the topic for his/her own group, zfiles if there are articles to read, and probably cafe to catch up with any social chat.

b.)MA TESOL

The table below shows the structure of one 10-week term of the degree. There are 5 subject areas, each of which is covered in a session lasting 2 weeks. The 24 students are allocated to one of two groups for each subject. In addition there is a noticeboard, 000 for general discussion, and a cafe.

TOPIC	**DESCRIPTION**
notices	Noticeboard
000	General discussion
cafe	Social chat
theory1	group 1 to discuss Nature of theory
theory2	group 2 to discuss Nature of theory
aspects1	group 1 to discuss Aspects of language
aspects2	group 2 to discuss Aspects of language
disc1	group 1 to discuss Discourse Analysis
disc2	group 2 to discuss Discourse Analysis
levels1	group 1 to discuss Levels & Scope of Linguistics
levels2	group 2 to discuss Levels & Scope of Linguistics
lexis1	group 1 to discuss Lexis
lexis2	group 2 to discuss Lexis

For this course, there is an elaborate arrangement which inolves the following components:

i.   Two days at the Institute at the start of each term, during which the students have introductory lectures and discussions to start the term's work.

ii. A pack of videos of the main f2f sessions for each of the 5 subjects. Students receive about 1.5hrs of video material for each subject. The videos were made quite informally during the normal f2f classes, and show the lecturer talking to the students, answering their questions, using the OHP, etc. They were edited to include only the most important parts of each session. For instance, students do not receive any video of workshop activity during the sessions.

iii. A list of readings, including set textbooks and recommended books and articles. Some copies of articles are provided if it is known they are hard to come by.

iv. A set of Tasks adapted from worksheets used in the f2f sessions. They are more detailed and also more explicit than the originals, and in many cases contain some brief explanatory notes.

   Students are expected to do all the Tasks, but only one student will put up a suggested answer. A list is put on the Noticeboard to say who should do each Task. The students contribute their answers to their group at some time during the 2 weeks that the session runs, and other students comment on them as they see fit. Some Tasks specifically relate to the readings, some stimulate students to draw on their own experience, others are exercises to reinforce learning of the subject.

   The topic 000 for General discussion allows the tutor and students to move beyond the Tasks to more general issues.

v. A set of past examination papers. Students are encouraged to put a sample answer into the conference for everyone to comment on.

vi. A collage of photos of all the students and tutors so that they can relate faces to names on the computer.

DISCUSSION

There are many educational issues that arise out of this mode of delivery. What seems evident to us already is that cc is a suitable mode of course delivery for the two types of course we have attempted, ie for educators to learn the mode itself, and for a higher degree in a humanities subject (in this case post-initial training of English teachers). Its great advantage for distance education lies in the opportunity for constant and unlimited interaction among students and tutors.

In fact, this interaction has proved so rich, that students complain of "overload". The reason is that unlike a f2f seminar in which only a small number of students manage to say anything, this medium allows everyone to put in as many messages as they wish. Typically, students who miss a week come back to find that they have a vast number of messages to read. Because the medium is print, people are much more anxious not to miss a word than they ever are in an aural situation. Also, they tend to want to transfer the whole conference onto printed paper. This is not usually necessary or worthwhile, but it takes quite some time and self-discipline before students get used to skimming and ignoring some messages.

There are also interesting consequences of the fact that nobody knows when anyone else will log on and read or write messages. If two tutors are working together on the same course, they may unintentionally step on each other's toes, for instance by intruding into each other's space, unless they have very clearly defined their respective roles in advance. In a f2f situation, because people can see each other and gauge what the other might be about to say or do, there is the possibility of negotiation of roles, or even of heading the other person off if necessary. But in cc, a tutor might step in and deal with a matter that his colleague actually wanted to handle differently but had not yet come to.

Among the many issues that still need research are:

Ways of training tutors and students in the new technology.
Developing useful interaction skills in the medium of writing.
Integrating cc with other media in course delivery.
Integrating cc with f2f teaching.
Keeping special materials to a minimum.
The new language skills required.
The most cost-effective way of using the medium.

34. The Use of Computer-based Best Practice Delivery Mechanisms in Education

P.A. Smart and D.R. Hughes, *University of Plymouth*

Summary

This paper reports the results of research aimed at the development of computer based tools to deliver 'best practice' to small and medium sized manufacturing enterprises (SME's). The research led to the development of a methodology which takes SME's through a structured improvement process whilst, at the same time, educating company personnel in the concepts tools and techniques essential to success. From this latter work the development of a computer based tool to support undergraduate education is reported.

The CBT Tool and methodology makes extensive use of recent research findings which have highlighted the importance of securing the full involvement of people at all levels in a company in the improvement process. Only in this way can companies fully ensure that staff own and commit to the solutions developed. Recognising that significant and sustainable improvements in performance cannot be achieved without a fundamental rethink of the business the methodology, supported by a simple to use, easy to understand CBT Tool provides the strategic context in which this rethink can take place. Drawing extensively on the lessons of international manufacturing best practice the methodology incorporates well proven tools and techniques to guide companies through the improvement process.

In addition, to offering the opportunity to secure significant improvements in company performance, attention is focused on the role of the CBT Tool in educating and developing company staff. The nature and extent of the learning process is described explaining the rationale for partitioning activities between the CBT Tool and company staff.

In using the methodology and CBT Tool with undergraduates the approach makes extensive use of role playing in carefully designed workshops to generate contributions, make decisions and agree actions. Because many of the decisions are complex and judgmental the most effective action can only be determined by generating a wide range of contributions from the individuals involved. All are encouraged to feel they have a valid contribution to make. The process is made more productive and effective by the assignment of carefully tailored preworks to be completed prior to each workshop session. To assist in completing prework activities detailed information is provided in the form of Toolkits and proformas which can be used to collect and analyse data.

The use of the CBT in three alternative modes for undergraduate teaching are described; interactive in *Tutorial mode* where the Tool is able to adapt its instructional sequences to the needs of the learner, *Tool mode* - when functioning in this mode, it is not instructing, but educating the learner by enabling a hands-on learning activity, and finally *Tutee mode* - where the learner is able to exercise full control of the computer.

INTRODUCTION

In order to provide a mechanism for delivering knowledge of best practice to company staff or undergraduate and postgraduate students one must start by first defining what is meant by the term "best practice".

BEST PRACTICE

Although a number of authors have emphasised the importance of adopting best practice to regenerate business and advocated its adoption as almost a universal panacea few have attempted to define precisely what it means. A useful starting point is to clarify what is understood as 'best' and 'practice'.

An analysis of the individual terms which make up the phrase 'best practice' revealed the following (Oxford English Dictionary, Cambridge English Dictionary):

Best: applicability within a certain category or in certain circumstances, comparison with all others.

In addition it was reasonably deduced that best does not imply perfection. The underlying notion is one of comparison with all others in a sufficiently homogeneous set to make comparisons meaningful. With regard to **all** others, this may prove impractical in practice. It is also important to note that none of the definitions examined states or even implies that what might be considered to be 'best' cannot be improved upon.

Practice: a physical action or activity of some kind, repeating or pursuing an action.

Clearly, then 'practice' is not theory. It has a physical manifestation, this is not to suggest that the activity or action is unconnected or unsupported by theory, but in so much as it relates to theory, it is applied theory.

THE DELIVERY OF BEST PRACTICE

Essentially, in practice, this means the delivery of *knowledge* relating to best practice. Traditionally such knowledge has been "transferred" by consultants to their clients in the form of advice or assistance in diagnosing company needs, identifying appropriate best practice to meet the needs and assistance in implementing the best practices identified.

Unfortunately, whilst larger and medium sized businesses may already have, or be in a position to buy in required expertise small businesses are known to suffer from resource poverty. Resource poverty is characterised by immense constraints on financial resources, a lack of human resource expertise, and a short range management perspective imposed by a volatile competitive environment (Ibrahim and Goodwin 1986).

Other means by which small companies can acquire knowledge of best practice include attendance at seminars and conferences, television, trade and popular press, technology vendors, books and workbooks, each of which have significant drawbacks.

Attendance at conferences and seminars rarely provides the depth or detail required to inform appropriate action and can be best considered only as raising awareness of best practice. Whilst raising awareness is an essential first step it does not provide an appropriate framework for a coherent programme of action. The same rationale can be applied, to a greater or lesser degree, with respect to articles in the trade or popular press and television programmes.

Vendors of technology not surprisingly suffer from problems of bias, of seeing the clients problems in terms of their technical solutions. Apart from the significant problem of bias the current ethos in manufacturing argues for a focus on simplification, before automation and integration and thus mitigates against the acquisition of best practice via this route.

However, books and in particular workbooks can provide valuable awareness and instructional material. Their availability and relatively low cost provides a reasonable opportunity to acquire knowledge of best practice, especially for those smaller firms restricted by the lack of resources. Methods and techniques may be transferred to the reader/learner of the literature in the form of frameworks used for analysis, supported by relevant case study results to relate those techniques to a comprehensible situation and environment.

Process methodologies, in workbook format, seem to at least fulfil some of the requirements for transferring knowledge of best practice to the target audience. However, though accessible, such materials at best provide a static, predominantly textual mechanism for the delivery of best practice knowledge. Their static nature is unlikely to provide instruction in the practically based, applied methods frequently found in manufacturing regeneration. This is supported by the perceived deficiency of textually based exploded diagrams found in technical manuals, the objective of which is to illustrate the assembly/disassembly of component parts.

In addition, books or workbooks are restricted in the nature of the support they provide lacking the means for automatic calculation, the ability to update, maintain and disseminate information, facilitate analysis and not least facilitate the management of the regeneration process. Declining costs of computer technology, and the advent of well structured, simple to use designs are influencing more small businesses to use computers (Cooley et al 1987). The use of the computer for the provision of 'interactive' learning provides the possibility to both optimise and facilitate the accessibility of human learning (Gotz 1991). This optimisation is characterised by a number of key attributes:

- A computer assisted learning mechanism may be produced by a team of experts (both in content, presentation and design).
- The learner may designate the time and place for the learning interaction to take place.
- Advanced mechanisms offer varying paths of instruction depicted by a self assessment of possessed skill by the learner.
- The learner may request the assistance of help modules to provide support in the learning module.
- Classification of test results may be integrated into the delivery mechanism.
- The learning sequences may be repeated as often as is needed and may take place directly at the workplace when and where a learning need arises.

In addition to these attributes, the dynamic nature of the computing medium and the recent technological advancements and capabilities provide the potential for a learning environment to be created which far surpasses the boundaries of traditional linear computer based training mechanisms (Houldsworth 1992). The advent of 'multi-media' and the use of both animation and simulation techniques for the transfer of practical knowledge enables an environment to be created which may represent the reality of the learners environment, thus facilitating comprehension of complex activities.

SECURING THE FULL INVOLVEMENT OF PEOPLE

Considerable recent research has highlighted the value of securing the full involvement of company staff in any improvement process. Without such support it is debatable whether or not any improvement programme can succeed. This ethos puts company staff at the forefront of the improvement process making all of them responsible, and not their consultants, for the success of the business. Such a philosophy arguably mitigates against the use of consultants and highlights the need to develop existing internal expertise. To achieve the best results staff should be involved at the earliest possible stage so that their knowledge and experience can be fully harnessed.

FEASIBILITY AND DESIRABILITY

Two major considerations arise from the above in terms of the nature and scope of the CBT required. First, the need to train staff in the new techniques, technologies and tools (best practice) so they may fully contribute to the success of the company. Secondly, to support staff in managing and making the necessary decisions and undertaking the types of tasks required in a regeneration programme. This latter issue leads inevitably to decisions on which tasks should be carried out by the CBT and which should be undertaken by company staff.

PARTITIONING TASKS BETWEEN THE CBT AND THE USER

A decision was taken to only use the CBT to manage the regeneration programme, perform any required analysis and to maintain and update information and for management development and training. Quite deliberately it was felt vital that the role of company staff was to weigh and judge the information presented to them and collectively arrive at some consensus on an appropriate course of action. The CBT was not allowed to make decisions.

DUAL ROLE OF THE CBT

An important characteristic of the methodology developed is its ability to not only offer the opportunity to secure significant improvements in company performance, but to use the CBT Tool in educating and developing company staff. Consequently, the Tool, via a tutorial facility whilst providing detailed instruction on the content and structure of the regeneration methodology also provides instructions on the use of the individual tools and techniques contained in the methodology. This capability enables users to learn about the techniques without affecting the company's programme of improvement.

USE OF THE TOOL FOR EDUCATION AND DEVELOPMENT

Little attempt was made to compare computer based training methods with those traditionally used in human to human interactions. Clark (1983), suggests that there is no theoretical reason for comparing computer and traditionally delivered instruction. But advocates the benefits for comparing instructional designs themselves. "As a field, it has finally been accepted that technologies do not mediate learning. Rather, knowledge is mediated by the thought processes engendered by technologies." Therefore, when attempting to use technology as a delivery mechanism to stimulate learning the primary focus is placed on the instructional designs that result in the most productive thought processes. Learning is therefore more directly affected by the soft technologies than it is by the hard technology.

In contrast, a number of studies (Kearsley et al 1983, Kulik et al 1980, Kulik et al 1983, Kulik et al 1984) have compared computer based with more traditional methods of instruction, where significant improvements in learning from computer assisted instruction (CAI) prevailed. However, the popularity of CAI as a new technology may have stimulated much enthusiasm which would doubtlessly contribute much to its relative effectiveness (Jonassen 1988). The reasons that Clark (1986) provides for confounding the success of CAI packages (Courseware) are that the amount of instruction, method and content were uncontrolled. This, it is suggested, is due to the deficiency of the instructional design for producing such courseware and not to the technology itself.

A most useful and lasting taxonomy of educational computer applications is that suggested by Taylor (1980). He places the use of computers for this purpose into three categories: Tutorial, Tool and Tutee.

(i) Tutorial - This category involves a high degree of interactivity from the users, a focus is on the learning needs of the recipient thus requiring the instructional sequences to adapt as the learning need changes. This may be achieved by altering both pace and content to fit the learners requirements, and via the provision of alternative levels of difficulty, or items of interest.

(ii) Tool - The objective of the tool mode is to supply a mechanism in which the user may accomplish a task more efficiently and effectively. When the computer is functioning in this mode, it is not instructing, but educating the learner by enabling a hands-on learning activity.

(iii) Tutee - In this mode the user controls the computer. Most of the functions include programming languages or translators which the user instructs to achieve a desired task. Thus, the learner uses the computer to solve a particular problem. In order to achieve this a more comprehensive understanding of the particular problem is required. This itself constitutes a learning activity.

Bentley (1992) suggests learning is conducted via direct interaction between ourselves and our environment and that learners know 'how to learn'. This concept therefore makes possible the provision of a computer based environment which enables the recipient to learn in their own 'personalised' way.

The use of a computer based tool for teaching may be viewed as following two of the three paths suggested by Taylor (1980). First, the provision of 'tools' which enable the learner to conduct experimental learning (Bentley 1992).

For example, a module was designed which provided a tool for the learner which was based on environmental scanning and stakeholder concepts. Providing a 'tool' in this way ensured that the learner consciously took a holistic view of the relative performance of the key stakeholders (customers, competitors, suppliers) in the context of the business information supplied.

In addition, support must be provided for this method of learning. Information was supplied in a set of 'tutorial' style modules which provided the background knowledge and context for the objective of the tool. This included the provision of information on origin, rationale and supported worked examples directly relating to the experimental learning exercise presented in the tool mode. This information was stored in varying degrees of complexity where each item of information would have associated items based on the following criteria: possibly of interest, probably of interest, more specific, more generic (Bentley 1992).

Furthermore, the identified 'best practice' was partitioned into discrete modules to facilitate the comprehension of its content and provide visible goals to enhance the motivation of the learner.

CONCLUSIONS

The paper has presented a number of considerations necessary for effectively delivering best practice to both industry and undergraduate students. The utilisation of technology provides a formidable opportunity for instigating learning experience in a number of circumstances. This include cost, time and safety considerations to mention a few. In addition, the approach presented attains a direct compatibility with the ethos of making companies responsible for the emerging activities relevant to successful business improvement. This concept is further supported by the identification of the need to involve personnel in the learning/educational process and by their participation in judgmental decision making. The approach focuses on the importance of the instructional design of such mechanisms to mediate learning in the intended target audience as opposed to a focus on the capabilities of the hard technologies.

References

Bentley, T., (1992), *Training to Meet the Technology Challenge*, McGraw-Hill.

Clark, R. E., (1983), Reconsidering Research on Learning from Media, *Review of Educational Research*, 53, 445-460.

Clark, R. E., (1986), Research on Student Thought Processes During Computer Based Instruction, *Journal of Instructional Development*, 8(3), 2-6.

Cooley, P. L., Waltz, D. T., and Waltz, D. B., (1987), A Research Agenda for Computers and Small Business, *American Journal of Small Business*, *12*, (3), 31-42.

Gotz, K., (1991), Interactive Learning with the Computer, *Educational Training and Technology International (ETTI)*, *28*, (1), 7-14.

Houldsworth, E., (1992), Technology Based Training as a Potential Aid to Competitive Advantage: A Survey of Small and Medium Enterprise & Training and Enterprise Councils, *Working Paper Series, Henley Management College*.

Ibrahim, A.B. and Goodwin, J.R., (1986), Perceived Causes of Success in Small Business, *American journal of small business*, 41-50.

Jonassen, D. H. (Ed) (1988), *Instructional Designs for Microcomputer Courseware*, Lawrence Erlbaum Associates.

Kearsley, G., Hunter, B., and Sidel, R. J., (1983), Two Decades of Computer Based Instruction: What We Have Learned?, *THE Journal*, 10, 88-96.

Kulik, C., Kulik, J., and Bangert-Drowns, R., (1984), Effects of Computer Based Education on Secondary School Pupils, Annual American Educational Research Association Meeting, New Orleans.

Kulik, J., Bangert, R., and Williams, G., (1983), Effects of Computer Based Teaching on Secondary School Students, *Journal of Educational Psychology*, 25,19-26.

Kulik, J., Kulik, C., and Cohen, P., (1980), Effectiveness of Computer Based College Teaching: *A Meta-Analysis of Findings, Review of Educational Research*, 50, 525-544.

Taylor, R., (1980), *The Computer in Education: Tutor, Tool and Tutee*, New York: Teachers College Press.

35. Developing an Alternative Mode of Delivery for the B.A. Hospitality Management at the Robert Gordon University

Richard W Barnes, *Robert Gordon University, Aberdeen*

Summary

A shift in the emphasis of government higher education policy, changes in higher education funding models, wider access programmes and the demographic shift changing the market profile are amongst the main catalysts for the development of alternative modes of delivery of the degree course in hospitality management.

Market research has been undertaken to ascertain the demand amongst hospitality employers and employees for a part-time/distance learning route into the existing degree programme and to identify areas of synergy with continuous development programmes of organisations. It is anticipated that these results will be presented and discussed at the conference.

In conjunction with the development of the course, new modes of delivery, such as teleconferencing and remote computer based learning will be appraised to ascertain their viability as an appropriate support and teaching mechanism.

This paper will identify and discuss the major influences for change and characterise the key factors of developing a new mode of delivery around an existing full time course.

INTRODUCTION

The B.A. Hospitality Management, a 3 year full time unclassified degree and 4 years full time Honours degree is offered at the School of Food and Consumers Studies, part of the Faculty of Health and Food at the Robert Gordon University, Aberdeen. All the courses within the School have been extensively developed over the past 25 years and now all courses are based on a modular, continuously assessed design in which students study an establish group of modules which collectively constitute a named course.

The B.A. Hospitality Management currently on offer was validated in 1990. A major factor in the changed course design was to facilitate a smooth articulation for students, from the SCOTVEC validated H.N.D. in Hospitality Management also offered by the School. This innovatory move was the first time such an articulation process in hospitality management had been offered in Scotland.

Currently there are 196 students studying the B.A. (all years) of which 83 students have entered through the articulation process. 16 students have entered the degree programme with H.N.D. or H.N.C. qualifications from other institutions.

The success of students articulating from H.N.D. has been high with 31 graduating with unclassified degrees and 2 graduating with honours in 1993.. In the initial year of the honours programme, the very first student to graduate with a first class honours was of the first cohort to articulate from H.N.D. to B.A.

WHY DEVELOP A DISTANCE LEARNING FORM OF THE COURSE ?

The Robert Gordon University is committed to a wider access programme for students. In recent years the School has sought, successfully, to increase student numbers to the hospitality management degree as per the Universitys' corporate plan. However, the shift in emphasis of government policy towards science and engineering courses has brought into question the continued funding of hospitality management students at the current levels. This means that one of the few areas available for expansion is the provision of full cost courses.

The benefits to the Robert Gordon University of developing a distance learning mode of the hospitality degree were identified as increased liaison between the University and the hospitality industry and the opportunity provided by a closer relationship in working together to identify and address the future training needs of the industry.

Following the successful conversion of the certificate and diploma in Occupational Health Nursing at the Robert Gordon University, Ellington H. I. & Lowis A. (1992), the B.A. Hospitality Management was identified as an ideal course for development into distance learning mode due to its modular design and the equivalence of the first two years to a certificate and diploma respectively.

METHODOLOGY UNDERTAKEN

It was decided to conduct market research to assess the viability of the proposed conversion by the following methods;

- Conduct an open forum between local senior hospitality managers, personnel practitioners and staff of the School of Food and Consumer studies to elicit opinions and ideas.
- Conduct a national market research survey of hospitality managers to gauge opinion on the development, content and likely take-up.
- Conduct a national market research survey of hospitality employees to gauge opinion on aspirations, need and likely take-up.

The open forum was held in mid November 1993. The general consensus of the hospitality practitioners attending was that distance learning *and* part time routes were desirable. It had originally been intended by the planning team, that the distance certificate and diploma would potentially lead some students to undertake a third phase of 6 months full time attendance at the University to gain a degree. However, it was suggested that the development of this third qualification also be considered for development in a distance learning mode.

The main areas of discussion were as follows;

- Costs to students and employers needed to be identified at an early stage in order to ascertain likely take-up. Employers identified this as a critical area.
- Access to funding routes needed to be identified and clarified. Use of the Grampian Enterprise innovatory 'Skillseekers' programme was cited as potentially providing a major impetus for local employers.
- Employers identified the need to create and provide support networks for students undertaking distance learning. This point was related to the students ability to maintain self discipline outwith the normal educational environment.
- The need for group activity, therefore some form of attendance at the University was stressed.

This latter point is currently being addressed via the formulation of either summer schools or course induction programmes. As the hospitality industry is service oriented and 'people focused', social interactivity and personal presentation skills underpin a great deal of the current full-time course. A priority of the development of the distance learning mode is the maintenance and integration of these key elements.

Following the open forum, two questionnaires were developed to elicit the views of employers and employees in a range of hospitality units nation-wide. The main aim of the employer survey was to ascertain employers requirements and preferences for staff development towards recognised management qualifications in the hospitality industry. Following an initial evaluation of the employer responses (81 organisations), the major factors to emerge were;

- time spent away from the workplace could place severe restraints on any training and development initiative.
- training & development was identified as important in developing the industry further and keeping pace with continental competitors.
- 95% of employers approached would be willing to support a member of staff on such a programme.

The aim of the employee survey was to ascertain if staff currently employed in the hospitality industry wished to further their careers by obtaining educational qualifications through distance learning. Initial responses (n=154) indicate;

- Almost 80% wished to move to, and progress within management.
- 80% felt that securing a management qualification is extremely important.
- Of those who wished to further develop their qualifications, over 85% opted for a distance learning approach due to difficulty in travelling to the education/training provider.

IDEAS INTO ACTION

Following consideration of the market research results, the academic course team developed a more focused aim for the project, this being;

"To provide an updating route for the hospitality industry leading to the award of a recognised academic qualification via a distance learning mode with minimum periods of attendance at The Robert Gordon University".

In developing this programme it is planned to provide a series of co-ordinating elements to suit individuals at various stages in their careers. Courses may be stand-alone or may lead from one stage to another through certificate and diploma to degree level.

THE PRACTICAL APPROACH

In order to prepare the course for the market, it was decided to utilise the model developed by Professor Henry Ellington of the Educational Development Unit at the Robert Gordon University, Ellington H. I. & Lowis A. (1992), as a new course did not need to be 'written from scratch' but a new mode of delivery developed from the existing validated course. The development model is summarised in figure 35.1.

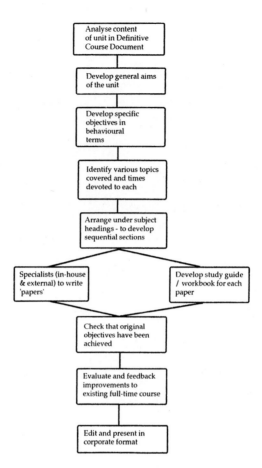

Figure 35.1

Key elements

An important aspect in the development of the model is the question of Accreditation of Prior Learning (APL) and Accreditation of Prior Experiential Learning (APEL). Certain units which are basic to this vocational course cannot be offered by distance mode. These include the practical food service and food preparation elements. Therefore it has become necessary to develop APL and APEL criteria to offer exemption from these units. It is anticipated that the criteria for these exemptions will be closely linked to the NVQ/SVQ frameworks. A working party has been initiated to consolidate this complex area. It is anticipated that entrants to the distance learning course will all be current practitioners within the industry and may have experience in the aforementioned areas. Should this not be so, then intensive summer schools and/or masterclasses may be developed.

The initial suggested model for the distance version of the course is presented in figure 35.2;

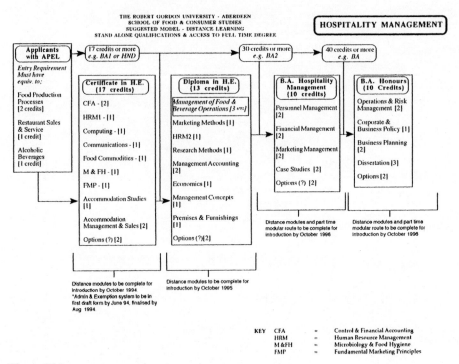

Figure 35.2

ASSESSMENT

A key factor in any award bearing course is that of obtaining feedback and assurance of competence - assessment. In order to maintain the validity and integrity of the host course, alternative assessment mechanisms which display achievement of the relevant specific objectives are being developed. It is important that assessments test knowledge and competences equivalent to those of full time students. Any disparity would be contentious - especially if students studying by distance learning were to eventually articulate to full time attendance.

OTHER DEVELOPMENTAL ISSUES

Areas highlighted for further investigation and development within the project are;

- Production of innovative course materials
- Production of video/interactive video and audio cassette materials
- Development and production of CD-Rom based learning materials
- Cross secondment of academic staff and industry practitioners to update expertise.
- Teleconferencing
- Remote computer based learning
- Tutorial support by telephone
- Arrangements for student networking

CONCLUSION

As with any major new development, commitment to the projects' success is dependent upon support at all levels, from senior management of the University, academic staff, external writers and hospitality employers. Any new or diversified product must also meet the needs of the consumer. The flexibility of the unitised hospitality degree allows for a great deal of versatility in creating and further developing this new version of an already successful product. It has already been clearly established that the development of this distance learning course will be of great value for further developing the host course by encouraging academic updating and improving the standard of teaching materials used.

References

Ellington H. I. & Lowis A. (1990)Converting a conventional taught course into Distance Learning form - a Case Study. In "*Aspects of Educational and Training Technology XXV*" (D. Saunders & P. Race, eds.); Kogan Page, London; pp 88-92 (1993)

Ellington H. I. (1990) Teaching in-post college lecturers by open-learning methods - a novel approach to staff development in the Scottish Central Institutions in Eastcott D., Farmer R. & Lantz B. *Aspects of Educational and Training Technology XXIII;* Kogan Page, London; pp 99-102

36.   Video autoEditing System for Open Learning (VESOL)

Chris O'Hagan, *University of Derby*

Summary
By the 21st Century it could be common practice for lecturers, presenters, demonstrators to video their work in real time, editing it on-line, without technician or other human assistance. This paper describes VESOL, the system being developed at the University of Derby, which has the power to generate an enormous amount of material for resource-based open learning. The system is shown to have the potential to break the tyrannies imposed by lecture schedules in higher education, as well as provide communication and training resources for industry and commerce.

INTRODUCTION

The development of computer assisted learning has come rather to overshadow the development of video and television in education and training, to the point where video is now seen as somewhat old-fashioned by enthusiasts of instructional technologies, or at best as just another digitised element within the multimedia format.

This is unfortunate, but not surprising. The history of audio-visual methods in education is full of examples of discarded systems displaced by the latest technological breakthrough before their full potential has been realised. Yet video is the most ubiquitous of all audio-visual technologies within the domestic environment, and very common in educational contexts. Diane Gayeski has surveyed research into the success and failure of information technologies, and has found that video is one of the very few unequivocal successes in education (Gayeski 1989).

The problems in further developing the use of video lie more in the difficulties in originating good material, than in access to delivery platforms - the VHS videocassette machine is common in the home and in education and training, and these days can often cope with different standards (for the UK) such as SECAM and NTSC. Elsewhere I have described how much better educational use can be made of off-air recordings (O'Hagan 1994a), but it is still difficult and relatively expensive to create one's own material from scratch.

Part of the problem in originating material is that programme makers can seem quite technocratic to the layperson with their obsessions with equipment, formats and broadcast standards. On the other hand, educational developers can seem quite technophobic to the educational technologist. Yet technology should empower both teacher and student, not an elite group of producers; and educational techniques should inform technology, not resist it. Video in educational establishments suffers from such a technocratic background. There are few opportunities for staff or student control, for real customisation. Even where expensive studio, editing and technical support is provided, the feeling of ownership is not strong.

THE INVENTION OF VESOL

At the University of Derby, the Directorate were seeking efficiency gains to cope with the costs of rapid expansion. The videoing of lectures to save lecturing time where lectures are repeated in the same or subsequent years was suggested. However, the problem was to do this without incurring great expense, without requiring a lot of technical support and without seeming to deskill or diminish the lecturer's role. The system had to be cheap enough to install in every lecture theatre and simple enough for any lecturer to use. The sense of lecturer control, of educational control over the whole process was essential.

Within this framework the idea of VESOL, Video auto-Editing System for Open Learning was conceived as a system for lecturers to record their lectures and presentations without technical assistance, empowering them completely through fuss-free technology to produce on-line, fully edited programmes in real time, with or without an audience, and of any chosen length.

Recording of lectures in sound and vision is not new. That it is not done more frequently and consistently has both technical and educational explanations:

a) Complicated staging for the lecturer
b) Intrusive equipment
c) Technical support required
d) Expensive in equipment and support staff
e) Lectures frequently lack visual interest and variety
f) Lack of a strong educational rationale

In fact, the lack of an educational rationale is to a large extent a consequence of unwieldy technology. VESOL solves most of the technical and cost limitations, and so opens the way to a strong rationale which is reinforced by the convergence of analogue and digital technologies in multimedia, and particularly by a strong push in higher education towards open and distance learning techniques.

THE VESOL SYSTEM

Two different systems have been installed at the University of Derby, to explore the kind of configurations that lecturers from different subject areas would find most appropriate.

The first system is illustrated schematically in Figure 36.1. It is a four camera system with an option to add another camera if required. The lecturer selects a camera using the switched mixer mounted on the top of the lectern. Just above the mixer, a monitor shows what the selected camera is seeing, and therefore what is being recorded to tape. A wall mounted monitor gives the same information, which is particularly useful when the lecturer moves away from the lectern (in long shot, or when using the whiteboard). With judicious lecture planning and preparation, the lecturer can produce quite a varied programme, with close and long shots of herself plus visual illustrations. If required, the system can take computer data directly using a transcoder (genlockable) while outputting to the live audience through a video projector. Similarly video can also be introduced into programmes, (subject to copyright restrictions, of course).

It might be said that this is rather a lot for the lecturer to cope with. In practice, it is much simpler than it sounds, assuming that the lecturer is skilled at using the presentation methods included, like overhead projectors and slide projectors, and that the slides for these have been well made using a good point size for the lettering (maximum 40 characters to a line on the TV screen). Some individual experimentation is required to discover what works well in terms of colours, lines and letters. Handwritten slides can be used, but are best avoided.

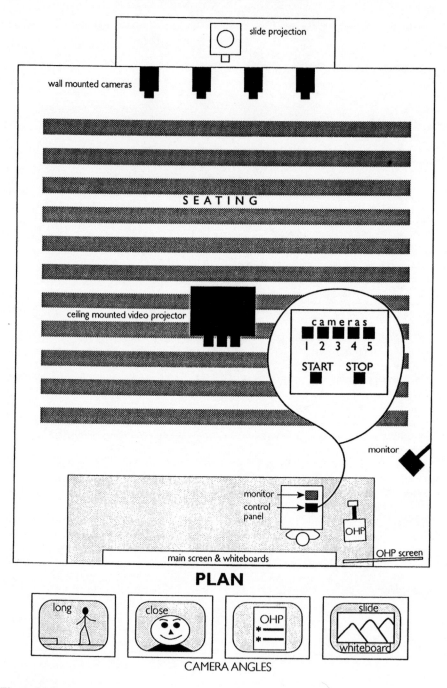

Figure 36.1

An experienced lecturer habitually reviews the process of a lecture as it proceeds, so that the addition of an extra element in that review, "which camera at this moment?" is soon accommodated, particularly if some thought is given to it before the lecture. Indeed, it is remarkable how well people manage the first time they use the system, particularly if they have watched the introductory videos which have been produced using the system itself - "What is VESOL", "Uses of VESOL" and "Getting the Best from VESOL". The beginner starts by making a short video of 10 to 15 minutes without an audience and progresses to a live recording when he feels confident. Because no technician support is necessary, lecturers can practise at times to suit themselves and the availability of the system. A variation on the system described above uses a rostrum camera in place of the more conventional overhead projector. The signal from the rostrum camera goes direct to tape and to a video projector, which is how a live audience accesses this input.

Both systems in basic form cost around £8,000, assuming the auditorium is already equipped with slide, video, and overhead projection.

TECHNICAL ISSUES AND QUALITY

The relatively low cost has been achieved by using top-end domestic equipment rather than professional. However, there must be at least one professional recorder in the system - Hi-Band UMatic, Betacam, S-VHS etc. This produces a master for making VHS copies, or for post-production editing, or for transferring to digital formats such as multi-media.

At Derby we have begun with two recorders, one VHS, one S-VHS. This means two recordings can be made simultaneously. The lecturer can take the VHS copy away with her for reviewing, and the S-VHS can be kept as master. The recorders operate simultaneously, and the controls have been tapped off to a set of basic buttons - EJECT, PLAY, STOP, REWIND, FAST-FORWARD - located above the recorders inside the lectern/console. On top of the lectern are just two buttons to control recording, START and STOP, which override all other controls. When the lecturer presses start, the monitor cues up START, and then MARK, at which point the tape is up to speed and the lecturer can begin.

Sound is recorded via a clip-on microphone and transmitter. The S-VHS recorder has a bar-graph to check that the sound system is working before beginning. All staff who have been trained to use the system access the console and microphone with a key, replacing the microphone before locking up after use. Getting going requires just 1 or 2 minutes in total from unlocking the console to pressing the start button, with experience.

The VESOL system is functional and meets its design criteria. So some of the main barriers to an educational rationale for videoing lectures have been overcome.

THE IMPACT OF VESOL

VESOL is associated with TOTAL, Tutor Only Transfer of Authored Lessons, a multimedia system which has the same ambition of stripping away the technocracy and giving lecturers some autonomy in creating computer-assisted learning tutorials. Short extracts from VESOL tapes are digitised into the tutorials, providing a resource which can replace the use of text. Too much text to read from a VDU has been a major flaw in computer-assisted learning packages.

What began with the idea of simply replacing repetitive lecturing time has developed into a system with enormous potential for open and resource-based learning. As Baxter (1989) has commented, " Ensuring a high quality and quantity of learning resources (is) one of the first steps in establishing a successful RBL programme. Such a rich resource base provides students with greater freedom in their learning, which in turn encourages learning for understanding." The beauty of VESOL is that potentially it can provide an enormous quantity of resources for RBL, building on resources which already exist - lectures - but which normally would be lost into the void.

More dramatically, it has the power to transform the way lectures are both given and used. It can break down tyrannies that the lecture system has erected. Firstly, the tyranny of the lecture schedule: it permits time-shift of either lecture or lecturer, liberating both lecturer and student. Secondly, the tyranny of the 'fifty-five minute slot': lectures can be broken down into sections, mini-lectures can be created, or several views from different experts included in a single tape. And perhaps most important of all, it can open up material to cross-disciplinary use, and allows students to explore more readily the interfaces between subject areas. All this can be done at very little added cost in time and resources. The uses, features and advantages of VESOL are summarised in Figure 36.2

VESOL

Uses:
• Time shift of lectures and lecturer
• Extending learning resources across courses and to part-time students
• Replacing repetitive lecturing time
• Generating mini-lectures to support other materials
• Lecture observation for self development and/or appraisal
• In distance learning packages
• In multi-media tutorials (eg. TOTAL)
• Recording guest or key speakers

Features
• Videotaping of lectures in real time
• Multi-camera for flexibility of presentation
• Other visual inputs (OHP, slide, video, film, solid objects, computer)
• LECTURER CONTROL
• Radio microphone for freedom of movement
• Two tape qualities (VHS and professional high quality)
• Can insert-edit off line
• Possibilities of other inputs (eg. audience response)
• Can be operated from rear for guest lectures

Advantages
• Better lecture planning and structure
• Better use of visual information
• More attention to support material
• Interactive uses
        for independent tutorials and tutorless group tutorials
        in study packs
        in multi-media programmes
• Short information videos on service providers and in industry
• Cable TV community channel programme potential

Figure 36.2

THE VESOL/TOTAL PROJECT

The joint development project has won a grant of nearly £200,000 over 3 years for the University of Derby as a part of the Higher Education Funding Council for England Teaching and Learning Technology Programme (Phase 2). It is a single institution project and not based on a consortium.

The project has several phases which may be summarised as follows:

i) To design and commission two different VESOL systems and to design a series of graded multimedia TOTAL shells to enable tutor-only authoring.

ii) To produce a staff development programme and train key users.

iii) To produce courseware in VESOL, TOTAL and VESOL/TOTAL.

iv) To evaluate the courseware in terms of effectiveness and efficiency - key outcomes for a TLTP funded project.

v) To disseminate the results, products and specification across the HE sector.

The project began in September 1993, and at the time of writing (March 1993) has reached phase iii) for VESOL.

EVALUATION

This is qualitative rather than quantitative at the moment.

i) The system works technically and is cheap enough to install in every lecture theatre, key laboratories and workshops over a relatively short period of time.

ii) The picture quality is not 'broadcast' but is fit for purpose provided simple guidelines are followed.

iii) The educational and creative quality depends on the lecturers skills. One of the advantages of the system is that it encourages the introduction of clearer structure, clearer delivery and more variety into the lecturer's presentation.

iv) Programmes have been produced in little more time than it takes to record them using the usual materials for presentation.

v) A spin-off has been the enthusiasm from areas like the Library and Student Services to use the system to produce short informational programmes.

Usage so early in the project is relatively light, but growing, and there is a lot of enthusiasm. Staff development materials have been created using the system and distributed across the University. Several staff development seminars have been organised to discuss the nature and implications of the system. To try to discover more about staff attitudes to the system and technology based learning in general a questionnaire has been distributed which is currently being processed. A superficial analysis suggests that it is not particularly technophobia or suspicion of senior management motives that deters involvement with technology in learning, but a lack of available time, training, and understanding. This would confirm other research that technophobia is not as prevalent as is often suggested by enthusiasts for new technology. "In a survey of teachers reactions to educational computing, it was found that different uses of computer technology elicit different concerns about the technology. Teacher's concerns did not address a total package of technology, but rather specific applications of the technology, demonstrating that computers per se were not troubling to them." (Gayeski 1989)

I believe that systems like VESOL and TOTAL are more likely to be successful than many technology based systems because they have a high level of teacher autonomy and ownership, as well as increasing the flexibility of student study (O'Hagan 1994b). However, an ongoing investigation at the University of Durham suggests there is an enormous gap between the aims and objectives of current development projects (e.g. TLTP) and the ability and readiness of academic staff and students to capitalise on these benefits (Adcock & McCartan 1994). One could also add that there are infrastructural problems posed as to how students will access learning opportunities in an expanding and more technological educational environment (MacFarlane 1992). For example, if VESOL diffuses to all lecturers in the University, how will the enormous quantity of tapes be stored and accessed? How will students gain access to playback facilities? These are issues which most systems claiming any degree of potential ubiquity must address before bottlenecks create disillusionment.

CONCLUSION

VESOL has enormous potential for opening up learning opportunities by breaking down barriers created by lecture schedules in universities and other educational establishments. It could be a major tool in developing new approaches to open learning. It could also have important uses outside education, in industry and commerce in both communication and training contexts. I would be pleased to discuss the system, its uses and problems via email, C.M.OHagan@uk.ac.derby.

References

Adcock D & McCartan (1994)   Enabling strategies to enhance the use of teaching and learning technologies in higher education: a national and institutional perspective in O'Hagan (1994b)

Gayeski D M (1989) Why Information Technologies Fail *Educational Technology* 29 (2) 9-17

MacFarlane A G J (1992) *Teaching and Learning in an Expanding Higher Education System* Scottish Centrally-Funded Colleges, Edinburgh

O'Hagan C M (1994a) The use and abuse of video in education R.Hoey ed (1994) Aspects XXVII: *Designing for Learning:Effectiveness with Efficiency* Kogan Page London

O'Hagan C M (1994b)   *Empowering Learners and Teachers Through Technology* Staff and Educational Development Association Birmingham (in preparation)

Baxter E P (1989) Problem-based Education *Higher Education* 18 p338

37. Campus-Wide Collaboration in the Delivery of Distributed Learning Technology

Hassan Khan, Wilma Strang, Vicki Simpson and David Slater, *University of Kent*

Summary
Hypermedia is a technology gaining prominence in its potential use as a learning tool. The flexibility offered by an information rich hypermedia environment, to people with different learning strategies is discussed, the inherent cognitive processes of hypermedia systems are also considered. Central to this new technology is the consideration of authors of applications using hypermedia systems, and the users. To this end the paper deals with the requirements of a specialist unit for support and development in computer aided learning (CAL) applications. It describes such a unit established at UKC and looks at its integration with other university services by way of examples.

INTRODUCTION

Hypermedia is now widely regarded as a premier vehicle for the presentation of information and creation of computer aided learning material. The term hypermedia describes information including text, graphics and other media linked via a series of nodes resulting in an information rich content environment that can be accessed or navigated via a number of different pathways. The obvious implications of this technology for teaching and learning, especially its potential for interactivity, continue to be explored and exploited.

Hypertext systems have often been compared to databases, but whilst there is a semblance of similarity, such systems are not subject to the rigorous structure laid down in traditional databases. The inherent navigational pracilities of typical hypertext systems allow for very overt movement through resource material, allowing users to apply different learning strategies to the material. Hypermedia is ".. a new form of information access which is highly attractive to users because it leaves them in full control of that access while at the same time making it extremely easy, on the surface at least. Hypermedia, in turning over control to the learner, puts more burden on him or her to seek out pertinent information without getting disorientated, as well as to provide a greater deal of the integration needed for comprehension." (Duchastel, 1990) Above all, the appeal of hypermedia is its use as a learning tool "..espousing a very constructivist approach tolearning." (Duchastel, 1990) Dufresne describes the advantages of CAL material as : "In the context of computer learning, interactive documentation has many advantages: dynamic figures; flexible detailing; the opportunity for the user to manipulate and make inferences; the opportunity to introduce tests and intelligent guiding of the user."(Dufresne et al, 1990)

The recent explosion of interest in hypermedia in universities, and participation in the World Wide Web (WWW -a global hypertext system) has reinforced the use of hypertext for the browsing of information in a distributed environment. Many institutions are now using Hypertext Mark language (HTML) in order to mark up various documents, including research papers and course information, so that they can be placed on the Web and be accessible.

Hypermedia allows the creation of teaching material which can be adapted for various cognitive styles, by not imposing a particular style of learning on individuals. Four cognitive process central to hypermedia interaction can be identified:

- browsing
- searching

- integrating
- angling (Duchastel, 1990)

Authors of hypermedia applications must take account of these process for they will dictate how much accessibility and flexibility will be allowed in their application. The last process namely angling is mainly user focussed in that it describes how a person using a hypermedia application can take a number of different navigational pathways to explore the same topic, thus seeing the same material each time with a different perspective.

Stanton and Stammers (Stanton and Stammers, 1990) state the advantage of hypertext as:

1) Allowing for different levels of prior knowledge ;

2) encouraging exploration;

3) enabling subjects to see a sub-task as part of the whole ;

4) allowing subjects to adapt material to their own learning style.

Hypermedia applications can be cost-effective through re-use, reduce training time and significantly enhance traditional teaching methods.

HYPERMEDIA: THE ANSWER TO THE SHAKE-UP?

The recent reorganisation of the educational structure, including the reduction of teaching time, increased student numbers and increased scrutiny of teaching standards has led to a complete rethink of teaching strategies (Strang et al,1993). The perceived need to introduce computer based learning material into British higher educational institutions has changed into a reality in response to which a concerted effort in the form of various initiatives is taking place. These efforts which, two years ago, were tentative are now proceeding apace through many Universities bringing on-board sceptics to accept the inevitability of the use of technology in teaching. Hypermedia based teaching material is seen to be a suitable solution to the constraints brought about by the reforms to HE. However, we are at a time when many of the initiatives have been running for some time and indeed some reaching conclusion. This should provide some interesting feedback regarding applications developed as part of the various initiatives. Quantitative and qualitative results are now needed to reassure academics and and funding bodies alike and to assess the implications of using hypermedia technology to assist in the reorganisation of HE.

HYPERTEXT SUPPORT UNIT

In August 1992 the Universities Funding Council announced 43 projects which were to be funded under the Teaching and Technology Programme (TLTP). The aim of the programme was "....to make teaching and learning more productive and efficient by harnessing modern technology. This will help institutions to respond effectively to the recent growth in student numbers, and to promote and maintain the quality of provision." (HEFC, 1993) One of these projects was the Hypertext Campus Project (HCP) from the Univerity of Kent (UKC). The aim of the HCP was to create a specific unit, the Hypertext Support Unit (HSU) that was to be responsible for introducing technology into teaching. The unit promotes the pervasive use of hypertext through staff support and development by offering assistance in all major hypertext systems on all major platforms. The university already has a fair expertise in hypertext, as KST UNIX Guide, one of the first hypertext systems was developed there by Professor Peter Brown. The creation of the HSU has centralised this expertise and provided a point of reference as an additional academic service.

The unit had a difficult role to achieve its objectives due to traditional intrinsic obstacles to the introduction of technology. Obstacles such as:-

- a general lack of awareness of technology and its implications
- a lack of resources for such activities
- a lack of recognition accorded to effort directed to courseware development

Early on it was realised that the majority of academics would be fairly new to hypermedia technology, and for the HCP to be successful it needed to really target such a group. This was reflected in that the staff recruited forthe project had computing knowledge but were not specialists, and above all were selected for their communication skills. In addition to this the unit has been set up as a distinct entity, a public office away from the Computing Laboratory is available as a first point of call for interested staff. This encourages staff who are apprehensive about and unfamiliar with new technology and find direct access to the Computing Laboratory rather forbidding. However, other members of the HSU are located within the Laboratory, this permits access to technical assistance from other computer support services.

The unit has been accorded a fairly high priority and is actually co-ordinated and managed as part of UKC's academic services. Academic staff involvement with the HCP and the HSU is actively encouraged through the Curriculum Development Sub-Committee and staff and HSU achievements are recognised at the University management level. With the involvement of the Curriculum Development Sub-Committee the problems of resources for the HSU's activities have been directly addressed. Participating staff have been able to gain in terms of personal and professional development and in some cases apply for and receive curriculum development (or research) grants for their self-initiated hypertext projects.

The work of the HSU includes supporting staff and students in developing applications, offering consultancy services across the campus, providing workshops and seminars on hypermedia and delivering a wide range of associated documentation. A fist draft of a guidelines document outlining good authorship practices has just gone into internal circulation and will shortly be widely available.

SOME EXAMPLES

The HSU in its second year has managed to integrate well within the university structure. It has played a middle role between the novices to technology and the experts in the field. It has filled a gap which traditionally has been difficult to bridge. The role of the unit and its interaction with other departments and units within the university are best highlighted by following the development of some of the applications the unit has been involved in.

A GUIDE TO CAREERS

The Careers service at UKC is a popular haunt of final year students who visit for information on job vacancies. However, the careers service is also a stop for people seeking information on letter-writing, preparing CV's, interviewing skills, and sitting company tests etc. Thecareers officer attended a couple of workshops, run by the HSU, on hypertext and was immediately struck by the potential of using hypertext for the presentation of general careers information.

The careers officer was keen to carry out the development of his ideas on his own and in that respect had a good idea about the application that he envisaged. HSU assistance was sought in introductory documents to PC-Guide the hypermedia package that was to be used, thereafter continuous support right through the development was available. Since the application was useful across the campus it was felt that it should be available on the PC campus network as opposed to a select few stand-alone machines. A specialist Micro-support unit at UKC services such needs on a permanent basis, however in order to deal with increased capacity of workload, the HSU liaised with the unit so that they could take the role of putting hypermedia applications on the network. In this manner the HSU was able to have access to technical assistance, and realise the requirements for the application to be networked, and communicate these to the careers officer. The result of this collaboration is a widely used package by students across the campus, and a careers officer familiar with authoring CAL material in a major hypermedia platform. The HSU was also able to work well with Micro-support and learn about networking future hypermedia applications.

In this example it is interesting to note that the officer retained a sense of ownership of the application and has since produced a version two. The application has also attracted the attention of other careers services and will be made available to them.

A STUDENT'S STUDY HINTS GUIDE

This application was developed in conjunction with another academic services unit, namely curriculum support. In this instance the proposers of the application did not know anything about hypermedia systems and left the entire development to the HSU. The approach taken by the HSU was one of incremental development, where a prototype was rapidly developed and then extended in stages to produce the final application. Whilst the HSU appreciated that the "clients" could not, for various reasons, undertake any development, they were kept very much involved in the creation of the application. The staff were invited to comment upon and make suggestions at every meeting, they were shown all versions of the application. This approach again contributed to the fact that the curriculum support unit still see the application as very much their own work.

A GUIDE TO THE CAMPUS

This application contained general information about the university, Canterbury town, bus schedules, places to eat etc. The material was contained in a handbook available from the Students Union. Although the development was carried out by the HSU alone, it was pre-development where a lot of discourse had to take place with the Student Union as regard their material. The Union officers had to be made aware of the concepts of hypermedia and the advantage of having their resource material in electronic format distributed across the campus.

Whilst no quantitative analysis have yet been conducted, it is known that these applications are being used quite frequently. There is no doubt that by having the same material available on the network a larger student base is being exposed to the information resources.

CONCLUSIONS

Several issues have been raised above but we now seek to consolidate our thoughts. Firstly hypermedia does have the potential to solve some of the problems facing HE. The technology is available and getting cheaper. The trend has already begun and we may find more and more technology pervading through some of the less obvious courses in the future, a culture change is underway. We do not suggest that the strategies employed at UKC for introducing technology are the optimum ones but we do stress that strategies are needed. Frustration and wasting of resources is an inevitable consequence of continued ad hoc developments. Given that a strategy is needed then the "think tank", support unit or whatever vehicle is used for implementing a change, should be centralised. In this manner the change that is effected has a chance to be uniform across the institution.

One crucial responsibility lies with the management of institutions, that is of co-ordination and support of a strategy for change and most importantly some form of recognition of people who try and improve the quality of their teaching through using technological resources. " Revolutionary improvements in the quality of teaching do not usually succeed in the context of one course, however. Many of the changes necessary need to occur at departmental or institutional level, or beyond." (Laurillard, 1993) The availability of units such as HSU need to be offered as another academic service and have a responsibility of collaborating with all those involved, rather than working in isolation. The benefits will manifest themselves in the success of the end-product.

References

Duchastel, P.C. (1990) Examining cognitive processing in hypermedia usage. *Hypermedia,* Vol 2 No 3.

Dufresne, A. Jolin, N. Sentini, A. (1990) Hypertext documents for the learning of procedures, *Hypertext State of the Art,* edited by McAleese, R. Green, C.

Higher Education Funding Council England, (1993) *Teaching and Technology Learning Programme:* Phase Two, circular13/93.

Laurillard, D. (1993) *Rethinking university teaching aframework for the effective use of educational technology.* Routledge, London.

Stanton, N.A. Stammers, R.B. (1990) Learning styles in a non linear training environment, *Hypertext State of the Art,* edited by McAleese, R. Green, C.

Strang, W. Khan. H.A. Simpson, V. Slater, D. (1993) From Hypertext to Hypermedia, *Promises and Challenges, Proceedings of the Second Annual Conference on Multimedia in Education and Industry,* Association for Applied Interactive Multimedia.

38. Development of a Distance Learning Course for Library Staff in Mauritius

David Craig, *Napier University*

Summary
This paper seeks to discuss the development and adaption of a United Kingdom course to meet the needs of Librarians in Mauritius. The course uses traditional print based study guides as the main method of delivering the subject content. Mauritius is a fast developing country but at present does not have widespread computer facilities or telecommunication networks and is therefore not suited to more sophisticated methods of course delivery. The paper will identify aspects of the development, delivery, support and management of the course which we believe have been important to the success of the course.

INTRODUCTION

Napier University, Edinburgh has been involved in the education and training of librarians and information personnel since 1973 and for most of those years it has used distance learning as the mode of delivery. This has proved to be very successful and an extremely effective system for providing education and training for people working in libraries. The first course offered by Napier ran from 1973 - 1981 (McElroy, 1981) and prepared students for the external professional examinations of the Library Association, during that time 150 students successfully completed the course. The second course is the Higher National Certificate in Librarianship and Information Science (Craig, 1988) which has been offered by the University since 1983. This has always been a distance learning course and has been reviewed and updated several times during the last ten years; the most recent review having taken place in 1992. The structure of the course is shown below and is based on a two year programme of study, where the University decides the order and pace of student learning.

Student Study Unit Title	Hours	Credit Value
Library Information Environment	40	1
Serving User Needs	80	2
Information Sources:		
1. Primary Sources	40	1
2. Information Flow	40	1
Information Handling:		
1. Literature searching and microcomputing	40	1
2. Cataloguing and classification	40	1
Managing the Resource:		
1. Staffing	40	1

2.	Finance	40	1
3.	Stock	40	1
Major Project		80	2
Problem solving in Libraries		40	1
Total		520	13

The course is designed for experienced non professional library staff and some 200 students have now successfully completed the course. An important feature is that it takes students who are currently working in libraries or information units and who have done so for at least two years. It provides a broadly based education on the objectives, tools and techniques of library/information work and builds upon the work experience of its students.

It is this course which was used to provide the basis for the course in Mauritius.

Support of student learning has always been an important part of the Napier course; each student is assigned a tutor who provides academic support and help when required. The only attendance requirement the course places upon students, is at the 'In University' week in each year. These weeks allow visits, practical work and demonstrations to be undertaken.

MAURITIUS AND ITS LIBRARY NEEDS

Mauritius is an island situated in the Indian Ocean, with a population of just over 1 million people from many different racial groups. It is an Independent country within the Commonwealth. Recently the government in Mauritius produced an Education Master Plan for the year 2000 (Ministry of Education and Science, 1992) which had specific recommendations for Information and Library provision. One area highlighted was the development of a good library service to support the educatio of

children. A good library services requires well qualified and educated staff, so a high priority was placed on producing a course to provide this education and training. The master plan also identified distance learning as a legitimate way of delivering courses. The Ministry of Education & Science had therefore some specific requirements.

1. they wanted to achieve a quick response to the plan.

2. they wanted to train/educate staff currently working in school libraries; many with several years experience.

3. they wanted to use distance or open learning if possible.

4. they wanted a qualification which would be recognised internationally.

5. they wanted the course provided to be as cost effective as possible.

COURSE DEVELOPMENT

The Mauritian need and our course provision and experience in using distance learning to teach librarians came together because of other contacts between Napier and Mauritius. The Minister of Education visited Napier in July 1992 to discuss other ongoing projects and at the same time indicated that he would be interested in the possibility of Napier providing a course for librarians. Napier thought that it might be possible to use the existing Higher National Certificate course as a basis for a course in Mauritius and indicated that the University would be willing to send staff out to Mauritius to investigate the possibilities with professional colleagues there.

The visit would also allow Napier to clarify some very important points.

    a)   the current level of library services in Mauritius.

    b)   the likelihood of being able to get people in Mauritius to write material for inclusion in the study guides.

    c)   the educational level of the potential students.

    d)   the general level of the technological develop in Mauritius and specifically in libraries.

We also looked at the literature on Distance Learning in Library education in other countries to try to identify problems and issues (Lally, 1993., Evans 1992., Williams 1992., Nawe 1991., Rao 1990) The Information from the literature and the situation we found in Mauritius would allow us to make a much better assessment of the likely success of adapting our course to meet the needs in Mauritius. Without local support we certainly did not believe that the project was viable. Equally, the library system in Mauritius had to be similar to that in the UK or our course would not be appropriate.

The exploratory visit was undertaken over an eight day period in October 1992. During this visit Napier staff met with a wide spectrum of people in Mauritius including government officials, professional librarians and educationalists.   A number of libraries were visited throughout the island ranging from the library of the University of Mauritius to small school libraries in rural areas. We discussed our proposal and at the same time assessed the actual situation in Mauritius. We had sent out to Mauritius before our visit outlines of our course and examples of course materials so that people in Mauritius could judge the level and scope of the Napier course. It quickly became obvious that Mauritius had some specific advantages.

- All the potential students could work and study in English. English is in fact the principle language used in education.
- The library structure in Mauritius was basically the same as that in the United Kingdom
- There was a very strong desire by library staff for a course at the right level and this desire was supported by the Government who were prepared to fund the course.

There were, however, some significant problems:

- The library profession in Mauritius has for a long time suffered from a lack of status which has demotivated and demoralised many of the professional librarians on the Island.
- There were only about 25 professional librarians - some of whom were nearing retiral age.

- There is not a strong library tradition in Mauritius, particularly at public library level.
- There had been several previous attempts to provide education and training for librarians. All of these had failed because they relied mainly on staff from abroad to teach on the courses, and when they left, the courses could not run. These experiences have created a rather a apathetic view of library projects.
- There had also been several reports from 'experts', most of them from abroad, on what was needed to improve library services (Harrison, 1990., Pope, 1988., Augustin, 1992). Many of the reports made reasonable recommendations but few of them have been acted upon. This has again caused library staff to become disillusioned.
- Libraries in Mauritius, while similar, were different in size and scope and, particularly, in their use of new technology.

The visiting team from Napier had with them a member of University staff who was born in Mauritius and who acted as a liaison officer for the visit. This role has proved to be important and will be discussed later in the paper.

At the end of the visit the following general proposals were presented to representatives of the Mauritian Government.

1. To use the existing Napier course as a basis for a course on Mauritius but it would be necessary to reflect practice and experience of libraries in Mauritius   The importance of addressing local practice and conditions was considered to be essential and other writers on distance learning in developing countries agree with this view (Nwakoby, 1990., Otike, 1989).

2. The course developed, would as an initial project, educate 100 library staff in two cohorts over a four year period; the first year being used to organise and produce the work required to provide the course and its materials.

3. The course would be a distance learning course based on printed study guides as this was best suited to the needs and experience of the student group.

4. There was a strong suggestion from all those who had been involved in the discussions during the visit that the development and delivery of the course should be a co-operative venture.

5. To use the same course structure, delivery and student support system which had been successfully developed in Britain.

6. To establish a partnership between Napier University and an education institution in Mauritius, who would administer and manage the course on the Island. A number of staff from that institution would act as local course co-ordinator.

7. Establish formally the role of liaison officer.

8. The financial cost of Napier provision and also the local costs were to be calculated and agreed by all parties.

These proposals were accepted in principle by the Government of Mauritius. Napier University provided detailed costing of their contribution and also the likely local costs of running the course. The parties agreed that the course would start in November 1993, only one year and one month after the initial investigation of the feasibility of the project.

Between October 1992 and November 1993 two further visits were undertaken by the course director. These visits established the work that had to be done and refined the timetable necessary to progress the project. The Mauritius College of the Air (MCA) was identified as the local educational centre for the course and its director and librarian took on administrative and management roles. A local team of professional librarians agreed to act as counsellors for the students and during the two visits by the course director the role and responsibilities of counsellors was discussed and agreed. A separate group of writers was also established and areas requiring material identified, together with a timetable for delivery.

The first cohort of students was identified and agreed and, during the visit in September 1993, the course director met the students and explained the course to them. He also discussed their role and responsibilities. This meeting in advance of the official start of the course in November 1993 was very valuable both for students and staff, as it allowed students to meet each other, their counsellors, and discuss issues that concerned them. During this induction meeting, students were also given a package of information about the course and help and guidance on developing effective study skills and techniques.

DISCUSSION

There are several important issues and factors which we believe have contributed to, or affected, the success of the course. They are:

1. Mauritius is not an underdeveloped country. It has a strong and growing economy and an education system for all children up to secondary school level. The country is, however, only just beginning to use new technology and although there is a reasonable telephone system, it is not universally available; with only a relatively small number of households having private telephones. Therefore, the temptation to use sophisticated technology such as computers or telecommunication networks to provide the course was never really a possibility. Our initial investigations quickly showed that students were happy with traditional print based course materials and these they could use easily at home. This said, we are exploring ways of using telecommunications systems; ISDN etc to transfer information between the two educational institutions involved.

2. The partnership between Napier University and the Mauritius College of the Air (MCA) has worked very well. The choice of partner is extremely important. The MCA has established a good management system to deal with delivery and receipt of course materials and student performance. It is also probably one of the most advanced educational establishment in Mauritius in terms of computer technology which may prove useful later in the project. The MCA have provided excellent leadership for the course in Mauritius. They have also supplied the local course co-ordinator, who has coped extremely efficiently with all the responsibilities placed upon her.

3. The wider partnership of Napier staff with professional librarians and educationalists in Mauritius has been very effective and has, we believe, overcome

some of the problems distance learning has encountered in other countries of the world (Arger, 1990).

The partnership divides responsibilities and uses the expertise of the two groups to provide th

Napier staff are responsible for:

- the editorial and production aspects of the study guides.
- printing of the required number of copies for students.
- providing course structure and timetable.
- marking and maintaining educational standards.
- providing documentation for Napier and Mauritius to demonstrate the level of the course and obtain permission to run the course.
  organising and teaching the 'In University's week.

Mauritius staff are responsible for:

- providing a local course co-ordinator.
- providing a local course support team.
- establishing a separate group of staff to write material for inclusion in the study guides.
  assisting in the work of the 'In University' week.

4. The course is successful because it is aimed at a specific group of students who are similar to the students in the United Kingdom. The ten years of development already invested in the course have resolved most of the problems and made the task of adapting it for Mauritius much easier. We were already aware of what was likely to work and, perhaps more importantly, what did not.

5. The students themselves are highly motivated and have good general levels of education. They also have a basic understanding of the subject being taught, having worked in libraries for a minimum of two years. The home environment of the students appears to be good and this is very important for students on a distance learning course.

6. The role of the local support team has been a very valuable one. They have set up a slightly different system from that used at Napier but it reflects local needs and conditions.

7. The writing and editing of material for the Mauritian course has generally worked well. The professional libraries in Mauritius have provided important articles on the practice and problems of library provision on the Island. They also read through our original study guides and made suggestions about what could be removed or reworded. The Mauritian study guides now contain an element of comparative librarianship showing practice in Mauritius along side a British or international view.

8. The role of the liaison officer has been very significant. In the initial stages of the course development, his local knowledge and understanding of the systems in Mauritius saved a lot of time and resolved problems we were not always aware of. He also sorted out potential confusion caused by language or custom.

9. The cost effectiveness of the course will only be fully tested at the end of the project but distance learning as a mode of delivery is certainly, initially cheaper than the alternatives. Providing the course in a traditional way with staff either from Mauritius, or more likely from abroad, and allowing the students to study on a part-time/day release basis was at least twice as expensive in provisional costings.

10. We also saw and discussed with staff in Mauritius a further benefit of a distance learning course and the partnership approach we had adopted. At the end of the initial project the course and its materials could be franchised to Mauritius, who would by then have a team of people able to run and support the course on their own.

CONCLUSION

The course officially started in the first week of November 1993 and, at the time of writing, the students had just started the third unit of the course. All the students have successfully completed and passed the first unit and their overall performance was very good. The second unit is currently being marked by Napier staff. The feedback from students on the first two units of the course has been positive.

The first 'In University' week has been planned and organised and will be held in April 1994.

The first eleven study guides of the course; that is the whole of year one, have been edited and material from Mauritius incorporated. Work has already started on year two.

We are currently ahead of all the targets set for the project and have been very pleased with the progress so far.

References

Arger, G (1990) Distance education in the third world: critical analysis on the promise and reality. *Open Learning* 5 (2), 9 - 18.

Augustin J A (1992) *Reading is fundamental: an action plan for the development of library services in Mauritius* Ministry of Education and Science

Craig, D D (1988) Higher Certificate in Librarianship and Information Science: a distance learning course for senior library assistants. *Learning Resources Journal* Vol 4 (3) p 113 - 122.

Evans, J (1992) Improving Education for Information at the University of Papua, New Guinea: The search for resources. *Education for Information* 10 (2) 105 - 114.

Harrison, K C (1978) *Libraries documentation and Archives services in Mauritius.* UNESCO

Lally, K (1993) Library School Without Walls: innovative in the teaching of Librarianship Information Studies in New Zealand. Wilson Library Bulletin - 67 (8), 43 - 45.

Ministry of Education and Science,(1992) *Mauritius Education Master Plan for the year 2000.*

McElroy, A R (1978) Professional qualifications in Librarianship by directed private study. Journal of Librarianship 10 (4), p 256 - 273.

Nawe, J (1991) Needs and priority areas for continuing education for sub professional information, library and archives personnel in Tanzania *IFLA Journal* 17 (3), 310 - 3143.

Nwakoby, M A (1990) Special curricula themes for library education in Nigera. International Library Review 27 (11), 213-224.

Otike, J (1989) Education of Information personnel in Kenya. *Outlook on Research Libraries* 11 (10) 9 - 12.

Pope, E (1988) *Final report and recommendations to the Ministry of Education, Arts & Culture on the development, reorganisation and modernisation of library documentation and archive services in Mauritius.* Ministry of Education, Mauritius.

Rao, P G (1988) Recent trends in education for Library and Information Science in South India. International *Library Review* 22 (3), 181 - 190.

Williams, P (1992) Library training in the Solomon Islands. *Focus on International and Comparative Librarianship* 22 (3), 69 - 72.

39.   Ten Tips for Using Technology in Distance Learning

Angela Lauener,   *School of Computing and Management Sciences, Sheffield Hallam University*

Summary

The School of Computing and Management Sciences in association with Sheffiled Business School is running a part time distance learning MSc course in Information Technology and Management.

From the beginning, it was proposed that students should be able to keep in touch with each other and with tutors using computer mediated communication, thereby reducing 'the loneliness of the distance learner'.

Now, two years from commencement of the course, much has been learnt from our experience. In this presentation, we aim to provide useful practical tips for others contemplating using CMC in distance learning by sharing our experiences. Tips will include advice concerning technical requirements, hardware and software choices, marketing the idea, managing user expectations, training users, ongoing use of the system, psychological issues and the need for preparatory research.

AIM

The aim of this paper is to draw attention to some of the practical issues which anyone should consider who is thinking of using computer mediated communication (CMC) in a distance or open learning programme. The advice given here is borne out of Sheffield Hallam University's (SHU) practical experience combined with research into the literature. This paper distils some of the most important advice; an extensive bibliography is given for those who wish to know more detail.

INTRODUCTION

Computer mediated communication (CMC) is the term used for all modes of communication made possible by use of computer networks, including electronic mail (a 1:1 or 1:many form of communication) and computer conferencing, a many to many form of communication where messages written by individuals can be read and responded to publicly by other users.

CMC is believed to be of benefit in distance learning because if successfully used, it can overcome the 'loneliness of the distance learner', i.e. it enables sharing and communication between students, tutors and administrative staff.

In May 1992, a new part time distance learning MSc in Information Technology and Management (IT&M) started, run jointly by the SHU School of Computing and Management Sciences (CMS) and Sheffield Business School and part of the Integrated Graduate Development Scheme (IGDS).

TEN TIPS

Here, the aim is to relate some of the wisdom gained by SHU from experience and hindsight. For each 'tip', there is a brief account of **SHU's experience** followed by some resulting **general advice.**

1. Do your homework

SHU's experience

We experienced some teething problems in the initial setting up and use of CMC which was later discovered to be typical for organisations doing this for the first time. Research into the literature and communication with others in the field have greatlyenhanced our understanding of CMC, drawn attention to typical teething problems and given good practical advice.

General advice

Extensive literature exists on practical experiences of other institutions' setting up and use of CMC. It also illustrates the scope of use of CMC - the degree of importance placed on it within a distance learning programme ranging from optional extra to compulsory, (Hartley et al), the range of uses and facilities which are useful (e.g computer conferencing, electronic mail and file transfer) and the subject areas found to be most suited to use of computer conferencing (e.g. Kaye ('87) believes that social studies and humanities lend themselves particularly well to conferencing).

The Open University has produced a number of papers relating its experience and much practical advice can be found there (Jones et al; Kirkup '91; Mason, 91a; Mason, 91b, Mason '92; Thomas, '89; Thomas, '90).

2. Set clear and feasible objectives

SHU's experience

The nature of the IT & M delegates and the programme is such that individuals from different organisations have a lot of experience to share with each other, so this was one of the underlying philosophies in our decision and plans to use CMC.

Agreement had been obtained from potential sponsoring organisations to provide their delegates with the necessary technology.

General advice

In the light of preparatory research, the feasibility of use of CMC can be discussed in an informed way in the widest possible context. Do you have adequate financial and technical resource? Is this means of communication appropriate for your course? Can you do the necessary groundwork in the time available?

Feasible objectives must be discussed involving participation by the highest level of management of the programme together with all potential types of user - academic staff, students and technical staff.

Do not be afraid to reject the idea if it will not fulfil the overall objectives of the course - there must be no technology push. CMC must only be used if it will serve the needs of the programme.

If you decide that CMC will be feasible, then a set of clear objectives may be agreed.

3. Take everyone along with you

SHU experience

Before the programme commenced, discussions took place between course designers and technical staff and a workshop for staff was held to give them some experience in using the system and to make them aware of the capabilities of the system.

General advice

Once objectives have been agreed, it is vital that they are communicated to all involved. Distance learning authors must incorporate use of the system in their writing accordingly; sponsors or students must be willing to obtain the necessary hardware and software; technical staff must understand the philosophy underlying the objectives; marketing literature must give a realistic impression of what is provided by the system and how it can benefit the programme; students must understand from the outset the purpose of the system.

4. Get the technology right

SHU's experience

In the IGDS programme, the expected number of users was about 30 per year for the three year programme - a comparatively small number, with no more than four users expected to be accessing the system simultaneously. Therefore, a relatively inexpensive bulletin board system running on a PC was agreed by the course designers and technical expert to be adequate.

All of the delegates have access to a PC, modem, communications software and telephone line. Sheffield Hallam University bought a software package called 'The Major BBS' - a professional bulletin board system supplied by Galacticomm, USA. This runs on a PC with four internal modems.

General advice

The choice of software and hardware must be appropriate for your intended use and it must be robust. Generally, all users will need access to a PC, modem, phone line and communications software. The host institution will need conferencing software, modems, a phone line and either a PC or mainframe, depending on the expected number of simultaneous users of the system. A range of technologies with various user interfaces, facilities and hardware requirements has been used by different institutions (Alexander, '92; Lauener, '93)

One of the crucial issues in deciding on the software and hence the hardware platform needed is the total number of users expected for the system, and the number of simultaneous users expected.

5. Get the system right

SHU's experience

The initial aims for IGDS NET were to provide basic facilities as simply and easy to use as possible, such as electronic mail and computer conferencing, arranged in a hierarchical menu structure of options. This fulfilled the programme objectives of enabling delegates to share experience through exercises in the learning material and to have some social contact via learning set forums. Files of relevant information such as references and articles were made available to conferences (with permission) as a highly up to date complement to the reading material issued by post. In addition, the programme administrator used the system for various administrative details concerning arrangements for residentials, reminding users to return feedback questionnaires etc. Some feedback questionnaires were issued and results published electronically using IGDS NET; ad hoc debates were set up as needed, such as a debate concerning delegates' views on accreditation for prior experience and learning.

Security procedures were built into the design to allow legitimate delegates only to gain access to the full range of facilities on the system. Marketing information was made publicly available. Virus checks and backups are made daily.

General advice

Once installed, the system needs to be configured and designed so it can become an enabler in meeting the agreed objectives of the distance learning programme.

6. Get the right technical resources

SHU's experience:

Two types of technical skill have been found to be necessary:

(i)   'hard' technical skill and knowledge of products available on the market, ability to install and set up the system initially and experitse in advising users on technical requirements and dealing, by phone, with problems when users are first setting up their equipment. Later, this expertise was necessary to upgrade, enhance and expand the system. This is a 'technology centred' role.

(ii)   'softer' skills in acting as 'system operator' (SYSOP) - a more 'user centred' role. This involves knowing in outline the content of the distance learning material and understanding the aims of using CMC in the programme. Initially, this involved configuring the software, writing a user guide and training delegates and staff, setting up conferences on relevant topics and providing a help facility. It also involves carrying out ongoing maintenance and housekeeping on the system and monitoring usage.

General advice

Full time technical expertise is not needed on an ongoing basis; needs fluctuate depending on which stage of the programme you are at, from full time to half a day a week. It is important that technical expertise is available in an advisory capacity in the early stages when discussing the feasibility of CMC and at any time when enhancement of the system is being considered. The level of input by SYSOP depends partly on how important a role   CMC plays in the running of the distance learning programme.

7. Know your users

SHU's experience

It has emerged from the first three intakes of delegates that our users are mainly from technical backgrounds and therefore are competent at using computer technology. Many come from organisations where they have technical support. A large number have previous experience of using CMC in the form of company e-mail systems and many are familiar with sophisticated groupware products such as Lotus Notes. The majority are middle managers in their 20s and 30s with busy work and family lives.

By nature, bulletin board systems demand unsophisticated technology as the underlying philosophy is to make them as widely available as possible, i.e. to cater for the 'lowest common denominator'. IGDS NET is keyboard driven; there is some scope for including colour and graphics in the interface and more recently, a new piece of software has been made available to users which provides a mouse driven interface with icons and buttons to click on.

User characteristics have implications both for the institution's and the users' expectations of CMC via IGDS NET in distance learning and hence the way we train them. We have had to manage our users' expectations of the system software, adjust our expectations of their use of the system to fit in with what they can realistically commit themselves to and have been able to assume a fairly low level of responsibility for technical support of delegates.

However, our users also include academic staff, not necessarily confident and experienced in using CMC. We have therefore included staff alongside delegates in IGDS NET training workshops and given technical support on a one to one basis as necessary.

General advice

It is advisable to do some research on characteristics of your users before deciding on what part CMC will play in a distance learning programme, how you will manage their expectations of your system, and how much training and support they will need. Ideally, this should lead to realistic objectives being set for CMC in the context of your course and your users, thereby avoiding a mismatch between your expectations and their commitment.

Research has shown that the majority of users are 'lurkers', ie they read messages but do not write, as opposed to enthusiasts who contribute greatly, or non-enthusiasts who do not like using CMC (Hartley et al).

8. Look after your users

SHU experience

We, and others (eg the TUDIC project) have found that a half day training workshop held two or three weeks before the programme starts is highly appreciated by delegates and encourages them to get their equipment set up in time for the beginning of the programme. The workshop includes a short talk on the benefit of using CMC in distance learning, some information on technical requirements and some practical exercises designed to familiarise users with the main features of the system (Lauener '93).

We have made efforts to proactively offer support for new users in the early stages. Users have found technical problems to be highly frustrating. Users who persevered without reporting problems have lost confidence and interest in the system. Similarly, efforts have been made to keep the system up and running 24 hours a day and to warn users in advance of plans to take it down.

Support in the early stages also includes providing adequate documentation, leaving friendly and welcoming e-mail messages and engendering an open, friendly atmosphere on the system.

We have realised that successful computer conferencing needs highly motivated users, stimulated by a conference 'moderator' who will start and maintain a discussion on a topic. Programme staff need extra training in moderating conferences (Kerr, '86; Mason, '91b).

General advice

Good training and support are imperative, especially in the early stages. Ongoing support is also important, including keeping users informed of maintenance in the system, providing documentation and minimising system down time. Enthusiastic, stimulating conference moderators need to be trained and appointed if you seriously intend to include computer conferencing a part of the distance learning programme.

9. Keep an eye on what is going on

SHU's experience

IGDS NET keeps an audit trail of user activity from which it is possible to derive statistical information. We use this information when a new intake of delegates has just started the programme, determine which users have not successfully logged on for the first time and need a phone call to find out if there are problems.

Questionnaires have also been used to gauge user opinion of the system and to elicit comments and suggestions for the system.

SYSOP logs on to the system daily and scans forums (conferences) periodically to monitor progress in conferences. It has been found that learning set conferences for social chat, discussion of assignments and mutual support are the most lively conferences. Delegates occasionally send draft assignments to tutors for comment and they use the system for simple questions regarding programme administration. Despite almost unanimous expression of the desire to use forums for advice on assignments, many prefer to discuss assignments over the phone with tutors.

General advice

Formal procedures to monitor activity on the system relevant to your objectives for it will indicate how successfully these objectives are being met and highlight areas which may need more support or an investigation of why certain features are not being utilised.

10. Do not be afraid to change

SHU's experience:

Over the two years that the programme has been running, we have amended our objectives for use of the system to more closely match the context in which we operate, i.e. the characteristics of the delegates, the software and the preferences of the tutors.

The high level of technical competence of delegates and has reduced the need for a foolproof but long-winded user interface and has enabled us to offer a more sophisticated range of facilities, suggested and installed by our technical expert. Compulsory group work over short time periods has proved to be unfeasible because of delegates' work commitments and occasional lack of availability so has been omitted. We are still working towards computer conferencing on relevant programme-related topics.

General advice

In theory, CMC may appear to be the perfect answer to problems in distance learning. High ideals may be sought, even in the light of extensive research and preparation. In practice, you may discover unforeseen features unique to your circumstances which render your plans lacking in some areas. It is important to keep an open mind on which plans will best suit your programme, to strive to meet the objectives which add value to the programme and not to be afraid to let go of original plans which prove not to be feasible.

CONCLUSION

The philosophy underlying use of computer mediated communication, and computer conferencing in particular, is that sharing widely with many others via the medium of text has numerous benefits. By the same token, sharing insights into CMC by means of papers and conferences should enrich and improve the experience of all who are engaged in the increasingly popular use of CMC in distance and open learning.

References and Bibliography

Alexander, G.(1992) Designing human interfaces for collaborative learning from *Collaborative Learning Through Computer Conferencing* ("Najaden Papers") Edited by Tony Kaye Springer-Verlagh

Barnard, J. Multimedia and the Future of Distance Learning Technology *EMI*,29,3

Boyd, G.M.(1987) Emancipative Educational Technology *Canadian Journal of Educational Communications,* 16(2), 167-172

Durham, M.(1990) Computer Conferencing: Students' Rhetorical Stance and the Demands of Academic Discourse *Journal of Computer Assisted Learning* 6, 265-272 1990

Galer, G (1990) *Computer Conferencing in a Multinational Company* Paper for AAAS meeting, New Orleans. Group Planning Shell International Petroleum Company Ltd., London

McAlpine, G. (1992) *Experiences with and Possibilities for the Use of Computer-Mediated Communication* The Danish Confederation of Trade Unions

Hartley, J., Tagg, A., Garber, B., Barry, D., and Fitter, M. *Computer Conferencing for Distance Learning* Final Report to the Learning Technologies Unit of the Department of Employment

Jones, A., Kirkup, G., Kirkwood, A. and Mason, R. *Providing Computing For Distance Learners: A strategy for Home Use*

Kaye, A. Introducing Computer-Mediated Communication into a Distance Education System *Canadian Journal of Educational Communications* Vol. 16, No. 2, pp. 153-166 1987

Kerr, E.B.(1986) *Electronic Leadership: A guide to Moderating On-line Conferences* In IEEE Transactions on Professional Communications, Vol. 29, No. 1, pp. 12-18

Kirkup, G.(1991) Computer Conferencing and Gender Computers in *Adult Education and Training* 2,2

Lauzon, A.(1991) *Enhancing Accessibility to Meaningful Learning Opportunities:* A Pilot Project in Online Education at the University of Guelph Research in Distance Education

Mason, R.(1991) Analysing Computer Conferencing Interactions *Computers in Adult Education and Training* 2,3

Mason, R.(1991) Moderating Educational Computer Conferencing in Paulsen, M. F. (Ed.): *Deosnews* Vol 1 no. 19 The Pennsylvania State University, College of Education, Pennsylvania, U.S.A.

Mason, R.(1992) Computer Conferencing for Managers *Interactive Learning International* Vol. 8. pp. 15-28

Skyrme, D. (1089) *Evolution of a Knowledge Network: Computer Conferencing at Digital* Digital Equipment Co. Ltd., Reading, U.K. 1989

Thomas, R. (1989) Implications for Conventional Institutions of Open University Experience in Use of Computer Conferences *Computers in Adult Education and Training*

Thomas, R. (1990) Benefits and Costs of Computer Conferencing in *Adult Education Intelligent Tutoring Media,* Vol. 1, No. 2

Rawson, J. H. (1990) Simulation at a Distance Using Computer Conferencing *Educational Training* Technology International 227, 3

Sorensen, E. and Kaye, T. *Online Course Design*

40. University-wide Integration of Open Learning: Implications for Staff Development

Stephen J Fallows, *Reader in Educational Development, University of Luton*

Summary

Throughout the United Kingdom, the University sector is faced with the dilemma of how to deal with greater student numbers without increased resource. Financial constraints act to preclude equivalent increases to the academic staff complement whilst for some institutions space constraints limit the potential to physically accommodate the additional numbers.

A variety of institutions are looking to an increased use of open learning (OL) to overcome these difficulties whilst continuing to offer students a worthwhile educational experience. The advent of academic audit and quality assessment require that standards are maintained if not enhanced.

Enhancement of standards requires that university staff are in a position to offer the best possible provision in a manner which utilises the potential of OL. for staff to be in this position there is a need for appropriate staff development programmes which take full account of the circumstances and experience of the individuals concerned to be in place.

The University of |Luton provides a prime example of an institution which is faced with very low levels of resources, an increasing and diversifying student population and an internal and external demand for quality enhancement. Open learning is seen by senior academic managers as a means to meet these demands. At the start of ` 1993, a target of 10% of course delivery was set for 1993-4 with 20% being the target for 1994-5. The University does not intend to act as a producer of OL; rather, materials will be purchased from appropriate higher education suppliers (principally the Open University).

Utilisation of OL in this manner sets the University aside from the standard model in which the educational institution is also the originator of the OL material. furthermore, since OL is to be integrated with other provision and the students are largely campus-based, in this context OL is not synonymous with distance learning.

The staff development needs arising from such a strategy are multiple a d range from exhortation of the concept to the logistical implications and onward into aspects of teaching, learning and assessment. The proposed paper will provide a summary of the staff development initiatives undertaken and will provide guidelines for other HE institutions considering the integration of OL into their mainstream provision.

CONTEXT

The United Kingdom university sector has recently undergone a period of very rapid expansion with a Government-led move towards mass higher education. Although the pace of increase has now been slowed considerably, the proportion of the population presently in higher education is now greater than at any time in the past. Whilst there has been a push to include more people within the system as students, there has not been a parallel increase in the numbers of staff employed by the universities. Consequently student to staff ratios are also at the highest recorded levels. Similarly, the university sector has had to cope with its increase in student numbers without major building programmes to expand the amount of teaching space. The constraints on staff numbers and space are likely to remain for some time as Government seeks to restrain the level of its expenditure on higher education.

The above changes have taken place against a background of increased external scrutiny and accountability. Academic audit and subject assessment have been extended to all universities and there are consistent demands for the quality of student learning experience to be at least maintained, if not actually enhanced.

The two issues outlined above have provided the context in many universities for a reconsideration of the style of educational provision. There has been a need for each institution to provide the best possible education from its available resources. The methods considered and chosen by different universities will reflect previous experience and expertise.

For many institutions a greater use of open learning materials (of all types) has been promoted as a route out of the dilemma.

Open learning provides a solution through a process of substitution:

- The lecture is replaced by an open learning package
- The student's own premises substitute for the lecture hall
- The tutorial replaces the lecture as the principal contact between teacher and student
- The rigid lecture timetable is replaced by each student's management of his or her own time for self-directed study

In an ideal world (in which constraints of time and budgets do not exist), the open learning materials would be specified in detail by the existing course teams and prepared as bespoke items by groups of professionals skilled in the preparation of educationally excellent materials which utilise (in the best possible way) all the available learning techniques and technologies.

In our real world, constraints of time and budgets do exist and so the luxury of bespoke open learning is available to only a few and even then it is often limited to a fraction of the teaching programme as an adjunct to other provision. In practice open learning is generally purchased piecemeal to provide specific elements of courses.

EXPERIENCE AT THE UNIVERSITY OF LUTON

The University of Luton is an institution which has moved rapidly into the higher education sector and which has grown fourfold (in terms of higher education student numbers) in the past five years. Although extra staff have been appointed and additional accommodation acquired there remains a major need to relieve the burdens placed on these two key resources.

The University has taken the decision to utilise the potential of open learning as a means of coping with its expanded student population. At the start of 1993 senior academic managers set a target of 10% of course delivery by open learning for academic year 1993-4 with 20% being the target for 1994-5. At the time the target was set there were certain pioneering fields of study which had provided a lead on open learning but for most of the University departments open learning had not been considered as a mainstream option.

In view of the time scales involved and the costs the University of Luton does not intend to become a major producer of open learning materials; rather the University will purchase materials from existing higher education suppliers. The principal United Kingdom provider of higher education through open learning is the Open University and its learning resource materials are recognised to be of high quality. The Open University has now become a significant supplier of course material to the University of Luton although other more specialist providers are also involved for professional courses particularly in management and health care.

The purchase of major quantities of open learning materials in this manner raises a number of observations and comparisons with the Open University and elsewhere in United Kingdom higher education.

- The Open University material was primarily prepared for well motivated adult learners working within a distance education model. Now the materials are being purchased by a campus based university for use by mainstream students with significantly different educational experience and expectations. In the case of the campus based university (such as Luton) open learning is not synonymous with distance learning and lecturing and other staff can maintain a day-to-day involvement with the students.

- Materials offered by the Open University are bespoke items prepared specifically for that institution's staff and students. Open University course teams have a direct input into the specification and production of the teaching materials. The utilisation of such materials within a second institution's course framework requires that academic staff overcome the commonly held "not invented here" prejudice and take the steps necessary to incorporate the purchased materials into their own courses perhaps by "topping and tailing" with additional materials.

The adoption of an "open learning by purchase" strategy provides significant challenges for the University particularly in the area of staff development.

IMPLICATIONS FOR STAFF DEVELOPMENT

The staff development requirements range from the promotion of the concept through to the practical teaching aspects and on to a consideration of the logistical needs of the institution. Experience has confirmed that it is essential that staff development be considered as an integral feature of the open learning initiative.

- The first consideration is the issue of the educational vision which underpins the open learning strategy. The decision to adopt the strategy may be taken centrally but the justifications must be promoted to all staff who will need (in their turn) to instil an understanding of this reasoning into their students. If the teaching staff are not motivated towards the use of open learning (or any other novel educational concept) then adoption will be slow and staff will not feel at ease when explaining the approach to their students. An enthusiastic champion (or team of champions) will be needed to win over the sceptics and encourage the early adopters.
- In order to incorporate purchased open learning materials into a university's existing courses of study it is necessary that course managers have the skills with which to assess the suitability of "off-the-peg" materials. The selection criteria will need to be stringently applied if educational quality is to be retained. Matters such as the reputation of the supplier and the educational quality control systems used by this organisation must be taken into consideration as must more basic aspects such as likely usefulness. The need to consider down to earth practical factors such as price and availability must also be brought to the attention of course managers. In making a decision to recommend purchase of open learning materials the course manager must always be able to justify the advantages of this material over the conventional alternatives.
- The incorporation of open learning materials into an existing course will require the course team to re-evaluate their role which must move from centre stage as lecturers / presenters to the more supportive role of tutor. There may also be a need to tailor materials (usually at the margins) to meet the course team's perceptions of additional need. Whilst there is a requirement to ensure that staff have the skills to provide the additional materials to steer the open learning towards the original course objectives and agreed curriculum, there is also a need to enhance course teams curriculum development skills to facilitate a revaluation of their existing objectives against the purchased open learning course. Where additional material is required it can generally be described as "enhancement" which: provides extra information (particularly local knowledge), alters the timings and adds skills or brings the published material up-to-date with further examples and reference material.
- The use of open learning requires that the benefits the student gains from tutorials must be maximised; it is necessary to provide staff development support to ensure that staff have

the skills necessary to provide this support. Similarly, there may be a need to utilise alternative assessment methods and to offer a greater degree of constructive feedback to the student than may have been the case in the past.

- Most open learning materials available today utilise conventional educational technologies of print, audio and video. However, the growing extent of interest in high-technology approaches to open learning, including multimedia will require that staff are provided with training and support in the use of these materials. The technologies involved in multimedia are now mature enough to provide useful educational systems although most universities would find economic constraints in utilising such systems for mass higher education in which several hundred students wish to utilise the equipment and materials concurrently.

- Effective learner support is essential to the achievement of a quality educational experience. Support for study skills may be provided by either a dedicated group of extra-faculty professionals or by the course team; whichever approach is adopted it is essential that all teaching staff are fully aware of the fact that students may not already possess the study skills necessary for success in self-directed learning. This will be particularly the case where the university has an established practice of encouraging diversity and thus recruits students from a wide variety of backgrounds.

- The achievement of academic quality is never merely a task for the direct teaching staff. The role played by the various supporting personnel must also be acknowledged and this is certainly the case in the development of an open learning by purchase strategy. There will be a need to establish a system whereby the logistics of ordering, receipt of orders, dispatch and perhaps receipt of returned material is dealt with in a professional manner. Staff concerned will need to be trained in the appropriate skills. Such staff will need to be included in the "champions' briefings" since it is likely to fall to them to explain many of the practical aspects of the open learning initiative to staff and students.

The above list is not intended to be exhaustive but rather serves as illustration of the issues involved. Staff development will continue to be required as the open learning procedures become embedded in the culture of the university. The corporate commitment to open learning is not intended as a short-term stop gap and so there will be opportunity to refine staff programmes in the context of experience. Similarly, as new staff are recruited by the university the use of open learning materials will provide a major focus for the induction training given to both those new to teaching and those transferring from other institutions.

Feedback from monitoring of student performance may provide additional themes for the staff development programme and the University will seek to incorporate these within the shortest period possible.

41. Providing Initial Training for University Teachers through Open Learning

Henry Ellington, *The Robert Gordon University* and Ray Land, *Napier University*

Summary

At the 1989 AETT Conference in Birmingham, the first-named author presented a paper on a novel approach to staff development being attempted in the (then) Scottish Central Institutions. This involved providing in-service training in basic teaching skills for lecturing staff by means of a self-study postgraduate certificate course that they could undertake on an open-learning basis. The course was first run in The Robert Gordon Institute of Technology (now The Robert Gordon University), and is now run in all four of Scotland's 'new' universities.

This paper describes the experience of running the course in the Robert Gordon and Napier Universities. It highlights the benefits that have resulted, providing data on 'value added' in respect of improved professional performance by participants. It also looks at some of the operational problems that have arisen, and shows how these have been addressed. Finally, it discusses how the course is likely to develop within the two universities, including the likely addition of a 'diploma' stage.

INTRODUCTION

The need for a course in basic teaching methods that is readily accessible to in-post university lecturers has long been recognised. It stems from the anomaly that there has never been a mandatory requirement for such staff to undergo any form of pre-service or in-service training in teaching methodology. Some, it is true, have traditionally availed themselves of the opportunities for improving their teaching skills presented through staff development workshops, short courses and (in a few cases) longer courses in education and educational technology. The great majority, however, have (until recently) had few opportunities to develop their teaching skills in this way, even in the process of acquiring considerable experience in the role of lecturer.

It was in order to satisfy the above requirement that the (then) Scottish Central Institutions developed their open-learning PG Certificate Course in Tertiary-Level Teaching Methods during the late 1980's (Ellington, 1990). The course was piloted in The Robert Gordon Institute of Technology in 1989, and was subsequently taken up by all the other Central Institutions that were to attain University status in 1992. This paper describes the experience of running the course in the Robert Gordon and Napier Universities, highlighting the benefits that have resulted and looking at some of the operational problems that have arisen and how these have been addressed. It concludes by discussing the likely future development of the course within the two Universities.

DESCRIPTION OF THE PG CERTIFICATE IN TLTM COURSE

The Postgraduate Certificate Course in Tertiary-Level Teaching Methods that is run in Scotland's 'new' Universities is primarily designed for new, inexperienced lecturers, although more experienced staff can also benefit greatly from undertaking it, as has been shown at both RGU and Napier. The overall aim is to provide course members with the basic knowledge and skills that are required to teach effectively at tertiary level. Specifically, the course is designed to enable them:

- to make effective use of **objectives** in planning their teaching;

- to select appropriate **teaching/learning methods** for achieving these objectives;
- to make effective use of the full range of teaching/learning methods that are appropriate to their discipline, including **mass instruction, student-centred learning** and **group-learning** methods;
- to make effective use of all the various **presentation techniques** and **instructional media** that are now available, including computers;
- to make effective use of the full range of **student-assessment techniques** that are now available;
- to make effective use of **evaluation** in course, curriculum and personal development.

Structurally, the course consists of eight self-contained modules, each dealing with a specific aspect of tertiary-level teaching. There are no formal classes, each module involving working through a self-study programme, presenting for a formative assessment tutorial, and then carrying out a (negotiated) terminal assignment on which summative assessment in respect of the module is based. The eight modules are listed below, together with the notional self-study times associated with each; these do **not** include the times needed to carry out the modular assignments, which effectively double the total study time for each module.

> **Module 1** : Educational objectives (10 hours)
> **Module 2** : Selection of instructional methods (10 hours)
> **Module 3** : Production of instructional materials (25 hours)
> **Module 4** : Student assessment (25 hours)
> **Module 5** : Use of mass instruction techniques (25 hours)
> **Module 6** : Use of student-centred learning methods (20 hours)
> **Module 7** : Use of group-learning methods (15 hours)
> **Module 8** : Evaluation (20 hours)

In order to obtain the PG Certificate, course members must demonstrate that they have acquired the full range of competences associated with each module - either by completing the work of the module and obtaining a satisfactory assessment in respect of the terminal assignment or by producing evidence of equivalent prior learning and achievement. All course members are assigned a personal Course Tutor, who is responsible for guiding them through the course, providing formative feedback on their coursework, negotiating their modular assignments and arranging for these to be assessed - normally by both an educational specialist and a subject specialist.

RUNNING THE TLTM COURSE - THE ROBERT GORDON EXPERIENCE

As we saw above, the Postgraduate Certificate in Tertiary-Level Teaching Methods has now been operating in The Robert Gordon University since 1989. The course is run by the Educational Development Unit, and plays a key role in the University's staff development programme, all new lecturing staff who lack a formal teaching qualification being encouraged to enrol. At the time of writing (March 1994), a total of 18 people have successfully completed the course, with current enrolments totalling 48 - 33 members of RGU staff and 15 members of staff at the Aberdeen Campus of the Scottish Agricultural College.

On the whole, the TLTM Course has proved extremely successful at RGU. It has, first of all, served as a useful pilot for all the other Scottish Higher Education Institutions (HEI's) who subsequently set up the course - all of whom were able to benefit from the RGU experience. Indeed, all the Universities and Colleges who now run the course have acknowledged their gratitude to the RGU course team for making them aware of the sort of problems that they were likely to encounter and providing advice on how to overcome them.

From an educational point of view, the course appears to be achieving all its aims and objectives. Feedback from people who have completed the course indicates that their effectiveness as teachers has been greatly enhanced, as is evidenced by the results of a survey carried out at the end of 1993. In this survey, all 17 people who had completed the course at the time were asked to rate their performance in respect of the various criteria for effective teaching covered by the course - 21 in all - (a) before they started the course and (b) after they had finished it. They were asked to do this by completing an amended version of the Teaching Skills Proforma that has recently been introduced in RGU to help staff carry out self-assessment of their teaching (Ellington and Ross, 1994). This requires staff to rate their performance in respect of each criterion covered by the Proforma using a four-point ordinal scale. The results of the survey indicated a significant improvement in performance in respect of all 21 of the criteria covered by the course, with course members moving an average of 1.5 places up the scale (range 0.9 - 2.3) as a result of undertaking the TLTM course.

Nor has the educational benefit of the course been limited to the people who have actually undertaken it. Feedback received both from course members and from Heads of Schools and Departments indicates that the course appears to be having a beneficial 'spin-off' effect in that course members are not only improving the quality of their own teaching, but, by talking to colleagues both informally and on committees such as Course Panels, are helping to increase general awareness of what constitutes 'good practice'. As more and more members of the University staff are exposed to the course, it is confidently expected that this 'domino effect' will increase.

From an operational point of view, the course has also proved largely successful. The RGU experience has shown that it is perfectly practicable to run such a course in any University or College that has the necessary specialist staff. All the informal and formal feedback received from course members also indicates that the course documentation - modular study guides backed up with course booklets and textbooks - is extremely 'user-friendly'. Indeed, no serious criticisms or suggestions for radical modification of the course documentation have yet been received. It has also been found that it is possible to complete the course within a period of one calendar year, as was envisaged by the designers. Six course members have already done so, although most take considerably longer. Feedback from course members also indicates that the average total study time needed to complete the course is roughly 170 hours - well below the notional figure of 300 hours (150 hours of self-study + 150 hours on modular assignments) envisaged by the designers. This is possible because most course members are able to use materials which they have already produced in carrying out their normal work (student resource materials, assessment instruments, etc.) in connection with many of the course activities. Indeed, some of them are able to gain exemption from entire modules as a result of prior work.

The only serious problems that have arisen at RGU have been the slow progression rate of many course members and the high drop-out rate - particularly among course members who were 'put on' the course by their Head of School rather than volunteering to enrol. This RGU experience parallels that of other establishments running open- and distance-learning courses, all of which tend to have poor completion rates. All the other Scottish HEI's running the TLTM Course, for example, appear to be having similar problems to RGU regarding progression and completion. In an attempt to improve its progression and completion rates, RGU introduced formal learning contracts for all existing and new TLTM course members in 1992. These specify the rate at which modules are to be completed and the amount of support (such as dedicated study time or remission from other duties) to be provided by the course member's Head of School. They are signed by the course member, his or her Head of School, and the Course Leader, and may be re-negotiated at a later date if they prove completely impracticable. Their introduction appears to have brought about significant improvements in both progression and completion rates.

RUNNING THE TLTM COURSE - THE NAPIER EXPERIENCE

Napier first offered the Postgraduate Certificate in Tertiary Level Teaching Methods in the Spring of 1992. The programme, as indicated above, was closely modelled on that offered at The Robert Gordon Institute of Technology (now The Robert Gordon University) and drew extensively on the open learning materials that were available through CICED, the Scottish Central Institutions Committee for Educational Development, now metamorphosed into SEDA-Scotland. The programme, based in Napier's Educational Development Unit, attracted wide interest, but for resourcing reasons was restricted to an initial cohort of 20 and was offered on a quota basis across faculties. With the expansion of the EDU in 1993 a second wave of participants entered the programme and the number enrolled has just reached 50. 24 university departments are represented on the programme and four participants are based in the Scottish College of Textiles in Galashiels. The majority of those enrolled are full-time staff and relatively new to teaching. Participants also include part-time lecturers, research assistants with systematic teaching duties and library services staff.

The course, like its RGU parent, operates through the use of self-paced open learning materials and study guides, supported by individual tutorials. Staff workloads and other professional commitments had ruled out any regular attendance-based model of professional development at Napier. Three Napier staff are currently involved in the tutoring of participants, each of the latter being asked to identify a mentor for support and guidance in areas of their subject specialism. Feedback to date, through questionnaire, tutorials and participant representation on the Board of Studies, indicates that the programme's strong focus on professional practice is generally fulfilling the requirements of the course members. There are, however, issues of implementation which have arisen and need to be considered.

As with flexible and self-paced models of professional development in other HEIs the rates of progress of individual participants can vary enormously. The first member of staff to complete the full programme graduated in November 1993 having taken just twelve months to achieve the award. It is likely that in the next batch coming up to completion there will be two or three others who will also have achieved the award in one year. A more 'comfortable' time-frame is more likely to be two years, which the majority of participants aim for. Certain course members, however, have maintained a very slow rate of module completion owing to a variety of extraneous factors and the attrition rate has been around 20%. Given that we are obliged, through current resource constraints, to restrict the programme to around 50 participants, it appears rather counter-productive to have people occupying a place when others, who might be in a better position to take advantage of the programme, might be excluded. In the current climate of Quality Assessment and Quality Audit there is no shortage of Heads of Department encouraging their staff to enrol. This raises the issue of whether further structural mechanisms need to be introduced to the way in which the course is currently operated and what the nature of such mechanisms might be. Moving the programme into the Napier Credit Accumulation Framework would certainly be an appropriate means for course members to take time out of the programme and re-enter when their schedules eased.

As stated earlier the preference amongst staff at Napier was for a flexible programme based on open learning. In terms of learning style, however, this approach does not suit all-comers any more than any other mode of provision. The open learning approach can lead to a certain isolation, particularly amongst part-time staff some of whom have rather tentative peer contact with their departments in any case. It is likely that at Napier EDU we will move towards the provision of a series of termly, voluntary workshops to complement the open learning programme. These would be offered at a twilight slot, each being focused on a specific module-related issue. It is hoped that the recent acquisition by the EDU of an attractive centrally-located resource centre should prove, (with the addition of light refreshments!) a useful venue for staff to meet other participants in order to share practice and ideas. The increasing availability of electronic mail within Napier also offers possibilities for contact between participants and their peers, and also with their tutors. The use of electronic mail as a medium for operating the programme is currently being tested with a course member who has returned to his home university in Sweden for a four month period.

The EDU currently runs a series of short induction workshops for new staff on a residential basis and there is inevitably some overlap in the areas of work covered by these sessions and the more substantial certificate programme. This raises the issue of whether all professional development activity should be credit-bearing and the further issues of how much credit, at what level, and how it would map on to the existing certificate and/or any future diploma programmes. It is likely that the induction workshops will soon become compulsory for new academic staff. As to whether the Postgraduate Certificate programme should also become compulsory gives rise to mixed feelings in the University. It is, however, an issue under consideration. Whether for good or ill this would significantly alter the prevailing climate of the programme.

All participants have identified mentors to perform the role described above. The use that is currently made of mentors differs widely however. There is certainly a need for more systematic training of the mentors - time permitting, of course - and a review of how they might be most profitably utilised would seem to be required.

The use of the RGU/Napier type of provision is becoming increasingly widespread in UK higher education establishments and the recently developed standards of accreditation for teaching in higher education developed by SEDA (the Staff and Educational Development Association) are a timely reminder of the need for compatibility between the provision of different institutions to facilitate credit transfer when and where this is required. Napier will be seeking such accreditation in the near future.

HOW THE TLTM COURSE IS LIKELY TO DEVELOP AT RGU AND NAPIER

During the past few months, the two authors of this paper (who are the Course Leaders for the TLTM Course within their respective Universities) have had lengthy discussions with regard to how the course might develop during the next few years. They have agreed to collaborate on the following broad programme.

(a) Upgrading of the present course to a 35 CAT-point Certificate

When the TLTM PG Certificate currently being run at RGU and Napier was developed in the late 1980's, there were no agreed criteria regarding the length of such a certificate course, since the former Council for National Academic Awards (CNAA), which validated most of their courses, had no PG Certificate in its portfolio. Since then, however, it has been generally agreed that such a PG Certificate should be equivalent to roughly 15 weeks of full-time study, and should qualify for 35 CAT points at 'M' level. The present course is only half this length, being rated at 18 CAT points, so it will be necessary to increase both its length and its CATS rating in order to comply with the new national criteria. In order to minimise the increase in workload for course members, it is proposed to do this by adding a limited amount of new material to existing modules and incorporating a period of 'supervised teaching practice' into the course.

(b) Adding an optional PG Diploma stage to the course

When the present PG Certificate course was developed, it was always the intention of the design team to add an optional 'PG Diploma' stage in due course. It is proposed that this should be done by developing new modules in areas such as curriculum development, quality assurance and quality enhancement, and introducing a new major project assessed via a dissertation. Such a PG Diploma would have the extended 35-point PG Certificate described above as its entry requirement, and would (along with the PG Certificate) be equivalent to roughly 25 weeks of full-time study; the combined PG Certificate/Diploma would be rated at 70 CAT points.

CONCLUSION

As was stated in the Introduction, it is one of the major anomalies of the present British educational system that there is no mandatory requirement for University teachers to have any formal training in teaching methodology. Judging by the signals presently coming from the new national bodies responsible for funding and quality assurance in the HE sector, however, this situation seems unlikely to continue. Both RGU and Napier have already made moves towards requiring new, inexperienced lecturers to undertake at least some basic training, and, through the developments described in this paper, will be well placed to implement any future mandatory requirement for more formal training for staff. The authors hope that the paper will encourage similar developments in other Universities.

References

Ellington, H I (1990) Training in-post college lecturers by open-learning methods. In Farmer, B, Eastcott, D and Lentz, B (eds.) *Aspects of Educational and Training Technology XXIII* Kogan Page, London 99-102

Ellington, H I and Ross, G T N (1994) Evaluating teaching quality throughout a University - a practical scheme based on self-assessment *Quality Assurance in Education 2* (in press)

42   Flexible Learning in Higher Education: Effective Methods of Staff Networking

Fiona Campbell, *Napier University* and Rachel Hudson, *University of the West of England*

Summary

At a seminar during the AETT 1993 Conference, the need for a network for staff involved in promoting and supporting open, flexible or distance learning developments within higher education was discussed. this session will sought to provide an update on network developments by providing:

- results of funded research carried out into effective networking methods.
- an overview of networking activities during the year including regional meetings and electronic mail
- a forum for participants to discuss the way forward for the network

The need for a network has arisen as a result of the increasing adoption of flexible learning approaches in higher education in order to meet the needs of potential students, cope with greater numbers and enhance the efficiency and effectiveness of the learning experience. As most of these developments are being facilitated by individuals and small teams, contact with others engaged in similar activities elsewhere would be very beneficial.

Such contact could facilitate the sharing of resources, exchange of information, marketing of courseware, fostering of links with industry and other educational sectors, investigation of opportunities abroad, collaboration on projects, co-ordination of research into flexible learning approaches and the provision of information to national bodies - such as Funding Councils - regarding flexible learning.

All participants will be provided with a copy of a unique listing of around 200 flexible learning practitioners in higher education compiled from the research which has been undertaken. The views of participants regarding the future form and nature of the network will be very welcome.

The paper summarised the findings of the authors' investigation into effective methods of networking staff involved in promoting and supporting flexible learning developments in higher education. The investigative methods employed were discussed together with the results obtained, conclusions drawn and the authors' resulting recommendations.

Flexible learning approaches are increasingly being adopted within higher education in order to meet the needs of potential students, cope with increased numbers and enhance the efficiency and effectiveness of the learning experience. Most developments in institutions are being facilitated by individuals and small teams who could benefit from contact with others engaged in similar activities elsewhere. The authors have carried out the investigation in order to gauge the extent of the need for networking and the most effective methods. The research was supported by funds from the Staff and Educational Development Association (SEDA) Small Grants Fund.

METHODS

The methods used for the investigation included:

    (a) a survey by questionnaire
    (b) analysis of interest shown in regional meetings
    (c) analysis of interest shown in the Electronic Mail Flexible Learning Mailbase

(a) Questionnaire

The questionnaire sought to locate individuals involved in flexible learning in higher education. As no existing list of such people exists, the questionnaire was despatched to:

- Educational Development / Continuing Education Units in all higher education institutions in Britain
- all individuals who had attended relevant conferences or other events and for which mailing lists were available.
- 200 recipients of the SEDA Newsletter who were listed as individual subscribers
- individuals who requested a copy after learning about the survey through the Flexible Learning Mailbase, regional meetings and the authors' contacts.

In total, 400 questionnaires were sent out in November and December 1993.

The questionnaire was carefully designed to facilitate quick completion. Its main features were:

- a brief information panel for contact details. Respondents were asked to sign that they were prepared for this information to be circulated
- free text section for details of post and responsibilities
- groups of questions asking about specific methods of networking - particularly regional meetings and electronic mail.

In order to encourage completion and return of questionnaires by a fixed date, respondents were tempted with:

- the chance to enter a prize draw to win a signed copy of the new edition of Phil Race's *Open Learning Handbook*
- the promise of a 'Who's Who' of open learning in Britain based on the information provided in the returns.

(b) Regional Meetings

Between October 1993 and March 1994, a number of meetings were organised by the authors in their regions.

In Scotland, four half-day meetings were held: in Edinburgh, Glasgow, Perth and Aberdeen. In the south west, a one-day event was held in Bristol.

(c) Electronic Mail

An Email Flexible Learning Mailbase was established on the JANET network in August 1993. Information about the Mailbase and how to access it was distributed to a range of individuals.

RESULTS

(a) Questionnaire

One hundred and fifty-five people returned the questionnaire in time to be included in the database. A further 44 questionnaires were returned after the cut-off date. The names and addresses of all the respondents have been added to the database but none of the data received after the cut-off date has been included in the following analysis. The front sheet of the questionnaire asked respondents to name other people whom we should contact in their institution. Most people answered this question, often listing 3 or 4 people. One person went so far as to give us the names of 13 other people.

1.   *Range of respondents*

The design of our questionnaire did not allow us to analyse the roles and responsibilities of the various respondents. However, inspection of the information available revealed that a very wide range of people had completed the questionnaire, including both support staff and academic staff from a variety of faculties and central service departments.

Questionnaires were returned from the following types of organisations:

- higher education institutions
- further education institutions
- educational publishers
- educational associations
- government departments
- funding councils
- TECs/LECs
- open learning delivery centres

Teaching staff returning questionnaires came from a wide range of subject areas and held a wide range of positions within faculties and departments, from directors of studies to project leaders and lecturers.

Support staff came from a range of central service departments, including:

- education development departments
- continuing education units
- enterprise units
- learner services
- open and flexible learning units
- marketing departments
- admissions
- computer services
- academic accreditation units
- libraries and information services

A number of replies came from central services with such titles as:

- inter-active learning centre
- learning resources centre
- centre for human service technology
- centre for technological education

The questionnaire asked for details of 'roles, responsibilities, special projects concerning flexible learning'. It was not possible to analyse this data in any way, but it did reveal a very wide range of activity, for example:

- writing/editing/producing/open learning material
- promoting open and distance learning
- promoting alternative methods of teaching and learning
- evaluating alternative methods of teaching and learning

- student managed learning
- personal/transferable skills
- effective learning
- study skills
- adult learning
- assessment
- role play, simulation, gaming
- experiential learning
- telematics
- computer-conferencing
- computer-mediated learning
- inter-active video
- staff development in IT in teaching
- multi-media development
- TQM and HRD
- Quality assurance
- Open learning databases
- Writing bids for funding
- APEL/APL
- Professional development in teaching and learning

2.   *Organisation of data on a regional basis*

Before the responses from the questionnaires were entered in the database, we divided a map of Britain into 15 regions and coded the questionnaires according to their geographical location. The regions are shown on the map in Figure 42.1. An initial inspection of the questionnaires had revealed that respondents were interested in attending regional meetings, and we felt that it would be useful to organise this data on a regional basis. It is difficult to predict the boundaries of regions which might form the basis of meetings and other activities, since these have to be organised around the limitations of our public transport system. For this reason we based our data on small regions which can be used in a range of combinations at a later stage.

The analysis of the data showed that our questionnaire had been answered by very few people in some regions, partly because there are less higher education institutions in these areas. However, North Scotland (15), Central Scotland (25), North West (13), Yorkshire (12) South Central (13) and South West (13) regions all have 12 or more people who have responded to the questionnaire. The two Scottish groups and the South West England group are likely to be larger because the two authors are based in these areas and sent questionnaires to their personal contacts as well as directly to each institution.

3.   *Regional meetings*

73% of respondents indicated that they would be likely to attend regional meetings concerning flexible learning in higher education. This level of commitment is reflected within each region - despite the fact some of the regions have very few people in them, an average of between 3 - 4 people per region stated that they are willing to organise regional meetings.

4.   *Newsletter*

Almost 50% of respondents indicated that they would be interested in contributing to a newsletter as a method of networking with people involved in flexible learning in higher education.

REGIONS

SCOTLAND
NS   North Scotland
CS   Central Scotland

IRELAND
I   Ireland

ENGLAND
NE   North East
NW   North West
Y   Yorkshire
EC   East Central
WC   West Central
SC   South Central
E   East
L   London and South East
S   South
SWe   South West

WALES
SWa   South Wales
NWa   North Wales

Figure 42.1: Regional groupings

5.   *National conferences*

Two thirds of respondents indicated that they would be interested in attending national conferences in order to network with people involved with flexible learning in higher education.

6.   *Electronic mail*

The remainder of our questionnaire concerned the possibilities for using electronic mail for networking between people interested in flexible learning in higher education.

72% of respondents indicated that they would join the Flexible Learning Mailbase if they were given clear joining instructions.

These results need to be put into the wider context revealed by our analysis of some of the other questions. Only 60% of respondents state that they are able to use electronic mail externally although 72% say they can network internally and 21% say there are plans to extend networking in their institution. Note that some of the questionnaires were sent by people working outside higher education institutions, most of whom would not be networked or have easy access to JANET. Our database did not record the number of respondents from outside the HE sector. However, 11 respondents stated that they were not networked at all. Only 17% of respondents stated that they can reach 100% of staff in their own institution via electronic mail reflecting the incomplete nature of networking within institutions.

The results of the analysis indicate that the number of active users of electronic mail are somewhat lower than the number who have access to it, and would like to use it for networking, probably implying the need for staff development and clear instructions. 39% of respondents are members of existing mailbase groups and 48% use electronic mail on a daily or weekly basis. These figures may be distorted upwards since we advertised the existence of the questionnaire to all members of the Flexible Learning Mailbase group.

(b)   *Regional meetings*

Meetings of people involved in flexible learning in higher education have taken place in the Scottish and South West England regions. The database provided a very useful mailing list.

Attendance figures for regional meetings in Scotland and the South West are as follows:

Edinburgh (October 1993):	6
Glasgow (December 1993):	8
Perth (February 1994):	21
Bristol (February 1994):	50
Aberdeen (March 1994):	23

Regional teams in these areas have now formed to make recommendations about how the regions should continue to operate and to ensure that the future of the regional network does not rely on an individual.

(c)   *Electronic Mail*

Current usage statistics (from April 1994) are as follows:

Number of subscribers:	99
Number of communications:	84
Number of communications per day:	0.365

CONCLUSIONS

The results of the investigation into networking are detailed below:

1. There are a large number of a range of individuals involved in various aspects of flexibility in course delivery in higher education and related sectors. These include staff from a wide range of roles within central service units and academic departments.

2. The term 'flexible learning' is interpreted in an extremely wide sense by higher education teaching and support staff who wish to network on a great range of issues concerning more flexible methods of teaching and learning.

3. Just under three-quarters of questionnaire respondents saw regional meetings as an effective means of networking. This was confirmed by attendance at organised meetings which has been high. Many individuals within each region have stated their willingness to organise such meetings. This commitment has been confirmed by the ease with which regional teams have found volunteers to organise meetings.

4. Over 70% of questionnaire respondents showed an interest in using the Flexible Learning Mailbase but many did not have access to the necessary facilities or experience in using electronic mail. The interest was not reflected in the actual usage of the Mailbase which has been fairly low.

5. Questionnaire respondents also supported other suggested methods of networking including the development and distribution of a newsletter and the holding of conferences.

RECOMMENDATIONS

1. The who's who in flexible learning

An address list has been created from the database of questionnaire returns. This is the only existing list of staff engaged in flexible learning in higher education in Britain and, as such, is an invaluable resource. Its availability has already had a direct impact on targeting the right individuals to advertise regional meetings etc.

The current database only contains names, addresses and contact information. The database could be more useful if organised by subject discipline or central service, expanded to include details of individual's role and details of areas of interest (eg topics for workshops, consultancy etc.)

It is recommended that an improved database be developed and maintained based on the results of a second questionnaire. The database could be developed from an address list into a Directory which is updated and distributed annually. Given its unique nature, such a publication is likely to be marketable.

Staff assigned to the HEFCE Flexibility in Course Provision Scheme kindly assisted us by creating the address list. However long-term ownership and maintenance of the Directory would have to be addressed.

2. Regional meetings

In order to strengthen regional meetings, all those who volunteered to organise events will be contacted by the authors with a recommendation that they form an organising team in each region. Each will be provided with a pack of information containing details of the respondents in their region and details of events which have already been held in other regions.

3. Flexible learning mailbase

To encourage greater use, the joining instructions need to be revamped to be more comprehensive and user-friendly. Usage protocols, will be developed and the authors will send out details to all respondents. Further activities on the Mailbase will be stimulated by the development of topics for discussion and by rotation of the list-holder.

The long term usage of the Mailbase needs to be monitored. Despite the growing interest in this method of communicating, the investigation revealed that little use was actually made of the facility probably because relatively few individuals have experience of electronic mail. Some staff development is probably necessary for staff to gain confidence in using this medium.

4. Conferences

The survey indicated that there is a high demand for national conferences in the area of flexible learning. Existing conferences often include flexible learning as a theme or stream but annual events are required which are wholly concerned with flexible learning. The survey has already carried out the market research for such an event and can provide a mailing list of 200 names for any organisation willing to take this on.

5. Newsletter

The demand for a newsletter is being met in the short term by the Open Learning Foundation which has kindly agreed to produce and distribute such a publication and it is proposed that it will be circulated on a termly basis. The publication will initially comprise information about activities and other relevant details based on the returns from each regional group.

6. National body

Regional meetings undoubtedly provide the most valuable method of networking but their success depend on the goodwill of the individuals involved and developments across the country are likely to be uneven if there is no over-arching body. Although a number of national organisations exist which concern teaching and learning, there is no representative body carrying out this function in respect of flexible learning developments currently.

Such a body could have a national voice concerning flexible learning developments, could liaise at national level, meet other national groups and advise national bodies such as the higher education funding councils. A body could be achieved by either:
- an existing body widening its remit to specifically include flexible learning
- the formation of a new body or association.

Although the formation of such a body would inevitably involve a certain amount of bureaucracy and additional costs, it would enable an essentially grass-roots organisation to flourish by providing material support for networking activities. The creation of a new national federal body would appear to be the most effective method of ensuring and facilitating networking opportunities for staff involved in flexible learning in higher education.

7. International links

The authors would like to explore possibilities for the development of similar federal bodies of regional groups based in EC countries. This could form an exciting basis for more extensive networking via newsletters, electronic mail and conferences.

43   Course Design for Resource Based Learning (RBL): Discipline Based Publications and Training

Professor Graham Gibbs and Stephen Cox *Oxford Centre for Staff Development*

Summary
The project was designed to:

locate examples of best practice in using learning resources

- write these up in a set of nine discipline-specific manuals
- deliver courses in nine discipline areas
- establish a team of trainers to support Departments who wish to use RBL methods and who need assistance in redesigning their courses to accommodate RBL

Funding from HEFCE was used for

- producing manuals,
- training the trainers,
- mounting national subject-specific conferences to launch the manuals and training provision.

Subsequently, the Oxford Centre for Staff Development will offer appropriate support to clients nationally on a self-funding basis.

The project was designed to make training available in the following subject areas:

- Accountancy
- Art and Design
- Built Environment
- Business
- Education
- Humanities
- Social Science
- Science
- Technology.

Each 50-60 page manual, one for each subject area, contains

- General material on alternative ways to design courses to exploit learning materials, including the teaching, learning and assessment methods and the organisational arrangements associated with these alternatives.
- Case studies of resource-based learning in the particular subject area, together with contact names and addresses.
- A full listing of available materials for the subject area (which will be updated).
- A bibliography concerning uses of the materials listed above and of resource-based learning methods in the subject area.

RATIONALE

There are two main barriers to the rapid extension of RBL in higher education:

- suitable learning materials are in short supply and many are difficult to locate.
- lecturers find it difficult to redesign their courses to make use of these materials.

Even where adequate resources exist (as with Open University materials) there has been little take-up due to lecturers' unfamiliarity with the kinds of course structure and teaching, learning and assessment arrangements appropriate for RBL in the context of face to face higher education. This project was not concerned with the production of new learning resources but with the exploitation of existing and new resources. It focused not on materials design but on the kinds of course redesign necessary to use learning resources effectively. It was concerned with RBL in the context of full and part time courses which take place on campus, not with distance learning.

In the past projects have tended not to influence practice once funding has ceased. In this project the funding has been used to establish a network of trainers that Universities and Departments will be able to draw on for support for many years afterwards, backed up by a permanent training unit.

The rapid expansion of higher education in the UK and the continued decline in funding have placed enormous pressure on conventional teaching and learning methods. These methods were developed in an era when there were far fewer students of a more homogeneous nature and far more generous funding allowing small classes, adequate contact between students and their tutors and reasonable library provision. In many institutions traditional methods are no longer resourceable and where they have been retained there are severe problems facing students. One potential alternative is Resource Based Learning (RBL). RBL has been enthusiastically adopted by senior management in many institutions, though sometimes with more optimism than understanding.

RBL is a difficult process to define. The traditional academic library is the major learning resource in most institutions and there is sense in which conventional course design, in which students attend lectures and then use the library to support much of their studying, involves RBL. An institution with an adequate and appropriately organised library might have little need for other forms of RBL. It is also possible to describe tutors or even students as learning resources. However here we are using a narrower definition of RBL as concerned with the use of mainly print-based materials written, collated or signposted by tutors to replace or substitute for some aspects of teaching and library use. This project is not concerned with distance learning or with part time open learning which takes place largely away from the institution. Neither is it concerned with information technology as a resource. Important developments in this area are being supported through the HEFC's parallel Teaching and Learning Technology Programme. Case studies used in the project may include technology as one component in an RBL course but technology will not be a central feature. The focus is on full time students learning 'on campus' but more independently through the use of largely print based learning resources.

TYPES OF COURSE DESIGN

Conventional course with additional resources

In conventional courses there are still lectures and seminars, or problem classes, or labs, but also a package or packages containing a range of supplementary material. The role of the package is to make everything else hang together and work and to compensate for poor lectures, inadequate library resources and limited tutorial support. The package plugs gaps and holds a weak course design together. The resource is seen as an extra rather than as the central feature. Specific variants include the lecture substitute, the library substitute, seminar support and the occasional use of resources for difficult topics.

Lecture substitute or enhancement

The resource is a replacement for the content delivery role of the lecture and so it contains information and explanation but maybe not much else. There may still be seminars, labs or workshops or other contact and the assessment may be unchanged. Students may still be expected to read around and find other sources independently.

Library substitute or enhancement

The resource is designed to cope with library inadequacies and/or the reluctance of students to buy key books. It might include copyright cleared materials or readers containing material which students might otherwise have been expected to find and read for themselves.

Seminar support

The resource enables students to prepare for seminars adequately and makes sure that every student has access to the basic reading where there are library resource problems. Seminar packages may also include key questions to be discussed in the seminar or even structured exercises which will be worked through in the seminar. Such packages can also be useful where there are tutors running seminars in parallel who need good briefing about what the seminar should focus on in order to ensure some consistency between seminar groups. In courses where there is a large team of part-time seminar leaders who are not otherwise greatly involved in the course there may also be a seminar guide for the tutors. Seminar packages can also be used for advanced courses where the seminars are the central feature of the course but where the availability of journals and other specialist materials is poor. In this context seminar packages might consist of a collection of key resources for each week's topic in a box-file or filing cabinet.

Difficult topics

The course operates conventionally except for one or two topics which are either traditionally 'hard to teach' or which lend themselves to other approaches. Students may work from a specially written package just for one or two weeks. Much CAL courseware use is of this kind, substituting just for particular topics. Even the biggest TLTP projects generally only provide enough materials for topics here and there, only one hour a week.

Distance learning on campus

The resource looks like an Open University course unit complete with almost all reading material, Self Assessment Questions and so on. Some students might do little more than read through this resource. There may still be lectures (perhaps on video) or even tutorials (as with the Open University) but these are the add-ons and the course unit is the central feature. Little use may be made of the library or of possibilities for student interaction.

Problem-based Learning

The central feature of the course is the problem or problems the students tackle, usually in groups. There may be tutored or tutorless problem sessions, but not, normally, lectures. The be only one resource set per problem and different student teams may be tackling different problems at any one time. The resource acts as a conduit to allow rapid routing of student attention and interest to other more widely dispersed material in the library and elsewhere.

Project

The central feature is a project, often extended and complex (as with a whole class simulation). The resource is an amorphous collection of material, even an entire filing cabinet, associated with the project topic (e.g. alternative energy sources). This resource may grow each year and even be added to by students as they discover new resources or write special materials. The filing cabinet is likely to be in a resource room in the Department rather than in the library.

Text book guide

Almost the entire course content is contained in a core text book - the problem is how to get students to work through it carefully enough. There is therefore a guide which contains objectives, questions, reading advice and sometimes supplementary material or explanations to cover gaps or poorly covered topics. There may still be lectures or other class contact elements but the text book and its associated guide is the central feature.

Keller plan

The central features are the unit objectives and self-paced testing system. The resources necessary to enable students to learn what is necessary to prepare themselves for the tests may be many and varied: a core textbook, lectures, specially written packages, a bibliography, practical sessions, or a mixture of these. The important feature of the resources is that they can be accessed at students' own pace and are focussed closely around the achievement of the objectives. Resources may be different for each Unit and economical Keller Plans will exploit whatever is available rather than producing anything new. The cheapest Keller Plans only have objectives, Self Assessment Questions (SAQs) and references.

Workshop

The central feature of the course is a series of extended workshops (perhaps two or three hours for 20-60 students). These may involve complex activities such as simulations, group tasks or case studies, perhaps spread out over several weeks or even a term. Students have to prepare extensively for these major activities. The resource is a guide to the content and process of these sessions. It may contain pre-reading, instructions on how to undertake the tasks, how the assessment activities associated with the workshops operate, extended bibliographies etc. The workshops are complex and without them the course would be threadbare so the resource is vital to the operation of the course. There may also be lectures or tutorials but these are less central. The extended lab guide is a variant of this, where the lab sessions are the central feature of the course and require much briefing and debriefing which can be done on paper.

Work-based learning

Students undertake a period of work placement, as before, but now a package is used to inform and structure this learning. The use of such packages can reduce the need for individual briefings at tutorials, help students to take more responsibility for their learning, standardise supervision practice and structure learning and assessment so that it is less variable between students. The main savings are in tutor time and travelling.

Additional packages may be employed for tutors who prepare students, negotiate with work-based supervisors, visit students and their supervisors while on placement or who assess students and their reports on work-based learning, or for work-based supervisors on the University's expectations, their responsibilities, the negotiation of learning contracts, assessing their students etc.

Fieldwork

The central feature of the course or section of the course is that students undertake learning activities in the field. In the past this might have meant a coach load of students led by a tutor. The resource-based alternative provides students with a package which provides a guide and commentary together with instructions for activities and questions. Students may be in small autonomous teams. They may spend the whole day independently and only meet up with other teams in the evening, or even find their way to and from the field site alone and undertake a de-briefing with a tutor only after they return to their University.

Study skill or transferable skill development

Tutorials and study skill exercises concerned with, for example, undertaking a final year dissertation are replaced by a guide providing details such as deadlines, criteria, bibliographies and advice on how to go about the dissertation. Students may be required to monitor the development of their transferable skills, such as communication, group work and IT skills by using a skills profile or by building up a portfolio of experiences involving the use of these skills. The resource may contain advice or instructions about the skills but more importantly will structure the processes through which student acquire and review the skills and may include checklists or criteria sheets for students to use in the self or peer assessment of skills.

CONCLUDING REMARKS

The case studies in the nine subject specific booklets will each illustrate the use of at least one of the foregoing, and demonstrate how this technique has been integrated into the day-to-day learning experiences of students on the courses concerned. These materials form the basis of the workshops for this national staff development programme in resource based learning.

44.   A Course Administration System for Remote Access

S D Benford, E K Burke and E Foxley *University of Nottingham*

Summary
The basis of this paper is the Ceilidh courseware system, one of the largest in the UK, currently distributed to approximately 70 universities in the UK and 15 other countries. The Ceilidh system provides tools for the administration of academic courses, and the automatic marking of student work, and comes as a controlling system, together with such courses as the user requires. The courses currently available are mainly computer related, since this is the environment in which the system was developed. It runs on computer networks in which students, tutors and teachers have access to the particular networked file system supporting Ceilidh. The Ceilidh system in various forms has been in use at Nottingham since 1988, where it is used to support courses in both C and C++ programming with classes of up to 160 students with administration and marking of student work all fully automated. It is also used to administer other courses, where it controls the submission of work for marking by hand, and the administration of the marks thus generated.

This paper describes the features and implementation of the system, and summarises some of its educational implications, and the experiences of using it.

The administration and some of the development work is funded by the Teaching and Learning Technology Project (TLTP) of the Higher Education Funding Council. Most of the development work is performed by the contributing universities.

INTRODUCTION

There are three main areas involved in teaching, and therefore in what we refer to as courseware, i.e. software to support the complete teaching/learning process. These are

- The administration of courses
- The assessment of student achievement
- The presentation of information to students

All of these represent areas in which computers can assist teacher and the student, and will be discussed further below.

The first two of these increase in proportion to student load and class size. Since we are being asked by government to work with larger classes, but without extra staff, it must be these areas on which we concentrate first.

AN OVERVIEW OF CEILIDH

The operations supported by Ceilidh in each of the above areas are summarised below.

The Administration of Courses

Under this heading the Ceilidh system performs the following operations.

- Monitoring individual student progress (on one course, or across all courses)
- Monitoring overall progress of a particular course (class strengths and weaknesses)
- Informing tutors of relevant information (defaulting or weak students)
- Collection of on-line work of any sort (questionnaires, essays, ...)

- Searching for evidence of plagiarism
- Appropriate security control

These are all aspects which incur significant staff effort when class sizes rise above 100. We should make as much use of computers as possible.

In addition to the assessments performed by Ceilidh (see the next section), marks generated by staff in other ways can be entered by hand. These marks may be either amendments to existing stored marks (perhaps overriding a computer assessment to allow for a student with particular difficulties), or marks for associated work (such as essays or reports) which has been marked by hand. In addition work in the form of essays/reports can be submitted on-line by the students (having been generated using a word processing system), stored under Ceilidh, marked by hand on or off the machine, and the marks then entered by hand. The convenience of collecting 160 essays on-line, with no boxes of paper, and no possible complaints of "But I DID hand it in!" is very valuable.

The teacher can then look at all of the pieces of work submitted by any student for any exercise, or at the mark statistics for a particular class of students, any particular exercise or an individual student, find who has not submitted a particular exercise (and perhaps email them and/or their tutors), look at overall class program metrics, and check for plagiarism in submitted work. The overall metrics for a given item of automatically assessed coursework are useful in keeping the teacher in touch with the current performance of the class as a whole; this is more important when the teacher is not hand marking student work. The plagiarism pattern over a series of exercises can be significant; a single occurrence of similar submitted items may not be significant. In general the known presence of plagiarism tests acts as a considerable deterrent to copying.

There are considerable security problems in the above; students must not be able to view each others work or achievements, perhaps tutors should not be able to see the work of students other than their own tutees. These are handled by Ceilidh system features acting in addition to the normal operating system protection mechanisms. Ceilidh also provides audit trail facilities for monitoring activity on a per-student or per-facility basis. A pro-active trail analyser may be provided later.

It will be immediately apparent from the above summary that the system is ideally suited to remotes access. The students, tutors, teachers and course developers can all be at different sites, with access to networked computer systems.

The assessment of student achievement

We use the computer to perform automatic marking of student work submitted in various forms such as

- Computer programs
  in various languages
  marked with static and dynamic metrics
- Multiple choice questionnaires
- Question/answer natural language exercises
- Essays or reports

The first of these is currently the most significant. The term language includes traditional serial compiled programming languages such as Pascal, C and C++ as well as database query languages such as SQL, interpreted languages such as shell programming, and functional languages such as SML.

With a typical class of 150 students, the marking of student work was in the past divided between members of staff and postgraduate students. This often resulted in slow response to the students, and in the absence of uniform standards; teachers tended to minimise the quantity of work set simply to keep the marking load to a minimum. The computer caneasily mark several exercises per student each week, with a response time of seconds, and with absolute impartiality.

The original version of Ceilidh was developed at Nottingham as a system for marking programs written in C. The student would (on-line) read this week's question defining what was required (then simple ASCII text), obtain a skeleton outline of the solution program (and any associated header files etc), develop a solution program using "edit", "compile" and "run" options from a menu, and finally submit the program for marking.

The marking uses a variety of techniques for dynamic testing of the program for correctness and efficiency, as well as static analyses of the source. The static features may include general features such as

    program layout
        indentation
        choice of identifiers
        quantity and positioning of comments
    program structure
        use of denotations
        complexity metrics
        the division of the program into functions
    "lint"-type warnings
        suspicious constructs

as well as features specific to the question being solved. For further details see Zin and Foxley (1991), also available as a Ceilidh document.

The "edit, compile, test, submit" steps can be repeated if the teacher so wishes, so that the student can have several attempts at refining a solution, with the system providing feedback about the weaknesses in each submission.

The ability of Ceilidh to assess the quality of submitted work produces a dichotomy in certain requirements. The process of marking in education fulfills two distinct roles; one is to provide feedback to the student, to help in the leaning process. The other is to provide an assessment for the teacher, to count as part of the student grading process for the award of qualifications. The assessment facilities of Ceilidh can also be considered in both of these capacities.

- From the student learning view, we would like extensive feedback on weaknesses and errors, and the possibility of repeated resubmissions.
- From the teacher's point of view, student assignments which count towards the course assessment should perhaps be completed with less help given to the student, and perhaps without the possibility of resubmission.

The system is designed so that the teacher or course developer can modify it's appearing to conform to either of the requirements.

The presentation of information

The early versions of Ceilidh were aimed mainly at the administration and assessment areas. The information available to the students on-line consists only of text files, accessible through a simple browser, but with no hypertext facilities. The student views either ASCII text or PostScript, depending on their terminal capabilities.

The information available to students includes a number of documents relevant to Ceilidh (software quality papers, student and teacher guides, design documents, currently totalling 11000 lines of text), the course notes for each course (divided into one chapter for each unit, ranging from 6000 to 11000 lines of text for different courses) and numerous help files (approximately 2000 lines in total).

Future versions will include a hypertext interface being developed at Manchester Metropolitan University, with the possibility of accessing the hypertext information from Ceilidh (to look for additional information or teaching help), or to access Ceilidh assessment facilities from the hypertext level.

Implementation

Ceilidh runs on UNIX-based machines. Most of the current implementations of Ceilidh work with a centralised information base, accessed through a networked file system. The information base consists of the Ceilidh system itself, and a filesystem for each course which is required. The course filesystem will initially contain notes, exercises, marking data, and will later contain all the student submitted work and mark details. Audit trail information is stored in the Ceilidh system file area. To use Ceilidh, a student must have access from a terminal to a computer which mounts the Ceilidh filesystem under NFS.

A site intending to install the Ceilidh system uses FTP to take the system, and then takes such courses as are required. There are courses in C, C++, Pascal and SQL, and more are being built. Tools are provided to enable courses in other disciplines to be built.

Experimental versions have been built in which the course information base may be at a different site (Hassan, 1993; Kwong, 1992) and accessed by FTP over the network (fast) or email (slow). The quantity of information to be stored locally is being researched.

USER VIEWS OF CEILIDH

We will briefly summarise the view of current versions of Ceilidh, as seen by different categories of user. Ceilidh is a single system, but looks at the identity of the person who has logged on, and offers them different facilities depending who they are, and whether their name appears on certain lists of people designated to supervise a particular course.

All these categories of user can work remotely, provided they can log in to a system supporting the Ceilidh NFS.

Student view

See the Ceilidh student guide (Benford et al, 1992) for full details. Originally the emphasis of Ceilidh was on computer program marking.

The student each week

- Reads the question(s) defining problems to solve
- Asks for skeleton program outline

- Develops a solution and tests it
- Submits it to the system for assessment

The last two steps can be repeated if the teacher permits. The marking provides as much helpful feedback on weaknesses as the teacher specifies.

Other types of work besides computer programs can easily be administered withing the system providing marking programs are provided. Programs for marking mathematical algebraic functions are already available (the marking works be evaluating the formula at a number of distinct points, and comparing the results with those for the teacher's model answer), and for various logical operations (evaluating truth-tables, simplifying formulae). Multiple choice, simple numerical and short sentence answers are already built in.

Tutor view

Another category of user is the *tutor* who can look at the progress of tutees, and look at their submitted work. At Nottingham, the tutor may be a member of teaching staff or a postgraduate student, with responsibilities for monitoring a particular group of up to about 20 students. Other institutions may have different roles for tutors.

The teacher's view

The *teacher* can then look at the mark statistics for a particular class of students, exercise or individual student, find who hasn't submitted (and perhaps email them and/or their tutors), look at overall class program metrics, and check for plagiarism in submitted work. The overall metrics for a given programming exercise are useful in keeping the teacher in touch with the current performance of the class as a whole; this is more important when the teacher is not hand marking student work. The plagiarism pattern over a series of exercises can be significant; in general the known presence of plagiarism tests acts as a considerable deterrent to copying.

Each week the teacher will

- Open some new exercises
- Make some open exercises late
- Make some late exercises closed
- Compute metrics/plagiarism
- Print this week's marks
- Print marks so far
- Set new defaults

In earlier versions, the teacher and developer (see below, essentially developing a course, its notes, exercises and marking metrics) were not distinguished; it became quickly apparent that teachers did not want to risk accidentally changing the exercise metrics or notes. These two roles are now distinguished.

Course developer's vew

The last category, generally requiring the highest privilege, is the course developer.

The course developer's task with an existing course is to set up new exercises (there are many tests and metrics to set up, see Benford et al (1994) for details). The developer may also need to set up additional metrics tools for an existing course if they are deemed necessary, or, for a completely new course, the complete set of notes, exercises and metrics tools.

For technical security reasons, it is also in the developer's facilities to set and analyse audit trails. It is possible to monitor the use of a given Ceilidh function to see which students are making most use of, the compilation facilities, or to monitor particular students to see how active they are.

CEILIDH DEVELOPMENTS

The current version of Ceilidh runs under UNIX, and works using a networked file system, in which the distribution of a UNIX file system across machines is invisible to the users. A network version for PCs with a UNIX fileserver has already been developed in Portugal (Francisco Moura, UMINHO, Portugal) and a pure PC network version is under development at Lancaster University, UK.

Research students have developed versions which use FTP to fetch information and submit work over a general set of networked machines with independent filesystems. This work is proving successful, and will be developed into a general client-server system, in which the client systems can implement a variety of different *look-and-feel* approaches to the central system.

It should be possible soon to distribut the Ceilidh system itself, with different courses being held at different sites.

EXPERIENCE IN USING CEILIDH

Ceilidh provides an integrated environment for learning to program whose core is an automatic assessment facility. Experience of using Ceilidh for over three years has provided us with a number of interesting insights into the advantages and pitfalls of introducing such a system into the teaching process, and has resulted in a number of enhancements to the system. Perhaps the most significant feature of Ceilidh is the ability for students to re-mark their work and obtain feedback as many times as they like and so work towards a quality target.

We have found that Ceilidh brings many advantages. First, there has been a much increased dialogue with the students arising from a combination of

- provision of an on-line comments facility,
- the fact that marks are obtained while the problem remains fresh in the mind and
  the observation that students seem happier criticising machine awarded marks than theyare human awarded marks. This more active dialogue (there are more interactions than in other non-Ceilidh courses) has produced an overall consciousness raising effect with discussion focusing on issues of program correctness and style. In particular, we have had detailed discussions with the self-taught "tweakers", the very group who often suffer from previously obtained bad programming habits and who we most need to convince of the need for quality standards in programming. Ceilidh has also helped build the confidence of the novice and weaker students.

Ceilidh also gave rise to some interesting student personality revelations including

- the "perfectionist" students who seemed unable to stop work until they have reached mark of 100% and
- the "gamblers" who played the system as if it were a fruit machine, making random changes to the program to see if the mark went up or down.

These problems motivated us to add several additional features to Ceilidh.

- The introduction of a configurable minimum time delay between markings.
- The introduction of a maximum number of submissions.
- A coarser scaling of the marks. Instead of giving percentage marks out of 100, we can give marks out of for example 5. This reduces the urge to tweak for another mark. The marks are still stored internally to full accuracy.
- The ability to draw graphs of detailed student progress and their number of marking attempts in order to spot the problem cases. In particular for exercises with more than a few submissions we introduced an automatically calculated statistical measure called the Development Ratio. This is the ratio of the number of mark increases minus the number of decreases to the total number of attempts which we believe affords an overview of whether a student is making progress on a given exercise or not.

On one course this year the weighing of the exercise is set high if the maximum number of permitted attempts is one,.LP and low if it is a larger number. Ceilidh has also been of great benefit to staff by reducing administration and marking time, thereby allowing greater effort to be focused on effective teaching. Perhaps surprisingly, one result of introducing automated assessment appears to be increased contact with students, and it has certainly increased the level of discussion of software quality in tutorials. Teachers also appreciated the improved progress monitoring facilities.

One problem area concerns the tension between criterion (summative) and normative assessment. Ceilidh uses the former with the pleasing result that final marks tend to be high and most students achieve desired standards of programming proficiency. However, this can cause problems if Ceilidh is used as part of formal assessment combined with modules using normative assessment, particularly on the later stages of a course, as there tends to be less separation between marks as there might have been from a traditional examination. The automatic weighting and scaling facilities go some way towards relieving this tension, but a general solution has yet to be found. Students would like to know the scaling factors in advance, so that they can set their own programming achievement standards relative to the standard they would want to reach over the whole course.

Finally, a number of issues in the area of standards and formats need to be addressed for the exchange of course resources between different Ceilidh users.

CONCLUSIONS

The Ceilidh system represents the largest known project to date using computer assessment as part of a student grading system. The educational implications have been more significant than we thought.

We believe that, by focusing on course management and automated assessment, Ceilidh represents a novel computer supported learning system. We have found Ceilidh to be of great benefit to both students and teachers, although some new techniques were required to solve a few unexpected problems. We will certainly continue to use Ceilidh as part of our teaching and anticipate that it will continue to spread to other organisations. We suspect that aspects of Ceilidh may also be transferable to other disciplines.

Finally, we would like to stress that the latest release of Ceilidh is freely available to academic organisations through the authors.

References

Benford S, Burke E, and Foxley E (1992) *Student's Guide to the Ceilidh System,* LTR Report, Computer Science Dept, Nottingham University.

Benford S, Burke E, and Foxley E (1994) *Course Developer's Guide to the Ceilidh System,* LTR Report, Computer Science Dept., Nottingham University,

Hassan M R (1993) *Remote Access to the Ceilidh, Coursework Assessment System,* MSc Dissertation, University of Nottingham, UK.

Kwong SSY (1992) *Remote access to the Ceilidh Assessment System,* MSc Dissertation, University of Nottingham, UK.

Zin A M and Foxley E (1991) Automatic Program Quality Assessment System, *Proceedings of the IFIP Conference on Software Quality,* S P University, Vidyanagar, INDIA.

Section 5: Additional Abstracts

The papers listed in this section were presented at the AETT 94 International Conference. Unfortunately, shortage of space precludes publication of these papers in full, and abstracts only have been included. Full copies of most of these papers were produced and are available either from the authors themselves or from the editors of these Proceedings.

LABORATORY COURSE SYSTEM USING PERSONAL COMPUTER

Yoshikazu Araki, *Saitama Institute of Technology, Japan*

The author has developed a new practical teaching and learning system on the "Electronic Engineering Laboratory Course" consisting of CAM (Computer Assisted Measurement) together with CAL (Computer Assisted Learning) systems. The system is schematically shown in Figure 1. The system is called RECALL (Real-Experience-Computer-Assisted-Laboratory-Learning) system. At the beginning of the laboratory course, the pre-Lab-CAI is done to check basic knowledge of experimental theories, equations and methods. In the laboratory, students measure voltage-current and switching characteristics of semiconductor devices such as BJT, JFET and MOS FET using personal computers. After taking the measurements students learn the characteristics of the devices by using their own data to answer questions such as calculation of input resistance, output resistance, mutual conductance and switching speed of the devices.

After all the processes mentioned above are finished, the post-Lab-CAI is done to check understanding of the completed section of the laboratory.

The author developed the whole system.

DESIGNING MULTIMEDIA EDUCATIONAL PROGRAMMES

Antonio R Bartolome, *University of Barcelona*

The aim of this paper is to present a framework for designing Multimedia programmes for self-learning purposes.

Several models are presented. In the domain of *Information Presentation Programmes I* 4 models are included: Data Base, Object Oriented, Electronic Book and Intelligent Hypermedia. In the domain of *Learning Activities Programmes,* four other models are shown: Practice, Tutorial, Problem Solving and Simulation.

Each one is studied through actual applications. The author will consider suitable objectives, specific design rules, possibilities, and other elements.

EXPLOITING INFORMATION TECHNOLOGY IN ELECTRONIC BOOKS

Ian D Benest, *Department of Computer Science, University of York* and **Philip G Barker,** *School of Computing and Mathematics, University of Teesside*

Electronic books of various sorts are now often used for the delivery of pedagogic material. Of course, developing material to be delivered through an electronic book system simply to provide what could be produced on paper is a poor exploitation of information technology. Furthermore the production process usually consumes more effort for the author than would the paper alternative, and it is probably less efficient for the student. This paper briefly identifies some of the situations where information technology can be usefully exploited and thus usurp the conventional book's superiority for conveying material. For example, the demonstration of sequential or temporal activity, for which the animation itself contains information or provides insight, that would otherwise be conveyed in a complex paragraph. Another example is the provision of a spoken narrative to describe a diagram, which removes the need for the student to look backwards and forwards at both the diagram and its description. The use of a specific simulator to enable users to test their models of a concept with particular instances to ensure that they have correctly understood the concept. The incorporation of colour pictures (which, in comparison are expensive to print in a conventional book) and the integration of video clips into courseware with additional authored observations, are further examples where information technology can be exploited to good effect.

But one of the most difficult aspects of any electronic book design is the provision of a user-interface that is sufficiently compatible with the human being for it to appear to be natural, instinctive, and above all transparent to use. While lecturers are fully conversant with the material that is being taught and the best way of explaining the concepts, they are less experienced in determining how the material should be accessed. Pointing and clicking is easy, putting material in a window and providing menu access is easy; remembering and finding a piece of material that is hidden from view in a hierarchical network is not, and it distracts the student from the primary task. By means of illustration, this paper will examine some of the user-interface issues that arise when developing electronic books for pedagogic use.

TRAINING BEGINNERS TO CREATE MULTIMEDIA: A FRESH APPROACH

Sandy Bloomer, *Dunblane High School* and Blue Stevens, *Vocational Technologies*

The purpose of this experimental workshop is to enable delegates to create their own multimedia presentation inside an hour. Inevitably, this will be limited in scope, but will include at least sounds (either recorded live or chosen from a compact disc sound library), graphics (chosen from Clip Art and/or edited/draw) and text, with hypertext links created by the delegates. Delegates do not require any previous experience of computing let alone multimedia, however they will need a sense of humour and the willingness to take a mild risk. (Delegates with relevant skills are also welcome, and may be recruited to assist the presenters.)

To help novices to accelerate up the learning curve, special short-cuts, software tools and job aids have been designed. There will be at least one computer per two delegates, and printouts may be made available later as a souvenir. While the tools used will be HyperCard on Apple Macintosh, what delegates will learn about the multimedia creation and editing process should be generalisable.

Because the presenters represent an unusual collaboration, the workshop addresses a further issue, namely it tests an alternative model of how such skills can be transmitted. In a world where hardware obsolescence cycles are increasingly rapid and teachers who lack the necessary confidence and skills effectively act as gate-keepers, should we try to liberate the teaching potential locked up within the pupils' heads?

The presenters are Sandy Bloomer, a first-year pupil at Dunblane High School, and Blue Stevens, a non-specialist who has learned much of what she knows about sound, graphics and HyperCard from Sandy. Blue will be responsible for ensuring that the workshop is well organised and enjoyable, while Sandy is in charge of all technical preparation and support. Both will provide hand- and mouse-holding as needed. If demand exists, the workshop will be run for a single hour and be repeated; if not, and delegates wish to continue, the process can be continued for a further hour. Since places are strictly limited, early enrolment is advised.

AN INTERACTIVE AUDIENCE RESPONSE SYSTEM - ITS APPLICATION TO TEACHING AND LEARNING

Denise Brough, *Department of Biological Sciences, Manchester Metropolitan University*

As with most other institutions of Higher Education we face the problem of the ever-growing class size, high SSRs and a consequent loss of interaction between staff and students. This is very much the case in the lecture theatre where student numbers are often in excess of 60. The lecture remains a very important teaching method but educational research has shown that for a lecture to be a useful learning experience it must involve the students in some form of intellectual activity. In the past this could be achieved through questions being asked during the lecture, and knowing the students well enough to identify when learning was not taking place. As class numbers have grown this form of activity has become increasingly more difficult and student interaction and feedback increasingly less frequent. Lectures can become very much more passive and sterile.

In an effort to overcome some of these problems we have been piloting an audience response system which depends upon the use of a projected PC image to display questions or information to the students during a lecture. Each student is provided with a digital handset which is interfaced with the PC, this allows each student to register his/her attendance and to respond to questions posed during the lecture. Response data is collected, stored, analysed and displayed to give immediate feedback. Responses can be stored either anonymously or named.

All students are required to respond to questions asked in class. Students are continuously assessed which means students with problems can be identified early, and tutorial support can be targeted more efficiently. Individuals can anonymously assess their progress against that of the whole group which can often improve motivation. Staff are also able to continuously assess the effectiveness of their teaching, as they can see when a large proportion of the group are having common difficulties. All this at the press of a button during the lecture.

These are just a few of the applications we have so far found for the system. No doubt others will present themselves as we become more familiar with the system.

What we appear to have is a tool, which can help make teaching and learning more fun and more effective, and assessment of large groups more meaningful and less time-consuming. So far staff and students have found the system enjoyable and useful.

The workshop will provide an opportunity to experience the system and comment on its effectiveness in teaching and learning and to suggest additional applications.

INCORPORATING LEARNING ISSUES INTO COMPUTER - ASSISTED EDUCATION

Susan Bull, *Department of Artificial Intelligence, University of Edinburgh* **and Tim Musson,** *Department of Computer Studies, Napier University*

Traditional computer - assisted learning (CAL) programs take very little account of real learning issues such as the following:

- What happens if the learner does not understand material in the manner it is presented?
- What should the programme do if students react differently from what expected?
- How do you take account of the different background knowledge and different approaches to learning which will necessarily be found among any group of students?

Most CAL software packages are either simple linear programs with no provision for adjusting to the needs of the individual student, or the - only slightly more sophisticated branching - programs which lead learners down particular pre-determined routes, depending only on the previous answer offered by a student. Hypertext applications allow the learner some choice as to the material covered and the order in which this is viewed, but the system itself does not react knowledgeably to individual student input.

The linear and branching types of program are adequate only for drilling or testing the student, but not as methods of improving students' learning as they lack individualised explanation techniques. Hypertext systems are likewise limited, as they also fail to take account of a student's learning needs beyond the provision of greater learner choice. Therefore a different type of system is required if the aim is to ensure the facilitation of learning, an issue which necessitates consideration of the student as an individual rather than students as a mass group expected all to behave in a similar manner. Intelligent Tutoring Systems (ITS) come much closer to this idea as, in addition to domain information, they also construct an individual model of each student. It is on this information that the tutoring strategy module bases its decisions regarding future system action. Thus teaching and explanation can be tailored to the individual. However, despite these benefits, the conventional ITS still suffers limitations. A major problem is the underlying assumption that the function of the system is simply to communicate knowledge. It does little to encourage a student's active involvement in learning.

This paper will describe an intelligent computer - assisted language learning system which seeks to overcome this limitation for a student-modelling perspective. This is achieved by allowing the learner to become an active agent in the construction and repair of the student model, both to obtain a more accurate model and to promote learner reflection, and therefore enhance learning. In addition, important issues in the field of second language acquisition are incorporated into the student model and the system as a whole, as these learning issues are clearly relevant to student modelling. The issues are:
1. acquisition order of the target grammatical rules.
2. language transfer.
3. learning strategies.
4. language awareness.

USING HYPERTEXT AS A LEARNING AID

Joseph K Campbell, *University of Wales*

Because of its vast storage capacity, CD-ROM technology promises to improve education by increasing the amount of resources available to teachers and students. Making use of this new technology is dependent upon a system that will allow users to access and manage the vast stores of information contained in a CD-ROM. Hypertext has been proposed as the key that can unlock the power of this new technology.

This paper traces the development of hypertext within the context of educational computing and reviews research that has been undertaken to investigate the use of hypertext as a learning resource. Early research has shown that hypertext is not a suitable medium for the learning of declarative knowledge. More promising research points to the use of hypertext as a resource to promote higher order thinking skills.

In the final section the author reports on a case study that evaluates the use of hypertext as a learning aid. The author concludes that hypertext is an effective resource for learning under certain conditions and suggests how to make the use of hypertext effective. The suggestions include the following:

1. Make sure users have some familiarity with the concepts covered in the hypertext.
2. Use hypertext for a definite purpose; avoid browsing.
3. Structure learning activities around complex problems which demand analysis, synthesis and evaluation of the hypertext database.
4. Try to contextualise the use of hypertext; give students authentic problems to solve.
5. Implement overt learning strategies which mimic expert learning strategies.

APPLICATION OF DESKTOP ISDN SYSTEMS TO REMOTE TEACHING

Colin Christie, *Department of Design, Napier University*

Background to ISDN

Telecom companies throughout Europe are making heavy investments in digital communication technology (ISDN). The networks being created will a standard method of high speed data transfer which can be readily accessed by any computer hardware platform. There are huge opportunities for the development of remote teaching networks, not simply the sharing of data but also interactive teaching and video communications.

Digital communications will provide the electronic arterial system to the new field of remote teaching. Cheap, effective hardware and software support systems provide readily usable platforms on which to build remote teaching practices where the exploitation of specialist knowledge and skills is not limited by traditional methods of communication and, most especially, distance.

ISDN desktop systems allow real time video, voice and software interaction - indeed everything except the user's physical presence. However as with all computer technology the user interface which gives access and control is vitally important. For ISDN technologies to become an effective tool for distance learning the software interfaces must not interfere with the learning process.

Trials of ISDN systems

Since mid 1993 a series of system trials have been carried out at Napier University. The aim was to ascertain the working limitations of desktop ISDN systems when confronted with the problems of remote teaching. The working problems discussed in this paper were identified as a result of these trials.

Paper contents

This paper will discuss the requirements, possible configurations, use and interfaces of typical desktop systems suitable for remote teaching over ISDN networks.

The discussion will review, in detail, the methods and types of remote teaching possible within the parameters of desktop ISDN systems. Moreover it will propose possible software configurations and software combinations which, based on the trials and the existing products under development, will begin to answer remote teaching requirements.

SETTING UP AND MANAGING A COMPUTER-BASED OPEN ACCESS CENTRE

Andrew K Comrie, *Perth College*

FOLIO (Flexible and Open Learning Individual Opportunity) has been established in its present form at Perth College since August 1992. The College has been actively involved in developing and running Open Learning courses, however, for over 10 years through what was originally the College's Centre for Open Learning.

FOLIO provides a curriculum support function to all Departments in the College to help develop and embed Flexible and Open Learning across the Curriculum Portfolio.

As well as continually adding to the range of Open Learning Courses offered, FOLIO is currently adopting a flexible approach to its whole curriculum. Part of this exercise has resulted in setting up 3 Computer-based Open Access Centres.

The Open Access Centres are open to all students in the College as well as to external customers on a bookable basis. The Centres can be used for:-

- Access to Software for private study or project work
- Completing the Computer element of a course
- Developing Skills in new Technology Software
- Computer-based training using Multi-media software.

The Centres provide the opportunity to enrol for all computer/computer software courses available on a "roll-on-roll-off" basis and students with a facility where they can learn at a time and pace which meets their needs.

Workshop content

The workshop will deal with setting up and running an Open Access Centre. The topics covered will highlight:-

> Hardware/Software Available in the Centres
> Materials Development (including multi-media courseware)
> Tutor Support in the Centres
> Administration
> Assuring Quality

THE ROLE OF TECHNOLOGY IN FACILITATING THE INTRODUCTION OF OPEN LEARNING WITHIN THE UNIVERSITY OF HUMBERSIDE

Mike Cook, *School of Social and Professional Studies, University of Humberside*

In common with most higher educational establishments within the UK, the University of Humberside is subject to increasing pressure to become more financially efficient, and to increase the quality of its educational performance. This pressure is forcing the University to examine its teaching and learning methods, and find new, more efficient ways of delivery. The paper will describe how the University is embracing `open learning' methods in its drive to increase efficiency and enhance the quality of its teaching. The use of technology will play a key role in these developments in terms of releasing staff time, and increasing access to learning material. The University is vigorously pursuing a number of projects in this area, which are expected to have widespread ramifications for its mainstream teaching and learning activities, e.g.

- The 'Learning to Learn' project seeks to allow all new students at the University to 'audit' their knowledge in key areas of the curriculum and take remedial 'crash courses' as necessary to make up any shortfalls. They will also be able to discover their own optimum learning style, and use this information to increase their personal learning efficiency. This project is dependent on the use of the University's computer networks, with students being responsible for working through the scheme independently.

- A number of projects have been completed (or are under way) to use CBT to deliver course material, or provide information about courses. Notable amongst these is a plan to use CBT to deliver those topics which students have found most difficult and to provide on-line selective access to model answers for mid-course tests.

The University is encouraging the examination of all course modules to see which are best suited to delivery via open learning methods. As part of this initiative I have devised a tool for 'rating' the suitability of each course unit for open learning delivery. This tool, the 'open learning index', is currently being developed and tested.

DEVELOPING AN "ELECTRONIC" COURSE

Dympna Copley, Stuart Kent, Keith Parramore, Jane Southern, *Faculty of Information Technology, University of Brighton*

The paper reports work arising from a pilot project currently being undertaken at the University of Brighton in the Faculty of Information Technology. The aim of the project is to redevelop an existing course (HND in Mathematical Studies for Business Applications) based on the assumption that every student and member of the teaching staff has personal, 24-hour access to information technology. The motivation for such a course is to improve its overall delivery, by making the students more responsible for their own learning and improving the range and accessibility of learning resources. It is intended that this should be a pilot "electronic" course, and it is hoped that, if successful, the experience may be repeated on other courses, both within and outside the University.

In particular, the paper describes:

- the status of current and relevant technology in IT.
- the specific areas in which we think IT has a role to play in the management and delivery of a course and individual modules, including examples of how this might be done.
- the likely problems that will need to be addressed both at a technical and social level.

The paper focuses on problems rather than solutions, although it describes progress to date and future directions which we expect our research to follow. The paper also briefly considers how the project, itself, will be evaluated.

TEACHING AND LEARNING THROUGH CAL DEVELOPMENT: AN HCI PERSPECTIVE

Alison Crerar and Kirsteen Davidson, *Napier University*

This paper focuses on pedagogical aspects of a collaborative study between the Departments of Computer Studies and Mathematics at Napier University. The aim of the research was to develop an interactive graphical linear programming package that would support exploratory learning in novices. However, this report is concerned less with the resulting software product than with the process of software development, which itself formed the basis of a multi-dimensional computer-based teaching and learning experience for students other than the target users.

The first part of the paper is concerned with outlining the approach taken to the design and implementation of this package and introducing the academic context in which the project was undertaken. We consider the implications of recent graphical user interface (GUI) development tools for production of computer-assisted learning (CAL) materials, in particular, Microsoft's Visual Basic which was used for this work.   The complex network of teaching/learning inter-relationships forged between the authors and a group of nine postgraduates studying human-computer interaction (HCI) is sketched.   This, in itself, constitutes a novel teaching/learning experience.

The second part of the paper concentrates on an empirical evaluation of the usability of the software by the postgraduate group, prior to its piloting with the target population. This study is of interest for a number of reasons: the task provided a rich learning experience for the programmer and the testers; the techniques used yielded a high volume of feedback from relatively few subjects and new insights were gained into the value of testing CAL software independently for usability *before* piloting it with intended users for teaching effectiveness.

The usability study centred round a set of structured tasks designed to exercise the software. These were completed simultaneously by six subjects under observation in the laboratory and individually by a further three subjects in a TV studio. All subjects completed a questionnaire after taking part. A summary of the findings will be presented, indicating how they affected the quality of the product.

The presentation will be illustrated by video material showing the graphical linear programming package developed and the split-screen technique with speaking aloud protocol that was used to elicit feedback from filmed subjects.

MODULAR APPLICATION ARCHITECTURES FOR MULTI-DISCIPLINARY MULTIMEDIA COURSEWARE - THE LANCAL SYSTEM

Roy Currie, *Computing Services, University of Central Lancashire*

The management of multiple large-scale multimedia courseware development projects, relating to different subject areas, has enabled the identification of generalisable application components which can be easily adapted to deliver materials for new subject areas. Multimedia teaching materials require a high development overhead both in the development of application architecture and the creation of media content. Development overheads are particularly high in initial projects. If they are to be significantly reduced for subsequent projects, it is essential that as much as possible, in terms of development practice, application structures and code, from the initial project can be redeployed in novel contexts.

The LANCAL (Lancashire Computer Assisted Learning) project commenced through the development of high-end multimedia applications for teaching midwifery. At an early stage in the midwifery project it was decided that a flexible development strategy should be pursued. This strategy is now being applied to the development of further courseware in midwifery, waste management (as part of an EEC funded consortium) and marketing (TLTP consortium). These applications all make use of digital video, animation, sound and full colour images and are highly interactive.

The courseware for all subjects consists of a mixture of three types of component: Tutorial Manager - responsible for presentation of primary content and courseware navigation, Hypertools - which allow the user to browse interlinked textual, image, video and animation files (these also include a variety of user support tools) and Content Interaction components - which can involve formative evaluation and simulations. The architecture for the first two components, in the form of application templates and codes of development practice - including the selection and preparation of media, can be generalised to new subject areas allowing a high proportion of the development effort for new projects to be directed to the creation of subject-specific modules dealing with interaction with course content.

SUPPORTING THE NOVICE IN THE LEARNING OF PROGRAM DESIGN

Martyn Davies and Tom Boyle *Department of Computing, Manchester Metropolitan University*

This paper will describe the design and evaluation of an integrated hypermedia system that aims to support novice progammers in doing and learning program design. The system, called Braque, seeks to address a number of factors which we believe inhibit students from engaging in the process of program design. Specifically it aims to support them by providing them with:

- a model of the design process which is derived from research into how programmers actually carry out the process of design.
- an environment that integrates the processes of design and implementation to reflect the essentially investigative and iterative nature of the programming process.
- a set of design representations which are specifically oriented towards the needs of novice programmers.

Consequently Braque has been developed on two layers. The first layer is a CAD environment specifically constructed to support the acquisition of program design skills. This layer provides three interactive views which support the design process at different levels of abstraction. These views deal with goal decomposition, control flow and the mapping to code respectively. The system is integrated such that changes made to one view e.g. goal decomposition, are automatically reflected in the other views. This CAD environment is supported by a full set of editing and navigation tools. The second layer consists of a series of multimedia tutorials which use the CAD environment to teach design skills. The paper will describe the principles underlying the two main layers and their integration.

The design environment is at present being used to teach program design to over 60 first year university students. The feedback received from using the environment with these students will be described, and the implications for multimedia tutorial design highlighted.

ACADEMIC MANAGEMENT SYSTEMS

Denis Edgar-Nevill, *Department of Computer Studies, Napier University*

Using a computer program to remove clerical/administrative drudgery has been the foundation stone of IT developments in industry and commerce. In education also, many sophisticated (and some not so sophisticated) management information systems exist to assist with admissions, assessment recording and analysis etc. Clearly we still fail to realise their full potential. For example, how many departments fail to use a standard spreadsheet for examinations boards? How many departments do analysis on those spreadsheets to display graphical information? All too often we fail to exploit the full potential of the medium. There are many opportunities to exploit the information available. Where simple mistakes in accounting or predictive processes can result in student problems not being recognised early, leading to eventual course failure, or dramatic resource over/under commitment, we must employ every means at our disposal. Even simple systems can help. Many HJE courses put great emphasis on the use of modern techniques in managing commercial systems. Yet another instance of us failing to practise what we preach.

This paper considers the role computers can play in departmental administration and planning. A whole departmental model of information sources and IT opportunities is given. Some examples of the simple computer models developed in the Department of Computer Studies at Napier will be displayed, which were developed for strategic long-term planning.

The paper concludes with guidelines on the introduction of IT in academic management.

ARTMASTER - A PACKAGE FOR SPECIAL NEEDS EDUCATION

J R Fowler and S Swales, *School of Computing and Information Systems, University of Sunderland*

This project sets out the progress made towards the construction of a specialised art package known as Art Master.

This package is in the form of a simple to use art package with a speech-synthesised help system, to take the burden out of teaching children to use computer art packages. Through this system, the needs of special needs children are especially catered for.

Firstly, there is a discussion of the background to the project which sets the stage for the development and the reasons behind the writing of that art package. Then the paper investigates the different aspects of the computer system chosen and discusses its special features which make it ideal for use in special needs areas, including user interfaces, special graphics features and the "narrator" speech synthesis system.

Secondly, there is a section on the feedback that arose from the prototype package being tested at a local special needs school, and from this there are conclusions which provide some indication about where the development of this art package system could continue in the future and how the same could be applied to other types of software, such as databases and word processors.

DEVELOPING A STRATEGY FOR CAL AND OPEN LEARNING

Elizabeth Frondigoun, *School of Computing, Staffordshire University*

Although many institutions have committed resources and money on quite a large scale to the development of technology in the classroom, and outside it on a student-centred basis, it is also the case that in many places the impetus for development has to come from a small band of researchers and developers, with a primary role in mainstream teaching, who work from a very limited remit and budget.

This paper will deal with ways in which growth in the areas of CAL and open learning may be developed from a very small initial base, and strategies will be illustrated via case studies which will also touch on wider issues in educational research. The case studies will involve a project to carry out comparative evaluation of tutorial strategies and an investigation into needs for tailored distance learning preparatory material. Wider issues will include the problem of recognising and handling the divergence of expectation which can be identified in student and staff expectations of particular units of learning.

MAKING A CASE FOR THE TEACHING OF SOFTWARE DEVELOPMENT

Richard Gelvin and José M Munoz, *Department of Computer Studies, Napier University*

A CASE tool, originally designed to develop communications protocols (Howie and Munoz 1993), has been used in the Department of Computer Studies at Napier University to teach senior undergraduate and postgraduate students. Primarily due to its character mode interface, the original package had pedagogical limitations, and a new tool, with enhanced functionality, has been designed and developed under Microsoft Windows. This offers a fully integrated learning environment without losing any of the features of the original CASE tool. This paper presents the new package and discusses its features and educational values.

Both tools teach the principles of software design using the concept of Finite State Machine (FSM) or Automaton. This paper discusses the pedagogical values of the new tool and its fully integrated Windows environment which allows the interactive design of an FSM in three different exchangeable modes: textual, diagrammatic and tubular. Provision is made for semantic checking and animation of the FSM in each of these modes.

The value of integrated Windows CASE tools used as a learning environment is explored by comparing the results of a survey of groups of students using the new and original tools. Preliminary user tests show that features of the new tool, such as its user-friendly interface, on-line tutorials and the capability to describe an FSM in different modes allows for individual cognitive differences in modelling software. Finally the educational and training values of combining the features of CASE and CAL tools are discussed.

THE MAGICAL MULTIMEDIA MYTH: NOTES FOR A HISTORY OF MEDIA AND TECHNOLOGY IN EDUCATION AND TRAINING

Donald J Gillies, *Film and Photography Department, Ryerson Polytechnic University, Toronto*

The author is a recycled revolutionary in the campaign to enhance teaching and learning by the use of media and technology. In the last thirty years he has moved from chalk-and-talk at a teachers' college through slides, films and filmstrips, records, phonotapes, television, multimedia Mark I (tapes/slides/ programmer), overhead projectuals, videotape, CAL, CBI, CBT, CMI, and videotex, with two years as an acolyte at the altar of McLuhanism and two years as chief executive of a private-sector international telecommunications management training institute.

In 1992-93 he participated in the distance education multimedia (Mark II) trial of IBM Canada's PARIS - Packetized Automated Routing Integrated System - a one-gigabit ultra-high-speed networking technology carried on a 2.4 gigabit fibre optic network. His multimedia work continues as a member of an R & D team in the Rogers Communications Centre of Ryerson Polytechnic University at work on "Multi-News", a multimedia news service, in a consortium comprising the Canadian Broadcasting Corporation/Societe Radio Canada (radio and television), the Canadian Government's Centre for Information Technologies Innovation, the Society Nationale d'Information (publishing), and Southam, Inc., a national publisher and supplier of business communications, information technology and services, magazines and newspapers. The project, which is in the proof-of-concept stage, will provide news-on-demand through PC-networked workstations through distributed multimedia.

The author will examine the history of this whole realm of education and training using, as a visual aid, his personal kaleidoscope comprised of the above elements and will offer a personal perspective on the past and an outlook on the future.

RIGHT OR WRONG, YOU AND I, KNOWLEDGE AND MEANING? THE INFLUENCE OF STUDENT ATTITUDE ON LEARNING.

Jen Harvey, *Department of Biological Sciences, Napier University*

This paper will describe an educational research project which has over the last three years been investigating the relationship between student attitude and the quality of their thinking.

Using the Perry Model of Intellectual Development as a theoretical basis for the research, the project has identified a number of factors which affected the quality of students' thinking while at University. These included the students' concepts of the subject area, their perceived roles for the student and the lecturer within the learning environment and their stage of intellectual development.

This paper describes how this project identified a number of individual developmental changes, as well as several class trends which appeared common to particular stages of Higher Education courses. This paper discusses some of these findings and by considering the implications of different teaching and assessment methods suggests ways in which the quality of student thinking might be improved.

TWO ALTERNATIVE APPROACHES TO DEVELOPING CAL COURSEWARE

Simon B Heath and Clive P L Young, *Centre for Computer-Based Learning in Land Use and Environmental Sciences, University of Aberdeen*

Lecturers in UK university departments teaching the agricultural sciences and other Land Use related subjects are increasingly aware of the benefits of using computers to enhance students' learning. We envisage two complementary approaches to courseware development in the future. The **team approach** involving lecturers (as subject experts) working with educational technologists, graphic designers and programmers, and a **low technology approach** with lecturers working alone and largely unsupported. This Centre is leading two TLTP projects, the consortium for Land Use and Environmental Sciences (**TLTP-CLUES**) and project **LoCAL**, which will allow us to examine the strengths and weaknesses of both approaches.

The **team approach** to courseware development is a costly activity, and consequently the key objective must be to maximise the uptake of a computer-assisted learning (CAL) package by as many lecturers as possible across institutions. To achieve this, firstly the same course content must be widely taught, and secondly lecturers must have flexibility in how they integrate the package into their own course and in how it is presented to students. Fortunately in our subject area lecturers from different universities teach the same core subject material opening up the opportunity for shared specification and use of courseware. One way of achieving flexibility is to produce courseware in a stand-alone modular format, with each module focusing on a discrete topic. **TLTP-CLUES** is developing a library of 26 such CAL modules. The modules are designed to be self-supporting dynamic tutorials from which activity-rich simulation models, databases and multimedia applications can be launched. Each module is specified by the relevant group of lectures drawn from the Consortium with the software development carried out by a team based at one site.

However, it is difficult to envisage how this **team approach** will be able to meet by itself the expected demand for CAL courseware in the future. The strategy, which incurs high development costs, is often dependent on grant funding with all the limitations that implies. Therefore the challenge is to develop a strategy for expansion which includes the individual lecturer working alone. It is unlikely that many lecturers will wish to attempt to develop the skills embodied in the team approach, nor do we believe that the modern **authoring tools**, such as Toolbook or Authorware, are a likely solution except for straightforward tutorial courseware. Unless a solution is found, these issues could prove to be a major limitation to the future expansion of CAL.

The **LoCAL** project provides one such alternative approach. The project will develop a methodology which will enable lecturers to develop educationally effective and visually stimulating courseware using generic application software, such as spreadsheets. The recent advances in the modern Windows spreadsheet and word-processing software, with the addition of the customised Help facility, allow a **low-technology**, low-investment route to courseware through their every day work. It will enable individual staff, with the minimum of resources and new skills, to develop CAL courseware packages which meet their own teaching needs. The **LoCAL** project will extend the current use of computers in teaching, and enable the production and implementation of new courseware to become a more mainstream activity for lecturers in the natural or social science departments in higher education.

TEACHING AND LEARNING STRATEGIES FOR A COMPUTER-BASED ALGEBRA TUTOR

Anne Groat and Tim Musson, *Department of Computer Studies, Napier University*

The idea that a person has a preferred way of learning has been acknowledged since the beginning of the century. It is only much more recently, however, that its importance in education has been recognised. Learning style refers to the way in which information is processed by an individual, independent of intelligence. There have been a number of attempts to measure learning style, not all of which have been useful in prescribing pedagogical tactics or strategies. Empirical data and experience in the classroom support the notion that a student will learn more effectively when the instruction strategy employed by a teacher matches the learning style of the student.

If the relationship holds for a computer-based learning environment, the task then is to match learning style and teaching strategy in such a way that learning is optimised. The aim of this project is to explore the relationship using a computer-based tutor for simple algebra; to determine

a)   whether it is possible to identify the learning strategy used by a given student in a way that can be used to guide the selection of an appropriate teaching strategy and

b)   whether the use of a teaching strategy that matches the student's learning style will result in more effective learning.

USE OF INTERACTIVE MULTI-MEDIA AS AN EFFECTIVE RESOURCE

John Hall, *Video Consultancy Service, Blackheath* and David Anderson, *Gloucestershire College of Arts & Technology.*

The theme of the presentation will consider the organisational as well as the learning considerations which need to be taken into account when setting out to use interactive multimedia as an effective resource.

GLOSCAT have well-developed flexible learning centres using interactive multimedia. The presentation by David Anderson will describe the way in which the interactive learning resources were structured and organised both for use by internal as well as external students.

Considerations about access to courseware, the availability of suitable courseware and the relationships between the flexible learning services and teaching staff would be explored.

John Hall has acted as consultant and project manager for a number of interactive multimedia programmes including a package produced for the National Council for Vocational Qualifications (NCVQ). He has also carried out a study commissioned by NCET and Further Education Unit on the use of interactive videodisc programs in colleges.

His presentation will complement that of David Anderson through drawing on this study which suggests a number of reasons for the under utilisation of interactive multimedia when compared to the potential benefits which the technology has to offer.

The essence of the presentation will be to point to the lessons which need to be drawn from experience in utilising interactive multimedia, so as to avoid, if possible, repeating the mistakes of the past when implementing the newer, emerging technologies.

BUT WE USED TO LAUGH: WHERE'S THE DIGITAL DELIGHT IN LEARNING?

Professor Stephen Heppell, *Ultralab, Anglia Polytechnic University*

Technology is at the heart of many new promises about learning in our future institutions. Learning Productivity suggests faster, better and cheaper learning and much is made of the flexibility that new learning technologies offer to vary both the time and place of learning and open up both asynchronous and distributed learning opportunities. Multimedia promises, and delivers, a broad spectrum of information, content cues and clues that enrich the learning environment. Hardware increasingly offers both speed and quantity in unimagined bounty.

Not surprisingly much of our focus in the heady technology rush of the last two decades has been on what the technology can do and what we might be able to do with it. However learning has been around a lot longer than learning technology and over the last few millennia we have begun to evolve a model of what helps learning along and what doesn't. Some of that experience is useful as we plan for our future learning environments and this paper will address firstly the need for new learning environments to learn from these experience of the past, good and bad.

However, as technology has accelerated we have averted our eyes from something else that is developing equally fast: the users. This paper's second focus is on the observable changes in that population of technology-resourced learners and on the lessons we can learn from them.

There are many components of successful learning: need, intention, delight, challenge, participation, cultural support. It is time to start matching the experience of the past to the climate of expectation that accompanies our new learning generation in a way that builds successful computer assisted learning.

"PASSPORTS ARE NO LONGER REQUIRED" MANAGING PAN-EUROPEAN DISTANCE LEARNING PROGRAMMES

JCH Jennings and R Findlay, *CECOMM, Southampton Institute*

Many educational and training organisations are looking to achieve more flexible educational provision in response to changes in demography, organisational objectives, work practices and evolving market factors. At the same time, developments in information technology and telecommunications are offering opportunities for these organisations to implement telematic-based solutions to educational needs.

The Multimedia Tele-School (MTS) has been established and is funded by DGXIII of the Commission of the European Communities under its DELTA (Developing European Learning Through Technological Advance) Programme. Focused on distance education and new technologies, it has as its aim the demonstration, thorough large-scale pilot projects, of the integration of advanced communication technologies in the delivery of interactive distance education to learners across Europe. Currently, courses are being delivered to learners in the UK, France, Germany, spain, Italy, Greece, Belgium, Finland and Russia. The MTS uses live satellite broadcasts (with feedback to tutors in the studio) supported by group-centred telematic "virtual seminars" to provide a fully interactive environment for distance learners.

This paper examines the management issues raised (and strategies developed to address them) in the telematic delivery and support of a group of language courses within the MTS. Managing the learning of a multi-national group of distance learners has been made an easier task by using structured design methodologies, software management tools and thoughtful adaption of pedagogies for these new learning environments.

COMPUTER SIMULATED EXPERIMENTS

Jerome J Leary, *Department of Mathematical Sciences, University of Brighton*

The paper describes the early results of a new research programme investigating the use of the three dimensional computer-aided design (3D CAD) packages to simulate science experiments in the teaching of Energy Studies. Through the new Modular Science at the University of Brighton, larger numbers of students are now choosing to take science modules which need a degree of practical work. This has traditionally involved experimental apparatus, taking measurements, and so on.

The option of fitting out laboratories with new equipment has obvious drawbacks, the main one being that it is costly and uneconomic, as each piece of equipment is used relatively infrequently; some of the experiments can also be quite dangerous and need to be well-supervised. Rotation of experiments can result in theory and practical work getting out of phase. However, practicals can't simply be done away with: in science teaching a practical element is considered necessary to support learning so that the student reinforces his or her knowledge through active experimentation.

The proposed solution is to use computer-based simulations. A typical experiment would show, for example, the inner workings of a gas calorimeter as an animation in three dimensions. This would be complemented by a mathematical model simulating the experiment, such that the student would be able to operate the machinery and obtain results as if operating the real calorimeter and obtaining real measurements with real instruments.

All the computer-based practicals run under the Microsoft Windows environment on PC compatibles. The paper describes the method of construction of the graphics using AutoCAD 3D Studio and Animator Pro. The mathematical model is written in C++, for speed of execution, but Visual Basic is also used. A simple example of code is given to show the principles of parallel execution of animation and simulation, and the means of synchronising the two. The paper is illustrated by pictures of the resulting animations.

A number of experiments have already been set up in this way and tested with second year science students. Student feedback has shown clearly that the students were better motivated, learned the inner workings of the equipment, and felt they understood the theory behind the experiment more quickly than if they had performed the real experiment.

COLLABORATIVE COURSEWARE FOR SYSTEMS ANALYSIS AND DESIGN D

P Linecar, D Siviter, *South Bank University, London* and P Siviter, *University of Brighton*

In August 1993 the Higher Education Funding Council England (HEFCE) funded a second round of projects in their Teaching and Learning Technology Programme. WISDEN was one of the successful bids in this second round of TLTP. WISDEN comprises a consortium of seven developer universities (Sheffield Hallam, Heriot-Watt, Teesside, Loughborough, Glamorgan, South Bank, and Brighton) and numerous evaluation sites. The collective aim is to produce Computer-Assisted Learning material which teaches about Software Systems Design in three main streams i.e., Structured Methods, Formal Methods and Object Oriented Methods; all aimed at undergraduate computing courses. A major feature of the courseware design is that it will encourage collaborative study (groupwork) and will be implemented in an environment which provides computer support for this collaborative work.

South Bank University is leading the development of the courseware for Structured Methods and Brighton University is leading the development of courseware for Object Oriented Methods.

The themes for the session are general courseware development issues rather than issues specifically relating to the courseware in Software Systems Design.

SUPPORT FOR LEARNING: VISUALISING AS AN ADJUNCT TO LEARNING

Ray McAleese, Cathy Gunn and Geir Granum, *Heriot-Watt University*

Along with the developments in CBL has come a realisation that learners need to acquire new skills to make the most of the new technology. This paper addresses the need for students to acquire appropriate study skills - in particular the ability to re-present learning ideas using a visualisation technique based on concept mapping (Auto-monitoring - A/M). The work reports on one aspect of the Courseware for Learning and Study Skills -(CLASS) TLTP (1) project that has developed a study module on Auto-monitoring. The paper will concentrate on the model that supports the A/M module. In addition a demonstration of the module will be made. The paper will make the following points.

1. In general the need for an A/M module in the CLASS project is supported by educational and psychological literature in two respects. Firstly the need for better learning and study skills in a significant sector of the student population is identified in the Howie Report (1992), the MacFarlane Report (1993) and Edinburgh University CRLI Report on the Transition from School to Higher Education in Scotland (1991). Secondly the educational effectiveness of the 'knowledge processing' approach to deep level learning and understanding of subject material is reported by many including Kommers et al. (1991), Heeren & Collis (1993).

2. In order to achieve deep level processing and to integrate new information into existing knowledge structures learners must adopt an active metalevel approach to what they read and hear and record (including notes). Tasks are devised to make explicit the nature of arguments in lectures and to show inconsistencies in different perspectives from different sources. In addition, by allowing different perspectives of what is known and what is to be learned, the learner will be able to negotiate a new meaning from amongst the inconsistencies.

3. A useful starting point is what has been called "situated cognition" (Brown, Collins & Duguid (1989). The most useful contribution is the claim that concepts are both situated and progressively developed through activity. Knowledge is claimed to be like tools. Thinking occurs when the tools are used for some task. Brown et al and Carroll (1989) along with many others have provided a stable raft of research supporting the idea of conceptual tools. A/M is the executive control and operation of such tools. A/M is the craft that the "apprentice" is acquiring in formal and informal education. That is, the learner is acquiring the skills needed to operate with and on concepts. Some would argue that this is also the function of language - a means by which we can operate on concepts. Learning, seen in this way, is the outcome of learner activity. It is something that learners cause by their actions.

4. In general, the learner is engaged in an active process in an environment which supports the manipulation of "knowledge" -ideas, concepts etc. The general process can be called "Engagement". The "Learning Arena" is the space where operations on entities occur. In this space the learner is able to engage with information, ideas. This accession is dynamic - that is it occurs while operations are ongoing in the arena. Ideas are "created" on the fly, concepts are recalled when appropriate etc. The learner has both tools and processes to use. In addition, the learner has available a number of models that constrain the operations performed.

5. The principal model is the "net" consisting of nodes and links. The net is n-dimensional. The tools are the computer related operations using a WIMP interface. Tools change with the instantiation of different models. In general, tools will allow representation of elements of models to be manipulated. For example "nodes" can be moved, created, deleted, etc.. Although the net is the most popular model, the "outline" of constrained net is also useful. The outline is a heiranhy and the freedom to manipulate concepts is pre-determined by relations that are generally is-a (B - is-a -A -> B has attributes of A). Processes are cognitive operations. Processes are dependant on the model of operation selected. For example in a model, there is a cybernetic influence on the operations. Dependencies are created and effects are transmitted through the underlying structure.

The paper explores these issues and describes the nature of the computer application that helps learners come to know.

PREDICTING THE DEVELOPMENT EFFORT AND COST OF MULTIMEDIA COURSEWARE

I M Marshall, W B Samson and P Dugard, *Department of Mathematical and Computer Sciences, Dundee Institute of Technology*

The availability of low cost multimedia production and delivery systems has resulted in an increase in interest in their use for computer-assisted and open access education. However, despite the reduction in cost of hardware and improved functionality of authoring software, the development effort required to produce multimedia courseware is still substantial. The authors will argue that some of the current major projects in this area should be used to collect accurately development and delivery data. Based on this data, accurate methods of estimating development effort and cost can be developed for use with future projects.

Critical review of development effort and cost estimation methods

A critical review of the informal methods used to estimate courseware development effort and cost will be presented. Existing methods for estimating courseware development effort and cost such as CEAC will be discussed. Early research by the authors indicates that, although some multimedia development effort estimating systems exist within commercial companies, these tend to be specific to the company concerned. Effort estimation within educational producers is almost non-existent even within large funded projects.

Multimedia Effort Estimation Model (MEEM)

This paper will discuss the development of a metrics based model for predicting the development effort and cost of multimedia courseware. The techniques used in the development of MEEM are well established in Software Engineering and are being adapted by the authors to suite courseware. The average number of training hours is used as the basis for the effort estimate. The use of cost drivers allows the effects of media, objectives, instructional design method and authoring system to be incorporated into the estimate of effort and cost.

Future research

The authors will propose that many of the assumptions of educational technology related to courseware development are not proven because they have not been objectively measured. The paper will discuss the potential for further research in this area. As well as producing a method of estimating multimedia development effort and cost, the team hope to be able to identify the effects on the development effort and cost of:

- instructional design method
- authoring method
- author and development team experience

TOWARDS A DISCUSSION-BASED INTELLIGENT TUTORING SYSTEM

D Moore and D Hobbs, *Leeds Metropolitan University*

This paper documents work concerned with the design of an intelligent tutoring system that will engage students in competitive debate on controversial issues.

A prerequisite for the computer to act as a participant in such a dialogue is a computational theory of co-operative dialogue. It has been suggested that dialogue game theory might form such a computational theory, and the main thrust of the research to be reported here is concerned with an investigation of this possibility. There are three essential stages of such an investigation. First, it is necessary to characterise the nature of the theory; an overview of the field will therefore be presented, and a case made for the dialectical system "DC" as the most promising model to facilitate computer-based debate. Next, the validity of the model needs to be established, and an overview of empirical work consequent upon this will be presented. This work, which suggests that the model can be readily assimilated and used to generate fair discourse, forms part of the unique contribution of this research. Finally, it is necessary to establish whether the theory is computationally tractable. In order to establish this, a design for a computer based system incorporating the framework offered by DC, based on strategic heuristics derived from the empirical work, and utilising rhetorical structure theory, will be presented and justified, and a program conceptualisation discussed.

The argument is that since the empirical work suggests that DC can be regarded as a valid prescriptive model of dialogue, then this sanctions its use as the prescriptive basis for a computer based dialogue system. Since, furthermore, the design work suggests that the model is sufficiently formal to be utilised computationally, the feasibility of such a system has thereby been demonstrated.

By having both the machine and user well-regulated by the strictures of the model, a major improvement in human computer interaction becomes possible.

The major theoretical contribution of this research is the linking together of dialogue game theory, artificial intelligence, and rhetorical structure theory.

APPROACHES TO TEACHING SEQUENTIAL LOGIC

H M Powell, D Palmer-Brown and B Hanson, *The Nottingham Trent University*

Logic circuits form the basis of computers and as such are covered in the first year of most computing courses in the Department of Computing. The treatment of the subject varies between the courses as they are at different levels (HNC/D to MSc) and have different emphasis (business/technical). In order to improve the quality of the teaching, several computer-based packages running under Windows have been produced. These include a tutorial-style 'Introduction to Combinational Logic', a sequential logic demonstrator ('SeqDem') and a logic simulator ('SeqSim').

Our work so far has led us to conclude that interactive simulation is a better way to meet varied pedagogical needs than a computer-based tutorial. A full simulation package provides the lecturer with a medium which they can tailor to meet their own requirements as any situation can be created and simulated. In contrast, tutorial packages suffer from their specificity and inflexibility, when considered for use by someone other than the producer or designer.

A third style of package has been developed. This provides an environment for experimentation with predefined examples and for browsing in hypertext. The workshop will provide participants with experience of using both a browsing/experimentation package and a full simulation package to learn about sequential logic. Their use of these packages will be guided to cover similar subject matter. Participants will be asked to provide some feedback on this experience on paper and there will be a discussion at the end to consider the relative merits of the two approaches.

The participants will be asked to consider the effectiveness of the two packages in terms of their user friendliness, the depth, breadth and nature of the understanding they encourage, the extent to which they stimulate the user to learn more and the extent to which they are enjoyable to use.

THE NAPIER EDITOR/ANIMATOR FOR PETRI-NETS (NEAP)

R C Rankin and P Bradbeer, *Napier University*

Teaching concurrent programming presents a particular set of challenges due to:

- the conceptual difficulty of envisaging the simultaneous execution of two or more processes
- errors in design being obscured by their unpredictable manifestation during execution on conventional programming bases
- the time penalty and the high skills-level demanded by conventional bases.

The last point is emphasised in a modular teaching system where students from different backgrounds may be familiar with different languages not all of which may support concurrency.

Petri-nets offer a means of addressing a large number of these difficulties, by providing in a visual form (using uniform symbolism), the design and representation of concurrent programs.

However, final implementation requires translation to a conventional base. Alternatively manual "execution" of the net is tedious.

The development of NEAP, as part of the COMETT PAPILLON project has simplified the teaching of concurrent programming to a number of disparate groups of students. The product runs under Windows in an MS-DOS environment. It allows creation, editing and storing of Petri-nets. These may be "executed" using a range of scheduling strategies, and speed of execution is under user control.

ANALYSIS OF LEARNING DESIGN - A RETROSPECTIVE APPROACH

Stephen Richards and Philip Barker, *School of Computing and Mathematics, University of Teesside*

In many computer-based learning applications relatively little emphasis is given to the underlying pedagogic strategies that are needed to support successful learning. All too often, learning product development is oriented towards what can be achieved with the technology rather than the learning needs of users. In order to address this problem a model of learning design has been developed specifically for the creation of interactive learning materials that are to be published on compact disc.

This model has been used as a basis for the implementation of a number of prototypical learning and training products. The learning products that were produced have been evaluated in order to find out how effectively the model of learning design has been embedded within them and also to discover the impact of using this model on the pedagogic uses of the resulting applications.

In order to undertake these evaluations a suitable evaluation tool was developed. This allowed various attributes of the quality of the learning software to be compared with the learning strategies that they contained. It also enabled weaknesses in the implementation of the learning software to be isolated and areas of potential improvement identified. This paper describes the evaluation tool which was developed and the results which were obtained as a result of applying it to various interactive learning products.

HYPERTEXT FOR ALL: THE STAFF AND STUDENT EXPERIENCE

Catherine Scott and Sarah Holyfield, *University of North London*

In the Faculty of Humanities and Teacher Education at the University of North London hypertext has featured on the programme for students for several years. Partly as a consequence of that, a significant number of staff have also become increasingly familiar with various forms of hypertext (predominantly **Guide** and **HyperCard**), and now there are several development projects underway which use hypertext and multimedia to provide Computer Assisted Learning and reference materials for use in an open learning context.

This paper reports on both staff and student projects and developments in hypermedia, illustrated (if practicable) with samples of products from different areas. It will also discuss the difficulties and advantages inherent in embracing hypermedia as a major development tool.

COMPUTER-BASED LEARNING AND SUPPORT FOR DYSLEXICS

Chris Singleton, *Dyslexia Computer Resource Centre, University of Hull*

Dyslexia is an unexpected difficulty in acquiring literacy skills. It is sometimes referred to as *Specific Learning Difficulty* or SpLD for short. It occurs in approximately one in every twenty five of the population, which means that, on average, there will be one child with dyslexic difficulties in every classroom. Computers are increasingly being seen as one of the most cost-effective ways of tackling many of the learning problems of dyslexics, and computers are now being widely purchased by schools, parents and charities for use by dyslexics at home, school and college. Education authorities can supply grants for computer purchases by dyslexics in higher education, and training agencies are doing the same for dyslexics on vocational training programmes.

This workshop will look at software in each of the main areas of computer-assisted learning and computer support. Emphasis will be on a small range of good software which exploits the technology to the full whilst meeting essential educational requirements, and which is practical for use in a variety of educational environments. The implications for policy and practice at school, home and university will be considered.

DEVELOPING A METHODOLOGY FOR THE EVALUATION OF AUTHORING TOOLS

Jayne Smith, *Staffordshire University* and **Bernard Williams,** *UEA Norwich*

This paper outlines the choice of authoring tools for the development of multimedia courseware in higher education.

Part of the motivation for the Teaching And Learning Technology Programme (TLTP) is a recognition that during the past 30 years, information technology has advanced considerably in terms of its capabilities and its much reduced cost. One aspect of this is the development of desktop technology that has vastly outstripped the lumbering mainframes of the 1960's. Another, which is the focus of this paper, is the development of high-powered software tools that both enhance usability and provide a means of a more rapid software production. Of these, Computer-Based Learning (CBL) has evolved its own specific set known as authoring tools. These vary in scope from dedicated authoring languages such as Authorware and Toolbook, to more general purpose tools such as HyperCard or Guide and other tools such as Excel which were designed for a different specific purpose but which are used for authoring purposes in a CBL context. One of the problems facing any potential courseware developer is how to choose an appropriate authoring platform. The main choice appears to be between either a computer language or one of the range of authoring tools outlined above.

There is a trade-off between the time required to develop courseware in a computer language and the loss of functionality or flexibility from the use of an authoring tool. For this reason, it is necessary to evaluate thoroughly the capability of authoring tools. This paper documents an account of the search for a suitable authoring platform, including authoring tools that took place in TLTP Phase I project, BITE (Business Education with Information

Technology). In doing so, it highlights some of the key issues that need to be addressed in formulating a methodology for this purpose.

The paper suggests that the form of a methodology for evaluating authoring tools cannot resemble a checklist or a set of concrete procedures since it needs to take account of the highly contextual nature of the area of activity. On the contrary, it needs to be in the form of a rational framework that provides the basis for stimulating and encouraging enquiry.

CALM - INTEGRATING COMPUTER ASSISTED LEARNING INTO NON-ACCOUNTING MODULES

Grahame J Steven , *Department of Accounting and Law, Napier University*

The Problem

Educational institutions are under pressure to devise new teaching strategies which will meet the following objectives:

- Enable the expansion of higher education to be achieved without a corresponding increase in resources.
- Promote student-centred learning.
- Provide more flexible modes of delivery.

A Solution?

While computer-assisted learning material has been developed -EQL, PEER etc - and is being developed - BITE project, INTERACTIVE etc - it has proved difficult to integrate this material into accounting modules for non-accounting students since this material was either developed principally for accounting students or it is not sufficiently correlated with syllabi to avoid it being looked upon as another recommended text. It is, therefore, doubtful if this material will enable the achievement of the above objectives unless modules are substantially re-written to conform with CAL material - tail wagging the dog?

The Solution?

In recent years, software has been developed which enables users to create bespoke CAL materials. While a wide variety of software is available, the proposed workshop will focus on GUIDE and QUESTIONMARK and how material developed for MANAGERIAL FINANCE 1 utilising these packages can enable the achievement of the above objectives.

GUIDE enables users to create interactive computer-based "books" which can be accessed from a floppy disc on a wide variety of PCs within an educational establishment and/or at home.

QUESTIONMARK enables users to create, mark and analyse objective tests for students which can be accessed by individual students or groups of students within an educational establishment and/or at home.

A NEW EDUCATIONAL TOOL - MODULES AND PARAMETERS

Grace Stewart and Marianne Farrell, *Glasgow Caledonian University*

This educational package is intended to assist students' understanding of the concepts associated with the implementation of modules, and in particular with the use of parameters. It is designed to involve the student interactively, and so differs from traditional text-based CAL delivery material.

The product was developed in Assymetrix's TOOLBOOK.

Students can easily become confused by the volume and complexity of information to be assimilated when learning about modules and parameters - formal/actual parameters, parameter passing mechanisms, local/global variables, procedures vs functions, etc.

The package supports the lecturer's teaching by using a mixture of visual demonstrations, textual explanation, and interaction from the student. Animation is used where appropriate, eg to show the flow of logic through code as modules are accessed, the use of memory in storing values for parameters and variables, the effect upon parameters of different supporting mechanisms.

The package is menu-driven, with the following major topic areas:

> Introduction to Using the Package
> General concepts of modularity
> Parameter Concepts
> Parameter Mechanisms
> Functions vs Procedures

On quitting the product, the user is required to 'log out' so that student access to the material can be monitored, and to provide the user with the opportunity to feedback suggestions/problems to the support programmer.

HYPERTEXT ACROSS THE DISCIPLINES: AN ANALYSIS OF READERS' APPROACHES TO A MULTI-DISCIPLINARY HYPERTEXT TUTORIAL

Wilma Strang and Gillian Tardivel, *Hypertext Support Unit, University of Kent*

Much has been written about the interactive and individualised nature of computer-assisted learning, in particular recently of hypertext documents. It is unusual for a hypertext document to be applicable across a wide range of disciplines. However, a long-term study at the University of Kent has monitored the use of just such a document. This paper analyses readers' approaches to the Xtutor document and presents findings in the following areas:

- patterns of use by discipline and status
- learner pacing
- interactivity
- use by non-native English speakers

- open learning.

Xtutor, a hypertext introduction to the X Windows system, has been used by over 400 people at the University of Kent in the past 20 months. Over 100 of these users, working on Xtutor on an open access machine, have had their sessions recorded in fine detail for the purposes of this major study.

Analysis of data has illustrated the following points -

- wide variations in session length
- wide variations in number of accesses
- 'feeler' access
- comparisons of use by individuals within/between disciplines
- wide range of users by status and discipline

The implications of these findings for higher education institutions investing in the provision of hypertext materials is discussed.

TECHNOLOGY AND THE ASSESSMENT OF MANAGEMENT COMPETENCIES

Richard Thomas, *Southampton Institute*

Recent initiatives such as those from the Management Charter Initiative (MCI) and BTEC including new courses adopting the NVQ standards, have all advocated the Competence-based approach to management training and development.

This research project involves the evaluation of technology-based media in the assessment of management competencies. A variety of such material is already commercially available, including the Computer-based Assessment System (CAS) developed by Mast Learning Systems Ltd in collaboration with the MCI. Other packages are being introduced incorporating sophisticated laser-disc technologies eg CD-I. Such material will be critically appraised and evaluated in terms of its effectiveness in the management competence assessment process.

Technology-based assessment methods will be compared with more 'traditional' methods such as the production of portfolios, undertaking written tests, interviews and participation in role plays and simulations. The validity of the current technology-based methods will be considered and new dynamic technological approaches to the assessment of management competencies (such as work-based simulations, case studies and profiling systems) will be explored. Such methods have implications for management training and development in addition to the assessment process.

SUPPORTING THE LEARNER WITH TECHNOLOGY-BASED SOLUTIONS

Julie Wright, *NCET, Coventry*

Academic research, NCET's own developing expertise, and guidance materials such as the Framework for the Inspection of Schools, all agree that there are critical factors which determine learner success. Such factors include tutorial time for the learner, the development of organisational skills and effective study skills. Furthermore it is possible to frame these factors in terms of learner needs and to provide a checklist for anyone wishing to offer support to the individual learner.

As new technological solutions are encountered and offered, this framework also ensures that the technology is not judged purely on its innovative appeal but on its effectiveness in relation to the critical factors above.

In this paper the framework is tested against innovations where new technologies have been applied to learner support, including: the use of satellite broadcasts to isolated school-based students on initial teaching practice in Wales, desk-top conferencing to deliver in-service training in schools in the Exeter area and the use of IV discs to raise awareness of the appraisal process in a medium sized organisation.